RETHINKING
the NEW DEAL COURT

RETHINKING
the NEW DEAL COURT

The Structure of a
Constitutional Revolution

BARRY CUSHMAN

New York   Oxford • Oxford University Press   1998

Oxford University Press

Oxford   New York
Athens   Auckland   Bangkok   Bogota   Bombay   Buenos Aires
Calcutta   Cape Town   Dar es Salaam   Delhi   Florence   Hong Kong
Istanbul   Karachi   Kuala Lumpur   Madras   Madrid   Melbourne
Mexico City   Nairobi   Paris   Singapore   Taipei   Tokyo   Toronto   Warsaw

and associated companies in
Berlin   Ibadan

Copyright © 1998 by Oxford University Press, Inc.

Published by Oxford University Press, Inc.
198 Madison Avenue, New York, New York 10016

Oxford is a registered trademark of Oxford University Press

Library of Congress Cataloging–in–Publication Data
Cushman, Barry 1960–
Rethinking the New Deal court: The structure of a constitutional
revolution / by Barry Cushman.
p.   cm.
Includes index.
ISBN 0–19–511532–5; 0–19–512033–7 (pbk.)
1. Constitutional history—United States. 2. United States—
Economic policy—1933–1945. 3. New Deal, 1933–1939. I. Title.
KF4541.C873   1997
342.73'029—dc21   97–8904

1 3 5 7 9 8 6 4 2
Printed in the United States of America
on acid-free paper

For Patty

Preface

This is not the book I set out to write. After watching me engage in more than the usual amount of fumbling around for a dissertation topic, my graduate adviser mercifully pulled me aside and suggested one. My subject was to be the evolution of constitutional culture during the decade of the 1920s. In order to elucidate the range of constitutional constraints and opportunities within which policy makers confronting the economic crisis of the 1930s worked, I was to undertake a set of case studies designed to determine the contours of contemporary thought concerning the commerce power, the spending power, and substantive due process on the eve of the depression decade. My story would stop with the death of Chief Justice Taft in 1930, and it would be for someone else (if anyone at all) to unpack the implications (if any) of my findings for subsequent events.

I began with the commerce power study, and with the legislative history of the Packers and Stockyards Act of 1921. In perusing the debates over the bill's constitutionality, I found the legislators discussing commerce clause doctrine in ways that seemed odd and unfamiliar to me. I recognized that there was something going on that I didn't fully appreciate, but I couldn't dope out exactly what it was. Walking home from the gym one day, under the influence of an unusually heavy dose of endorphins, it occurred to me that the debates in question had seemed peculiar because they had assumed relationships between commerce clause jurisprudence and substantive due process doctrine that had previously eluded my attention. As I probed deeper into my study, I began to notice more such interdoctrinal connections. Eventually, I came to the conclusion that the story of these connections—their formation, development, and disintegration—might help to explain some of the constitutional change of the New Deal period. It is that story that I seek to tell in this, the book I inadvertently wrote.

In the course of this misadventure I have accumulated a great many debts and made a great many friends. My greatest intellectual debt is to Charles McCurdy. In addition to teaching me how to run the West Coast offense, he was the merciful graduate adviser who initially suggested the project and guided it to completion as a dissertation. Throughout the process he brought to the enterprise the keen critical and synthetic capacities and the staggering breadth and depth of knowledge of an exemplary scholar, as well as the patience and enthusiasm of an exemplary friend. It was the analytical equipment earlier provided by his lectures that enabled me to conceptualize the questions studied here as I have. Though he is to blame for none of its shortcomings, his influence on the book is unmistakable.

I have also profited tremendously from the advice of two of Chuck's colleagues at the University of Virginia, Michael Klarman and G. Edward White. Mike managed the admirable feat of remaining unstintingly encouraging while at the same time gently yet persistently confronting me with the critical insights of one inclined (at least initially) to see things differently. To the extent that I have persuaded him, it is because he has helped me to do so. Ted gave me a critical shot in the arm at an early juncture, and has throughout generously shared with me his uncanny sense for the big picture and the way that a book "works." I'm deeply grateful to both for their friendship and counsel.

I'm deeply grateful as well to Bill Nelson, who characteristically called me out of the blue at 11 o'clock one night to invite me into a world of scholarly fraternity I had never known existed. During my year as a Golieb Fellow at the New York University School of Law, and in subsequent visits to the NYU Legal History Colloquium directed by Bill and John Philip Reid, I benefited from the suggestions, criticisms, and friendship of an extraordinary group of legal historians. I hesitate to name any lest I inadvertently forget someone, but particularly deserving of thanks are R. B. Bernstein, Chris Eisgruber, Louise Halper, Larry Kramer, Eben Moglen, Don Nieman, Bill Offutt, Reuel Schiller, and especially Bill LaPiana and Ed Purcell. Many other friends and colleagues, both here and around the country, have generously given me their time and counsel: John Attanasio, Melvyn Dubofsky, Dan Ernst, Tony Freyer, Rich Friedman, Chris Frost, Roger Goldman, John Griesbach, John Harrison, Alan Howard, Laura Kalman, Joseph Kett, William Leuchtenburg, Joe McCartin, Michael Parrish, Doug Williams, and the members of the Legal Studies Workshop at the University of Virginia School of Law.

I have been the beneficiary as well of the gracious assistance of librarians at St. Louis University, the University of Virginia, the University of Kentucky, the University of Michigan, and the Library of Congress. Brian Elsbernd and William Sultemeier provided able research assistance in the latter stages, and Martin Onwu and Stephanie Haley assisted in the final preparation of the manuscript.

Finally, it is a delight to thank my crackerjack assistants, Helen and Lydia Cushman, who spent hours lovingly illustrating innumerable previous drafts of the manuscript while I worked on yet another, and generously granted me release time to complete it. My most profound debt, however, is to their mother. She has scrutinized and edited every page of manuscript more than once, rescuing the reader from myriad infelicities. More impressively, she has for more than seven years endured the Promethean ordeal of my diurnal discourses on the public/private distinction with singular grace and good humor. It is to her, with love and gratitude, that I dedicate this book.

St. Louis   B.C.
Thanksgiving 1996

Acknowledgments

The author has previously published portions of this book in the following journals:

"Doctrinal Synergies and Liberal Dilemmas: The Case of the Yellow Dog Contract," *Supreme Court Review* (1992). © 1993 by The University of Chicago. All Rights Reserved. Published by permission of the University of Chicago Press.

"A Stream of Legal Consciousness: The Current of Commerce Doctrine from Swift to Jones & Laughlin," 61 *Fordham Law Review* 105 (1992). Published by permission of Fordham University.

"Rethinking the New Deal Court," *Virginia Law Review*, Vol. 80, No. 1. Published with permission.

Permission has also been granted by Hugo L. Black Jr. to quote from documents pertaining to the 1939 case, *NLRB v. Fainblatt*, found in Box 255 of Justice Hugo Black Sr.'s collection.

Contents

RETHINKING
the NEW DEAL COURT

Introduction

The story of the "switch-in-time" is among the most enduring chapters of our constitutional history. It is repeated every year in countless courses in government, history, and constitutional law in our nation's high schools, colleges, and law schools. One of the great morality plays of American civics, it is both celebratory and cautionary. A vast and remarkably homogenous literature built by legions of lawyers, historians, and political scientists recounts and reiterates the story with varying degrees of subtlety and sophistication. In truncated, composite, and only mildly caricatured form, it goes as follows:

Once upon a time, in the dark days of the Great Depression, there was a great liberal president (Franklin Roosevelt) who fought valiantly against rich and powerful economic royalists in a noble effort to better the lot of the common man and save the country from economic ruin. His plan, which he called the New Deal, enjoyed widespread public support but was repeatedly rejected by the Supreme Court. The president was aided in his crusade by three wise and visionary liberal justices (Brandeis, Stone, and Cardozo), who generally supported his program and voted accordingly in the cases that came before the Court. Their efforts were frustrated, however, by four reactionary conservative justices (the "Four Horsemen" — Van Devanter, McReynolds, Sutherland, and Butler), whose jurisprudence was driven by their devotion to the anachronistic tenets of laissez-faire economics and their sympathetic subservience to the interests of rich and powerful people and institutions. The conservatives were too frequently aided in their obstructionist enterprise by two waffling moderates (Hughes and Roberts), whose business-class origins likewise disposed them against the New Deal. In the general election of 1936, however, the American people forcefully repudiated the jurisprudence of the Court's majority and wholeheartedly embraced the constitutional theories of Franklin Roosevelt. Emboldened by his landslide victory, Roosevelt soon thereafter announced his plan to pack the Court. Fearing institutional evisceration, the moderates, in an act spurred by a mixture of cowardice, "statesmanship," and newfound constitutional enlightenment, decided to switch rather than fight. Upholding the National Labor Relations Act, the Social Security Act, and the minimum wage,

3

they pledged their allegiance to the liberal cause. Thus was a new constitutional order born.[1]

The staying power of this story is truly remarkable. Despite recent substantial and successful revisions of longstanding accounts of the Gilded Age and Lochner Era Courts,[2] the conventional wisdom on the New Deal Court persists. Even as these exciting reappraisals of earlier Courts have been emerging, the constitutional history of the New Deal Court has remained almost moribund.[3] This has caused one recent commentator to lament that "contemporary scholarship exploring the constitutional dimensions of the New Deal remains weak. . . . considering its importance, the subject remains incredibly underresearched."[4]

The dominance of the conventional wisdom is itself an historical artifact and is largely inertial. The "Constitutional Revolution of 1937"—the Court's decisions in *West Coast Hotel v. Parrish,*[5] the Wagner Act cases,[6] and the Social Security cases[7]—occurred at a point in American history when the field of constitutional commentary was dominated by scholars inclined to predominantly political explanations of judicial behavior. Their accounts of the revolution, written in its immediate wake, quickly erected a virtually monolithic externalist interpretation[8] that persisted in the postwar era of New Deal consensus culture.[9] New Left historians of the 1960s and 1970s offered extensive reappraisals of various aspects of the New Deal, but seldom focused their attention on its constitutional dimensions.[10] A few commentators of a generation ago expressed some dissatisfaction with this conventional historical wisdom,[11] but their critiques were neither adequately sustained nor sufficiently powerful analytically to blunt the withering counterattacks of their professional foes.[12] As a consequence, the reign of the received account has now spanned more than two generations.

This conceptualization of the decisions of 1937 in externalist terms, as a political response to political pressures, has deflected scholars from inquiry into the plausibility of an internal—legal and intellectual—component to a more comprehensive explanation of the actions of the New Deal Court. Moreover, the externalist account has obscured interesting lines of development in constitutional thought and doctrine. The plausibility (indeed hegemony) of the externalist explanation rests on the assumption that no plausible internal account might be forthcoming. This view is crystallized in the image of a "switch" in time, suggesting a simple binary system of constitutional law. Before 1937, the Court was "anti-regulation" and opposed to "activist national government,"[13] constructing a "doctrinal defense of laissez-faire capitalism"; from 1937 on, however, "the Court accept[ed] liberal nationalism,"[14] and "began to build new constitutional foundations for activist national government."[15] Such abstract terms hardly begin to capture the complexity of the positions taken by the justices on a wide variety of issues. Moreover, to think about constitutional issues in these terms is to substitute the language of political science for the legal language in which the justices discussed these issues in conference, in which they wrote about them in their opinions, and which, we may presume, played at least some role in the ways in which they actually thought about the cases that were brought before them. To embrace the thoroughgoing externalist account as the last word on the New Deal Court is to deny the constitutional jurisprudence of the period any status as a mode of intellectual discourse having its own internal dynamic. It is to dismiss the efforts of the lawyers defending the constitutionality of New Deal initiatives as irrelevant and redundant, to deprive Hughes and Roberts of a substantial measure of intellectual integrity and personal dignity, and to suggest that sophisticated legal thinkers casually discard a jurisprudential worldview formed over the course of a long lifetime simply because it becomes momentarily politically inconvenient.

The conventional wisdom is therefore long overdue for some serious scrutiny, for two reasons. First, there is good reason to doubt that it offers an *accurate* account. The nature of the external account and the evidence available preclude it from being *conclusively* disproved in its entirety. There is no utterly irrefutable smoking gun: both the conventional wisdom and its critique necessarily rest on circumstantial evidence. Nevertheless, there is ample evidence to suggest that the external account is not nearly as compelling as has conventionally been thought, that it certainly has been overstated, and that it may very well be just plain wrong. Second, the conventional account of the "revolution" requires reexamination because it is certainly not a *complete* account, insofar as it neglects serious exploration of the internal dimensions of the phenomenon.[16]

The conventional historical wisdom makes two distinct claims: first, that the Supreme Court suddenly and substantially reversed its position in the cases decided in the spring of 1937;[17] and second, that this reversal was a political response to such external political pressures as the 1936 election and the Court-packing plan.[18] The second claim is dealt with in Part I; the first is scrutinized in Parts II, III, and IV. Chapter 1 examines the contention that the Court's behavior in the spring of 1937 was either a reaction to the threat of FDR's Court-packing plan or a response to the results of the 1936 presidential election. Chapter 2 criticizes the conventional claim that the jurisprudence of the New Deal Court can be adequately understood through generic political categories, and then discusses the importance of the role that lawyering played in determining the fate of particular New Deal initiatives.

The burden of Part I is thus critical; its objective is to create sufficient intellectual space to develop the kind of alternative internal account necessary to an improved understanding of the shape and trajectory of the New Deal Court's constitutional jurisprudence. Chapter 2 concludes with a brief prescription for producing that sort of account, and Parts II, III, and IV are each attempts to fill that prescription. Part II evaluates the conventional claim that the Court's decision upholding minimum wage regulation in *West Coast Hotel v. Parrish* was revolutionary. New light is shed on *Parrish* by reconstructing the intellectual history of the various strands of substantive due process that converged in that decision. In Parts III and IV, a similar method is employed to evaluate comparable claims concerning the Court's resolution of the due process and commerce clause issues presented in the Wagner Act cases. The conclusions reached in each of these three parts take issue with the conventional tale of an abrupt *volte face*, and in turn support Part I's critique of the conventional externalist story line.

The objective, however, is not to deny that the New Deal era witnessed dramatic changes in constitutional jurisprudence. It is instead to recharacterize both the jurisprudence that changed and the mechanics by which it changed, approaching the phenomenon examined as a chapter in the history of ideas rather than as an episode in the history of politics. The pudding produced by this recipe may be described briefly. The story identifies three different impulses undergirding the Court's constitutional jurisprudence between the Civil War and World War II. One impulse, rooted in the republican fear of the tendencies of centralized authority toward tyranny and corruption and the desire to preserve liberty through the broad diffusion of power, was to maintain the boundary between the respective spheres of state and national legislative competence. Another impulse, similarly grounded in concerns over legislative corruption, as well as in solicitude for "vested rights," sought to ensure governmental neutrality among citizens by maintaining a boundary between a sphere of authority to enact "public-regarding" legislation and a sphere in which the private sector might operate presumptively free from governmental regulation. And a third and related impulse, resting on the Lockean precept of a man's property right in his own toil most trenchantly expressed in abolitionism and "free labor" ideology, sought to maintain the boundary between private rights of contract and legitimate regulation of the employment relationship in the public interest.

Each of these impulses, translated into juridical idiom, found expression in various doctrines of constitutional law. During an era in which legal thought was deeply influenced by analogies to mathematics and the natural sciences, the drive to systematize constitutional law produced a high level of doctrinal integration. During the chief justiceship of Melville Fuller (1888–1910) and thereafter, the doctrinal expressions of these three impulses became integrated in particular ways, producing a system of constitutional jurisprudence in which doctrines were structurally interrelated and developmentally interdependent. Over time, in a series of responses prompted both by external pressures and the internal dynamics produced by this interdependence, this integrated body of jurisprudence eroded and ultimately collapsed.

Our view of this doctrinal integration has long been obscured by the way we learn and think about constitutional law. In our casebooks and courses on the subject, we study the development of *lines* and competing lines of doctrine. We do not devote ourselves to understanding the ways in which these strands of doctrine were woven together into an interdependent *web* of constitutional thought. Instead, our pedagogy sunders older interdoctrinal connections, aggregating various doctrines into the categories comprising the modern constitutional sensibility. So, for example, the police power is examined in the context of the doctrine of "liberty of contract," an "implied fundamental right" cognate of the right of privacy or sexual autonomy. Such a coupling is of course pedagogically valuable in the context of late twentieth-century constitutionalism. Yet at the same time it obscures the fact that late nineteenth- and early twentieth-century constitutional thinkers adjudicated questions of the scope of the police power within the same conceptual matrix with which they approached eminent domain, takings and contracts clause issues — areas of the law we today learn about in another chapter, or perhaps even another course. A similar fire wall separates our treatments of the development of commerce clause jurisprudence and the evolution of economic substantive due process. We examine "structural" issues like federalism (perhaps in "Constitutional

Law I"), then we "move on" to discuss "individual rights" issues such as substantive due process (perhaps in "Constitutional Law II"). Seldom if ever do we pause to identify the points of contact between these two areas of doctrine, and the ways in which those intersections made those doctrines developmentally interdependent parts of a larger jurisprudential structure.

An appreciation of the structure of these doctrinal edifices can help to expand our understanding of the *context* within which the legal actors in this drama were situated. Over the past several decades, legal historians have significantly enhanced our understanding of the legal past by locating legal events within the political, economic, social, cultural, and intellectual contexts in which they transpired. Recreating the doctrinal context within which these legal actors behaved is no less important an endeavor. It illuminates the contours of constraint confronting and the channels of opportunity beckoning those policy makers and advocates who sought to accommodate transformative statutory initiatives within the structure of contemporary doctrine. It also helps us to see how these pressures of statutory innovation and efforts at accommodation worked to reshape existing doctrinal structures over time, thereby reconfiguring the constitutional terrain facing subsequent legal reformers. Moreover, identifying doctrinal structures enables us not only to understand the ways in which legal issues were conceptualized by contemporary legal minds, but also to appreciate the internal dynamics of doctrinal development. For where the elements of one constitutional doctrine had become integrated into and partially constitutive of another, modifications in the former doctrine entailed changes in the latter. The story of the 1930s is in part the story of how this integrated body of jurisprudence disintegrated when the Court, in response to a particular statutory initiative, abandoned a doctrinal formulation that had become a central nexus of such integration.

The decision in which that abandonment transpired was *Nebbia v. New York*,[19] which occupies center stage in each of the stories told in Parts II, III, and IV. In that case, decided in 1934, the Court upheld a New York statute regulating the price of milk. The claim that a decision issuing such a comparatively pedestrian holding could have very much to do with the collapse of laissez-faire constitutionalism may seem at first blush fantastic. It is my contention, however, that the highly integrated body of jurisprudence referred to as laissez-faire constitutionalism was an interwoven fabric of constitutional doctrine. Within that body the distinction between public and private enterprise performed a critical integrative function. When the Court abandoned the old public/private distinction in *Nebbia*, then, it pulled a particularly important thread from that fabric.[20] As we shall see, it was only a matter of time before that fabric would begin to unravel.[21] When that fabric lay in tatters, those who mourned its demise were in no position to reweave it, and the new milliners had already embraced the next generation of constitutional fashion.

PART I

RETHINKING
THE NEW DEAL COURT

Roosevelt's Shadow

The Court-Packing Thesis

On February 5, 1937, President Roosevelt sent Congress a proposal to "reorganize" the federal judiciary. Buried in the text of the bill was a provision that would have permitted the president to appoint to the Supreme Court an additional justice for each sitting justice who had not retired within six months of his seventieth birthday. Because six of the Justices then sitting were over seventy, this provision would have permitted the president to appoint six additional justices immediately.

In his accompanying message, Roosevelt offered a disingenuous rationale for his proposal, one that was to come back to haunt him. "[T]he personnel of the Federal judiciary," the president contended, "is insufficient to meet the business before them." Roosevelt pointed out that in the preceding year, the Court had denied petitions for certiorari in 695 of the 803 cases presented for review by non-governmental litigants. "[C]an it be said," Roosevelt queried, "that full justice is achieved when a court is forced by the sheer necessity of keeping up with its business to decline, without even an explanation, to hear 87 percent of the cases presented to it by private litigants?" The reason for this failure to achieve full justice, the president opined, was the advanced age of the justices. "The modern tasks of judges call for the use of full energies. Modern complexities call also for a constant infusion of new blood in the courts. . . . A lowered mental or physical vigor leads men to avoid an examination of complicated and changed conditions. Little by little, new facts become blurred through old glasses fitted, as it were, for the needs of another generation; older men, assuming that the scene is the same as it was in the past, cease to explore or inquire into the present or the future."[1]

Because each of the decisions comprising the revolution was handed down after Roosevelt's February 5, 1937 announcement of the plan, commentators quite naturally posited a causal link. Chief Justice Hughes vigorously denied any such connection, but "cynical and sober" observers refused to take him at his word.[2] Some historians have been inclined to attribute the Court's behavior solely to the impending threat of Roosevelt's proposal;[3] others have been more circumspect, listing the plan as one of a number of circumstances inducing judicial capitulation.[4] In all of these accounts, however, the Court plan figures as, if not a sine qua non, a substantial factor influencing the Court's decisions. Upon closer examination, however, it appears unlikely that the Court-packing plan can shoulder the heavy explanatory burden it has been asked to sustain.

The recent history of legislative attempts to control judicial behavior was not one from which Roosevelt could draw much encouragement. There had been regular agitation for the election of federal judges and the limitation of their tenure at least since the 1890s. Some proposals would even have required sitting Supreme Court justices to vacate their offices. None of these proposals had ever achieved enactment. Between 1913 and 1921, Congress had rebuffed measures to curtail or abolish judicial review, as well as proposals for the impeachment of or automatic forfeiture of office by any justice attempting to nullify federal legislation.[5] After the Supreme Court had handed down its decisions in *Bailey v. Drexel Furniture*[6] and *Adkins v. Children's Hospital*[7] in 1922 and 1923, numerous bills designed to limit the power of the Court to declare acts of Congress unconstitutional were introduced in Congress. All of these bills had died in committee. Comparable proposals had foundered again in the early 1930s.[8]

Following a series of decisions striking down New Deal initiatives, several proposals to restrain judicial power were introduced again in 1935. Some would have required a supermajority of the Court to invalidate legislation; others would have deprived the Court of the power to review questions of social and economic policy. A Gallup poll taken in September of that year showed that only 31 percent of the population favored limitation of the Court's power of judicial review, and again these proposals came to naught.[9] Similarly, in early 1936, in the wake of the Court's decision striking down the Agricultural Adjustment Act (AAA), congressmen introduced more than one hundred bills designed to restrict the federal courts. Among these was the Cross bill, which sought to strip the federal courts of the power of judicial review; a measure sponsored by Ernest Lundeen of Minnesota, which would have increased the number of justices on the Supreme Court to eleven; and a bill introduced by Representative James L. Quinn, which would have increased the number of justices to fifteen.[10] Representative Joseph P. Monaghan of Montana backed a bill to remove from office any justice voting to strike down the Tennessee Valley Authority (TVA). Senator Lynn J. Frazier of North Dakota offered a bill that would have forbidden the justices, on pain of impeachment, to invalidate any congressional statute. Senator Peter Norbeck of South Dakota introduced a measure that would have permitted such invalidations only by a majority of seven justices, and Senator James P. Pope of Idaho sponsored a similar measure. Senator George Norris of Nebraska advocated an amendment that would have permitted invalidation of federal statutes only by a unanimous vote of the justices. Such national luminaries as Karl Llewellyn and Norman Thomas publicly supported comparable Court-curbing proposals.[11] None of these bills gained congressional approval during 1936 (nor, indeed, thereafter); yet the Court continued, while these bills were pending, to eviscerate the New Deal.[12] The Hughes Court had successfully ignored congressional threats in 1935 and 1936, and if the recent past were to be read as prologue, the justices had reason to believe that they could do so again in 1937.[13]

The Court could likewise draw confidence from the size and vehemence of the opposition to the plan. From the beginning, the press voiced near-unanimous outrage and disdain. Joining the chorus of protest were numerous bar associations across the nation, including the prestigious American Bar Association. Resolutions opposing the Court bill were introduced in several state assemblies. The plan was denounced by numerous civic, patriotic, fraternal, professional, political, and religious organizations. The plan also encountered opposition from such eminent liberal reformers as Oswald Garrison Villard, John T. Flynn, and Morris L. Ernst; from college presidents like Harold W. Dodds of Princeton; from law school deans such as Young B. Smith of Columbia; from such eminent journalists as Dorothy Thompson; and from such prominent former members of the administration as erstwhile presidential aide Raymond Moley. "No day passed without some more or less eminent citizen, often one who had favored the President for re-election, bitterly denouncing his court plan." The voices of these eminent citizens were supplemented by the propagandistic efforts of several organizations: Frank Gannett's "National Committee to Uphold Constitutional Government"; "America Forward," a religious adjunct of the Republican National Committee; and various "Associations to Preserve Our Liberties." Conservatives and liberals alike denounced the plan as a threat to civil liberty and democratic rule.[14]

While the opposition was extensive and well organized, key constituents of the New Deal coalition failed to get solidly behind the plan. Roosevelt had decided not to consult with labor or farm leaders before springing his plan on the country, and their consequent alienation was to cost him their needed support. Despite official endorsements from the American Federation of Labor (AFL) and the Congress of Industrial Organizations (CIO), organized labor failed to deliver any real support for the president's proposal. But while labor damned the plan with faint praise, the farm bloc mounted a concerted campaign against the president. The radical Farmers' Union, the progressive National Cooperative Council, the Farm Bureau Federation, and the Grange all publicly opposed the plan. E. E. Everson of the Farmers' Union and Louis Taber and Fred Brenckman of the Grange testified in opposition to the plan in the hearings before the Senate Judiciary Committee. The Grange, which denounced the plan as a threat to fundamental liberties, took the extraordinary step of conducting a campaign against the bill over the radio and in the farm press.[15]

The strength of the opposition was most trenchantly expressed by the general public. "Perhaps no presidential message," wrote one historian, "has excited such an immediate and enraged outcry." Almost immediately after Roosevelt's announcement, the Congress was deluged with letters and telegrams.[16] One historian estimates that senators received an average of 10,000 letters each in the first two weeks of the struggle.[17] Nine of every ten were opposed to the plan.[18] Polls taken between February and May of 1937 indicate that the first major domestic initiative of Roosevelt's second term was consistently opposed by a majority of the same American people who had so overwhelmingly returned him to office the preceding November. Indeed, polls taken during the same period reveal a steady decline in Roosevelt's personal popularity.[19]

The justices were not left unaware of the public's sentiments toward the plan. The thousands of letters and telegrams sent to the Court were nearly unanimous in their opposition to the president's proposal. Justice Brandeis received hundreds of letters from a diverse collection of correspondents: women, children, lawyers, doctors, farmers, and grocery clerks all wrote "the original New Dealer" to outline their views on the Court bill. Ninety percent of his correspondents expressed opposition to FDR's plan. "If there had been any doubt as to the standing of the court with the people," wrote Merlo Pusey, "the flood of mail that went both to the court and to Congress quickly removed it." The "roar of protest," wrote Joseph Alsop and Turner Catledge, "was unified, reverberant, and clearly meant business."[20]

This roar of protest was heard and echoed in the halls of Congress. Opposition from the Republicans was to be expected. But the president also faced potential opposition from within his own party. Approximately twenty conservative Senate Democrats were openly hostile to the New Deal, and "could be expected to leave the party reservation on the first major issue." Many congressional Democrats, believing that Roosevelt would step down after the customary two terms as president, "had that second-term feeling of independence which comes with the knowledge that another name will head the ticket at the next voting." Moreover, the enormity of the Democratic majorities in both houses diminished the partisan cohesiveness characteristic of more nearly balanced Congresses.[21]

The initial signals from Congress were ominous. Every Republican came out against the plan in the first few days. Conservative Democratic senators also quickly lined up against the plan. Edward Burke of Nebraska, Harry Byrd and Carter Glass of Virginia, "Cotton Ed" Smith of South Carolina, Walter George of Georgia, Peter Gerry of Rhode Island, David Walsh of Massachusetts, and nearly a dozen others joined the opposition shortly after the president's announcement.[22]

But the president also faced early opposition from less expected quarters. The president had consulted neither his cabinet, nor party leaders, nor members of Congress before revealing the plan to the American public. His decision to eschew the counsel of congressional chieftains not only deprived Roosevelt of an important sounding board for his proposal; it also left many Democrats feeling disgruntled at having been excluded from the process of making a decision of such import.[23] Thus, shortly after the president's announcement, his own vice president, John Nance Garner, was to be seen outside the Senate chamber flagrantly brandishing the "thumbs-down" sign while holding his nose in distaste. Senator Nathan Bachman, of Tennessee, expressed misgivings about the bill the very day it was introduced and ultimately became an opponent of the plan. George Norris, the highly regarded liberal senator from Nebraska, similarly announced his opposition February 5. Norris was to recant his opposition after a White House meeting with Roosevelt, but as Alsop and Catledge noted, "his first distaste had been too public; his subsequent lack of enthusiasm was too marked. A deal of damage was already done."[24]

Perhaps the most devastating defection in the early going was that of Hatton Sumners of Texas, Democratic Chairman of the House Judiciary Committee. His famous February 5 remark to his congressional colleagues, "Boys, here's where I cash in my chips," was not merely the first announcement of Democratic opposition to the plan;[25] it also augured two important maneuvers that were to sap the plan of much of its initial vitality.

Sumners' first move concerned judicial retirement policy. It was widely rumored that both Van Devanter and Sutherland had wanted to retire before 1937. Van Devanter had been on the Court for twenty-six years, and at the age of seventy-eight was anxious to leave the bench. Sutherland suffered from high blood pressure, and as a result was required to write most of his opinions while lying in bed. Both were discouraged from retirement, however, by the treatment Justice Holmes had received from Congress after his retirement in 1932. Shortly after Holmes had resigned Congress had enacted the Economy Bill of 1933, which had the effect of reducing the retirement compensation of all retired Supreme Court justices. The ironic effect of this measure was to keep judicial opponents of other New Deal legislation on the Supreme Court longer than they otherwise would have remained.[26]

In 1935, Sumners' committee had reported out a bill to allow Supreme Court justices to retire at full pay. Perversely, the House rejected the bill when it came to the floor for a vote.[27] But once the extreme measures contained in the president's bill had been proposed, Sumners' bill found new life. Seeking to obviate the president's bill, Sumners managed to rush his retirement bill to passage by the House within five days of the president's announcement.[28] The bill was quickly hustled through the Senate and signed by Roosevelt on March 1.[29] The Congress' alacrity in enacting the previously moribund Sumners bill surely sent both Roosevelt and the Court a powerful early signal of legislative hostility to the president's plan.[30]

Sumners' second blow to Roosevelt's proposal was also delivered in his capacity as chairman of the House Judiciary Committee. Sumners was quickly able to line up a comfortable majority of the members of the committee against the president's bill. "Such a state of affairs in the usually servile House was a severe blow." It meant not only that the administration would be unable to control the committee's hearings on the bill, but also that the bill could be brought to the floor only by extraordinary parliamentary techniques requiring a public display of administration strongarming. House leaders Speaker William Bankhead and Majority Leader Sam Rayburn strongly opposed the resort to such tactics. "They could, they argued, dragoon the bill through the House, but they judged that they would leave the House sore and angry and all the more ready to rebel once the bill came back from the Senate." Bankhead and Rayburn therefore prevailed upon Roosevelt to follow the unusual course of initiating the bill in the Senate rather than the House.[31] But even if the bill managed to pass the Senate, the obstacles created by Sumners' opposition remained lurking in the House. Again, Sumners had sent a strong signal to the justices that the president's plan was in trouble.

Meanwhile, the Senate opposition was planning its strategy. The Republicans recognized that they could defeat the president's plan only if they were able to draw over a sufficient number of moderate and liberal Democrats. Realizing that their purpose would best be served by remaining in the background while the Democrats fought among themselves, they hoped in the early days to find a liberal Democrat to champion their cause. By February 13, they had found him. That day Senator Burton Wheeler, liberal Democrat of Montana, publicly announced his opposition to the plan and thereafter became the leader of the opposition forces.[32]

Wheeler's decision was a coup for the opposition. The White House had been counting on young Bob LaFollette to recruit the independent leftwing votes of the

Northwest. Wheeler was able to bring Gerald Nye and Lynn Frazier of North Dakota, and Henrik Shipstead, Farmer-Laborite of Minnesota, over to the opposition before LaFollette had a chance. By mid-February, Joseph C. O'Mahoney of Wyoming and Tom Connally of Texas had both announced their opposition to the bill.[33] Shortly thereafter, eighteen Democratic members of the opposition met for dinner at the home of Senator Millard Tydings of Maryland for the purpose of forming a steering committee for the opposition forces.[34]

Meanwhile, the signs of congressional coolness continued to proliferate. Such freshmen Democratic senators as Prentiss Brown of Michigan, John Overton of Louisiana, and Charles Andrews of Florida all remained noncommittal.[35] The resistance of these freshmen, brought in on Roosevelt's considerable coattails, to the first major domestic initiative of the president's term, amplified the signal sent to the Court by the noncommittal or antagonistic posture of many other Democrats. Senator Robert Wagner of New York, who had made a tremendous personal investment in the National Labor Relations Act and the Social Security Act and thus had a great stake in seeing the Court uphold them, might have been expected to be a voluble supporter of the president's bill. Yet Wagner privately opposed the bill from the start, censuring the president through silence on the matter.[36] As of February 15, Henry Morgenthau, Roosevelt's secretary of the treasury, gave the plan at best a fifty-fifty chance of passage.[37] By February 19 there were approximately thirty senators committed to support the plan, approximately thirty committed to oppose it, and the remainder undecided. However, the unanimity of the Republicans and the conservative Democrats, the defection of such regulars as O'Mahoney and Connally, and "the painfully evident lack of enthusiasm among the rank and file, all suggested that the situation [in the Senate] was doubtful."[38]

By late February, administration support had further deteriorated. At that time Roosevelt had a falling out with leading southern senators over the issues of deficit relief spending and the handling of the sit-down strikes. As a result of this split, such influential figures as Pat Harrison of Mississippi, James Byrnes of South Carolina, and Vice President John Nance Garner of Texas would no longer do any heavy lifting for Roosevelt on the Court bill. After Roosevelt defended the plan during a March 9 fireside chat, writes William Swindler, "[i]t was quite evident—to everyone but the President and his hard core of advisers—that the scales were beginning to tip permanently toward the opposition."[39]

When the Senate Judiciary Committee opened its hearings on the bill March 10, eight members of the committee supported the plan,[40] eight opposed it,[41] and two were as yet officially undecided.[42] Recognizing that time was on the side of the opposition, the administration forces sought to expedite the hearings by suggesting that each side take no more than two weeks putting on its testimony. The opposition refused to agree, and Chairman Ashurst declined to force the issue. The opposition took full advantage of Ashurst's aversion to haste. The American Bar Association, which opposed the plan, had put together a staff of researchers to aid the opposition in their cross-examination of the administration's witnesses. Each witness was questioned exhaustively, and most were caught in some sort of inconsistency. The senators' lengthy interrogations and elaborate orations consumed nearly as much time as the witnesses' prepared testimony. At the end of two weeks, the administration had managed to put on fewer than half of its witnesses.[43]

Members of the administration were privately convinced that the opposition was conducting a filibuster. When the opposition offered to give the administration more time to put on its witnesses, the proponents of the bill saw the offer as an attempt to trap them into helping the opposition to draw out the hearings. The offer was accordingly refused. In retrospect this proved to be a serious error, for it allowed the opposition forces to dominate the news headlines for the next month.[44]

The opposition was to open its testimony Monday, March 22. Wheeler and his Senate colleagues William King of Utah and Warren Austin of Vermont approached Chief Justice Hughes on Thursday, March 18, requesting that he appear to testify before the committee. After consulting with Brandeis and Van Devanter, the chief justice informed Wheeler that his colleagues on the Court were strongly opposed to any justice appearing before the committee. Wheeler was undeterred, however, and on Saturday, March 20, he called on Brandeis. Brandeis, who as the Court's only octogenarian was profoundly offended by Roosevelt's charge that the elderly justices were incapable of dispatching their duties promptly, suggested to Wheeler that he ask Hughes for a letter answering the charges Roosevelt had leveled against the Court's efficiency and management of its caseload. Wheeler telephoned Hughes from Brandeis' home, and Hughes agreed to prepare the letter to be read by Wheeler before the committee on Monday, March 22. Brandeis and Van Devanter both read and approved the letter Sunday, March 21, and Wheeler picked up the letter at Hughes' home later that afternoon.[45]

Wheeler's dramatic recitation of Hughes' letter before the committee was staged the following morning. The letter rebutted point by point each of the arguments deployed by Roosevelt in his February 5 message. "There is no congestion of cases upon our calendar," wrote the chief justice. "This gratifying condition has obtained for several years." To the contention that the Court had been stingy in granting petitions for certiorari, Hughes replied that the Court had instead been, if anything, overly generous. Most of the petitions denied, Hughes contended, were so utterly without merit that they ought never to have been presented for review. The addition of new justices, Hughes wrote, "apart from any question of policy, which I do not discuss, would not promote the efficiency of the Court. It is believed that it would impair that efficiency so long as the Court acts as a unit. There would be more judges to hear, more judges to confer, more judges to discuss, more judges to be convinced and to decide. The present number of justices is thought to be large enough so far as the prompt, adequate, and efficient conduct of the work of the Court is concerned."[46]

"On account of the shortness of time," Hughes confessed in the final paragraph, "I have not been able to consult with the members of the Court generally with respect to the foregoing statement, but I am confident that it is in accord with the views of the Justices. I should say, however, that I have been able to consult with Mr. Justice Van Devanter and Mr. Justice Brandeis, and I am at liberty to say that the statement is approved by them." This final paragraph created a widespread impression that the Court endorsed the letter unanimously.[47]

This impression of unanimity was what gave the Hughes letter its pivotal impact. Wheeler claimed that after the letter had been read, Vice President Garner telephoned FDR at Warm Springs, where the president was vacationing, and said: "We're licked."[48] Associate Justice Robert Jackson, who was assistant attorney general and one of the key administration witnesses during the Senate hearings, later remarked that Hughes' letter "did more than any one thing to turn the tide in the Court struggle."[49] Brandeis biographer Melvin Urofsky notes that "the reading of [Hughes'] letter marked the end of the Court-packing bill."[50] It is worthy of note that this pivotal event in the already-troubled life of the Court-packing plan occurred before the Court had handed down any of the decisions comprising the constitutional revolution, and indeed before the Social Security cases had even been argued.[51]

On March 29, the Court handed down its 5 to 4 decision upholding Washington State's minimum wage law for women.[52] The new majority consisted of Brandeis, Stone, Cardozo, and Hughes, all of whom had voted to uphold similar laws in the past, and Justice Owen Roberts, who had voted to strike down a similar New York law the previous term.[53] Despite the appearance at the time, however, the decision in *West Coast Hotel* was not influenced by the pendency of the Court-packing plan. The case was actually voted on by the justices in conference on December 19, 1936. The vote was 4 to 4, with Roberts joining Hughes, Brandeis, and Cardozo. Justice Stone was unable to attend the conference due to a severe bout with amoebic dysentery, which kept him away from the Court for more than three months. All of the justices knew how Stone would vote, however, and Hughes decided that it would be better to affirm the lower court's decision by a 5 to 4 vote rather than by the vote of an equally divided Court. The case was therefore held until Stone could return to the Court and cast his deciding vote. Stone did return and cast his vote at the beginning of February, and Hughes set about drafting the opinion of the Court. Roosevelt shortly thereafter announced his Court-packing scheme, however, and Hughes decided that if the Court were to hand down the *Parrish* opinion so soon after the president's announcement, it would convey the false impression that the Court was capitulating to political pressure. He therefore decided to hold the opinion for release at a more propitious date. That date was to be March 29, exactly one week after Wheeler's dramatic reading of Hughes' letter before the Senate Judiciary Committee.[54] Though Hughes was largely unsuccessful in his attempt to avoid conveying the impression that *Parrish* was an act of judicial obeisance to an aggressive executive, it is amply clear that the constitutional revolution was actually initiated more than six weeks before the Court-packing plan, a very closely guarded secret, became public knowledge.[55]

The impact of the minimum wage decision on the fate of the Court-packing bill was, arguably, substantial. "[I]t was obvious," writes Leonard Baker, "that the decision upholding the minimum wage would make it more difficult to push FDR's Court plan through the Senate." "Particularly after the Roberts switch, there was no nationwide desire for altering the Court, and, as a result, no great desire in Congress either."[56] "By April," reports James MacGregor Burns, "the chances for the court plan were almost nil."[57] The justices could no doubt have anticipated the effect that the *Parrish* decision would have on the plan's chances for passage. And they knew, even as they were deliberating over the Wagner Act cases, what the decision in the minimum wage case would be.

Even before Wheeler's presentation of Hughes' letter and the Court's decision in *Parrish*, there was good reason to doubt that the president's proposal would ever be approved by the Senate. The Democrats' overwhelming majority in the upper house did appear to give the plan a significant leg up, and there were times, especially early in the Court fight, when the proponents of the plan thought that they had a slender majority of the votes in the upper house.[58] But as Alsop and Catledge pointed out, these optimistic estimates were always subject to serious question. Among the proponents

> [t]here was no orderly daily pooling of information. . . . They could not even manage an accurate list of their own supporters—and this in a fight in which the opposition had admirably prepared, carefully checked, semiweekly lists from their whip, Gerry, who was able to say at a moment's notice whether any Senator was sure, inclined to the opposition, wavering, inclined to the administration or sure for the administration.
>
> Robinson and Keenan both tried to make lists. So did Corcoran. . . . But Robinson carried all his information in his head, and some of it was confidential and not to be revealed even to the White House. And some Senators talked double, giving one impression to Keenan and Corcoran and quite another to James Roosevelt when they called on the President. And other Senators would not talk at all, and no two could agree on how they should be counted. . . . The administration actually never possessed a reliable list of its friends and enemies until the very final weeks of the struggle.[59]

Not in even their most optimistic moments, however, did the plan's proponents believe that they had the sixty-four votes necessary to prevent a filibuster. The leaders of the opposition recognized that delay would permit them to extend their propaganda and to augment their forces. They also realized that the consumption of time entailed by a filibuster might persuade uncommitted senators to oppose the plan for the purpose of getting rid of that bill and on to others. Accordingly, the leaders of the opposition had always considered the option of mounting a filibuster to defeat the bill, and "were obviously prepared" to do so. Their determination to employ tactics of delay in order to weaken the bill was demonstrated by the quasi-filibuster they conducted, with Ashurst's complicity, in the Judiciary Committee hearings.[60]

Even before the hearings began, plans for a filibuster had already begun to crystallize. Senator William Borah of Idaho "made plans to filibuster the Court bill to death if enough Democrats did not defect from Roosevelt. He would talk about constitutional law and history for a month if necessary. One of his associates declared many years later that Borah had planned to fight the Court bill with his voice until he fainted with exhaustion." Journalists encountered Borah at his Senate desk preparing a filibuster speech as early as March 4.[61] On March 8, a prominent Republican wrote to William Allen White, "unless there is a change of attitude caused by the tremendous propaganda of the Administration, there are enough senators pledged to speak against the President's proposal to prevent a vote upon it."[62] This view was confirmed by Senator Arthur Capper, who on February 26 wrote, "I think the Roosevelt program in its present form is blocked. I feel quite sure we have enough votes to upset him."[63]

Throughout most of the Court fight, members of the opposition were in close touch with certain of the justices. The justices doubtless suspected, if they did not in fact know, that a filibuster was in the offing. The opposition kept very accurate lists detailing the various senators' leanings,[64] and it does not seem at all unlikely that certain members of the Court were privy to some of those lists. We know, for example, that an agent of the opposition informed Hughes in late February that thirty-seven senators were "hostile" to the bill and that twenty more were "doubtful."[65] We do not know what else was said in the conversation, but we do know that Hughes could count, and surely recognized that thirty-seven senators were four more than the thirty-three that would be required to prevent cloture of floor debate on the bill. Members of the Court were therefore aware as early as late February, and probably at other times as well, that the opposition had enough votes to sustain a successful filibuster, if not to defeat the bill outright. It is therefore likely that the justices never saw the president's bill as a serious threat to the Court's independence, because the administration forces never held a card capable of trumping what appeared to be the opposition's one sure ace—the filibuster.

All of this was clear by the time the Court upheld the National Labor Relations Act in a series of cases handed down April 12.[66] Here the Court gave the government far more than it needed to in order to avert the Court-packing threat. As Richard Friedman has argued, "the Court might have held for the NLRB [National Labor Relations Board] in its case against Jones & Laughlin and the giant Fruehauf Trailer Company, but held against the Board in its case against the smaller Friedman-Harry Marks Clothing Company. Such a result would greatly weaken any argument that the Court was trying to scuttle the New Deal. . . ."[67] Yet Hughes and Roberts voted to grant the NLRB victory in each of the five cases. Moreover, Hughes' opinion upholding the Act offered a more expansive conception of the commerce power than was required to reach such a result.[68]

The Four Horsemen were presumably as devoted as were their brethren to the Court and its preservation as an independent institution. Yet the Court-packing plan not only did not intimidate them, it appeared to harden their resolve. In *Parrish* and all but one of the Wagner Act cases,[69] the Horsemen filed ringing dissents.[70] As noted earlier, the announcement of the plan actually persuaded Van Devanter and Sutherland to *delay* their retirements. If the plan had this effect on the Four Horsemen, one must wonder whether it would have had any different effect on Hughes and Roberts. It was by no means obvious that upholding the Wagner Act would dampen congressional support for the plan. In addition to deflating a justice's self-image, a manifestation of cowardice in a time of crisis might well have diminished the prestige and public support that were the Court's principal defenses against the plan.[71] Hughes was surely mindful of this possibility when he delayed release of *Parrish* to avoid giving the appearance that it was the sacrificial offering of a timorous Court cowering before the prospect of institutional evisceration.

Had the Court wished to hold against the government but to avoid releasing an adverse opinion in the midst of the Court fight, it had options. It could have delayed release of the opinion, as it did in *Parrish*, until later in the term when the plan was in still deeper trouble. It could also have done what it later did with such controversial cases as *Wickard v. Filburn*[72] and *Brown v. Board of Education:*[73] ordered reargument and held the cases over until the next term, by which time the plan would have presumably lost most, if not all of its momentum. Awarding the government victory in all five of the Wagner Act cases in mid-April was not the only way to defeat the plan, and it probably was not even the best. This suggests again that the decisions were not a direct response to the Court-packing threat.

Within ten days of the Wagner Act decisions Senator Joe Robinson of Arkansas, floor manager of the bill, knew of at least forty-five senators committed to vote against the president's bill.[74] The opposition now clearly had the votes to sustain any attempted filibuster. When the Judiciary Committee's hearings finally ended April 23, it was clear that a majority of the committee opposed the bill and was preparing to write a critical report.[75] The following day Chairman Ashurst admitted to reporters, "[E]verybody knew from the start that the committee was not for the bill."[76] Roosevelt summoned Ashurst to the White House to try to persuade him to report the bill to the Senate "without recommendation." Ashurst and Robinson looked into the possibility and discovered that such a course of action was "not feasible."[77] On April 28 Senators McCarran and Hatch, the two undecided members of the committee who, along with Senator O'Mahoney, had tried unsuccessfully to persuade Roosevelt to agree to a compromise bill, publicly announced their opposition to the plan.[78] The vote was now eight in favor, ten opposed.

The opposition, however, was not to be contented with the parliamentary advantages entailed by a victory in committee: it was their intention to defeat the bill in a roll-call vote on the floor of the Senate. "Everywhere waverers were beset by members of the opposition, who wheedled, persuaded, threatened and cajoled until waverers wavered no longer."[79] A poll taken near the end of April showed forty-four senators in favor, forty-seven opposed, four doubtful, and one seat vacant.[80] By the beginning of May, more than three weeks before the Court was to hand down its opinions in the Social Security cases, the steering committee of the opposition concluded that they commanded an absolute majority in the Senate.[81] Even the optimistic backers of the bill soon had to face the fact that they simply did not have the votes. Five different polls of the Senate taken in May had all spelled defeat for the Plan.[82] The lack of senatorial support for the bill was mirrored by public opinion. By May 12 a Gallup poll indicated that only 31 percent of the public supported the president's plan.[83] And on May 18, the Senate Judiciary Committee, by a vote of 10 to 8, determined to report the bill out with an unfavorable recommendation.[84]

In the meantime, Justice Van Devanter had finally decided to retire. After consulting with his close friend Senator William Borah, a prominent member of the opposition, Van Devanter decided to send his letter of resignation to Roosevelt on the very day that the committee was to issue its adverse recommendation.[85] The timing could not have been more exquisite. Already facing defeat in the Senate, the president's plan was rebuked by a Democratic committee on the very day that one of its principal *raisons d'être* submitted his resignation. The retirement for which both Roosevelt and Van Devanter had thirsted so long had sealed the fate of the Court-packing plan.

Roosevelt managed to undermine the bill's chances even further in the days following Van Devanter's retirement announcement. It was widely known that Roosevelt had promised Joe Robinson the first vacant seat on the Supreme Court. On the day of Van Devanter's announcement, Robinson's colleagues gathered round the popular senator's desk and congratulated him heartily. But the expected announcement from the White House was not forthcoming. Because he saw Robinson as a conservative, Roosevelt was loath to appoint him to Van Devanter's seat. The replacement of one conservative with another would result in no net gain for Roosevelt's constitutional agenda. Rather than facing the inevitable with grace, the administration hemmed and hawed for nearly two weeks before calling Robinson to the White House. Members of Roosevelt's staff even began to circulate reports that Robinson would not be appointed. Robinson was incensed by such shabby treatment and made no secret of his anger among his Senate colleagues. His outrage was shared by many of his fellow senators, and their disgust at Roosevelt's graceless handling of the situation undoubtedly further compromised the bill's chances for passage.[86]

It was on May 24, in the midst of Roosevelt's mishandling of the Robinson appointment, that the Supreme Court handed down its decisions in the Social Security cases. In *Carmichael v. Southern Coal & Coke Co.*, a majority composed of Hughes, Roberts, Brandeis, Stone, and Cardozo upheld the Alabama Unemployment Compensation Act, which had been enacted by the State of Alabama pursuant to the unemployment compensation provisions of the Social Security Act. Here the solidarity of the Four Horsemen, who had stood shoulder to shoulder in dissent in *West Coast Hotel* and the Wagner Act cases, began to unravel. Justice McReynolds dissented alone without opinion. Justice Sutherland, joined by Justices Van Devanter and Butler, contended that certain provisions of the Alabama statute violated both the due process and equal protection clauses of the Fourteenth Amendment. Theirs was not a blanket condemnation of unemployment compensation legislation, however. Rather, these justices opined that, were the Alabama legislature to redraft the objectionable provisions so that they more resembled the Wisconsin unemployment compensation act, then the Alabama act's constitutionality would be beyond cavil.[87]

In *Steward Machine Co. v. Davis*, the same five-man majority upheld the unemployment compensation provisions of the Social Security Act. Here again the Four Horsemen broke ranks. Justices McReynolds and Butler dissented, contending that the Act invaded the powers reserved to the states by the Tenth Amendment. Justice Sutherland, joined by Justice Van Devanter, again wrote separately, objecting only to certain easily correctable provisions of the Act.[88] And in *Helvering v. Davis*,[89] Sutherland and the retiring Van Devanter actually joined the majority in sustaining the old-age pension provisions of the Social Security Act. These largely superfluous gestures of support for the New Deal were offered when backing for the Court-packing plan was at its ebb. If the Court-packing plan had been the efficient cause of the Court's decisions in the spring of 1937, one might have expected the Court's receptivity to the New Deal to vary in direct proportion to the plan's chances for passage. Yet the relationship was, if anything, inverse: the compliance of the justices appeared to increase even as the fortunes of the plan waned.

Even disregarding the weakness of the plan when the Social Security cases were decided, there are chronological reasons to doubt that the president's proposal influenced the decisions. Sutherland's *Carmichael* dissent[90] suggested that the deficiencies plaguing the Alabama act were those that had prompted the Four Horsemen to vote to strike down its New York counterpart in *Chamberlin v. Andrews*. There the lower court decision upholding the New York statute had been affirmed by an equally divided Court on November 23, 1936.[91] The missing justice was again the ailing Stone. Hughes and Roberts must therefore have joined Brandeis and Cardozo in *Chamberlin*, as they did in *Carmichael*, in voting to uphold a state unemployment compensation act enacted in accordance with the provisions of the federal Social Security Act. And they did so more than two months before the unveiling of the Court-packing plan.

In sum, then, *Parrish* was decided six weeks, and the first Social Security case ten weeks, before the Court-packing plan was known to any but the most intimate of Roosevelt's advisers; the Wagner Act cases were handed down six weeks after it was clear that the opposition had sufficient support to sustain a successful filibuster against the bill; and the remaining Social Security cases were handed down over three weeks after it was widely known that the committee would issue an adverse report and that the opposition had enough votes to defeat the bill in a vote on the Senate floor. Because the justices had ample reason to doubt that the Court-packing plan had sufficient public and congressional support to pose a genuine threat to the Court as an institution, the plan is unlikely to have been the proximate cause of the Constitutional Revolution of 1937.

Roosevelt did have opportunities for compromise. There were numerous proposals to deal with "the Court problem" on Capitol Hill;[92] and though none of them had thus far garnered much support in either house, they might have been invigorated by the backing of a popular president seeking a reasonable accommodation with opponents of his bill. But it became evident very early in the struggle that the president was in no mood to compromise.

Roosevelt and his advisers had contemplated many alternative proposals when framing the Court bill and had rejected almost all of them. Thoughts of amending the Constitution were abandoned early.[93] In the first place, it was Roosevelt's view that the Court, not the Constitution, was the problem.[94] Amending the Constitution would appear to be conceding that the Court's decisions against the New Deal had been correct.[95] Second, there was considerable dispute within the administration and the liberal legal community over whether an amendment ought to be offered at all, and if offered, what it should look like. The framing difficulties were manifest in the failure of two years of Justice Department efforts to render an acceptable proposal.[96] Moreover, an amendment would have to receive a two-thirds vote in each house of Congress and the approval of thirty-six state legislatures. The administration doubted that any acceptable amendment could run such a gauntlet at all, let alone with satisfactory celerity.[97] Finally, any legislation enacted pursuant to the authority of a constitutional amendment enlarging regulatory power would be subject to judicial review and interpretation.[98] Efforts to amend the Constitution, even if successful, might turn out to have been squandered on a Pyrrhic victory.

Having abandoned the constitutional amendment approach, the administration considered a variety of statutory remedies. Proposals to require a supermajority of the Court to invalidate legislation were rejected for two reasons. First, such a measure was of doubtful constitutionality and would almost certainly be voided by a Court jealous of its prestige.[99] Second, such a statute would dilute the Court's power to protect citizens from infringements of their civil liberties.[100] A proposal to restrict the Court's appellate jurisdiction was similarly rejected. Again, the reasons were twofold. First, the Court would still have original jurisdiction in cases involving conflicts among the states. Second, the lower federal courts, which had not been particularly hospitable to the New Deal, would retain the power of judicial review.[101]

The rejection of all of these alternatives left the administration with only one acceptable solution: enlargement of the Court by statute. Even within these constraints, however, Roosevelt had room to negotiate. His proposal would have resulted in the immediate addition of six justices to the Court. Even if he could not get a majority of the Senate behind his bill, there was reason to believe he could get a majority to support a compromise bill that would add two or perhaps three new justices. But throughout the Court fight the president spurned this and all other offers of compromise. In mid-February a group of congressional leaders headed by Vice President Garner approached Roosevelt and proposed a compromise "probably on the basis of two or three rather than six additional justices." The president responded by laughing in their faces. Against the urging of White House advisers, Roosevelt publicly reaffirmed his commitment to his bill, as drafted, in a speech delivered at the Democratic victory dinners on March 4, and again in a fireside chat broadcast March 9. Even after the Wagner Act decisions came down, Roosevelt rejected compromises promising two or three immediate appointments to the Court. Not until June 3, after the Court had concluded its term, did Roosevelt finally consent to allow Robinson to secure the best compromise possible.[102]

Though born in part of the arrogance of his great electoral victory, Roosevelt's intransigence was not entirely irrational. First, Roosevelt wanted to regain control over his own party. He wanted to give the conservative Democratic apostates who opposed him on the Court bill and other initiatives a thorough thrashing, and a compromise would not achieve this desired effect. Second, and perhaps more troubling, was Roosevelt's well-known promise to Robinson of an appointment to the first available vacancy on the Court. If, as Roosevelt suspected, Robinson returned to his conservative roots once vested with lifetime judicial tenure, a two-judge compromise would get the president nowhere. What had been 5 to 4 and 6 to 3 decisions against the New Deal would now be adverse votes of 6 to 5 or 7 to 4. Even a three-judge compromise held little allure. A 6 to 6 decision might well affirm by an equally divided Court an unfavorable decision of a lower federal or state court; and if Hughes, Roberts, and Robinson all voted with the Four Horsemen, the administration would be handed defeat by a vote of 7 to 5.[103]

The justices of course could not be certain that Roosevelt would not grasp one of his compromise alternatives. But even if Roosevelt had been prepared to agree to a compromise bill, it would have had to run the gauntlet of a Senate filibuster. In fact, when a compromise bill finally was introduced in early July, Robinson knew he was not even close to having the votes necessary to impose cloture, and he expressed doubt over how long his support would hold in the face of a filibuster. There were between forty-two and forty-four Senators lined up to speak against the measure. "At no time in the history of successful filibusters," wrote William Leuchtenburg, "could the foes of a piece of legislation count so many Senators in their ranks as were aligned against the Court bill. . . ."[104] About half of these senators had pledged to make two full-dress speeches not only against the bill itself, but also twice again on each of the 125 pesky amendments that the opposition had prepared in order to prolong the filibuster.[105] These full-dress speeches could last anywhere from two hours to two days each. Had support for the bill not crumbled later that month, observed Alsop and Catledge, "[t]he oratory might have flowed on until the 1938 election. . . ."[106]

Of course, no one could be sure that the Senate opposition's filibuster lines would hold. But even had the imposition of cloture managed to spare the country this deluge of prolixity, the bill still had to negotiate the House. This of course meant reckoning with House Judiciary Committee Chairman Hatton Sumners, who on July 13 made an ominous speech on the subject of the bill's merits and its chances of passage in the lower house. "[I]f they bring that bill into this House for consideration," Sumners predicted to the wild applause of his colleagues, "I do not believe they will have enough hide left on it to bother about."[107] Sumners' tirade and the congressmen's response confirmed Vice President Garner's long-held suspicion that the bill could not pass the House. As Garner had suspected, "Sumners would bottle the bill up in his Judiciary Committee, and the House members did not appear very anxious to dislodge the bill from his grasp."[108]

From the outset and throughout the fight, then, it was clear that Roosevelt would cling stubbornly to his own bill rather than seizing on any of a number of possible compromise measures. Moreover, it was doubtful that even a compromise bill could survive both a Senate filibuster and the House Judiciary Committee. The justices had ample reason to be confident that constitutional capitulation was not necessary to avert the Court-packing threat. Certainly they had reason to doubt that immediate, total, and unconditional surrender was required.[109]

The Electoral Theory

It was perhaps in recognition of these deficiencies in the Court-packing thesis that many historians turned to additional or alternative explanations for the Court's behavior. At the ready was a thesis that held considerable charm for the Progressive mind, namely Mr. Dooley's aphorism, "the Supreme Court follows th' iliction returns." Like its cousin the Court-packing thesis, the electoral theory is sometimes offered as the sole explanation for the Court's behavior, but it is more often presented as one of two or more political factors driving the Court's decisions. And like the Court-packing thesis, it is conventionally argued to be one of the two most significant factors in inducing the Court to accept the New Deal.[110]

The 1936 general election was indeed a tremendous victory for Roosevelt and the New Deal. In an electoral landslide, Roosevelt took every state but Maine and

Vermont. Moreover, Roosevelt's coattails brought the Democrats six additional seats in the Senate, raising the party's majority to seventy-five of the ninety-six seats in that body.[111]

But this electoral explanation for the Court's behavior encounters several difficulties. Initially, one might reasonably wonder what it means to say that the Supreme Court decided a particular case a particular way in response to the results of a particular election. Federal judges hold their offices "during good Behaviour,"[112] and none of the justices had been accused of the commission of an impeachable offense. The electorate was powerless to touch the Court directly. The announcement of Roosevelt's Court-packing plan was more than six weeks away at the time *Parrish* was decided, and no other bill to restrict the Court's behavior was going anywhere in Congress. Moreover, the justices had taken an oath to uphold the Constitution, as they understood it, despite the vicissitudes of public opinion. The 1930s was not the first time that the Court had flouted the popular will, and it would not be the last.

In evaluating the electoral theory, it is also instructive to examine the Court's reaction to the results of other elections. Consider, for example, the election of 1934. In that year the nation held off-year elections in the midst of the severest depression in U.S. history.[113] The party in power traditionally loses a number of seats in off-year elections and, in light of the economic conditions prevailing in 1934, the Republicans were widely expected to rout the Democrats at the polls. Rather than picking up the expected few dozen seats, however, the Republicans lost thirteen in the House. When the dust had settled, the Republicans held fewer than 30 percent of the seats in the House, the lowest percentage in the party's history. The drubbing in the Senate was even more devastating. The Democrats picked up nine additional seats, swelling their total to sixty-nine. The Democrats now held better than a two-thirds majority in the Senate, the greatest margin either party had ever held in the history of the upper house.[114]

"If there was an issue in the [1934] campaign," wrote William Leuchtenburg, "it was Roosevelt: the election was a thumping personal victory for the President. Even Republicans had invoked Roosevelt's name to get elected."[115] "There has been no such popular endorsement since the days of Thomas Jefferson and Andrew Jackson," wrote William Randolph Hearst. The New Deal, wrote Arthur Krock, the veteran political reporter of the *New York Times,* had won "the most overwhelming victory in the history of American politics."[116] "William Allen White, who had watched political pretenders and practitioners of all seasons for almost half a century, would comment after the spectacular returns in the 1934 Congressional elections that the President had 'been all but crowned by the people.'"[117] "The elections," continued Leuchtenburg, "almost erased the Republican party as a national force. They left the GOP with only seven governorships, less than a third of Congress, no program of any substance, no leader with popular appeal and none on the horizon."[118] The Congress elected in 1934, noted William Swindler, was "unmistakably returned by the voters to continue the program Roosevelt had inaugurated."[119]

The Supreme Court clearly did not follow the election returns of 1934. Indeed, in the two years following the 1934 election, the Court routinely struck down legislation enacted by the overwhelmingly Democratic Congress.[120] If the Court felt no compunction about gutting the New Deal in the wake of the Democrats' spectacular success in 1934, one is led to inquire, why would the Court respond so differently to the election of 1936?

Moreover, it is difficult to see how the Court could have construed the 1936 election as a constitutional referendum. In the wake of 1934's debacle, the Republicans recognized that they would have to liberalize their party if they were to have a political future. Their selection of a nominee in 1936 reflected this recognition. Alf Landon of Kansas, allied with the Progressive wing of the party since the days of Theodore Roosevelt's Bull Moose crusade, was the only Republican governor in the nation to survive the 1934 election. Landon had been private secretary to progressive Kansas governor Henry Allen in 1922, had voted for Robert M. LaFollette in 1924, and had been a progressive governor in his own right. During Landon's administration Kansas had abolished the poll tax, enacted graduated income and corporate taxes, passed a farm mortgage moratorium, and beefed up utility and securities regulation. Landon favored the redistribution of wealth, criticized industrial plutocracy, and contended that government power had to increase as civilization grew more complex. The Kansas governor "had offered to enlist with Roosevelt in 1933, supported the administration's agricultural and conservation programs, endorsed the principle of social security, had never criticized the securities or banking or holding company or labor legislation, and seemed to hold against the New Deal chiefly its administrative inefficiency and its fiscal deficits." In the national radio broadcast inaugurating his campaign in January of 1936, Landon proclaimed himself a "constitutional liberal."[121]

Roosevelt assiduously avoided raising either the Constitution or the Court as an issue in his campaign.[122] His platform had pledged the administration to meet the economic and social problems of the day "through legislation within the Constitution" or, if that should prove impracticable, through a "clarifying amendment."[123] Though Landon occasionally remarked that the Court had held numerous New Deal initiatives unconstitutional, he did not seek to identify himself with the positions taken by the justices in recent cases; he stood instead behind a platform that generally called for national solutions to economic problems.[124] Nor did the Republican candidate frame the minimum wage and the Wagner Act as partisan issues. On the contrary, the Republican platform explicitly endorsed minimum wages for women and children, as did Landon in his telegram to the convention accepting his party's nomination.[125] The Wagner Act, which was not a Roosevelt initiative, to which Roosevelt was initially opposed, and to which the President offered virtually no support until after the Senate had approved it by an overwhelming margin and its passage in the House was certain,[126] was opposed by only half of the Senate members of the GOP.[127] The Republican platform, far from criticizing the Act, pledged the party "to protect the right of labor to organize and bargain collectively through representatives of its own choosing without interference from any source,"[128] a position to which Landon adhered throughout his campaign.[129] In his speech accepting the nomination, Landon pledged both full protection for the right of labor to organize and government mediation of disputes between management and labor.[130] On the issues of the minimum wage and the Wagner Act, the justices might well have taken from a Landon victory a message not significantly different from that they are alleged to have taken from the Roosevelt landslide. Certainly decisions in 1937 upholding minimum wage legislation and the Wagner Act could not have been seen as a judicial repudiation of President Landon, any more than decisions striking down such legislation could have been seen as concessions to a Landon "mandate."

On the issue of Social Security, Landon sent mixed signals. He accepted the basic philosophy of social security, and resisted the urgings of some Republicans that he repudiate the idea. When the Social Security bill had been under consideration in the Senate, Democratic Senator Harry Byrd of Virginia had "tried to enlist Landon's support in opposing it, because the states could not afford to match its federal grants, but Landon wired back saying the states must match federal social security funds. . . ." In July of 1936 Landon called the Kansas legislature into special session for the purpose of authorizing state constitutional amendments enabling Kansans to receive federal Social Security benefits. At Landon's urging, the amendments were passed with only one dissenting vote. In a speech before the Ohio Chamber of Commerce in November of 1935, the Kansas governor declared that "unemployment relief was neither a vested right or a charity but a common obligation," and "called for genuine cooperation between national and state governments . . . preferably on a pay-as-you-go basis." And in his acceptance address before the Republican National Convention in July of 1936, Landon promised to continue federal unemployment grants. Landon similarly declared his approval of social security in a national radio interview with H. V. Kaltenborn on May 7, 1936. Landon, who favored old-age pensions, personally did not like the compulsory insurance features of the Social Security Act, but was resigned to such a system.[131]

As the campaign wore on, the nature of Landon's reservations toward the Social Security Act became clearer. In a speech at Milwaukee on September 26, 1936, Landon leveled several criticisms at the Act. First, he noted, payroll taxes to finance the old-age pensions would begin to be levied in 1937, while no pensioner would receive any payments until 1942. Second, only about half of the nation's workers would be eligible for pensions under the Act. Third, even at full coverage the pensions were, in Landon's view, parsimonious. Fourth, the Act's taxes were a "cruel hoax," because the costs of rising payroll taxes imposed on employers would be passed on to their employees in the form of reduced compensation. Yet Landon did not dispute the Act's objectives. "We can afford old-age pensions," he declared. ". . . [I]n a highly industrialized society they are necessary. I believe in them as a matter of social justice." Landon proposed legislation giving "every American citizen over sixty-five the supplementary payment necessary to give a minimum of income sufficient to protect him or her from want." Landon defended such a program as "much less expensive than the plan of the present administration, because we will not create a needless reserve fund." Such pensions would be administered by the states and would be financed not by a regressive payroll tax, but by a direct federal tax levied over a broad base. Finally, Landon invoked Brandeisian rhetoric in contending that unemployment insurance was an appropriate matter for state experimentation.[132] These were hardly the remarks of a laissez-faire ideologue.[133]

Landon reiterated these themes in the final week of the campaign. In Newark, New Jersey, on October 28, he warned the crowd that about 50 percent of the workforce was excluded from the Act's old-age and survivors' insurance program, and that the payroll deductions would fall "almost entirely on workers." He "repeated the Republican platform pledges to assist the needy, blind, and crippled, to promote child welfare and state unemployment-insurance programs, and to improve public health services." "To these," he concluded, "—our old people and our workers struggling for better conditions I will not promise the moon. I promise only what I know can be performed: economy, a living pension and such security as can be provided by a generous people." At Madison Square Garden the next day, Landon charged that the Social Security Act gave the nation "an unworkable hodgepodge, which only partially covered the people and would lead to unfair taxation and fiscal waste." At a stop at Charleston, West Virginia, in the last, desperate days of the campaign, however, Landon went off the deep end. Warning that workers would bear a disproportionate part of the tax burden of Social Security, Landon added that "keeping track of those covered under the program would lead to 'federal snooping,' perhaps even fingerprinting, photographing, and the wearing of identification tags."[134]

Though some Republican operatives, especially in the waning days of the campaign, volubly opposed the Act,[135] the posture of the broader party was also far from decidedly reactionary. Three times as many Republicans had voted for the Social Security Act as had voted against it.[136] The Republican platform declared that "Society has an obligation to promote the security of the people, by affording some measure of protection against involuntary unemployment and dependency in old age." The platform proposed a federal-state cooperative system of old-age pensions financed on a pay-as-you-go basis from the proceeds of "a direct tax widely distributed," and encouraged the states to adopt "honest and practical measures for meeting the problems of unemployment insurance." What criticism the Republican platform leveled at the Act came as much from the left as the right.[137] In light of Republican congressional support for the Act, the platform's position, Landon's numerous pronouncements in favor of a social security program, and the many other issues at stake in the campaign,[138] a vote for Landon in 1936 couldn't be read unequivocally as a vote against Social Security. The claim that the election was a referendum on the Social Security Act thus seems overdrawn.[139]

Let us assume, however, that the 1936 election is properly read as a referendum on the issue of Social Security. Let us assume that a vote in a multi-issued presidential election is a sufficiently subtle form of expression to yield an informed understanding of the electorate's views with respect to a particular piece of legislation in all of its details.[140] The claim that the Court's decisions in the Social Security cases were responses to the results of the 1936 election nevertheless remains problematic. First, nothing in the justices' papers suggests that they interpreted Landon's defeat as a "mandate" for Social Security. Moreover, if the justices were looking to the electorate for cues concerning the constitutionality of legislation, they might very well have taken the 1932 election to be determinative of public sentiment. Anyone familiar with Roosevelt's gubernatorial record and with the Democratic platform knew that he favored social insurance for the elderly and the unemployed, at least at the state level. And by the time voters went to the polls in 1934, they knew that FDR favored and the next Congress would take up a federal social security measure.[141] The overwhelming victory of Democrats in that election therefore might have been taken as a mandate for a national social security program. Would a vote for Landon in 1936 have signaled the justices that the country had abruptly changed its mind on that issue? As I have just suggested, such a conclusion would hardly have been irrefragable.

In evaluating the causal relationship between the 1936 election and the Social Security cases, we should also look to the behavior of the Four Horsemen. In view of their dissents in *Parrish* and the Wagner Act cases, it would be implausible to claim that they were responding to political pressure in the spring of 1937. Yet even "conservative" justices were receptive to social security. In *Carmichael v. Southern Coal & Coke Co.*,[142] Sutherland, Van Devanter, and even Butler expressed the view that Wisconsin's state unemployment compensation statute was constitutional. In *Steward Machine Co. v. Davis*,[143] Sutherland and Van Devanter took the position that it was possible to achieve a constitutional system of federal-state cooperation for insuring against unemployment, and that with a few revisions the Social Security Act could be such an acceptable scheme. Finally, Sutherland and Van Devanter actually joined the majority opinion upholding the old-age pension provisions of the Act.[144] It seems unlikely that these justices came to these positions only as a result of the 1936 election, and it is therefore improbable that Hughes and Roberts needed such electoral prodding to induce them to vote as they did.

The electoral theory and, more generally, the political response theory, suffer additional setbacks when one considers the fortunes of President Roosevelt as reflected in the events leading up to and culminating in the election of 1938. In July of 1937 the Senate utterly repudiated the Court-packing plan, voting to recommit the Court bill with directions that the provisions pertaining to the appointment of additional justices be removed. A substitute measure containing procedural reforms for the lower federal courts was enacted in August. That same month, the economy again slid into recession, while resentment over New Deal relief spending and Roosevelt's handling of the sit-down epidemic continued to build. The concatenation of these events undermined Roosevelt's authority with Congress, and indeed precipitated the dissolution of the New Deal coalition and the formation of a bipartisan anti-New Deal coalition.[145] By the end of 1937, Roosevelt had gotten almost nothing of what he had asked of Congress that year.[146] Apparently Congress did not take the same message from the election that the Court is alleged to have. "A year after his overwhelming triumph in the 1936 election," wrote William Leuchtenburg, "Roosevelt appeared to be a thoroughly repudiated leader."[147]

As the recession deepened in 1938, Roosevelt's personal popularity continued to slip, and congressional resistance stiffened. "By the spring of 1938, the prospects for reform had diminished perceptibly." Indeed, "[a]s Roosevelt's power waned, Congress began to handle him more roughly." For example, on April 8, 1938, the House voted down FDR's executive reorganization bill by a vote of 204 to 196, with 108 Democrats voting against. Roosevelt opened further the breach within the party by campaigning, largely unsuccessfully, against anti-New Deal Democrats in the 1938 primary elections. This failed attempt to purge the party of Roosevelt's opponents was compounded by the results of the 1938 election. That November the GOP picked up a whopping eighty-one seats in the House, eight seats in the Senate, and thirteen governorships. Some of the most prominent liberal governors, including Frank Murphy of Michigan, Elmer Benson of Minnesota, and Philip LaFollette of Wisconsin, failed to win reelection. A more thorough repudiation of Roosevelt and the New Deal would have been difficult to imagine. "The GOP had been resuscitated as a national power. Roosevelt's political career seemed all but ended. The 1938 outcome, wrote the usually astute newspaperman Raymond Clapper, showed 'clearly, I think, that President Roosevelt could not run for a third term even if he so desired.'" The depth and persistence of the recession had undermined the confidence of the voters in the capacity of the administration to restore prosperity. By the end of 1938, even New Dealers had lost confidence that the New Deal could bring the economy out of its stagnant state. And by 1939, "Congress was moving aggressively to dismantle the New Deal. It slashed relief appropriations, killed Roosevelt appointments, and . . . eliminated what was left of the undistributed-profits tax."[148]

Yet despite the defeat of the Court-packing plan, the recession, the loss of voter and congressional confidence in the New Deal, and the resounding victories of Republicans and anti-New Deal Democrats in the 1938 elections, the Supreme Court, with Hughes and Roberts voting with the majority, continued to sustain the constitutionality of New Deal measures.[149] As William Swindler noted, the Court "had, indeed, saved the New Deal after Congress had declared its independence of the White House."[150] Lest this be construed as a general capitulation by these justices to the New Deal in response to the political pressures of 1936–37, it should be noted that both Hughes and Roberts continued occasionally to vote against the interests of labor well after 1937;[151] that both justices continued occasionally to cast votes against the New Deal farm program;[152] that Justice Roberts remained unreconstructed in cases involving delegation of congressional power to the executive branch;[153] that in the non-unanimous labor cases involving the National Labor Relations Act heard before the Court between 1941 and 1946, Roberts voted with labor only 7 percent of the time; that Roberts voted against labor in each of the thirty non-unanimous labor cases involving the Fair Labor Standards Act heard by the Court during the same period; and that between 1941 and 1946, even after Roosevelt had won reelection to his third term, Roberts remained "in almost continuous opposition" to the claims of the administrative agencies that were integral to the New Deal vision of government.[154]

At the very least, it should be apparent that the claim that *Parrish* was precipitated by the Court-packing plan is untenable, and that the theory that the decision was prompted by the 1936 election is highly problematic. It is worthy of note at this juncture that *Parrish* was the only one of the decisions comprising the "Constitutional Revolution of 1937" that required the Court to overrule one of its own precedents. The Wagner Act cases and the Social Security cases were (not disingenuously, I contend) distinguishable and distinguished from earlier decisions. The fact that the only case that required the Court to eat its words was a response neither to the Court-packing plan nor to the 1936 election ought to give us pause when considering whether these political events were the proximate causes of decisions requiring no such *volte face*.

The Court-packing and electoral theories are often accompanied by the listing of other extrajudicial factors alleged to have influenced the Court's decisions in 1937. Some commentators have argued that public opposition to some of the Court's decisions was a significant factor.[155] Others have argued that the epidemic of sit-down strikes between 1935 and 1937 caused the justices to rethink their attitude toward regulation of labor relations.[156] Edward Corwin complemented the leading theories with the argument that Justice Hughes was converted because of his concern for his reputation as a liberal.[157]

All of these theories have at least some facial plausibility, and it is not surprising that some commentators have found them at least somewhat persuasive. Like the Court-packing thesis and the electoral theory, these conjectures cannot be conclusively disproved on the evidence available. By the same token, however, each of these supplementary theories remains a speculative hypothesis for which no evidence (other than temporal coincidence with the decisions) has been adduced. For lack of evidence of a causal relationship, these hypotheses necessarily take the form of the familiar logical fallacy, *post hoc ergo propter hoc*. Indeed, these hypotheses are no more supported by any evidence than would be theories that the Court decided cases the way it did because of an act of divine intervention, because of a peculiar alignment of the celestial bodies, or because the Yankees won the 1936 World Series. The only direct evidence we have on the issue of why the justices decided the cases the way they did is the cases themselves and a few autobiographical remarks by Chief Justice Hughes and Justice Roberts. The opinions themselves offer *legal* reasons for the results reached, and with the express exception of *West Coast Hotel v. Parrish*, for which a technical procedural explanation is offered,[158] claim to be rendering decisions consistent with existing precedent. Both Hughes and Roberts denied that political events or circumstances had anything to do with the way the cases were decided, and none of their colleagues contradicted them.[159] One can of course easily imagine reasons why these justices would have wanted to be perceived as not having succumbed to political pressure, and were there evidence to impeach their claims, one would be inclined to dismiss their proffered explanations. But in the absence of such impeaching evidence, it seems a rather curious historical method to blithely dismiss the only direct evidence we have of the Court's motivations on the unsubstantiated ground that the justices were either lying or deluding themselves.

The durability of the various political response theories scrutinized in this chapter is not, however, the simple product of the plausibility of their particular causal claims. These specific causal stories are each undergirded by a set of assumptions about what it was that the New Deal Court was "really" up to. The next chapter evaluates the capacity of those assumptions to generate a persuasive descriptive account of the New Deal Court, and offers an alternative way of understanding the New Deal legal saga that promises greater explanatory power.

Judging the Image of
New Deal Court Judging

The notion that the Court's behavior in 1937 was a response to political events is symptomatic of a larger view of the relationship between constitutional thought and partisan politics. Under this view, constitutional doctrine is entirely superstructural, indeed downright disingenuous, little more than a beard for what are at bottom judicial evaluations of the wisdom of legislative policy. When a judge reviews the constitutionality of a given piece of legislation, he first decides whether it embraces a political, social, or economic policy with which he concurs. Having made this essentially political determination, he then instructs his law clerk to go out and find the precedents that will support the result he desires. Under this view, then, the role of the judge is essentially that of a policy-making legislator—with the exception that the judge (or, more often, his law clerk) is inconvenienced by the professional requirement that he dream up some technical mumbo-jumbo to justify his decision.[1] Judges may accordingly be classified, deified, or vilified using the richly descriptive language of our political taxonomy: "moderate," "liberal," "conservative."[2] This view of judicial history has frequently been adopted by historians inclined to Progressive views, with the result that the judicial history of the New Deal (and of other eras) often depicts the Court as the conservative handmaiden of industrial and financial elites, advocating the interests of the wealthy and powerful at the expense of farmers, laborers, and debtors.[3] Only as a result of the Court-packing plan and/or the 1936 election, the story goes, was the Court persuaded to uphold legislative measures designed to ameliorate the condition of these common people.

But a purely political model, particularly a class politics model, can adequately account neither for the behavior of the New Deal Court as an institution, nor for the behavior of the individual justices. Consider the following examples. In 1930, to the delight of labor and the consternation of management, a unanimous Court upheld the collective bargaining provisions of the Railway Labor Act of 1926. In the Gold Clause Cases, decided in 1935, the Court upheld the power of the federal government to reduce the gold content of the dollar and to nullify the gold clause in private contracts. The Court thus upheld a government initiative that had the potential to induce radical inflation and promised to insulate debtors from a potential consequence of currency devaluation—this to the chagrin of creditors across the nation. In *Home Bldg. & Loan Assn. v. Blaisdell*, decided in 1934, the Court upheld a Minnesota law declaring a limited moratorium on mortgage payments. Again, this decision worked to the benefit of homeowners and farmers, and to the detriment of lending institutions. In *Nebbia v. New York*, also decided in 1934, the Court effectively overturned nearly sixty years of precedent in upholding a statute designed to aid dairy farmers who had been reduced to selling their milk at prices below the cost of production. And in *Ashwander v. Tennessee Valley Authority*, decided in 1936, the Court held by a vote of 8 to 1 that the TVA had the constitutional authority to compete with private power companies in the sale and distribution of electric power to consumers. "The decision, clearing away so many of the clouds hanging over us, makes me feel very humble," wrote TVA Director David Lilienthal. "We are given an almost incredible grant of power." The TVA was about the closest thing to socialism that the New Deal had to offer, and it was sustained by a nearly unanimous Court of putatively reactionary justices. The significance of this decision was noted by Carl Swisher:

> In a sense, the TVA decision, nominally the one bright spot in the Supreme Court record for the term, constituted an embarrassment for the administration. It indicated that the Court had not set out maliciously to batter every major feature of the New Deal program, and that, if New Deal legislation could be brought within the traditional lines of constitutional interpretation, it might be upheld by the Court. In spite of the conviction of many administration leaders that the Court had set out deliberately to sabotage their program, the line-up of decisions conveyed the suggestion that it was the program and not the Court that was wrong.[4]

Indeed, in light of these decisions (all, incidentally, handed down before both the 1936 election and the Court-packing plan), the claim that Supreme Court jurisprudence in the 1930s was all politics, and more specifically the politics of class, is difficult to sustain.

Moreover, there is reason to doubt the conservatism of certain decisions striking down New Deal measures, precisely because there is reason to doubt the liberality of the New Deal programs they invalidated. For example, by 1934, less than a year into its short life, the National Industrial Recovery Act (NIRA) was under heavy attack. Consumer prices got higher while workers' wages stayed low; employers ignored wage, hour, and collective bargaining provisions with impunity; blacks were routinely forced to accept lower wages than whites; and code authorities were dominated by representatives of larger enterprises, who promulgated regulations restricting production and reducing competition, both to the detriment of smaller businesses. When the Supreme Court invalidated the NIRA in May of 1935, unemployment was higher than it had been a year earlier, the program had few friends, and prospects for congressional extension of its two-year charter were gloomy.[5]

Similarly, the principal beneficiaries of the AAA were large commercial farmers. Consumers, forced irrespective of income to bear the brunt of higher food prices, were horrified by its policy of enforced scarcity. The food processing taxes used to fund the program were likewise passed on in a regressive fashion to consumers in the form of higher prices. Many large landowners complied with their acreage reduction contracts by evicting sharecroppers and tenant farmers, who could then be exploited as cheap farm labor, conveniently unprotected by the collective bargaining provisions of NIRA and the National Labor Relations Act. Members of the AAA who sought to remedy this situation were purged, and the plight of displaced tenants remained largely unaddressed even after it attracted the attention of the national media in 1936. There was no shortage of contemporary liberals who thought that the AAA was a sellout to the commercial farm lobby and a policy disaster.[6] Indeed, a Gallup poll printed in the *Washington Post* the day before the *Butler* decision was handed down revealed that a majority of the American public opposed the AAA.[7] Even farm leaders hailed the *Butler* opinion.[8] New Deal architect Raymond Moley remarked years later, "we all did the best we could in May 1933 and God was good to us and the farmer and the country when the Supreme Court destroyed the processing tax."[9]

Moreover, we know that the justices did not always vote their policy preferences. Stone and Brandeis disliked both the NIRA and the AAA;[10] they voted to strike down one and to uphold the other.[11] Stone disapproved of the railway pension bill and the gold clause legislation, yet he voted to uphold them both.[12] Brandeis opposed the Government's gold policies yet voted to uphold them;[13] he had great sympathy for the Frazier-Lemke Act, which provided relief for farm mortgage debtors, yet he authored the unanimous opinion declaring the Act unconstitutional.[14] Harold Ickes noted in his diary that he encountered Justice Roberts at a dinner party during the week that the Court had handed down its 8 to 1, adverse decision in the Hot Oil case. On that occasion, Ickes wrote, Justice Roberts (who had voted with the majority) "assured me that he is entirely sympathetic with what we are trying to do in the oil matter and that he hoped that we would pass a statute that would enable us to carry out our policy."[15]

Considering the frequent divergence of judicial behavior from political preference, one may well wonder whether such conventional political labels as "liberal," "moderate," and "conservative" are very instructive ways to think about these justices and the decisions they rendered. Were Brandeis, Stone, and Cardozo being "liberal" in voting to uphold the AAA,[16] the Guffey Coal Act,[17] and the minimum wage,[18] yet "conservative" in voting to strike down the NIRA[19] and the Frazier-Lemke debt relief legislation?[20] Were Van Devanter and Sutherland being "conservative" in voting to strike down minimum wages,[21] farm price supports,[22] and price regulation,[23] yet striking a liberal posture in voting to uphold the Railway Labor Act,[24] the TVA,[25] and the Social Security Act?[26] Thinking about these justices in such a vocabulary would seem inevitably to result in an across-the-bench diagnosis of intellectual and political schizophrenia.

The justices themselves certainly considered such political categories problematic. Stone profoundly disliked being called a "liberal," contending that the label had "a connotation which ought not to be applied to a judge."[27] And indeed, in light of his own policy preferences, the application of the label to Stone was simply inaccurate. Brandeis, his former clerk Paul Freund tells us, always considered himself a conservative.[28] Paul Conkin has noted that labeling the Four Horsemen "conservative" is profoundly problematic in light of their comparatively strong civil liberties records; and it needs to be emphasized that their voting records in cases involving economic and regulatory policy, which include several votes in favor of New Deal initiatives, hardly offer a portrait of unmitigated reaction.[29]

Examination of the political career of George Sutherland, purportedly the leading judicial expositor of laissez-faire conservatism, is instructive. His endorsement of the Chinese Exclusion Act and the protective tariff may lead one to question his devotion to laissez-faire, but even the charge of conservatism loses much of its force when one considers the following indictment: in the 1890s he supported free coinage of silver, and in fact in 1896 crossed party lines to support William Jennings Bryan's candidacy for president; as a Utah legislator he supported the law establishing an eight-hour day for miners, which was upheld by the Supreme Court in *Holden v. Hardy*; as a U.S. senator he supported the Employers' Liability Act, the Pure Food and Drugs Act, the Hepburn Rate Act, the eight-hour day for laborers employed by the United States, the Children's Bureau, the Seamen's Act of 1915, and Postal Savings Banks, which many decried as socialistic. It was Sutherland who introduced in the Senate Susan B. Anthony's resolution to extend the suffrage to women. Sutherland also chaired the special commission that prepared a federal workmen's compensation bill, for which he was a fervent advocate.[30] During floor debate on the bill, Sutherland was even brought to declare that "the individualistic theory has been pushed with too much stress upon the dry logic of its doctrines and too little regard for their practical operation from the humanitarian point of view . . . a good many people perversely insist upon being fed and clothed and comforted by the practical rule of thumb rather than by exact rules of logic."[31]

Chief Justice Hughes perhaps best summed up the attitude of the justices toward political labels. Asked in 1932 whether he considered himself a liberal or a conservative, Hughes replied, "These labels do not interest me . . . such characterizations are not infrequently used to foster prejudices and they serve as a very poor substitute for intelligent criticism."[32] If Hughes was right—if, as the foregoing discussion suggests, the attempt to comprehend the New Deal justices and the decisions they rendered in purely political terms is unlikely to prove particularly illuminating, then how are we to go about trying to understand the New Deal Court?

The answer to this question, curiously enough, may turn out to have something to do with law. Consider Senator Burton Wheeler's report of a conversation he had with Hughes at the chief justice's home on March 21, 1937. "What, [Hughes] mused, might have been the story of New Deal legislation of the past few years if 'we had an Attorney General in whom the President had confidence, and in whom the Court had confidence, and in whom the people had confidence.' As it was, Hughes declared, 'the laws have been poorly drafted, the briefs have been badly drawn and the arguments have been poorly presented. We've had to be not only the Court but we've had to do the work that should have been done by the Attorney General.'" "The fundamental thrust of the comment," noted William Swindler, "was that the Chief Justice had often found no means of upholding hasty legislation which had been poorly drafted," frequently under the supervision of Attorney General Homer Cummings.[33] Indeed, there is no dearth of evidence to suggest that the fate of the First New Deal can be explained by the fact that the statutes were drafted with scant attention to (and even flagrant disregard for) existing constitutional law; that inadequate attention was given to the selection and cultivation of promising test cases; and that the legal arguments offered in its defense were poorly framed and infelicitously presented.[34]

Senate Judiciary Chairman Henry Ashurst wrote of the first Hundred Days: "We ground out laws so fast that we had no time to offer even a respectful gesture toward grammar, syntax and philology. We counted deuces as aces, reasoned from non-existent premises and, at times, we seemed to accept chimeras, phantasies and exploded social and economic theories as our authentic guides."[35] "Under pressure from an impatient Roosevelt and an equally impatient Congress," reports Peter Irons, "the NIRA drafters gave little thought to the constitutional questions raised by their far-reaching proposal." Indeed, the only member of the drafting team who raised troubling questions about the NIRA's constitutionality was Charles Wyzanski, the young Labor Department solicitor who was to play such a prominent role in the government's victory in the Wagner Act cases four years later.[36] "The most striking fact about the NIRA," reports Ronen Shamir, "was that even its drafters and staunchest supporters did not believe it could survive a constitutional test."

> It was passed with the implicit understanding among the administration's senior legal advisers that since it would be in effect only two years, judicial review by the Supreme Court might be avoided. Donald Richberg, the general counsel of the National Recovery Administration . . . and Homer Cummings, the United States Attorney General, were so convinced that the NIRA was unconstitutional that the former constantly attempted to avoid judicial review and the latter refused to defend it before the Supreme Court.[37]

General Hugh Johnson, administrator of the agency, was hamstrung by his own and his adviser's doubts concerning the statute's constitutionality, and rumors circulated that he, too, feared a test before the Court.[38] In the wake of the *Schechter* decision, Justice Stone wrote: "The general sloppiness of everything that has been done in connection with this effort is disheartening. Let us hope that Congress will now undertake to do its job and that ultimately we may find solutions of what in any aspect must be regarded as serious problems."[39]

Lawyers in the AAA similarly blamed their early defeats in the lower courts in part on the inadequacies of the statute itself.[40] The act had been hastily framed by Secretary Wallace and his aides, and was passed by the House after only five and a half hours of debate.[41] Jerome Frank, while a lawyer with the AAA, himself doubted that the statute was constitutional.[42] The Senate Judiciary Committee, in its report criticizing the Court-packing plan, noted that of the twelve decisions overturning New Deal statutes, six were unanimous, and two others were dissented from by only one justice.[43] At least one of the committee's members, Senator Joseph O'Mahoney, a New Deal Democrat, "had a strong conviction that the Court would soon change its position on New Deal legislation. Never an admirer of Homer Cummings, he believed that much of the problem of constitutionality arose simply because the legislation was poorly drafted. The Justice Department, in his opinion, had not performed its homework."[44] Roosevelt himself appeared to concede the weakness of the First New Deal's draftsmanship when, in the wake of the Hot Oil decision, he told reporters, "You and I know that in the long run there may be half a dozen more court decisions before they get the correct language, before they get things straightened out according to correct constitutional methods."[45]

The drafting of the Second New Deal provided a study in contrast.

> Significantly, all of the Wagner Act draftsmen were lawyers. In this regard, the drafting process differed sharply from those which produced the NIRA and the AAA, in which lawyers took a back seat to politicians, bureaucrats, and lobbyists. In these earlier hectic and contentious sessions, interest groups with antithetical programs carried their battles from drafting sessions into the White House, and the resulting legislation bore the scars of awkward compromises. And, in these earlier sessions, troubling questions of legal precision and constitutionality were given short shrift.[46]

The drafters of the Wagner Act, by contrast, framed its provisions with both eyes firmly fixed on contemporary constitutional doctrine. Indeed, they advertised this deferential nod to constitutional niceties by peppering the Wagner Act's "Declaration of Policy" with language taken from favorable Supreme Court commerce clause cases.[47] Charles Fahy, general counsel to the National Labor Relations Board, felt that his job in preparing test cases for the Wagner Act "was immeasurably assisted by the careful draftsmanship of this beautifully drafted statute."[48] Despite the Court's recent invalidation of the Guffey Coal Act on Tenth Amendment grounds, Fahy was confident that the superior draftsmanship of the Wagner Act would allay the concerns of Hughes and Roberts.[49] The framers of the Social Security Act similarly paid greater attention to constitutional considerations. Labor Secretary Perkins' consultation with Justice Stone concerning the preparation of the Act was admittedly brief and probably inconsequential;[50] but the degree of Brandeis' participation in the framing of the Act, which included not only extensive consultations with the bill's drafters but also intervention with Roosevelt himself, is by today's standards simply astounding.[51]

Poor attention to constitutional detail at the drafting stage was not the only disability under which early New Deal initiatives labored. In addition, the lawyers defending the NIRA had virtually no strategy for selecting and preparing test cases. "The direction the NRA took," reports Thomas Emerson, "was not influenced by fear of constitutional challenges."

> For the first year we assumed that, in the emergency of the Great Depression, with a public demand that something be done, and the unanimous support of all groups, the Supreme Court would have to accept the situation. Hence, although we realized that many undecided constitutional problems existed, particularly those relating to the commerce power, the agency made no effort to conform its operations to any strategy for testing the constitutional issue.[52]

The Justice Department was forced, because of doubts concerning the lumber code's constitutionality, to withdraw the only case they had worked up to test the validity of the NIRA. As a result, the government lost the initiative in selecting cases with which to test the recovery program before the Court. The Schechter brothers, who had lost their appeal before the Second Circuit, brought their case before the

Court, and the Justice Department had no alternative but to defend the NIRA in the context of the preposterous "sick chicken case." Lawyers in the Department were well aware that *Schechter* was "the weakest possible case," and Stanley Reed tried to prepare Roosevelt for an adverse decision.[53] By contrast, the cases brought to the Supreme Court to test the constitutionality of the Wagner Act were carefully selected and cultivated by NLRB lawyers precisely because they presented fact patterns that fit nicely into the doctrinal formulations outlined by the Court in opinions sustaining exercises of the commerce power.[54]

These deficiencies in statutory craftsmanship and case preparation were aggravated by what many saw as inadequate defenses of the New Deal by an incompetent Justice Department.[55] Brandeis and Stone both "expressed concern over the Department's competence to Roosevelt shortly after Cummings assumed office."[56] Felix Frankfurter shared this low estimate of Cummings.[57] Under Cummings the Justice Department was "at its lowest ebb of any time during the New Deal period, in terms of the capacity of its personnel." The department was generally considered "a haven for political hacks," "a patronage agency," "staffed by many with first-rate political credentials but with second-rate legal ability," "hardly interested in or capable of carrying on an effective enforcement program." J. Crawford Biggs, Roosevelt's first solicitor general, "was an outstanding example of incompetency," "did only mediocre work and is generally blamed for the poor representation the administration received on constitutional issues before the Supreme Court." Thomas Emerson, who at the time lived with a law clerk to Justice Cardozo, "heard constant reports that the members of the Supreme Court were extremely dissatisfied with the government arguments in the cases, and particularly with the arguments of Mr. Biggs himself."[58] "I would not have any confidence in decisions from the Department of Justice," wrote Harold Ickes in his diary. "That Department is simply loaded with political appointees and hardly anyone has respect for the standing and ability of the lawyers over there."[59] Shortly after the Court's adverse decision in the Hot Oil cases, Ickes wrote, "It makes me sick when I think of the way Special Assistant Attorney General Stevens handled our oil case before the Supreme Court last week, and yet men on my legal staff think he was the best man in the whole Department to handle it."[60] Lawyers in the AAA blamed their early setbacks in the lower courts in part on the inexperience of Justice Department lawyers,[61] and Burton Wheeler, the leader of the Senate opposition to the Court-packing plan, was convinced that Roosevelt's difficulties with the Supreme Court never would have developed if Attorney General Cummings had been a better lawyer.[62] Indeed, Cummings devoted the bulk of his attention to the reform of federal crime legislation and the unification of practice and procedure in the federal courts rather than to the defense of the New Deal, and he did not inaugurate a much-needed reorganization of the Justice Department until March of 1935.[63]

Unlike political appointees such as Cummings and Biggs, unlike the "Legal Politicians" of the NIRA and the "Legal Reformers" of the AAA, Charles Fahy and his NLRB lawyers were "Legal Craftsmen" with legalistic mind-sets.[64] "The First New Dealers were characteristically social evangelists. . . . The New Dealers of 1935 were characteristically lawyers, precise and trenchant." The First New Dealers disdained legal exactitude, while the men and women of the Second New Deal valued and embraced it. "The difference," wrote Arthur Schlesinger,

> emerged in the contrast between the sweeping and rhetorical strokes of, say, Donald Richberg, and the exquisite craftsmanship of Ben Cohen. Richberg, moved by a passionate feeling that the imperatives of history required drastic social reorganization, wanted to draft laws and fight cases in terms of prophetic affirmations. He resented the whole notion of pussy-footing around to avoid offending the stupid prejudices of reactionary judges. But Cohen, who felt it more important to make a particular statute stick than to promote a crusade, thought through every point with technical punctiliousness and always showed a meticulous regard for legal continuities. The laws drawn by the First New Deal tended to perish before the courts because of loose draftsmanship and emotional advocacy. The laws drawn by the Second New Deal were masterpieces of the lawyer's art; and they survived.[65]

Fahy's NLRB attorneys, wrote Peter Irons, "were as much meticulous technicians as partisan advocates. They winnowed and selected cases with care; scrutinized records with a fine-toothed comb; chose courts with a shopper's discriminating eye; and wrote briefs to draw the issues narrowly and precisely."[66] Moreover, the lawyers defending the Second New Deal before the Court wowed even the lions of the bar with their forensic prowess. After hearing Charles Wyzanski's argument in the Social Security cases, the redoubtable John W. Davis told Francis Perkins, "In my palmiest days, I could not have touched that argument."[67] The lawyers of the Second New Deal were aware, as we should be aware, that their task was not merely to persuade the justices of the wisdom of a particular legislative policy; and the care and skill with which they drafted and defended their initiatives immeasurably enhanced their prospects for success before the Supreme Court.

Felix Frankfurter summarized this lawyerly view nicely in a letter he wrote to Roosevelt in the wake of the *Schechter* decision. Seeking to boost the president's sagging spirits, Frankfurter reminded him of "how much you can still do . . . and what a difference it makes in the Court's application of 'the law' how statutes are drawn, how they are administered, how they are tested by the right selection of cases, how these cases are treated in lower courts by judges, district attorneys and government counsel, how they are handled and argued before the Supreme Court itself."[68]

THE HISTORIOGRAPHICAL APPROACH critiqued here has for many years been subjected to criticism from several quarters. In his magisterial treatment of American slavery, Eugene Genovese noted how "the fashionable relegation of law to the rank of a superstructural and derivative phenomenon obscures the degree of autonomy it creates for itself." Robert Gordon, perhaps our leading observer/philosopher of legal historiography, finds prevalent among histories written by Critical legal scholars the view that "legal forms and practices don't shift with every realignment of the balance of political forces. They tend to become embedded in 'relatively autonomous' structures that transcend and, to some extent, help to shape the content of the immediate self-interest of social groups." "This relative autonomy," Gordon continues, "means that they [legal forms and practices] can't be explained completely by reference to external political/social/economic factors. To some extent they are independent variables in social experience and therefore require study elaborating their peculiar internal structures. . . ."[69] Duncan Kennedy has contended more particularly that our understanding of the judicial history of the period between 1850 and 1940 has been impoverished by liberal historians' model of "an unmediated interplay of purposes and outcomes." In order to offer a more powerful explanation of the judicial history of the period, argues Kennedy, we must take into account "the existence of legal consciousness as an entity with a measure of autonomy. It is a set of concepts and operations that evolves according to a pattern of its own, and exercises an influence on results distinguishable from those of political power and economic interest . . . [it is] the body of ideas through which lawyers experience legal issues."[70]

These insights are not the exclusive province of Gramscian Marxists and Critical anti-functionalists. Hints of these ideas surface in Roscoe Pound's ruminations on the "tenacity of a taught legal tradition," and in Frederic Maitland's equally alliterative aphorism, "taught law is tough law." Writing specifically about the New Deal Court in 1947, Charles Curtis argued:

> It is absurd to think that these Justices would have reasoned as they did in these opinions, if they had been asked to give, not judicial opinions, but solutions of our national problems. . . . The Legal Tradition makes it very difficult, almost impossible to talk sensibly about these questions by expecting, almost prescribing that a court treat them as purely judicial questions. . . . the Tradition required these Justices, or so they thought, to argue empirical problems as if they were analytic, as if the predicate they were seeking could be spun wholly out of what was implied in the subject, that is, the constitutional doctrines they had been brought up on.[71]

These scholars have all been trying to remind us that legal history is not simply political history, or social history, or economic history; legal history is also intellectual history. Judges are participants not merely in a political system, but in an intellectual tradition in which they have been trained and immersed, a tradition that has provided them with the conceptual equipment through which they understand legal disputes. To reduce constitutional jurisprudence to a political football, to relegate law to the status of dependent variable, is to deny that judges deciding cases experience legal ideas as constraints on their own political preferences. As I have attempted to demonstrate, such a reductionist model simply cannot explain the behavior of the New Deal justices.

The history of the Supreme Court during the New Deal is not a simple tale of the unmediated interplay of judicial purposes, external political events, and case outcomes. A much more plausible case might be made that the fate of New Deal legislation rested on the capacity of statutory formulations, test case fact patterns, and legal theories to resonate with the set of doctrinal categories comprising the constitutional consciousness of the individual justices. In order to understand why some statutes succeeded where others failed, we must attempt to reconstruct that consciousness. We must abandon our crude attempts to comprehend the New Deal Court in purely political terms, and instead undertake an earnest effort to appreciate the various dimensions and subtleties of the justices' jurisprudential postures. We need to explore the question of how a tradition that had generated a "formidably plausible"[72] system of constitutional thought underwent a transformative change in the first forty years of the twentieth century.

The plausibility of the system, I suggest, lay principally in two of its features: first, the persuasiveness of its constituent premises as descriptive accounts of the underlying external reality they purported to govern; and second, the structural relationships among its constituent premises, which gave the system the appearance of symmetry and internal coherence.[73]

With economic development and integration, certain of the system's premises ceased to be persuasive descriptive accounts of the world; this prompted the Court to reassess and revise those premises. For example, the notion that the public had no interest in regulating providers of food and fuel (*Wolff Packing v. Industrial Court*, *Williams v. Standard Oil Co.*) was reassessed and revised in *Nebbia v. New York*. The premise that the activities of traders and keepers of stockyards in the nation's major livestock trading centers were entirely local matters exerting no appreciable impact on interstate commerce (*Hopkins v. United States*) was reevaluated and revised in *Swift v. United States* and *Stafford v. Wallace*. The premise that a railway's refusal to permit its employees to join a labor union could not possibly exert any impact on interstate commerce (*Adair v. United States*) was reevaluated and revised in *Texas & New Orleans R.R. Co. v. Brotherhood of Railway and Steamship Clerks*.[74]

This reassessment and revision of constituent premises exerted two distinct kinds of impacts on the structure of the system of thought. First, as the Court elaborated doctrine in cases presenting fact patterns that challenged the underlying premises of the system, the system lost its appearance of coherence and symmetry, becoming unwieldy. Some businesses were affected with a public interest, others were not; some economic activities affected interstate commerce directly, others only indirectly. The problem was that there were an increasing number of cases in which one could not with confidence predict the outcome *ex ante*. Moreover, the system began to generate seemingly paradoxical outcomes: lottery tickets,[75] adulterated food,[76] prostitutes,[77] and stolen cars[78] moving in interstate commerce could be regulated by Congress, but interstate commerce in goods made by child labor could not;[79] the production and sale of oleomargarine[80] and narcotics[81] could be regulated through the power of taxation, but child labor[82] and sales of grain futures[83] could not. Such paradoxes made the system appear increasingly indeterminate and politically charged, and fueled external academic critiques that sought further to undermine the system's plausibility.[84] In the common law such paradoxes and asymmetries prompted the efforts to synthesize the particularities of existing law into more general "Restatements"; in constitutional law, they played a role in prompting such synthetic opinions as *Nebbia v. New York* and *Jones & Laughlin*.[85]

The second distinct type of impact that reassessment and revision of constituent premises had on the system was a function of the system's structure and internal dynamic. Due to the structural interrelation of the system's constituent premises, revision of one premise often implied reassessment of another. Transformations in one area of doctrine not only foreshadowed but entailed, through structural ripple effects or interdoctrinal synergies, transformations in structurally related areas of doctrine. Thus, for example, the reevaluation of the public/private distinction in

Nebbia had consequences not only for price regulation, but for liberty of contract doctrine and commerce clause doctrine as well.[86] Similarly, the reevaluation of the impact of labor relations on interstate commerce in *Texas & New Orleans R.R. Co. v. Brotherhood of Railway and Steamship Clerks* exerted an impact not only on commerce clause jurisprudence but also on the doctrine of liberty of contract.

The story of the New Deal Court, then, is not a simple tale of how "laissez-faire" constitutionalism was summarily jettisoned for political reasons in the course of a couple of months in the spring of 1937. It is instead the more complex story of how a structurally interdependent system of thought gradually unraveled over the first forty years of the twentieth century, and how, after it had unraveled so far as to become completely unserviceable, it was abandoned by a generation of jurists with no stake in salvaging its remains. It is to the telling of that story that we now turn.

PART II

A NEW TRIAL FOR
JUSTICE ROBERTS

The indictment of Owen Roberts for his ostensibly inconsistent behavior in the minimum wage cases is a staple of New Deal historiography.[1] In the spring of 1936, Justice Roberts voted with the Four Horsemen to strike down New York's minimum wage law for women. Yet in the spring of 1937, under mounting external pressure, Roberts joined Chief Justice Hughes' opinion upholding the state of Washington's minimum wage statute. This apparent *volte face* was the famous "switch in time that saved nine."[2]

It has long been recognized that Roberts' vote in 1937 was not influenced by the pendency of Franklin Roosevelt's ill-fated "Court-packing" plan. Roberts cast his decisive vote in conference on December 19, 1936, more than six weeks before the plan, a very closely guarded secret, was announced.[3] Several historians have speculated that Roberts' course might have been influenced by Roosevelt's landslide victory in the presidential elections held in November of 1936,[4] though there are good reasons to doubt this hypothesis as well.[5] Still others have ascribed Roberts' behavior in 1937 to the pressure of public opinion.[6]

Roberts himself maintained that his behavior had not been inconsistent. In a memorandum written at the request of Felix Frankfurter in 1945, and published posthumously, Roberts explained that his vote in 1936 had not been on the constitutuional merits of minimum wage legislation. He had instead joined the majority opinion on the narrow, technical ground that the New York statute was not distinguishable from the statute struck down in *Adkins v. Children's Hospital*, and that the state had not requested that *Adkins*, the governing precedent, be overruled.[7]

Several scholars writing in the two decades following World War II were prepared to accept Roberts' explanation.[8] Their acceptance was on the whole rather uncritical, however, and more recent treatments have greeted the explanation with a derisive skepticism.[9] Some of the believers have recognized that Roberts' case was strengthened by his authorship of *Nebbia v. New York*[10] in 1934, and have briefly noted as much.[11] Yet no one has yet adequately situated *Nebbia* in the intellectual history of economic substantive due process doctrine. A reconstruction of that history will better enable us to evaluate the nature of the jurisprudential commitments Roberts made in writing that landmark opinion, and an appreciation of the scope of those commitments will place us in a better position from which to judge Roberts' explanation. Such a reconstruction should also offer an improved vantage from which to assess the conventional claim that *West Coast Hotel v. Parrish* was the center-piece of a "Constitutional Revolution" in 1937.

In this part, I attempt to reconstruct such an intellectual history. In chapters 3 and 4, I seek to demonstrate that wage regulation was conceived not merely as a type of employment regulation, like statutes regulating hours of work, but also as a species of price regulation, governed by categories informing that strand of substantive due process jurisprudence. Chapter 4 then situates *Nebbia* within that intellectual history, and examines its ramifications for the issue of the minimum wage's constitutionality. Chapter 5 analyzes *West Coast Hotel v. Parrish*[12] as the culmination of that intellectual history, in which *Nebbia* played a pivotal role, and then undertakes a reevaluation of the Roberts memorandum in light of this history. For the unpersuaded skeptic, I offer some concluding observations on the historical significance of Roberts' "switch."

3

The Public/Private Distinction and the Minimum Wage

The Public/Private Matrix of Substantive Due Process

The distinction between public and private spheres was one of the fundamental concepts of nineteenth- and early twentieth-century American law.[1] The tendrils of the public/private distinction permeated everything from nuisance law[2] to contracts clause jurisprudence,[3] from the law of civil rights[4] to the law of riparian rights.[5]

Notions of public and private realms were central to the law of the police power, takings, taxation, and eminent domain.[6] In these areas, the public/private distinction played a critical role in the enforcement of what one scholar has called the principle of neutrality.[7] Rooted in the Madisonian aspiration to a faction-free politics and the Jacksonian revulsion against special privilege, the principle of neutrality dictated that legislatures ought not to play favorites. Proper legislation did not confer special benefits on any one group that were not conferred on the public generally. Legitimate statutes, in other words, were enacted for genuinely *public* purposes. Legislation that favored some groups over others in life's competition were condemned as impermissible "class legislation" or "special legislation." In enforcing this principle of neutrality, it was the duty of the judiciary to ensure that legislatures were not captured by special-interest groups, and that legislators refrained from dealing in pork-barrel politics.[8]

The seminal juristic expression of the American principle of neutrality was rendered by Justice Samuel Chase in the 1798 case of *Calder v. Bull*: "a law that takes property from A. and gives it to B.," he wrote, was "contrary to the great first principles of the social compact, and cannot be considered a rightful exercise of legislative authority."[9] One sees the expression of the principle in the nation's highest law even earlier, however, in the takings clause of the Fifth Amendment: "nor shall *private* property be taken for *public* use, without just compensation."[10] Two things should be noted concerning this statement of the principle of neutrality. First, the prohibition is only against takings of *private* property. Actions affecting property that was in some sense *public* did not fall within the principle's prohibition. An action of government that conditioned, regulated, or reallocated enjoyments of property that fell on the public side of the line did not take any property from A and give it to B. Accordingly, such actions gave rise to no right of compensation. Second, though expressed in the takings clause as a negative pregnant, private property could be taken with compensation to the owner, but only for a *public* use or purpose. To take property from its owner for a *private* use or purpose was to take property from A and to give it to B (who had presumably captured the legislative process), and this was impermissible special legislation.[11]

Considering the crucial role that the public/private distinction played across a broad spectrum of legal issues in maintaining the vision of a neutral state, it comes as no surprise that the distinction also held a pride of place in the Court's substantive due process jurisprudence, particularly in the closely related areas of price regulation, regulation of hours of work, and wage regulation.

Regulation of Prices

The Court first encountered the issue of the constitutionality of state price regulation in *Munn v. Illinois*. At issue was an Illinois statute regulating the rates charged by grain elevator operators. Munn contended that because the rate prescribed by the statute was lower than that which he might have obtained in an unregulated market, the regulation deprived him of property without due process of law.[12] The property of which Munn was being deprived was, of course, the difference between the regulated price and the presumably higher market price. Munn's argument resonated nicely with contemporary takings jurisprudence, for the state was in effect taking this property from Munn and giving it to his customers. The state could not take private property unless the property was taken for a public purpose, and even then only with just compensation.

The state of Illinois did not suggest that the price charged by any and all businesses might be regulated—it did not contend that the Fourteenth Amendment imposed no substantive constraints on price regulation. Presumably most enterprises were completely immune from such regulation. The state instead defended the statute on the ground that warehousemen for the storage of grain at Chicago were "engaged in a public employment, as distinguished from ordinary business pursuits." Like common carriers, they "'exercise[d] a sort of public office,' and ha[d] public duties to perform."[13] In order to justify regulation of the rates charged by grain elevators, the state's attorneys thought it necessary to relocate them conceptually from the private realm to the public.

In upholding the statute, the Supreme Court felt similar constraints. Chief Justice Morrison Waite's opinion for a 7 to 2 majority was no blanket blessing of legislative price regulation. The Court instead narrowly held that the rates charged by the grain elevators at Chicago might be regulated because the elevators were "businesses affected with a public interest."[14] "Property does become clothed with a public interest," wrote Waite,

> when used in a manner to make it of public consequence, and affect a community at large. When, therefore, one devotes his property to a use in which the public has an

interest, he, in effect, grants to the public an interest in that use, and must submit to be controlled by the public for the common good, to the extent of the interest he has thus created.[15]

Waite made clear, through the authorities he quoted with approval, that price regulation was the exception rather than the rule. Lord Hale, the fountainhead of the concept of the business affected with a public interest, had written in his treatise *De Portibus Maris*[16] that "[a] man, for his own private advantage, may in a port or town, set up a wharf or crane, and may take what rates he and his customers can agree for cranage, [etc.] . . . for he doth no more than is lawful for any man to do, viz., makes the most of his own. . . ." It was only where the wharfinger was operating under a license from the crown, or occupied a monopolistic position in the port, that his rates might be regulated.[17] Similarly, in *Aldnutt v. Inglis*, Lord Ellenborough had remarked, "There is no doubt that the general principle is favored, both in law and justice, that every man may fix what price he pleases upon his own property, or the use of it."[18] It was only where the owner held a monopoly over an enterprise to which the public had a right of access that his rates might be regulated. Only when "private property is devoted to a public use," wrote Waite, was it subject to price regulation.[19] In short, Waite had solved the takings problem by characterizing the property taken as in some sense public rather than strictly private. Shortly after the decision was handed down, Waite wrote privately, "The great difficulty in the future will be to establish the boundary between that which is private, and that in which the public has an interest."[20] The need to delimit the boundary was taken as given.

Justice Field believed the boundary lay elsewhere.[21] In a dissenting opinion for himself and Justice Strong that bristled with analogies to contracts clause and takings jurisprudence,[22] Field wrote:

> It is only where some right or privilege is conferred by the government or municipality upon the owner, which he can use in connection with his property, or by means of which the use of his property is rendered more valuable to him, or he thereby enjoys an advantage over others, that the compensation to be received by him becomes a legitimate matter of regulation. Submission to the regulation of compensation in such cases is an implied condition of the grant, and the State, in exercising its power of prescribing the compensation, only determines the conditions upon which its concession shall be enjoyed.[23]

Judged by this standard, Munn & Scott's grain elevator was clearly private in nature. Indeed, Field asserted that his theory—that government's conferral of a special privilege was *the* event by which an otherwise private business was made quasi-public and thus amenable to rate regulation—could account for nearly all of the instances in Anglo-American legal history in which such regulation had occurred. In the case of public turnpikes, ferries, bridges, mills, wharves, and warehouses, the owner had either "dedicated" his property to the public or had received a special license or monopoly charter from the crown or its agent. Draymen and hackmen had enjoyed the privilege of using the stands on public streets, "not allowed to the ordinary coachman or laborer with teams," and this constituted a sufficient warrant for regulation of their fares. Only with respect to usury laws did Field struggle;[24] and here he was subsequently aided by Justice Joseph Rucker Lamar who, thirty-seven years later, offered the rationale on which the regulation of rates of interest charged for the lending of money might be justified within a public/private framework. "[A]s the sovereign had the prerogative to coin money and make legal tender for all claims," he wrote, "he could fix the price that should be charged for the use of that money."[25] Here the sovereign was merely prescribing the conditions upon which the privilege of having a uniform medium of exchange—a privilege that he alone could confer, and might withhold—might be enjoyed.

Marginal disagreements concerning the precise location of the boundary between public and private enterprise persisted. There was, however, a broad measure of agreement concerning where the division lay; and the existence of such a division remained the major premise of substantive due process jurisprudence. The Court reaffirmed the constitutionality of rate regulation of grain elevators in 1892[26] and again in 1894.[27] Railroads were "engaged in a public employment affecting the public interest,"[28] and regulation of their rates was therefore repeatedly upheld.[29] The supply of water to consumers, over which private utilities often held a virtual monopoly, was similarly public in nature: "the character and extent of the use make it public; and since the service is a public one the rates are subject to regulation."[30] Where a private oil pipeline had been "devoted by its owner to public use," the line was "a public utility and its owner a common carrier whose rates and practices [were] subject to public regulation."[31] Stockyards in the nation's major livestock trading centers performed "work in which the public has an interest" and were therefore subject to rate regulation.[32] The Chicago Board of Trade was engaged in "a business affected with a national public interest," and was therefore amenable to legislation seeking to restrain manipulation of the prices of grain futures.[33] Because the business of fire insurance had become "clothed with a public interest," the premiums charged by companies selling such insurance could be regulated.[34]

Justice Holmes quipped in 1927 that the notion of businesses "affected with a public interest" was "little more than a fiction intended to beautify what is disagreeable to the sufferers."[35] The persistence with which the justices of his era earnestly struggled to locate the boundary between the public and private realms in cases involving price regulation suggests that the concept was more than a mere juridical cosmetic. Even Holmes himself was not above reasoning in the public/private idiom. Indeed, in *Terminal Taxicab Co. v. Kutz*, we see Holmes writing not in the vocabulary of his later dissent in *Tyson v. Banton*, nor in that of Justice Roberts' landmark opinion in *Nebbia v. New York*,[36] but instead within the conceptual framework sketched in *Munn*.

The case involved the District of Columbia's regulation of the fares charged by the Terminal Taxicab Company. At issue was whether the company was a public utility within the meaning of the Public Utility Act of 1913 and, of course, within the meaning of *Munn*.[37] Under a lease from the Washington Terminal Company, owner of the Union Railroad Station in the District, the taxicab company held the *exclusive* right to solicit livery and taxicab business from all persons passing to or from trains in Union Station. When so employed, the Court held, the company's cabs were "a public utility by ancient usage and understanding." The company also did a substantial portion of its business under contract with area hotels. Under these contracts, the company agreed to furnish enough taxicabs within certain hours to meet the reasonable needs of the hotel, receiving in return the exclusive right to solicit patrons of the hotel on and around the hotel premises. Here the company had dedicated itself to a public use—its "public duty" presumably prohibited it "arbitrarily to refuse to carry a guest upon demand"—and its service was therefore "public" in nature.[38]

A third portion of the company's business, however, consisted of furnishing cabs to individual customers from its central garage in response to telephone orders. Here Holmes equivocated, but ultimately found that this portion of the company's business was private.

> Although I have not been able to free my mind from doubt the Court is of the opinion that this part of the business is not to be regarded as a public utility. It is true that all business, and for the matter of that, every life in all its details, has a public aspect, and some bearing upon the welfare of the community in which it is passed. But however it may have been in earlier days as to the common callings, it is assumed in our time that an invitation to the public to buy does not necessarily entail an obligation to sell. It is assumed that an ordinary shop keeper may refuse his wares arbitrarily to a customer whom he dislikes, and . . . it is assumed that such a calling is not public as the word is used. In the absence of clear language to the contrary it would be assumed that an ordinary livery stable stood on the same footing as a common shop, and there seems to be no difference between the plaintiff's service from its garage and that of a livery stable.[39]

Even the generation's greatest legal skeptic could not fully escape the fact that he lived in a world that language and habits of mind had divided into public and private realms.

Holmes again beautified the disagreeable in *Block v. Hirsh*, decided in 1921. In light of the housing crisis precipitated by the demobilization of the armed forces after World War I, the District of Columbia had enacted legislation regulating the price to be charged under residential leases. Holmes authored the majority opinion upholding the statute against a due process challenge. "The general proposition to be maintained," he wrote, "is that circumstances have clothed the letting of buildings in the District of Columbia with a public interest so great as to justify regulation by law. Plainly circumstances may so change in time or so differ in space as to clothe with such an interest what at other times or in other places would be a matter of purely private concern." "Housing is a necessary of life," wrote Holmes. "All the elements of a public interest justifying some degree of public control are present."[40] Earlier cases[41] dispelled "the notion that what in its immediate aspect may be only a private transaction may not be raised by its class or character to a public affair."[42] The language of elevation by circumstances suggests an almost physical relocation of the business from the private to the public sphere.[43]

The concept of a business affected with a public interest was not the sole means by which the Court was able to characterize the subject matter of price regulation as public in nature. In *Highland v. Russell Car & Snow Plow Co.*, for example, the

Court upheld federal regulation of the price of coal during World War I. Highland had entered into a contract to sell coal to the Russell Snow Plow Company. Russell refused to pay the contract price and set up as a defense the federal price regulation. Highland contended that the price regulation was invalid because the coal-mining business was not affected with a public interest. The Court nevertheless held that the production of snowplows for the clearing of railroads during the war was "a public use for which coal and other private property might have been taken by exertion of the power of eminent domain." Because the regulated price was no lower than that to which the plaintiff would have been entitled had his coal been taken under the power of eminent domain, he had been deprived only of "the right or opportunity by negotiation to obtain more than his coal was worth." Though this liberty so to contract would ordinarily be secured by the Fifth Amendment, it had to yield "whenever reasonably necessary to effect any of the great purposes for which the national government was created," that is, for *public* purposes.[44]

In *Stephenson v. Binford*, the Court upheld a regulation of the Texas Railroad Commission requiring private contract carriers to charge certain minimum rates for transport. The regulation had been promulgated in response to the threat that competition from private carriers posed to the economic viability of the state's rail carriers. The Court declined to address the issue of whether this competitive threat alone justified legislative price regulation. Nor did the Court reach the issue of whether such carriers were conducting a business affected with a public interest. Yet the Court thought it necessary to find that the subject matter of the regulation was in some way essentially public rather than private. The justices found the rationale by shifting their attention from the private nature of the carriers to the public nature of the highways those carriers used, upholding the regulation as a constitutional exercise of the legislative power to regulate the use of public highways. "It is well established law," wrote Justice Sutherland, echoing Justice Lamar's defense of usury laws, "that the highways of the state are public property; that their primary and preferred use is for private purposes; and that their use for purposes of gain is special and extraordinary, which, generally at least, the legislature may prohibit or condition as it sees fit."[45] As Justice Field had written in his *Munn* dissent, "Submission to the regulation of compensation in such cases is an implied condition of the grant, and the State, in exercising its power of prescribing the compensation, only determines the conditions upon which its concession shall be enjoyed."[46]

Regulation of Working Hours

The public/private distinction played a comparable role in cases involving the constitutionality of statutes regulating hours of employment. Indeed, the first case in which the Court considered such a measure involved a congressional statute providing that eight hours should constitute a day's work for all laborers, workmen, and mechanics employed by or on behalf of the government of the United States. The statute was unanimously sustained.[47]

In 1891 the state of Kansas enacted a statute providing that, except in cases of extraordinary emergency, eight hours should constitute a day's work for everyone employed by or on behalf of the state, its political subdivisions, and any contractor or subcontractor in the execution of a contract with the state or any of its political subdivisions. Atkin, a contractor with the city of Kansas City, was convicted of employing laborers for ten-hour days on a municipal street repair project. Justice Harlan wrote the opinion of the Court upholding the statute in the face of claims that it deprived employer and employee of liberty to contract, and he hastened to locate the business regulated in the public sphere. "No question arises here as to the power of a State, consistent with the Federal Constitution, to make it a criminal offense for an employer in purely private work in which the public has no concern, to permit or require his employees to perform daily labor in excess of a prescribed number of hours." The work in question here was "performed on behalf of a municipal corporation, not private work for private parties." The street repair project was the kind of work that the state "could have taken immediate charge of by its own agents; for it is one of the functions of government to provide public highways for the convenience and comfort of the people." Accordingly, "the work was of a public, not private, character." Because it was "for the State to prescribe the conditions under which it will permit work of that kind to be done," the statute "[did] not infringe the personal liberty of anyone."[48]

Upon the authority of *Atkin* the Court upheld a federal statute limiting to eight hours per day the service of any laborer or mechanic employed by the United States, the District of Columbia, or any contractor or subcontractor upon any of the public works of the United States or the District of Columbia.[49] The Court similarly upheld federal legislation limiting the hours of labor of employees of the paradigmatic businesses affected with a public interest, railroads.[50]

Yet state legislatures were not content to regulate the hours of only those employees engaged in enterprises considered essentially public. Legislators also sought to limit the length of the workday in those employments in which it was thought that long hours might adversely affect the health or safety of the employees. Such businesses—mines, smelters, mills, factories, and laundries, for example—were thought of as private rather than public in nature. Indeed, in the first such case to reach the Court, *Holden v. Hardy*, the state supreme court had so resoundingly rejected the contention that mining was a business affected with a public interest that the Utah attorney general dropped it on appeal. The only cases in which such regulations of hours had been sustained, contended the plaintiff in error, involved either public employment, employment in a business affected with a public interest, or employment of "women, children, insane persons, and the like." In all other cases the number of hours to be worked per day was a private matter to be settled between employer and employee.[51]

Regulations of the prices charged by businesses affected with a public interest were not takings because the "property" taken was not fully private.[52] Limitation of the hours that could be worked in a public employment was neither a deprivation of liberty nor a taking of the property right one held in one's labor[53] and/or capital because no one had any right to public employment. Yet neither of these rationales was available to sustain limitations on the hours of employment worked in a private business not affected with a public interest.[54] If such regulations were to be upheld, it would be necessary to explain why they were deprivations of neither liberty nor property.

That rationale, of course, was found in the state's police power: its power to protect public health, safety, welfare, and morals. As Ernst Freund pointed out in his treatise on the subject, the police power was simply the proactive, legislative analog to the reactive judicial power to abate a nuisance.[55] One who was enjoined to abate a nuisance was not entitled to compensation for the costs of the abatement, nor for the diminution in property value that the abatement might entail.[56] Nor, according to the ancient maxim, *sic utere tuo ut alienum non laedas*, was one who was restrained from using his property so as to harm another deprived of any constitutionally protected liberty.[57] If, then, limitations on hours of work in certain employments constituted legitimate exercises of the police power, they were neither deprivations of liberty nor takings of property, and therefore did not violate the due process clause.

Accordingly, a Utah statute limiting the workday in underground mines and in smelters to eight hours was upheld against a Fourteenth Amendment challenge. There was ample reason to believe, the Court held, that prolonged exposure to the conditions of such employment—high temperatures, noxious gases, and lack of fresh air and sunlight—might be judged detrimental to the health of the employees.[58] Similarly, an Oregon statute prohibiting the employment of women in mechanical establishments, factories, or laundries for longer than ten hours per day survived constitutional attack. It was a matter of general knowledge, held the Court, that "woman's physical structure and the performance of her maternal functions" justified special measures to protect her health from the degrading rigors of "long-continued labor, particularly when done standing." And "as healthy mothers are essential to vigorous offspring, the physical well-being of woman becomes an object of public interest and care in order to preserve the strength and vigor of the race."[59]

But the police power could not be used as a mere pretext to disguise what was in actuality governmental favoritism.[60] Accordingly, working hours could be limited only by a statute having the "natural effect"[61] of promoting the proper *public purpose* of protecting public health. Maximum hours statutes without such a natural effect violated the principle of neutrality in two ways. First, they could be seen simply as measures "intended to alter the distribution of power or wealth between employers and their workers."[62] Second, such statutes might be viewed as designed to benefit one group of workers at the expense of another: "The real loser . . . was the worker who would have been willing to work longer hours. . . . The 'lazier' worker had used the power of government to protect himself from the competition of the more diligent."[63]

In *Lochner v. New York*, the Court declared unconstitutional a New York statute prohibiting bakers from working more than ten hours per day or sixty hours per week. Writing for a five-man majority, Justice Peckham opined that there was no valid public purpose served by the statute. The law did not protect the public safety, morals, or welfare.[64] Nor did the statute protect the health of the public generally,[65] or of bakers specifically: "To the common understanding the trade of a baker has never been regarded as an unhealthy one."[66] The act therefore was "not, within any fair meaning of the term, a health law." Statutes limiting working hours were "not saved from condemnation by the claim that they are passed in the exercise of the police power and upon the subject of the health of the individual whose rights are interfered with, unless there be some fair ground, reasonable in and of itself, to say that there is material danger to the public health or to the health of the employees, if the hours of labor are not curtailed." Without such searching scrutiny by the judiciary, "the claim of the police power would be a mere pretext" for class legislation, "and it would be enough to say that any piece of legislation was enacted to conserve the morals, the health or the safety of the people; such legislation would be valid, no matter how absolutely without foundation the claim might be."[67]

> It is impossible for us to shut our eyes to the fact that many of the laws of this character, while passed under what is claimed to be the police power for the purpose of protecting the public health or welfare, are, in reality, passed from other motives. We are justified in saying so when, from the character of the law and the subject upon which it legislates, it is apparent that the public health or welfare bears but the most remote relation to the law. The purpose of the statute must be determined from the natural and legal effect of the language employed; and whether it is or is not repugnant to the Constitution of the United States must be determined from the natural effect of such statutes when put into operation, and not from their proclaimed purpose.[68]

Justice Harlan, dissenting for himself and Justices White and Day, accepted the majority's mode of analysis. The liberty of contract guaranteed by the due process clause of the Fourteenth Amendment constituted a limitation on legislative authority;[69] the police power could be exercised to curtail this liberty only in order to attain certain kinds of ends, such as the preservation of the public health, safety, or morals, or the abatement of public nuisances;[70] and the judiciary must scrutinize putative exercises of the police power to ensure that such statutes were not merely pretexts for special legislation.[71] But Justice Harlan differed with his colleagues in the majority over one thing: how to decide close cases. Where a statute could be plausibly characterized as either a health measure or special legislation, which characterization should the Court adopt? Harlan's answer was unequivocal: "If there be doubt as to the validity of the statute, that doubt must . . . be resolved in favor of its validity, and the courts must keep their hands off. . . ."[72] "It is enough for the determination of this case," wrote Harlan, "and it is enough for this court to know, that the question is one about which there is room for debate and for an honest difference of opinion." "In other words, where the validity of a statute is questioned, the burden of proof, so to speak, is upon those who assert it to be unconstitutional." Such a burden, in Harlan's view, was not easily met. Reviewing the evidence tending to support the determination that long hours of work in bakeries was unhealthful,[73] Harlan concluded:

> If such reasons exist that ought to be the end of this case, for the State is not amenable to the judiciary, in respect of its legislative enactments, unless such enactments are plainly, palpably, beyond all question, inconsistent with the Constitution of the United States. We are not to presume that the state of New York has acted in bad faith. Nor can we assume that the legislature acted without due deliberation, or that it did not determine this question upon the fullest attainable information, and for the common good. We cannot say that the State has acted without good reason nor ought we to proceed upon the theory that its action is a mere sham. Our duty, I submit, is to

sustain the statute as not being in conflict with the Federal Constitution, for the reason—and such is an all-sufficient reason—it is not shown to be plainly and palpably inconsistent with that instrument.[74]

Unlike Harlan, Justice Holmes rejected the majority's mode of analysis at every point. Holmes did not agree that the due process clause provided special protection for contractual prerogatives; accordingly, he did not believe that contractual liberty could be curtailed only to attain the kinds of ends generally associated with the police power. As a result, he did not believe that it was incumbent upon the judiciary to scrutinize legislation to ensure that it conformed to the neutrality principle. Indeed, Holmes' dissent virtually ignored traditional police power categories, and didn't even acknowledge liberty of contract as a legal concept. In his view, the Court ought to refrain from declaring legislation unconstitutional "unless it can be said that a rational and fair man necessarily would admit that the statute proposed would infringe fundamental principles as they have been understood by the traditions of our people and our law." As far as Holmes was concerned, class legislation, while perhaps inadvisable, was constitutional. As he said of the New York statute, "Men whom I certainly could not pronounce unreasonable would uphold it as a first instalment of a general regulation of the hours of work. *Whether in this latter aspect it would be open to the charge of inequality I think it unnecessary to discuss.*"[75]

Thus three modes of reviewing legislation curtailing contractual liberty emerged in *Lochner*. Eight of the justices shared common ideological commitments concerning liberty of contract and special legislation, and agreed on the analytic categories to be deployed to further those commitments. The dispute between Harlan and Peckham was over which branch of government should have the final say with respect to legislation that could reasonably be viewed as either consistent or inconsistent with those commitments. Holmes alone rejected the commitments, the categories and the vocabulary of substantive due process.[76]

Yet even the majority appeared to concede that the case would have been different had the business in question been public in nature: "It seems to us that the real object and purpose were simply to regulate the hours of labor between the master and his employees (all being men, *sui juris*), *in a private business.* . . ." "The *Atkin* case was decided upon the right of the State to control its municipal corporations and to prescribe the conditions upon which it will permit work of a *public character* to be done for a municipality."[77] Indeed, *Lochner's* brief had employed the public/private distinction to distinguish not only *Atkin* and *United States v. Martin*, but also *Munn v. Illinois.*[78]

Regulation of Wages

Despite the Court's embrace of liberty of contract in the employment law context, early legislative prescriptions concerning wages met with favorable judicial review. Between 1899 and 1920, the Court repeatedly upheld statutes regulating the time and manner of wage payment as legitimate exercises of the state's police power to prevent fraud and overreaching. In *Knoxville Iron Co. v. Harbison*, the Court upheld as a valid exercise of the police power a Tennessee statute requiring that all store orders or other evidences of indebtedness issued by employers in payment of wages be redeemable in cash.[79] Similarly upheld were statutes directing that, where miners' wages were determined by the weight of the coal they mined, the weighing take place before the coal was screened.[80] In *Patterson v. Bark Eudora*, the Court upheld as a proper exercise of the commerce power a federal statute prohibiting the advance payment of seamen's wages.[81]

Even in these cases concerning time and manner regulations, the public/private distinction occasionally played a role. For example, in *Erie Railroad Co. v. Williams*, the Court upheld a New York statute requiring semi-monthly, cash payment of railroad workers' wages not only as a valid exercise of the police power, but also as a permissible condition upon which the state-conferred privilege of doing business in the corporate form might be enjoyed. In *St. Louis, Iron Mountain & St. Paul Railway Co. v. Paul*, an Arkansas statute required any railroad company discharging an employee to pay him any unpaid wages on the date of discharge. As a penalty for nonpayment, the daily wages of the discharged employee were to continue to accrue until the date upon which payment was made. The Supreme Court unanimously sustained the statute against a due process attack. Railroad corporations, noted Chief Justice Fuller, "were organized for a public purpose; their roads were public highways; and they were common carriers." "In view of the fact that these corporations were clothed with a public trust, and discharged duties of public consequence," the statute was a legitimate exercise of legislative power.[82]

None of these statutes, however, prescribed the *amount* of wages to be paid. In cases involving that kind of regulation, the Court's attention tended to shift away from police power categories to the public/private matrix laid out by the *Munn* opinions and their progeny.[83] Regulation of the amount of wages to be paid was thus seen as more closely analogous to price regulation than to regulation of the time and manner of wage payment.

The relationship between regulation of prices and regulation of wage levels had been recognized as early as 1877. After all, what was regulated by the Granger laws was not the price of a good, but the fee for a service: storage of grain and carriage by rail. The services involved, however, entailed substantial investments of capital, and therefore regulation of the rate charged for the service could be seen as regulating a rate of return on property. Most of the historical analogies discussed by Waite and Field involved services requiring significant capital investments: gristmills, cabs, carts, ferries, wharves, cranes, and warehouses all had to be built before they could be employed to serve the public, and the fees charged for milling, carriage, cranage, and storage recovered sunk costs and secured a profit on capital investment in addition to providing compensation for the labor entailed by the provision of the service.

One of the services subject to regulation, however, involved a comparatively small, certainly not unusual, capital investment. Congress had in 1820 enacted a statute regulating the fees for sweeping chimneys in the District of Columbia.

Because chimney sweeps had been awarded no special privileges by Congress, Field believed that the statute was unconstitutional: "The chimney-sweeps may, I think, safely claim all the compensation which they can obtain by bargain for their work."[84] But the majority's citation of the statute as precedent for legitimate rate regulation[85] suggested that labor-intensive as well as capital-intensive businesses could be affected with a public interest, and that with respect to such businesses, compensation for labor might be regulated by the legislature.

Munn's suggestion that the legislature might regulate compensation for work that was public in nature was confirmed in subsequent decisions. *Frisbie v. United States* involved a conviction under an act of Congress forbidding any attorney engaged in preparing, presenting, or prosecuting a claim for a federal military pension to demand or receive a fee of greater than $10. Frisbie challenged the statute as a violation of his liberty to contract, and the Court unanimously rejected his contention. Justice Brewer's opinion acknowledged that, "generally speaking, every citizen has a right freely to contract for the price of his labor, services, or property." But the granting of a pension was "a matter of bounty" and, as Brewer's uncle Stephen Field had pointed out in his *Munn* dissent, acceptance of the privilege implied consent to regulation of the terms upon which the privilege might be enjoyed. No one had any right to a military pension, nor did anyone have a right to represent another in pursuit of largesse the government was free to withhold. "Congress being at liberty to give or withhold a pension, may prescribe who shall receive it, and determine all the circumstances under which any application therefor shall be prosecuted." Congress therefore possessed the power "to prescribe the conditions under which parties may assist in procuring pensions. . . ."[86]

Regulation of the compensation of attorneys performing "public" work was again upheld in *Ball v. Halsell.* A federal statute authorized suits against the United States arising out of Indian depredations to be pursued in the Court of Claims. Halsell, who alleged losses resulting from depredations of the Comanche and the Kiowa, engaged Ball to represent him. Their contract provided that Ball would receive 50 percent of whatever he recovered on Halsell's behalf. The statute authorizing suit prohibited assignment of any portion of any such claim, and authorized the court to allow out of amounts awarded attorneys' fees not to exceed 20 percent of such amounts. Ball succeeded in recovering $17,720 for Halsell, out of which the court awarded Ball $1,500, or less than 9 percent. Ball sued Halsell's estate for the balance due him under the contract. The Supreme Court unanimously denied Ball's claim, upholding that statutory limitation on attorneys' fees against the claim that it deprived Ball of property without due process of law. Quoting Chief Justice Taney's opinion in *Beers v. Arkansas,* Justice Gray wrote:

> It is an established principle of jurisprudence, in all civilized nations, that the sovereign cannot be sued in its own courts, or in any other, without its consent and permission; but it may, if it thinks proper, waive this privilege, and permit itself to be made a defendant in a suit by individuals, or by another State. And as this permission is altogether voluntary on the part of the sovereignty, it follows that it may prescribe the

terms and conditions on which it consents to be sued, and the manner in which the suit shall be conducted, and may withdraw its consent whenever it may suppose that justice to the public requires it.

The conferral of a privilege that the sovereign was free to withhold carried with it the prerogative of prescribing the conditions on which the privilege might be enjoyed. As Justice Gray concluded, "The restriction of the compensation of attorneys to the amounts so allowed by the court was one of the terms and conditions upon which the United States consented to be sued."[87]

Yeiser v. Dysart upheld a provision of Nebraska law limiting the fees chargeable by attorneys in cases arising under the state's workmen's compensation act. A unanimous Court upheld the statute against the contention that it interfered with liberty of contract. Employing a surprisingly low level of scrutiny, Justice Holmes' opinion held that the limitation was a reasonable means of protecting injured workers from making improvident contracts. It was perhaps at the insistence of colleagues who embraced a more robust concept of contractual liberty that Holmes added the following language: "When we add the considerations that an attorney practices under a license from the State and that the subject matter is a right created by statute, it is obvious that the State may attach such conditions to the license in respect of such matters as it believes to be necessary in order to make it a public good."[88] Such an utterance from Holmes was powerful testimony to the thrall in which the justices continued to be held by Fieldian conceptions of public and private spheres.

All of these cases involved regulation of the *maximum* rate that might be charged for labor. But the Court also made clear that where the work in question was public in character, the legislature might also prescribe *minimum* rates of compensation. The eight-hour law upheld in *Atkin* provided that "not less than the current rate of per diem wages in the locality where the work is performed shall be paid" to workers employed by or on behalf of the state of Kansas. Moreover, any worker legally working overtime due to extraordinary circumstances was to be paid for such overtime at the same hourly rate paid for the first eight hours. Atkin was convicted of violating not only the eight-hour limitation, but the wage provision of the statute as well. The current per diem rate of pay for comparable private work in Kansas City was $1.50 a day for a ten-hour day. Atkin hired a worker to work ten-hour days for $1.50 per day, rather than eight hours for the same amount as was required by the statute. Put another way, Atkin paid his worker 15 cents an hour when the statute required that he pay 18.75¢.[89] The Court upheld the convictions on both counts.[90] "We rest our decision," wrote Justice Harlan, "upon the broad ground that the work being of a public character . . . it is for the State to prescribe the conditions under which it will permit work of that kind to be done."[91] So long as the business regulated was public in nature, the issues of wage regulation and hours regulation were not seen as different in kind. But the majority opinion suggested that had the work in question been private, the outcome of the case might have been different. "Whether a similar statute, applied to laborers or employees in purely private work, would be constitutional, is a question of very large import, which we have no occasion now to determine or even to consider."[92]

The 1917 Trilogy

The Court would consider the constitutionality of wage regulation three times in the early months of 1917. In 1913 the Oregon legislature had enacted a statute limiting the hours of work in mills, factories, and manufacturing establishments to ten per day. The statute permitted an employee to work an additional three hours of overtime per day, provided that he was compensated for overtime at the rate of time and one-half of his regular wage. The constitutional attack on the statute, which reached the Court in *Bunting v. Oregon,* was two-pronged. First, the act was condemned on the authority of *Lochner* as an hours statute having no reasonable relation to the preservation of health. Second, the statute was challenged as a wage regulation masquerading as an hours statute. "The law is not a ten-hour law," Bunting argued; "it is a thirteen-hour law designed solely for the purpose of compelling the employer of labor in mills, factories and manufacturing establishments to pay more for labor than the actual market value thereof." Even if a ten-hour statute could pass muster as a health measure, the Oregon statute could not. "The provision for overtime at time and one-half of the regular wage robs the law of any argument that might be made to bring it within those grounds that justify an exercise of the police power. . . . Insufficiency of wage does not justify legislative regulation. The wage has no bearing upon health." Because this reallocation of wealth could not be justified under the police power, it violated the principle of neutrality. "The effect is to take money from the employer and give it to the laborer without due process or value in return." "Society may not force the employer to pay wages sufficient to support the employee upon the scale of his desire."[93]

The state of Oregon sought to limit the constitutional battle to one front. The businesses regulated were not affected with a public interest, so the *Munn* line of cases could offer no support for the statute's overtime pay provision. Hours regulations had previously been upheld as valid exercises of the police power,[94] but no statute prescribing wage levels in a private business had ever been faced by the Court, and the state court precedents were not altogether favorable.[95] The statute undeniably regulated hours, but the attorneys for the state believed that they might plausibly deny that it was a wage regulation. "The law is an hours law, not a wage law," argued Felix Frankfurter; "the provision for overtime work and extra pay being merely to allow a limited and reasonable flexibility in time of unusual business pressure." The state's brief then contended for a wide berth for the police power, and mobilized data concerning the adverse effects of long hours of work on employees.[96]

The Court was as anxious as Frankfurter to avoid characterizing the statute as a wage regulation. The statute's preamble had expressed the legislature's intent to protect the health of the state's citizens by limiting working hours in certain employments. Departing from Peckham's Lochnerian skepticism, Justice McKenna's majority opinion rejected the suggestion that this was a "pretense" to disguise an ulterior purpose. The overtime provision created an incentive—more flexible, and perhaps wiser than a rigid prohibition—for employers to limit the working day to ten hours. "The provision for overtime is permissive, in the same sense that any penalty is permissive. Its purpose is to deter by its burden and its adequacy for this was a matter of legislative judgment. . . ." As Oregon's Supreme Court had pointed out, "'The act makes no attempt to fix the standard of wages. No maximum or minimum wage is named. That is left wholly to the contracting parties.'" Accordingly, the validity of wage regulation need not be discussed.[97]

McKenna then considered Bunting's contention that the hours law was not "necessary or useful" for the preservation of workers' health. In a breathtakingly terse and unceremonious break with *Lochner*, McKenna dismissed this contention with the observation that "[t]he record contains no facts to support the contention, and against it is the judgment of the legislature. . . ."[98] The burden of proof, in other words, rested precisely where Harlan had located it in his *Lochner* dissent: on the party challenging the statute. As if this were not sufficient disrespect for a precedent of recent vintage, McKenna then quoted with approval a passage from the Oregon Supreme Court's opinion that was lifted from Harlan's dissent in the bakeshop case.[99] It was perhaps such gestures that prompted Chief Justice Taft to remark six years later, "It is impossible for me to reconcile the *Bunting Case* and the *Lochner Case* and I have always supposed that the *Lochner Case* was thus overruled *sub silentio*."[100]

But it is important to recognize that if *Bunting* overruled *Lochner*, it did so in a limited fashion. The Court did adopt Harlan's attitude toward resolving doubts about exercises of the police power. But the Court did not reject liberty of contract as a substantive constraint on legislative power, and it did not suggest that such liberty might be curtailed to achieve ends other than those associated with the police power. Moreover, the majority opinion did not disavow the Court's duty to expose special legislation masquerading under the guise of police regulation.[101] While the specific holding in *Lochner* may have been vitiated, the analytic framework from which that holding had emerged remained intact.

In another case before the Court in early 1917, however, the issue of wage regulation could not be dodged so easily. The 1913 Oregon legislature had also enacted a statute creating an Industrial Welfare Commission and empowering the commission to prescribe "standards of minimum wages for women in any occupation within the state of Oregon and what wages are inadequate to supply the necessary cost of living to any such women workers and to maintain them in good health."[102] Relying principally on *Muller* and on Harlan's *Lochner* dissent, the Oregon Supreme Court upheld the statute in two cases,[103] and appeals were taken to the U.S. Supreme Court.

The minimum wage cases were argued on the same day as *Bunting* and were decided on the same day nearly three months later. Justice Brandeis, who had earlier participated in all of the litigations as counsel to the state, recused himself in each instance.[104] Brandeis' recusal ironically permitted the Court to avoid deciding the constitutionality of wage regulation, thereby leaving the issue open, and at the same time to affirm the state court decisions upholding the statute. Four justices (McKenna, Holmes, Day and Clarke) were prepared to uphold the statute as a valid police measure, while the remaining four (White, Van Devanter, Pitney, and McReynolds) thought otherwise.[105] As a consequence, the decisions of the Oregon Supreme Court in the minimum wage cases were affirmed by an equally divided Court.[106]

The most important of the three wage regulation cases decided in 1917 was *Wilson v. New*. At issue was the constitutionality of certain provisions of the Adamson Act, which Congress had enacted in September of 1916 in order to avert a general railway strike. Section one of the act had declared that "eight hours shall, in contracts for labor and service, be deemed a day's work and the measure or standard of a day's work for the purposes of reckoning the compensation for services of all employees who are now or may hereafter be employed by any common carrier by railroad. . . ." Section two directed the president to appoint a commission to study labor relations in the industry for six to nine months, and within thirty days thereafter to report its findings to the president and Congress. Section three, which was the focus of the controversy, provided:

> That pending the report of the commission herein provided for and for a period of thirty days thereafter the compensation of railway employees subject to this Act for a standard eight-hour workday shall not be reduced below the present standard day's wage, and for all necessary time in excess of eight hours such employees shall be paid at a rate not less than the pro rata rate for such standard eight hour workday.[107]

In other words, employees whose compensation had previously been determined based on a ten-hour workday were now temporarily to receive the same pay for eight hours of work that they had previously garnered for ten.

The railroad contended that the statute violated the principle of neutrality: "On its face §3 is for the direct pecuniary benefit of a particular class of a community, to wit, the persons who are actually engaged in the operation of railroad trains. . . . It is a direct taking of the carrier's property without compensation and the transfer of the same to private individuals."[108] Justice Department lawyers defended the act as a valid regulation of interstate commerce. Foreshadowing arguments that would be put forward to defend the minimum wage as a police regulation, the government contended: "Physical efficiency is impossible without proper living conditions, which demand suitable food, clothing, housing, rest, and recreation. These, in turn, can not be secured without the payment of an adequate wage. An adequate wage, therefore, is essential to safe, regular, and efficient service in interstate commerce. . . ."[109] Moreover, because disputes over wages frequently led to interferences with the free flow of commerce, wage regulation bore a "close relation to the proper performance by carriers of their *public* duties."[110]

Chief Justice White's majority opinion upheld the Act as a valid exercise of the congressional power to protect and promote interstate commerce. Throughout his lengthy opinion, White repeatedly emphasized that the public nature of railroads made them peculiarly amenable to forms of regulation to which purely private businesses were constitutionally immune.[111] Legislatures had, after all, exercised their power to restrict the railroads' contractual prerogatives not only by rate regulation, but also by legislation dealing with railway employees and "the relation of such servants not only with their employers, but between themselves."[112] Yet even with respect to so paradigmatically public a business, the wage relation was a pre-sumptively private matter.[113] Thus, the amount of wages to be paid an employee was not rendered subject to regulation merely by virtue of the fact that the business in which the worker was employed was affected with a public interest. Legislative power "embrace[d] the right to control the contract power of the carrier," but only "in so far as the public interest require[d] such limitation. . . ."[114]

In this instance, however, such a limitation was required in order to protect the public's interest in the free flow of commerce, which the parties' wage dispute threatened.[115] As businesses affected with a public interest, the railways were under special duties to the public,[116] and accordingly the contractual prerogatives of both the carriers[117] and their employees[118] had to yield to the public interest.

> In other words, considering comprehensively the situation of the employer and the employee in the light of the obligations arising from the *public interest* and of the work in which they are engaged and the degree of regulation which may be lawfully exerted by Congress as to that business, it must follow that the exercise of the lawful governmental right is controlling. This results from the considerations we have previously pointed out and which we repeat, since conceding from that point of view the *private right* and *private interest* as contradistinguished from the *public interest* the power exists between the parties, the employers and employees, to agree as to a standard of wages free from legislative interference, that right in no way affects the law-making power to protect the *public right* and create a standard of wages resulting from a dispute as to wages and a failure therefore to establish by consent a standard. The capacity to exercise the *private right* free from legislative interference affords no ground for saying that legislative power does not exist to protect the *public interest* from the injury resulting from a failure to exercise the *private right.*[119]

Moreover, such regulation was permissible at all only because of the public nature of the business involved.

> And this emphasizes that there is no question here of *purely private right* since the law is concerned only with those who are engaged in a *business charged with a public interest* where the subject dealt with as to all parties is one involved in that business and which we have seen comes under the control of the right to regulate to the extent that the power to do so is appropriate or relevant to the business regulated.[120]

Justice McKenna, concurring, interpreted the statute as fixing only hours of labor, not wages. He made clear, however, that he concurred in the Court's view concerning the constitutionality of wage regulation.

> I speak only of intention; of the power I have no doubt. When one enters into inter-state commerce one enters into *a service in which the public has an interest* and subjects one's self to its behests. And this is no limitation of liberty; it is the consequence of liberty exercised, the obligation of his undertaking, and constrains no more than any contract constrains. The obligation of a contract is the law under which it is made and submission to regulation is the condition which attaches to one who enters into or accepts employment in *a business in which the public has an interest.*[121]

Indeed, McKenna appeared to be suggesting that Congress possessed the power to regulate the wages paid by interstate carriers by virtue of their public character alone. The effect of the impending strike on interstate commerce, he implied, was irrelevant. Holmes, not surprisingly, expressed a similar sentiment in private correspondence,[122] and one might infer from Brandeis' questions at oral argument that he held a comparable view.[123] It appears likely that White was the only member of the majority who believed that congressional power was more narrowly confined.[124]

In dissent Justice Day opined that because the act made no provision for a concomitant rate increase through which the increased cost to the railroads might be passed on to the public, it was arbitrary and confiscatory.[125] He did not, however, deny the power of Congress recognized by the majority. In fact, even Day appeared to concede to Congress broader power to regulate trainmen's wages than had White. It thus appears that it was perhaps only Day's collateral reservations that prevented the formation of a majority opinion recognizing a more expansive power in Congress to regulate wages in businesses affected with a national public interest. Wrote Day:

> I am not prepared to deny Congress, in view of its constitutional authority to regulate commerce among the States, the right to fix by lawful enactment the wages to be paid to those engaged in such commerce in the operation of trains carrying passengers and freight. While the railroads of the country are *privately owned*, they are *engaged in a public service*, and because of that fact are subject in a large measure to governmental control. . . . Congress has the power to fix the amount of compensation necessary to secure a proper service and to insure reasonable rates to the public on the part of the railroads engaged in [interstate] traffic.[126]

Only three justices disagreed with this proposition. Justice McReynolds contended that the subject matter of the statute was beyond the scope of the commerce clause. Justice Pitney, dissenting with Justice Van Devanter, thought the act unsupported by the commerce power and in any event an infringement of rights protected by the Fifth Amendment. As Justice Pitney put it, "The logical consequences of the doctrine now announced are sufficient to condemn it." If Congress may fix wages of trainmen in interstate commerce during a period of months, it may do so during a term of years, or indefinitely. "If it may increase wages, much more certainly it may reduce them. If it may establish a minimum it may establish a maximum."[127]

Justice McReynolds echoed Pitney's point: ". . . considering the doctrine now affirmed by a majority of the court as established, it follows as of course that Congress has power to fix a maximum as well as a minimum wage for trainmen. . . ."[128] Both this proposition—that the power to fix a minimum wage or rate entailed the power to fix a maximum—and its converse would continue to inform constitutional doctrine for the next twenty years.

Wilson v. New established the analytical model within which the Court would conduct its constitutional analysis of wage regulation throughout the 1920s. Under *Wilson*, the employer was shielded from wage regulation by two lines of defense. First, the amount of wages he paid his employees could be regulated by the state only if his business was in some sense public—most typically, if it was a business affected with a public interest. Even if his business was public, however, *Wilson* held that his wage relations with his employees were carried on within a private inner core presumptively immune from regulation. That second line of defense could be breached only if there were a peculiarly strong public interest in regulating the amount of his employees' compensation. The opinions in *Wilson* suggested that this second line of defense was the more tenuous, and in 1931 it would be the first to fall. With the collapse of the first line of defense three years later, the analytical impediments to minimum wage regulation would disappear.

4

From *Adkins* to *Nebbia*

1923: *Adkins* and *Wolff Packing*

In 1918 Congress enacted a statute creating a minimum wage board for the District of Columbia. The board was authorized to investigate the wages paid to women engaged in local occupations and to prescribe for those occupations minimum wages adequate "to supply the necessary cost of living to any such women workers to maintain them in good health and to protect their morals. . . ." The constitutionality of the act was questioned in *Adkins v. Children's Hospital.*[1]

Felix Frankfurter's argument defended the statute as a legitimate exercise of Congress' power to protect public health, morals, and general welfare in the District of Columbia. The "deficit between the essential needs for decent life and the actual earnings of large numbers of women workers in the District . . . impaired the health of this generation of women and thereby threatened the coming generation through undernourishment, demoralizing shelter and insufficient medical care." A declaratory section of the statute made its purpose plain: "To protect the women and minors of the District from conditions detrimental to their health and morals, resulting from wages which are inadequate to maintain decent standards of life."[2] Other cases upholding liberty of contract in the employment context were inapplicable due to the fact that the statutes there at issue had not aimed to achieve ends so clearly identified with the police power.[3] As a rebuttal to the general proposition that the wage relation was immune from regulation, Frankfurter cited the cases upholding statutes prescribing the time and manner of wage payment.[4]

The police power defense was not the only means by which Frankfurter sought to reconcile the minimum wage statute with the principle of neutrality. Though appearing only in embryonic form, Frankfurter's argument contained suggestions that the *absence* of minimum wage legislation would effectively result in special legislation. "A contract for labor below its cost must inevitably rely upon a subsidy from outside or result in human deterioration. To the extent of the subsidy or the deterioration the public is necessarily concerned. The employer has no constitutional right to such an indirect subsidy. . . ." As a result of the need to care for those who suffered from inadequate compensation, "financial burdens were imposed upon the District, involving excessive and unproductive taxation, for the support of charitable institutions engaged in impotent amelioration rather than prevention."[5] In other words, the tax dollars of the District's citizens were being used to subsidize the enterprises of those employers who paid subminimum wages, while other employers in the District, many of whom may have been in competition with subsidized employers, paid living wages and received no subsidy. Had this been done directly there would have been no question that it violated the principle of neutrality; the fact that it was done indirectly should have been constitutionally irrelevant. The minimum wage law was necessary in order to return the state to a position of neutrality. Assuming some form of state-supported poor relief,[6] the minimum wage law was not constitutionally suspect: it was constitutionally imperative. Frankfurter, however, made this argument neither forcefully nor explicitly.[7]

Opposing counsel, by contrast, forcefully contended that the law violated the principle of neutrality, characterizing the statute as "the taking of property without just compensation, and not even for a public purpose, but for private purpose. . . ." Attorney Wade Ellis' opening gambit was to assimilate wage-fixing to price-fixing, which was permissible only in businesses affected with a public interest. The minimum wage statute, argued Ellis, was "a price fixing law. . . . and no exercise of the police power justifies the fixing of prices of either property or of services in a private business, not affected with a public interest. . . ." Other cases in which wage-fixing had been upheld were clearly distinguishable. The measure upheld in *Frisbie v. United States* had involved government conditioning the terms upon which the privilege of receiving a federal pension might be enjoyed.[8] The Adamson Act upheld in *Wilson v. New* had imposed only temporary regulation of wages in a business affected with a public interest.[9] And the Court in *Bunting v. Oregon* had pointed out "with emphasis that [its] conclusion rested upon a finding that the law was not to be considered a wage law." Finally, Ellis dismissed the police power justification for the minimum wage. The statute could not be defended as a health measure, argued Ellis, because wages, unlike hours, affected health only "indirectly or remotely."[10]

The majority opinion explicitly accepted Ellis' conflation of wage-fixing and price-fixing, characterizing the statute as "simply and exclusively a price-fixing law." "In principle," wrote Justice Sutherland, "there can be no difference between the case of selling labor and the case of selling goods." Statutes fixing rates and charges had been upheld in the past, but only under two circumstances. First, in "contracts relating to the performance of public work." Such statutes had been upheld "as depending, not upon the right to condition private contracts, but upon the right of the government to prescribe the conditions upon which it will permit work of a public character to be done for it. . . ." The second circumstance involved "statutes fixing rates and charges to be exacted by businesses affected with a public interest." However, Sutherland opined, the statute here in question "does not depend upon the existence of a public interest in any business to be affected, and this class of cases may be laid aside as inapplicable." "It is not a law dealing with any business charged with a public interest or with public work. . . . It forbids two parties having lawful capacity . . . to freely contract with one another in respect of the price for which one shall render service to the other in a purely private employment. . . ."[11]

Wilson v. New was accordingly distinguishable: the Adamson Act "was sustained primarily upon the ground that it was a regulation of a business charged with a public interest."[12]

Nor, in the majority's opinion, was the statute defensible as an exercise of the police power.[13] The means chosen by the legislature were not reasonably related to the protection of public health and morals because they did not take into account a variety of factors relevant to the determination of the pay necessary to achieve those ends in individual cases. The statute was accordingly both overinclusive[14] and underinclusive.[15] Indeed, the majority suggested that a minimum wage statute capable of being sustained as a health and morals measure would create an impracticable administrative burden. "[T]he inquiry in respect of the necessary cost of living and of the income necessary to preserve health and morals, presents an individual and not a composite question, and must be answered for each individual considered by herself and not by a general formula prescribed by a statutory bureau."[16] For all practical purposes, the constitutional obstacles to minimum wage legislation were insurmountable.

This implication was confirmed in the ensuing portion of the Court's opinion, which characterized the statute as a violation of the principle of neutrality—a taking of private property from A, the employer, and giving it to B, the employee, for a private purpose and without just compensation.

> The law takes account of the necessities of only one party to the contract. It ignores the necessities of the employer by compelling him to pay not less than a certain sum, not only whether the employee is capable of earning it, but irrespective of the ability of his business to sustain the burden. . . . It compels him to pay at least the sum fixed in any event, because the employee needs it, but requires no service of equivalent value from the employee. . . . To the extent that the sum fixed exceeds the fair value of the services rendered, it amounts to a compulsory exaction from the employer for the support of a partially indigent person, for whose condition there rests upon him no peculiar responsibility, and therefore, in effect, arbitrarily shifts to his shoulders a burden which, if it belongs to anybody, belongs to society as a whole.[17]

The Court left open the possibility that a wage statute designed to prevent fraud or overreaching might be constitutional.[18] As a health and morals measure, however, the minimum wage was hopelessly unconstitutional.

Sutherland's peroration echoed the parade of horribles sketched by the dissenters in *Wilson v. New*. "Finally, it may be said that if, in the interest of the public welfare, the police power may be invoked to justify the fixing of a minimum wage, it may, when the public welfare is thought to require it, be invoked to justify a maximum wage. The power to fix high wages connotes, by like course of reasoning, the power to fix low wages."[19] This remark confirmed Sutherland's earlier suggestions that minimum wages might be fixed for businesses affected with a public interest. For presumably the connotation flowed both ways. And because maximum wages had already been upheld when imposed on businesses affected with a public interest, "by like course of reasoning" minimum wages could be as well.

If Justice Sutherland's opinion resuscitated Peckham's mode of analysis, Chief Justice Taft's dissent echoed Justice Harlan's. Noting that the majority opinion in

Bunting had vindicated Harlan's *Lochner* dissent with respect to hours regulation, Taft opined that the issue was thus reduced to whether wage regulation was constitutionally distinct. This question turned on whether the relation of health and morals to wages was less direct than their relation to hours. This was a matter on which reasonable people might disagree; and accordingly, the legislature was entitled to the final word.

> If it be said that long hours of labor have a more direct effect upon the health of the employee than the low wage, there is very respectable authority from close observers, disclosed in the record and in the literature on the subject quoted at length in the briefs, that they are equally harmful in this regard. Congress took this view and we can not say it was not warranted in so doing.[20]

Holmes dissented separately, again expressing his exasperation with "the dogma, Liberty of Contract." "Contract is not specially mentioned in the text that we have to construe," he wrote. "It is merely an example of doing what you want to do, embodied in the word liberty. But pretty much all law consists in forbidding men to do some things that they want to do, and contract is no more exempt from law than other acts." The only relevant questions were whether the end sought was within the scope of constitutional legislation, and whether the means adopted were reasonably related to that end. The end, "to remove conditions leading to ill health, immorality and the deterioration of the race," were clearly proper. And the fact that Congress, several state legislatures, and the governments of other nations had adopted such legislation disposed of the question of whether the means were reasonably adapted to the proper end: "When so many intelligent persons, who have studied the matter more than any of us can, have thought that the means are effective and are worth the price, it seems to me impossible to deny that the belief reasonably may be held by reasonable men."[21] Again, Holmes alone refused to converse in the language of substantive due process.

In 1920 the Kansas legislature enacted the Court of Industrial Relations Act. The act declared certain businesses to be affected with a public interest, and vested an Industrial Court with power to fix wages and other terms of employment in such businesses should it find that a dispute over such terms imperiled the peace and health of the public. The employer was bound to pay the wages fixed and was permitted to discontinue the business only if he could show that continuance under the terms imposed would result in collapse. An employee discontented with his wages was permitted to quit but forbidden to agree with his fellow employees to quit or to combine with others to induce his fellow employees to quit.[22] One of the businesses declared to be affected with a public interest was the manufacturing and preparation of food for public consumption.

The Charles Wolff Packing Company, a slaughtering and meatpacking concern, objected to a wage order imposed by the Industrial Court. The meatpacking business, argued counsel for the company, was private rather than public in nature. The fixing of wages in such an industry therefore both infringed the employer's liberty of contract and constituted "the taking of private property for private use without compensation, and in violation of due process of law." Lawyers for the state contended that the packing industry was affected with a public interest, rendering it peculiarly amenable to state regulation. The Court's dicta in *Adkins*, they noted, suggested that regulation of the wages paid to those working in businesses affected with a public interest was constitutional.[23]

Chief Justice Taft's opinion for a unanimous Court took as the central issue the character of the meatpacking business. Businesses affected with a public interest, Taft opined, fell into three categories:

> (1) Those which are carried on under the authority of a public grant of privileges which either expressly or impliedly imposes the affirmative duty of rendering a public service demanded by any member of the public. Such are the railroads, other common carriers and public utilities.
>
> (2) Certain occupations, regarded as exceptional . . . Such are those of the keepers of inns, cabs and grist mills. [citations omitted].
>
> (3) Businesses which though not public at their inception may be fairly said to have risen to be such and have become subject in consequence to some government regulation. They have come to hold such a peculiar relation to the public that this is superimposed upon them. In the language of the cases, the owner by devoting his business to the public use, in effect grants the public an interest in that use and subjects himself to public regulation to the extent of that interest although the property continues to belong to its private owner and to be entitled to protection accordingly. [citations omitted].[24]

The business of food preparation did not fall into either of the first two categories, and the Court's opinion cast grave doubt on whether it fell into the third. "It has never been supposed, since the adoption of the constitution," wrote Taft, "that the business of the butcher, or the baker . . . was clothed with such a public interest that the price of his product or his wages could be fixed by State regulation." There was no monopoly in food preparation: competition fixed prices.[25]

But even assuming *arguendo* that food preparation did fall within the third class, the regulation attempted by the Kansas statute was impermissible. This is where Taft's categorization became important. "To say that a business is clothed with a public interest, is not to determine what regulation may be permissible in view of the private rights of the owner. The extent to which an inn or a cab system [second category] may be regulated may differ widely from that allowable as to a railroad or other common carrier [first category]. It depends on the nature of the business, on the feature which touches the public, and on the abuses reasonably to be feared." Preparing to distinguish *Wilson v. New*, Taft continued:

> The extent to which regulation may reasonably go varies with different kinds of business. The regulation of rates to avoid monopoly is one thing. The regulation of wages is another. A business may be of such a character that only the first is permissible, while another may involve such a possible danger of monopoly on the one hand, and such disaster from stoppage on the other, that both come within the public concern and power of regulation.

The purpose of the Kansas statute was to secure continuity in the supply of food, fuel, and clothing.[26] But regulation designed to secure such continuity could not be validly imposed on businesses falling into the third category. As Chief Justice Waite had written of owners of such businesses in *Munn*: "*He may withdraw his grant by discontinuing the use; but so long as he maintains the use, he must submit to the control.*"[27] "These words," concluded Taft, "refute the view that public regulation in such cases can secure continuity of a business against the owner." Such regulation was permissible, Taft suggested, only with respect to the first category of businesses affected with a public interest.[28]

It was on this ground that *Wilson v. New* was distinguishable. "A common carrier which accepts a railroad franchise is not free to withdraw the use of that which it has granted to the public. . . . Not so the owner when by mere changed conditions his business becomes clothed with a public interest. He may stop at will whether the business be losing or profitable."[29] The fixing of wages in the meatpacking industry therefore violated the principle of neutrality, depriving the company "of its property and liberty of contract without due process of law."[30]

Wolff Packing confirmed the implications of Chief Justice White's opinion in *Wilson v. New*: the fact that the business regulated was affected with a public interest was not alone sufficient to warrant wage-fixing. To be sure, businesses affected with a public interest were more amenable to wage-fixing than purely private businesses, which were constitutionally immune from such regulation. But the proponent of regulating wages in a business affected with a public interest also had to identify the public interest to be served by the regulation. *Wolff Packing* made clear, at least with respect to Taft's third category of businesses affected with a public interest, that continuity of operation was not such an interest.

Taft's opinion left the impression that it was the Kansas legislature's *objective* in enacting the statute—that of employing wage-fixing as a means of securing continuity of operation in certain businesses—that most troubled the Court. The impression was confirmed when *Wolff Packing* returned to the Court two years later. Upon remand, the Kansas Supreme Court had vacated its original judgment, but had entered an order compelling the company to comply with the Industrial Court's directives concerning hours of labor in the meatpacking industry. The company again brought a due process challenge before the Court.[31]

Having lost *Wolff Packing I*, however, attorneys for the state no longer sought to justify the Industrial Court's order as a valid regulation of a business affected with a public interest. Instead, the state's lawyers defended the order as a valid exercise of the police power. "The Supreme Court of Kansas, from the start of this litigation," they contended, "has interpreted the statute as having among its purposes the protection of the health of the workers, and has recognized the fixing of hours of labor as a method of protecting their health."[32] "Hours of labor in packing plants [were] a proper subject for regulations under the police power."[33] This much appeared to have been settled by *Bunting*. Indeed, the order of the court pertaining to hours appeared to be modeled on the statute upheld in *Bunting*.[34] "[T]he provision of the statute declaring the packing industry to be affected with a public interest" could therefore "be ignored."[35] "The portions of the statute relating to hours" were, therefore, "valid despite the invalidity of the wage-fixing provisions."[36]

Despite a defense of the act resting on the recent authority of *Bunting*, the Court's opinion declaring the hours directive unconstitutional was unanimous. The act's "purpose," wrote Justice Van Devanter, "is not to regulate wages or hours of labor generally or in particular classes of business, but to authorize the state agency to fix them where, and in so far as, they are the subjects of a controversy the settlement of which is directed in the interest of the public. In short, the authority to fix them is intended to be merely a part of the system of compulsory arbitration and to be exerted in attaining its object, which is continuity of operation and production." "[N]either [wages nor hours] is to be fixed save in the compulsory adjustment of an endangering controversy to the end that the business shall go on." "The system of compulsory arbitration which the Act establishes is intended to compel, and if sustained will compel, the owner and employees to continue the business on terms which are not of their own making. It will constrain them not merely to respect the terms if they continue the business, but will constrain them to continue the business on those terms. . . . Such a system infringes the liberty of contract and rights of property guaranteed by the due process clause of the Fourteenth Amendment." "The authority which the Act gives respecting the fixing of hours of labor is merely a feature of the system of compulsory arbitration and has no separate purpose. It was exerted by the state agency as part of that system and the state court sustained its exertion as such." Accordingly, Bunting was distinguishable, and the police power rationale offered by the state inapplicable. "Whether it would be valid had it been conferred independently of the system and made either general or applicable to all businesses of a particular class we need not consider, for that was not done."[37]

The voting patterns in these two cases merit attention. Wolff Packing I was written by Taft, who had dissented in Adkins; was joined by Sanford and Holmes, who had likewise dissented; and was joined by Brandeis,[38] who would have dissented in Adkins had he participated. Wolff Packing II, similarly unanimous, was joined by Taft and Sanford; was also joined by Holmes, who had joined the majority in Bunting; was joined by Brandeis,[39] who would have joined in Bunting had he participated; and was joined by the newly appointed Justice Harlan Fiske Stone, who would later vote in favor of minimum wage regulation.[40]

The fact that so many supporters of the minimum wage opposed wage legislation designed to require business continuity suggests that these justices believed that there was a stronger public interest rationale supporting the former than the latter. Adkins, however, had foreclosed any rationale based on health and morals, and had indicated that such regulation of private businesses violated the principle of neutrality. Dicta in the Adkins majority opinion, however, had suggested that the peculiar amenability to rate regulation of businesses affected with a public interest might render them susceptible to minimum wage regulation. With this proposition the Adkins dissenters were presumably in accord. What remained was for proponents of minimum wage legislation to frame a rationale upon which its application to such businesses might be sustained.

The Road to Nebbia

After Adkins, it was clear that the only available route to sustaining legislation fixing wages was to argue that the business in question was affected with a public interest.

The next three opinions considering the validity of legislation regulating compensation for services accordingly took the character of the business involved as the central issue.[41] In the first of these three cases, *Ribnik v. McBride*, the Court struck down a New Jersey statute regulating the fees charged by employment agencies on the ground that the business in question was not affected with a public interest. Sutherland's majority opinion offered the most extreme statement of opposition to wage regulation yet articulated by the Court. Again conflating wage and price regulation, Sutherland wrote: "Under the decisions of this Court it is no longer fairly open to question that, at least in the absence of a grave emergency, . . . the fixing of prices for food or clothing, of house rental or of wages to be paid, whether minimum or maximum, is beyond legislative power."[42] This dictum announced a virtual per se rule against wage regulation, irrespective of whether the business regulated was public in nature. Such a strong formulation could not, and would not, long survive.

In fact, it would not last even two years. In 1921 Congress had enacted the Packers and Stockyards Act, authorizing the secretary of agriculture to regulate the business of meat packers done in interstate commerce, and forbidding the packers from engaging in any unfair, discriminatory, or deceptive practices in interstate commerce. Title III of the Act authorized the secretary to regulate transactions in the stockyards, including the rates to be charged for stockyard services and the fees to be charged by commission men making sales of stock in interstate commerce. In 1930, the Act weathered a due process attack in *Tagg Bros. & Moorhead v. United States.*[43]

In *Tagg Bros.*, a group of commission agencies doing business at the Union Stockyards in Omaha, and together comprising the membership of the Omaha Livestock Exchange, had established rules requiring all members to charge the same rates for their services. The Exchange had promulgated a rate schedule to govern fees charged by its members, effectively eliminating rate competition among Omaha commission agencies. Pursuant to his authority under the Act, the secretary of agriculture suspended the operation of the Exchange's rate schedule and supplanted it with a schedule of his own making. The members of the Exchange sought to enjoin the secretary's action.

The commission men conceded that they were engaged in interstate commerce at a public stockyards and were therefore subject to some Congressional regulation.[44] Indeed eight years earlier, in *Stafford v. Wallace*, the Court had held that the stockyards "conduct a business affected by a public use of a national character and subject to national regulation."[45] Attorneys for the commission men nevertheless sought to overcome this precedential hurdle by drawing a sharp distinction between wage-fixing and price-fixing, between compensation for personal services and returns on capital investment.[46] Indeed, they contended from the outset that the regulation in question was properly governed by previous cases concerning statutes governing compensation for personal services.[47] "Congress has no power to fix prices for purely personal services (such as that of the commission men, for selling and grading cattle)."[48] "The commissions are only wages for the labor of the commission men. . . . The business is wholly one of skill and labor, with the elements of capital or other property investment negligible."[49] "[H]is services are those of skilled labor and the commission paid him by the shipper . . . is his wages for his arduous toil." "To quote Jefferson's phrase in his first inaugural, this fixing of wages for personal service 'takes from the mouth of labor the bread it has earned.'"[50]

The fixing of rates for the commission men was impermissible because of "the vital distinctions, from the constitutional standpoint, in all legislative price-fixing between property and the use of property, on the one hand, and personal services, on the other." "First, property originates with the State and reverts to the State. . . . Liberty is not held at the will of the State. . . ." "Second, property may be taken by the State for public use. But liberty—personal services—may not be taken by the State for public use or any other use except as a punishment for crime or in a time of war." Property could be taken by due process and with just compensation. Liberty, however, "including personal services, can be taken by due process only, that is, by determining the commission of the crime for which punishment is required." There was, moreover, no way to provide adequate compensation for a deprivation of liberty. "When prices are fixed for personal services, there is no capital invested upon which an adequate and just return may be calculated." Accordingly, personal services, unlike property, could not be affected with a public interest. As a result, the prices charged for such services could not be regulated at all. "[T]he whole truth," concluded the commission men's brief triumphantly, "has emerged—that ordinary legislative price fixing for purely personal services is impossible under our Constitution—all the time, everywhere."[51] "[P]ersonal services are not subject to price-fixing by law unless, to use the language of this Court in a recent case, 'there is to be a revolution in the relation of government to general business.'"[52]

Attorneys for the government, mindful of the absolute prohibition on wage-fixing suggested by Sutherland's *Ribnik* dictum, denied categorically that the act fixed wages. They instead sought to characterize the statute as a regulation of prices. "The regulation of maximum commission charges under the Packers and Stockyards Act is not wage-fixing either in form or in substance," they contended, because "the service performed, the charge for which is regulated, requires the use of property and of personal services." The commission men employed the "very valuable property" of the stockyards in the conduct of their business. If the stockyards company itself had conducted the commission business, there would be no question that the statute regulated the rate of return on capital rather than compensation for personal services. "The power of the public to regulate is not lost because most of the property and facilities used in the business are leased, rather than owned, by those engaged in it." Nor did the statute fix wages merely because wages and salaries were the largest expense of the business. "The Secretary's rates prescribe the maximum charges for a business carried on, like other businesses, through the use of property and the complementary services of individuals." The maximum charges for this business could be regulated because it was, like those involved in *Munn* and its progeny, affected with a public interest.[53]

The Court, in an opinion authored by Justice Brandeis, unanimously rejected both the commission men's contentions that compensation for personal services could never be regulated and the government's suggestion that the regulation of compensation was here permissible only because the conduct of the business required the use of valuable property. "There is nothing in the nature of monopolistic personal services," wrote Brandeis, "which makes it impossible to fix reasonable charges to be made therefor; and there is nothing in the Constitution which limits the Government's power of regulation to businesses which employ substantial capital." *Tyson* and *Ribnik* had not held "that charges for personal services cannot be regulated." The Court there had held only that such charges could not be regulated where the business involved was not affected with a public interest. Here the business involved was so affected. Moreover, as *Wolff Packing* required, the regulation in question was reasonably related to the protection of a legitimate public interest: preventing the services of the commission men from becoming an undue burden on and an obstruction to interstate commerce in livestock.[54]

Brandeis sought to soften the blow to Sutherland's extravagant *Ribnik* dictum through a disingenuous characterization of the statute. "There is here no attempt to fix anyone's wages or to limit anyone's net income. Differences in skill, industry and experience will continue to be factors in the earning power of the several plaintiffs. For, the order fixes only the charges to be made in individual transactions."[55] True, the order did not limit anyone's net income. But prescribing the commission that could be earned on a sale was no less wage-fixing than prescribing the fee that could be earned for a service rendered by a lawyer or a chimney sweep, nor less wage-fixing than prescribing the fee to be paid for an hour's service in ordinary labor. The "heart of the contract"[56] was in all such situations the regulated term, and in *Tagg Bros.* it was permitted because the business in question was affected with a public interest. The decline of a per se rule against the regulation of compensation for personal services had begun.

O'Gorman & Young v. Hartford Fire Ins. Co., decided in 1931, concerned the constitutionality of a New Jersey statute regulating the commissions paid to insurance agents by fire insurance companies.[57] *German Alliance Ins. Co. v. Lewis* had held that the business of fire insurance was affected with a public interest and that its premium rates could accordingly be regulated. In defense of the statute, the appellees in *O'Gorman* filed a five-page brief relying almost entirely on *German Alliance*.[58]

The appellants denied that *German Alliance* supported the statute in question. Admittedly, the legislature could regulate fire insurance rates. But "[t]he power to regulate rates to be charged the public does not imply power to invade the field of private management." "The fact that the business of a company is impressed with a public interest does not subject its internal administration to legislative control." The New Jersey statute was "not a regulation of the relation of the insurance company to the public but regulation of one of the internal details of private management." Permitting regulation of such internal details would be to erode, and potentially to obliterate, the private zone of contractual liberty enjoyed even by businesses affected with a public interest and their employees.

> While it must be conceded that the legislature has the right to regulate the rates to be charged to the public, it does not follow therefrom that the detail cost of administration may be fixed and regulated by the government and the management of such business largely assumed by the government. If it be only necessary in order to sustain

an act of this character to show that it regulates one of the items of cost entering into the rendition of service to the public, then there is no detail of the business from the salary of the president to the wages of the charwoman, and the sufficiency of the services rendered by each, as well as the price of rent to the price of paper clips, which may not become the ultimate subject of legislative control.[59]

Upholding the New Jersey statute would be not only an unwarranted extension of *German Alliance*; it would be a repudiation of *Wilson v. New* and *Wolff Packing I*. Those cases had made clear that businesses affected with a public interest were public in some respects but private in others. In their relations with consumers, such businesses were public. In their internal operations, however, they were private. In all of the cases "dealing with internal contracts"—*Wilson v. New, Adkins* and *Wolff Packing I*—"all legislative power, to inhibit private contracts as to the amount of compensation to be paid for personal services, is denied." "No case brought before this court upholds any statute which seeks to substitute, as between employer and employee, a legislative rate of wage for a conventional rate or the right to arrive at a conventional rate. Wherever this court has dealt with this subject it has asserted the liberty of an individual to enter into service contracts for compensation agreed upon." *Wilson v. New* had permitted temporary wage-fixing as a means of ensuring continuity of rail service. It had repudiated the notion that fixing the wages of railway employees might be a legitimate means of regulating railroad rates. *Wilson* stood for the proposition "that there is no power in state or federal legislature to substitute a legislative standard of wages or remuneration for those agreed upon between employer and employee even in an occupation affected with a public interest." *Wolff Packing I* stood for the same proposition. The regulation upheld in *Tagg Bros.* had concerned not an "internal contract" between employer and employee, but "contracts with the public." That regulation had "dealt with 'the feature which touched the public.' It was like regulating insurance rates, but was not concerned with the regulation of salaries, fees or commissions within the internal organization of market agencies." Sutherland's *Ribnik* dictum "declare[d] against legislative price-fixing of maximum or minimum wages in all private activities in the absence of a grave emergency." "The Legislature," appellant's counsel concluded, "is without power to prohibit private contracts as to the amount of compensation to be paid by employers to their adult employees."[60]

Chief Justice Taft became ill in the autumn of 1929, and resigned February 3, 1930. He was replaced by Charles Evans Hughes, who took his seat on February 24, the very day that the decision in *Tagg Bros.* was announced. Justice Sanford died March 8, 1930. *O'Gorman* was argued April 30, 1930, more than a week before President Hoover nominated Owen Roberts to succeed Sanford. Presumably because the Court was deadlocked 4 to 4, the case was set for a reargument at which Roberts could sit the following term. Roberts took his seat June 2, 1930, and the case was reargued October 30, 1930.[61] When the Court's opinion was handed down the following January 5, the nation got its first indication of Justice Roberts' views on the constitutionality of statutes regulating compensation for personal services.

Hughes surely recognized that the opinion would be an important one, and he placed it in the capable hands of Brandeis. The majority opinion ignored the appellant's parade of horribles, refusing to engage the question of whether authorization of commission regulation entailed sanctioning regulation of the price of paper clips. For Brandeis, the matter was fairly simple. *German Alliance* had established that "[t]he business of insurance is so far affected with a public interest that the State may regulate the rates." Moreover, as *Wolff Packing I* required, regulation of agents' commissions was reasonably related to a legitimate public interest with respect to the business. "The agent's compensation, being a percentage of the premium, bears a direct relation to the rate charged the insured. The percentage commonly allowed is so large that it is a vital element in the rate structure and may seriously affect the adequacy of the rate. Excessive commissions may result in an unreasonably high rate level or in impairment of the financial stability of the insurer."[62] In other words, the regulation was reasonably related both to the public's interest in reasonable insurance rates and to the public's interest in the ability of fire insurance companies to perform their vital public function.

More important, Brandeis' opinion implicitly rejected *Wilson*'s holding that businesses affected with a public interest contained a near-inviolable private inner core, and that contracts between the business and its employees were negotiated and executed within that private, concentric inner sphere. Justice Van Devanter, dissenting for himself and Justices McReynolds, Sutherland, and Butler, pointed this out with chagrin.[63] "[I]t must be accepted as settled," wrote Van Devanter, "that the right to regulate a business does not necessarily imply power to fix the scale for services therein. . . ." "Congress has power, for example, to regulate interstate commerce; but generally, at least, it may not say what shall be paid to employees or interfere with the freedom of the parties to contract in respect of wages." The New Jersey legislature had done precisely that, and without the presence of an emergency to justify its action. "In order to justify the denial of the right to make private contracts," Van Devanter complained, "some special circumstances sufficient to indicate the necessity therefor must be shown by the party relying upon the denial. Here the right freely to agree upon reasonable compensation has been abridged; and no special circumstances demanding such action have been disclosed."[64]

The majority opinion further indicated that the Court was now taking the same approach toward statutes regulating compensation that it had toward hours regulation in *Bunting*.

> The statute here questioned deals with a subject clearly within the scope of the police power. We are asked to declare it void on the ground that the specific method of regulation prescribed is unreasonable and hence deprives the plaintiff of due process of law. As underlying questions of fact may condition the constitutionality of legislation of this character, the presumption of constitutionality must prevail in the absence of some factual foundation of record for overthrowing the statute. It does not appear upon the face of the statute, or from any facts of which the court must take judicial notice, that in New Jersey evils did not exist in the business of fire insurance for which this statutory provision was an appropriate remedy. The action of the legislature and of the highest court of the State indicates that such evils did exist. The record is barren of any allegation of fact tending to show unreasonableness.[65]

At least with respect to businesses affected with a public interest, there was now a strong presumption in favor of the constitutionality of statutes regulating even internal contracts for compensation. As one commentator predicted, "The instant case, decided on a realignment of the Justices, is further significant in that it may serve to stem the tide of decisions holding invalid legislative attempts at price- and wage-fixing."[66] As another noted, "Since a good case can be made out for most statutes sustained by the state courts, and particularly for those aiming to remedy social conditions, this alteration in the burden of proof will be decisive in the majority of instances. The basic premise of the *Adkins* case is seriously impaired." The "vigorous" dissent of the Four Horsemen showed "their appreciation of the bold change of front by the majority, and their disapproval."[67]

Brandeis' brief opinion addressed *Wilson* and *Ribnik* only obliquely, but it strongly suggested that both White's private inner core and Sutherland's absolute prohibition on wage regulation were dead. The compensation of those working in businesses affected with a public interest could be regulated if such regulation was reasonably related to the protection of the public's interest in the business; and there was thenceforth to be a strong presumption that any such regulation was so related. In this respect, however, the power to fix maximum wages did not necessarily imply the power to fix minimum wages. Any advocate defending a statute imposing a minimum wage regulation on businesses affected with a public interest would have to explain how that statute protected the public's interest in that business. Defenders of the minimum wage had articulated two public interests protected by such legislation. First, ensuring workers a living wage protected public health and morals. Second, requiring employers to pay the cost of sustaining their labor force prevented them from externalizing that cost to the public through poor relief. Neither of these public interests, however, was peculiar to businesses affected with a public interest: they pertained to all businesses, both public and private. *O'Gorman*, consistently with its ancestors, suggested that the public interest rationale supporting wage regulation must be custom-tailored to the business in question. The public interest rationales designed by minimum wage advocates were one-size-fits-all. If, however, the category of "business affected with a public interest" were removed as an initial obstacle to wage regulation—if, in other words, *all* businesses were affected with a public interest—these broad public interest rationales might be invoked to support the constitutionality of minimum wage legislation.

Nebbia v. New York involved a New York State Control Board regulation of retail milk prices. The regulation was an attempt to ameliorate the effects of cut-throat competition in the retail milk business, where price-cutting had reduced the income of dairy farmers to a level below the cost of production. Leo Nebbia, a retailer convicted of selling milk below the price prescribed by state regulation, argued that the regulation deprived him of property without due process of law in violation of the Fourteenth Amendment. Price regulation, Nebbia contended, was constitutional only as applied to a business affected with a public interest. For a business to be affected with a public interest, he argued, it had to be either a public utility or a natural monopoly. Because neither Nebbia's business itself nor the milk industry as a whole belonged to either of these categories, Nebbia contended that his business was not affected with a public interest and therefore was not subject to price regulation. As the Court had repeatedly held, price regulation of purely private business was constitutionally impermissible.[68]

Predictably, Nebbia's attorneys contended that *Adkins* controlled the instant case. In *Adkins*, they argued,

> the fixing of the minima was strikingly like the method here. The opinion emphasized as one of the principal faults of the statute that "the declared basis" of the minimum wage "is not the value of the service rendered, but the extraneous circumstance that the employee needs to get a prescribed sum of money to insure her subsistence, health and morals."
>
> Similarly in the case at bar, the laudable desire to see the dairy farmer happier and more prosperous has brought the New York Legislature to say that, regardless of the retail value of milk as fixed by oversupply and limited demand, the dealer must sell to his customers at a fixed minimum, or else not sell.[69]

Each regulation equally violated the principle of neutrality.

New York's attorneys dutifully sought to accommodate the regulation within conventional doctrinal categories. First, because the regulation was temporary, it was supported by the emergency doctrine set forth in *Wilson v. New* and *Block v. Hirsh*. Second, they contended, the business of milk distribution was a natural monopoly and a business affected with a public interest. Third, they maintained, overproduction of milk posed a hazard within the cognizance of the police power: "Milk is a perishable food and the presence of excess milk in a city market under ordinary conditions of human cupidity is a health menace."[70]

Justices interested only in sustaining the instant regulation without making any broader doctrinal commitments could easily have grasped on to any of these conventional, comfortable rationales. The case did not call for a revolution in due process jurisprudence. But Justice Roberts' opinion for the majority spurned all of the doctrinal vehicles offered up by New York, instead taking the revolutionary step of abandoning the public/private distinction as an analytic category in price regulation cases. "The Fifth Amendment," he wrote,

> in the field of federal activity, and the Fourteenth, as respects state action, do not prohibit governmental regulation for the public welfare. They merely condition the exertion of the admitted power, by securing that the end shall be accomplished by methods consistent with due process. And the guaranty of due process, as has often been held, demands only that the law shall not be unreasonable, arbitrary or capricious, and that the means selected shall have a real and substantial relation to the object sought to be attained.[71]

Roberts acknowledged that the dairy industry was not a public utility, that it was not a monopoly, and that those engaged in the business were not recipients of any peculiar government-granted privilege. "But if, as must be conceded, the industry is subject to regulation in the public interest, what constitutional principle bars the state from correcting existing maladjustments by legislation touching prices? We think there is no such principle." In words reminiscent of Holmes' *Adkins* dissent, words that would be echoed three years later in *West Coast Hotel v. Parrish*, Roberts observed:

> The due process clause makes no mention of sales or of prices any more than it speaks of business or contracts or buildings or other incidents of property. The thought seems nevertheless to have persisted that there is something peculiarly sacrosanct about the price one may charge for what he makes or sells, and that, however able to regulate other elements of manufacture or trade, with incidental effect upon price, the state is incapable of directly controlling the price itself.[72]

This, Roberts maintained, was nonsense. The term "'affected with a public interest' is the equivalent of 'subject to the exercise of the police power'; and it is plain that nothing more was intended by the expression."[73]

Of course, it had long been established that every business was subject to the police power. Accordingly, "The statement that one has dedicated his property to a public use is, therefore, merely another way of saying that if one embarks in a business which public interest demands shall be regulated, he must know regulation will ensue." Nearly all of the cases in which price or wage regulation had previously been upheld were reconceptualized as applications of this principle. "It is clear," wrote Roberts, "that there is no closed class or category of businesses affected with a public interest,"

> and the function of courts in the application of the Fifth and Fourteenth Amendments is to determine in each case whether circumstances vindicate the challenged regulation as a reasonable exertion of governmental authority or condemn it as arbitrary or discriminatory. . . . The phrase "affected with a public interest" can, in the nature of things, mean no more than that an industry, for adequate reason, is subject to control for the public good.

"[T]here can be no doubt," Roberts concluded, "that upon proper occasion and by appropriate measures the state may regulate a business in any of its aspects, including the prices to be charged for the products or commodities it sells."[74]

In words more reminiscent of Holmes' *Tyson & Brother v. Banton* dissent than of any previous majority opinion, Roberts asserted that earlier cases in which the term "affected with a public interest" had served as the criterion of the validity of price control legislation had admitted that the term formed "an unsatisfactory test" of constitutionality. Cases in which price control legislation had been struck down "must rest, finally, upon the basis that the requirements of due process were not met because the laws were found arbitrary in their operation and effect." As Justice McReynolds pointed out in dissent, this was not at all what those opinions had said: the statutes in those cases had been declared unconstitutional because they had regulated the prices of businesses that were purely private. But in light of Justice Roberts' opinion, such a characterization could no longer have its previous constitutional import. The category "business affected with a public interest" had been retired.[75]

Taken in conjunction with *O'Gorman*, this doctrinal development alone was probably sufficient to herald the demise of *Adkins*. But the balance of Roberts' opinion made clear that the Court was announcing a revolution in due process jurisprudence that extended beyond the narrow confines of price regulation controversies.

> So far as the requirement of due process is concerned, and in the absence of other constitutional restriction, a state is free to adopt whatever economic policy may reasonably be deemed to promote the public welfare, and to enforce that policy by legislation adapted to its purpose. The courts are without authority either to declare such policy, or, when it is declared by the legislature, to override it. If the laws passed are seen to have a reasonable relation to a proper legislative purpose, and are neither arbitrary nor discriminatory, the requirements of due process are satisfied. . . .[76]

"With the wisdom of the policy adopted, with the adequacy or practicability of the law enacted to enforce it, the courts are both incompetent and unauthorized to deal." And the hopes of minimum wage advocates who recalled Frankfurter's arguments in favor of the minimum wage surely soared as they read Roberts' peroration.

> The Constitution does not secure to anyone liberty to conduct his business in such a fashion as *to inflict injury upon the public at large,* or upon any substantial group of people. Price control, *like any other form of regulation,* is unconstitutional only if arbitrary, discriminatory, or demonstrably irrelevant to the policy the legislature is free to adopt, and hence an unnecessary and unwarranted interference with individual liberty.[77]

The analogical ramifications of Roberts' opinion were enormous, and the Four Horsemen grasped them immediately. After all, Sutherland had written in *Adkins* that there was no distinction in principle between "the case of selling labor and the case of selling goods." Indeed, Sutherland's condemnation of the minimum wage in *Adkins* had drawn an analogy to legislation regulating the price of groceries.

> The feature of this [minimum wage] statute which, perhaps more than any other, puts upon it the stamp of invalidity is that it exacts from the employer an arbitrary payment for a purpose and upon a basis having no causal connection with his business. . . . If one goes to the butcher, the baker or grocer to buy food, he is morally entitled to obtain the worth of his money but he is not entitled to more. If what he gets is worth what he pays he is not justified in demanding more simply because he needs more; and the shopkeeper, having dealt fairly and honestly in that transaction, is not concerned in any particular sense with the question of his customer's necessities. Should a statute undertake to vest in a commission power to determine the quantity of food necessary for individual support and require the shopkeeper, if he sell to the individual at all, to furnish that quantity at not more than a fixed maximum, it would undoubtedly fall before the constitutional test. The fallacy of any argument in support of the validity of such a statute would be quickly exposed. The argument in support of that now being considered is equally fallacious, though the weakness of it may not be so plain.[78]

If requiring the grocer to provide food at below-market prices because of the consumer's necessitous circumstances was a taking, then surely requiring the consumer to pay above-market prices because of the producer's necessitous circumstances was equally a taking. The instant regulation, wrote McReynolds, "takes away the liberty of twelve millon consumers to buy a necessity of life in an open market. It imposes direct and arbitrary burdens upon those already seriously impoverished with the alleged immediate design of affording special benefits to others. . . . The Legislature cannot lawfully destroy guaranteed rights of one man with the prime purpose of enriching another, even if for the moment, this may seem advantageous to the public." However, if such a regulation were not a taking, then neither would a regulation fixing maximum prices be; and by force of Sutherland's analogy, neither would the fixing of a minimum wage. These consequences the dissenters acknowledged explicitly. "The argument advanced here would support general prescription of prices for farm products, groceries, shoes, clothing, all the necessities of modern civilization, *as well as labor*, when some legislature finds and declares such action advisable and for the public good."[79] In other words, the expansive views expressed in Roberts' opinion committed the majority to the constitutionality of minimum wage legislation. *Adkins*, in the dissenters' view, had been effectively overruled.

This view was shared by a bevy of contemporary Court-watchers. *O'Gorman* and *Nebbia*, wrote Hugh Willis, were "a prophecy" that *Adkins* "will be overruled whenever a case giving the Supreme Court an opportunity to do so is presented to it." The change wrought by *Nebbia*, wrote one commentator, was "so great as to overrule for all practical purposes a host of cases decided in recent years under the due process clause." It was now "possible that a state may legally regulate all its businesses even to the extent of fixing prices, wages and hours of labor." *Nebbia*, wrote another commentator, "clinch[ed] the battle." "No longer may a man cry out 'Unconstitutional!' against every law that seems to restrict his freedom of contract or to deprive him of his property. . . . The gateway to social legislation has at last been opened. Labor laws, health laws, and other legislation that is sorely needed . . . now stand a good chance of being enacted." Thomas Raeburn White, in a piece whose title posed the question, "Constitutional Protection of Liberty of Contract: Does It Still Exist?" answered in the negative. The Supreme Court, he wrote, "has in effect surrendered its power to declare void acts of legislature on the ground that they infringe liberty of contract." It was now clear that state legislatures "may fix the rates of wages and the hours of labor."[80]

At the time of the *Adkins* decision, wrote Robert Hale, "it was the doctrine of the Court that any direct legislative interference with market prices was invalid, except in the cases of businesses labeled 'affected with a public interest.' This doctrine, however, was emphatically repudiated" in *Nebbia*. "In view of this decision," inquired Hale, "is it not possible that the views expressed by Taft, Sanford and Holmes in their dissents in 1923, have become the law of the court, and that a law forbidding the sale or purchase of women's labor for less than the minimum cost of living found by a board, would now be held to be a valid means of protecting the wage structure and the health of women?"[81] Wages, wrote another commentator, "are but the price of a commodity which is sold to employers, and the labor and health of women are easily as essential to the welfare of a state as is milk. Therefore, if the dairy industry may be protected by minimum price laws, the states should be permitted to extend similar aid to the far more helpless women workers."[82] The *Nebbia* decision, wrote Morris Duane, "practically overruled a number of cases in which the Court had held state price fixing a violation of the due process clause of the Fourteenth Amendment; also another number in which state control of hours and wages had been declared invalid—a very similar problem."[83] "The Nebbia case doctrine," wrote John Hannigan, "if applied to the *Adkins* case, would have sustained the law. . . ." *Nebbia*, Alpheus Thomas Mason agreed, "augurs well for minimum wage regulations."[84]

Another *Nebbia* commentator conjectured that had Hughes and Roberts "been on the court in 1923, it is highly improbable that they would have concurred in the *Adkins* decision." In light of *O'Gorman* and *Nebbia*, it seemed "probable that they will now refuse to follow the *Adkins* doctrine." That same commentator, however, looked into the future with preternatural clairvoyance:

> But I am instructed that Mr. Hughes is extremely reluctant to overrule a case expressly, especially when such action would result, as it almost certainly would here, in a five to four decision. Therefore, in order to placate the minority and to save the face of the court, it is my prediction that the *Adkins* case will be distinguished rather than directly overruled.[85]

As it would turn out, all of these commentators would be proven correct.

5

The Minimum Wage Cases Revisited

West Coast Hotel v. Parrish

In 1937, a Washington minimum wage statute virtually identical to the statute struck down in *Adkins* came before the Court in *West Coast Hotel v. Parrish*. Like the 1918 District of Columbia statute, the Washington statute was grounded in the police power. Section 1 of the statute declared that "The welfare of the State of Washington demands that women and minors be protected from conditions of labor which have a pernicious effect on their health and morals," and that "inadequate wages and unsanitary conditions of labor exert such pernicious effect." Section 2 made it unlawful to employ women or minors "under conditions of labor detrimental to their health or morals," and to employ women "at wages which are not adequate for their maintenance." Section 3 created a commission, which was to establish "such standards of wages and conditions of labor for women and minors . . . as shall be held hereunder to be reasonable and not detrimental to health and morals, and which shall be sufficient for the decent maintenance of women." Elsie Parrish, a chambermaid employed by the West Coast Hotel Company, had been paid less than the wage prescribed by the state commission. When she sued to recover the difference due her under state law, the hotel company contended that the Washington statute violated the due process clause of the Fourteenth Amendment.[1]

Faced with the claim that *Adkins* controlled the case, the Washington Supreme Court had suggested that the vitality of *Adkins* had been sapped by the intervening decisions in *O'Gorman* and *Nebbia*. *Nebbia* had indicated that if a deprivation of contractual liberty "is with due process, if it corrects a known and stated evil, if it promotes the public welfare — that is, if it is a reasonable exercise of the police power — it is constitutional and it is a proper exercise of legislative power." *O'Gorman* had held "that a state statute dealing with a subject clearly within the police power cannot be declared void upon the ground that the specific method of regulation prescribed by it is unreasonable, in the absence of any factual foundation in the record to overcome the presumption of constitutionality."[2]

The Washington court bolstered its claims for a more robust police power by employing the broader notion of affectation with a public interest innovated by Roberts' opinion in *Nebbia.* "[T]he controversy here," wrote the court,

> had an added element not found in the ordinary controversy between individuals. It was not wholly of private concern. It was affected with a public interest. The state, having declared that a minimum wage of a certain amount is necessary to a decent maintenance of an employee engaged in the employment in which the respondent was engaged, has an interest in seeing that the fixed compensation is actually paid.[3]

Because the state had determined that the public had an interest in the wages paid to "an employee engaged in the employment in which the respondent was engaged," and because *Nebbia* had indicated that legislative judgments concerning the affectation of a business with a public interest were entitled to a broad measure of deference,[4] the wage relations of the hotel's business were affected with a public interest. Accordingly, regulation of those wages did not violate the principle of neutrality. It was not a taking from A, the employer, and a giving to B, the employee, for a purely private purpose. As the court remarked, "The statute was not therefore intended solely for the benefit of the wage-earner. It was believed that the welfare of the public requires that wage-earners receive a wage sufficient for their decent maintenance." "The statute is protective of the public as well as the wage earner." The employer was not entitled to run his business so as to inflict injury on the public at large.[5] Legislative enforcement of the *sic utere* principle did not deprive anyone of a constitutionally protected right to liberty or property.

On appeal to the U.S. Supreme Court, the briefs defending the Washington statute relied heavily on *Nebbia* and *O'Gorman.*[6] As the Washington state attorney general pointed out in his amicus brief, "It seems very difficult to understand why minimum wages may not be fixed without violating due process, if prices can be fixed without violating due process. Both interfere with liberty to contract." "Whether there are adequate reasons for submitting certain types of contracts to the public control depends upon the economic policies of the states," he contended, and *Nebbia* had held that "'so far as the requirement of due process is concerned . . . a state is free to adopt whatever economic policy may reasonably be deemed to promote public welfare. . . .'" Those challenging the statute had not met the burden of proof imposed by *O'Gorman* and *Nebbia:* "no showing is made that payment at the rate prescribed by the welfare committee is unfair or unreasonable." Moreover, the business in question fell squarely within the second category of businesses affected with a public interest identified by Taft in *Wolff Packing I:* "a hotel or inn is a business affected with a public interest." Accordingly, there was "no factual basis for a general attack upon the constitutionality of the statute."[7]

Throughout his majority opinion upholding the statute, Chief Justice Hughes made clear his reliance on the principles of substantive due process forged by Roberts in *Nebbia.* "[T]he violation alleged by those attacking minimum wage regulation for women," he wrote, "is deprivation of freedom of contract. What is this freedom? The Constitution does not speak of freedom of contract. It speaks of liberty and prohibits the deprivation of liberty without due process of law."[8] "In prohibiting that deprivation the Constitution does not recognize an absolute and uncontrollable liberty. . . . Liberty under the Constitution is thus necessarily subject to the restraints of due process, and regulation which is reasonable in relation to its subject and is adopted in the interests of the community is due process."[9] Contractual liberty was thus no more sacrosanct than any other sort of liberty protected by the Fourteenth Amendment: "This essential limitation of liberty in general governs freedom of contract in particular."[10] As this rearticulation of the principles Roberts had set forth made clear, *Nebbia* had liberated the Court from the task of determining whether the business regulated was purely private. No longer would the constitutionality of regulation of the wage contract turn on whether the employment involved could somehow be conceptually located in the public sphere. No longer would the private nature of the business operate as an absolute bar to regulation of the price it paid for labor. In that sense, *Nebbia* had declared all businesses to be affected with a public interest. Now the only relevant inquiry was whether the regulation imposed was reasonable. *Adkins*, however, had held that the District of Columbia minimum wage statute was not a reasonable exercise of the police power. It had taken property from the employer and given it to the employee for a purely private purpose. The abandonment of heightened scrutiny for legislation impinging on contractual liberty did not necessarily entail the constitutionality of the minimum wage. It remained for Hughes to defend the reasonableness of such legislation.

Like Roberts' approach to price control in *Nebbia*, Hughes' rejection of the notion that contract was a domain of activity afforded heightened constitutional protection was drawn from Holmes. Yet adopting Holmes' mode of due process analysis in its entirety would have entailed disregarding conventional police power categories as superfluous and abandoning the principle of neutrality. The cautious Hughes was prepared to take neither of those revolutionary steps. Instead, he summoned his considerable skills at doctrinal synthesis,[11] combining Holmes' rejection of a special liberty of *contract* with Harlan's and Taft's solicitude for conventional police power categories, their deference to legislative judgments of fact, and their embrace of the principle of neutrality.

Hughes accordingly proceeded to demonstrate how minimum wage regulation might be reconciled with the principle of neutrality, deftly synthesizing the broad Nebbian public interest concept with the police power categories under which legislation restricting freedom of contract had been sustained. "[T]he liberty safeguarded," Hughes opined, "is liberty in a social organization which requires the protection of law against the evils which menace the health, safety, morals and welfare of the people." The "power under the Constitution to restrict freedom of contract has had many illustrations. That it may be exercised in the public interest with respect to contracts between employer and employee is undeniable." Here Hughes cited cases upholding workmen's compensation statutes, statutes regulating hours of work, and statutes prescribing the time and manner of wage payment. These cases illustrated the principle that the legislature enjoyed broad discretion to ensure "suitable protection of health and safety, and that peace and good order may be promoted through regulations designed to insure wholesome conditions of work and freedom from oppression."[12]

This principle was "peculiarly applicable in relation to the employment of women in whose protection the state has a special interest." *Muller v. Oregon* had made clear that due to "the performance of maternal functions," woman's "physical well being 'becomes an object of public interest and care in order to preserve the strength and vigor of the race,'" and that limitations upon her power to contract with her employer for longer hours were "'not imposed solely for her benefit, but also largely for the benefit of us all.'"[13]

Echoing Taft's and Holmes' assessments of *Lochner* in their *Adkins* dissents, Hughes concluded that "the decision in the *Adkins* case was a departure from the true application of the principles governing the regulation by the State of the relation between employer and employed." And where was one to find the true application of such principles? In the two recent price regulation cases of *O'Gorman* and *Nebbia*. *O'Gorman* had emphasized "the presumption of the constitutionality of a statute dealing with a subject within the police power," and the burden of proof borne by those challenging such a statute. And in *Nebbia*, which Hughes quoted far more extensively than any other case to which he referred in his opinion, the Court had declared that if laws limiting contractual freedom

> "have a reasonable relation to a proper legislative purpose, and are neither arbitrary nor discriminatory, the requirements of due process are satisfied"; that "with the wisdom of the policy adopted, with the adequacy or practicability of the law enacted to forward it, the courts are both incompetent and unauthorized to deal"; that "times without number we have said that the legislature is primarily the judge of the necessity of such an enactment, that every possible presumption is in favor of its validity, and that though the court may hold views inconsistent with the wisdom of the law, it may not be annulled unless palpably in excess of legislative power."[14]

Immediately following this lengthy examination of the principles enunciated in *Nebbia*, Hughes confirmed the inference that the Four Horsemen and contemporary commentators had drawn from Roberts' 1934 opinion: *Nebbia* had overruled *Adkins sub silentio*. "With full recognition of the earnestness and vigor which characterize the opinion in the *Adkins* case," wrote the chief justice, "we find it impossible to reconcile that ruling with these well-considered declarations." Again skillfully synthesizing police power categories with the broad public interest concept of which they were illustrative, Hughes asked, "What can be closer to the public interest than the health of women and their protection from unscrupulous and overreaching employers?" Applying the principles of *O'Gorman* and *Nebbia*, Hughes further queried, "And if the protection of women is a legitimate end of the exercise of state power, how can it be said that the requirement of the payment of a minimum wage fairly fixed in order to meet the very necessities of existence is not an admissible means to that end?" The Washington statute "cannot be regarded as arbitrary or capricious, and that is all we have to decide. Even if the wisdom of the policy be debatable and its effects uncertain, still the legislature is entitled to its judgment."[15]

In the concluding pages of his opinion, Hughes made clear that the Court was not abandoning the principle of neutrality: it was merely demonstrating how minimum wage regulation might be reconciled with the principle that property could be taken only for a public purpose. The expanded conceptions of the police power and the public interest that underlay the Court's opinions in *O'Gorman* and *Nebbia* of course provided the foundation on which such a reconciliation might be effected. But Hughes sought in addition to show, as Frankfurter had perceived some fourteen years earlier, that the requirement that employers pay a minimum wage was necessary in order to preserve state neutrality. At the time Hughes was writing, state and local governments were expending millions of dollars annually in poor relief. Hughes' opinion took "judicial notice of the unparalleled demands for relief which arose during the recent depression and still continue to an alarming extent. . . ." Human labor, like all physical work, required resources for its production. To the extent that an employer paid his employee less than was necessary for the employee to provide the labor contracted for, the difference had to be made up by poor relief. The employer paying subminimum wages was thus externalizing a portion of the cost of his business, and the burden was borne by the taxpaying public. Taxation, the effect of which was to subsidize the employer's business, could be seen as a taking from A and a giving to B for a private purpose. Unscrupulous employers were in effect raiding the public treasury for their own benefit, without any benefit accruing to the public generally. Paying women workers subminimum wages, Hughes wrote, was "not only detrimental to their health and well being but casts a direct burden for their support upon the community. What these workers lose in wages the taxpayers are called upon to pay. . . . The community is not bound to provide what is in effect a subsidy for unconscionable employers. The community may direct its law-making power to correct the abuse which springs from their selfish disregard of the public interest."[16]

Cass Sunstein has observed that this passage reflects a change in the Court's baseline for determining whether government action constitutes an impermissible redistribution. In *Adkins*, the Court had held that the minimum wage took property from the employer for the support of the partially indigent employee, "a burden which, if it belongs to anybody, belongs to society as a whole." Payment of subminimum wages gave rise to no externality, because the employer, by paying the market rate, was giving the employee (and because the transaction was private, hence the public) all to which she was entitled. Accordingly, requiring the employer to pay a wage above that dictated by the higgling of the market forced him to pay his employee a subsidy.[17] In *West Coast Hotel*, however, the Court characterized the payment of poor relief to those employed at subminimum wages to be a form of subsidy to their employers.

Two things should be noted about this relocation of the baseline from which to determine from whom a subsidy is being required. First, the notion that whether a subsidy is being extracted is constitutionally relevant presupposes the principle of neutrality. There was no reason for Hughes to characterize payment of subminimum wages as the extraction of a public subsidy unless he intended to pay homage to and work within a tradition in which such extractions were constitutionally problematic.[18] Relocating a baseline is far less revolutionary than abandoning a mode of analysis.[19]

Second, to the chagrin of the Four Horsemen who had formed the core of the *Adkins* majority, the Court had relocated the baseline three years earlier in

Nebbia.[20] There, after all, the Court had upheld a regulation requiring the consumer to pay an above-market price for milk. The majority had rejected the Four Horsemen's contentions that this was a subsidy from the consumer to the dairy farmer. Instead, Roberts had argued, it prevented the consumer and the retailer from conspiring to externalize a portion of the cost of their transaction by demoralizing the price structure and contributing to a collapse of the milk industry. To pay less than the regulated price was to extract a subsidy from the public. As Justice Roberts wrote in upholding the milk price regulation, "The Constitution does not secure to anyone liberty to conduct his business in such a fashion as to inflict injury upon the public at large. . . ."[21]

Professor Howard Gillman takes the view that "when the Court in *West Coast Hotel v. Parrish* (1937) gave 'fresh consideration' to the question of police powers and finally permitted the establishment of a minimum wage on the grounds that 'workers . . . in an unequal position with respect to bargaining power' were 'exploited' by their employers and 'relatively defenseless against the denial of a living wage,' the United States underwent a true constitutional revolution." The significance of *West Coast Hotel*, Gillman argues, is that the justices "expressed a willingness to allow government to intrude itself into market relations on the behalf of favored classes."[22] Gillman concedes that the Court was prepared to recognize inequality of bargaining power as a grounds for legislative regulation of a contractual relationship where that inequality might result in bargains compromising worker health and safety, as it did in *Holden v. Hardy* and *Muller v. Oregon*, or in fraud, as it did in the time and manner of wage payment cases.[23] Indeed, though Gillman's narrative neglects many of the time and manner of payment cases, it would be hard not to characterize them as cases in which it was thought that the employer was taking advantage of his employee because of inequalities in bargaining power: even Justice Sutherland characterized these statutes as preventing "unfair" methods of wage payment.[24] Yet Gillman contends that the prevention of fraud and the protection of worker health and safety were well-established, legitimate police power ends, whereas the redress of other consequences of inequality of bargaining power were not. Only in 1937 did the Court recognize inequality of bargaining power per se as a reason for the state to intervene on behalf of a class. It was in this sense, then, that *West Coast Hotel* was "revolutionary."

This view is open to at least two objections. First, as his majority opinion amply demonstrates, Hughes was at pains to show that minimum wage regulation was a legitimate means of protecting the health of women workers, and was accordingly no different from other police regulations that the Court had upheld. In other words, Hughes continued to work within the established police power categories.

Second, Gillman's almost total neglect of the cases involving price regulation obscures his view of the fact that the Court had long been using inequalities of bargaining power as a legitimate reason for upholding the constitutionality of legislative regulation of business. Minimum wage regulation, Gillman tells us, had been considered problematic because it appeared as though it "was primarily designed to improve the economic condition of one class at the expense of a competing class."[25] But this had always been precisely what rate regulation of railroads, grain elevators, gas, water and electric works, stockyards, fire insurance, taxis, attorneys, and rental housing had been designed to accomplish: to protect the interests of consumers at the expense of providers of goods and services. *Nebbia* had upheld a price regulation promoting the interests of producers at the expense of consumers. Non-neutrality had always been permissible where the business regulated was affected with a public interest. The issue had always been whether the business regulated was sufficiently public in nature to justify what would otherwise have clearly been impermissible instances of state non-neutrality. In *Wolff Packing I*, Chief Justice Taft had divided such businesses into three categories: (1) businesses enjoying special privileges granted by the state; (2) certain "exceptional" businesses, such as inns, cabs, and gristmills; and (3) businesses providing an indispensable service, and therefore capable of subjecting the public to exorbitant charges and arbitrary control.[26] In other words, businesses falling in this third category were subject to price regulation precisely because they occupied a position in the market that gave them unequal bargaining power over the consumers with whom they contracted.

Field's *Munn* dissent is a long explanation of why subjecting businesses in the third category to price regulation violated the principle of neutrality. The virtually uninterrupted enlargement of the category of businesses affected with a public interest between 1877 and 1923 was on this view an informal, back-door erosion of the principle of neutrality. What dissenters like Field and the Four Horsemen saw as takings of private property for private use, majorities were able to reconcile to the principle of neutrality by labeling the business in question "public." But as Taft had pointed out, it was precisely a business's disproportionate bargaining power that made it public. The debate between Field and Waite in *Munn* might initially have been seen as a disagreement over whether a business must be a de jure monopoly or merely a de facto monopoly in order to be subject to price regulation.[27] But with the Court's decisions in *Brass v. Stoeser* (upholding rate regulation of grain elevators where there was not even a de facto monopoly), *German Alliance* (upholding regulation of fire insurance premiums), and the post–World War I rent control cases,[28] it became clear that a business need not possess even a de facto monopoly to be properly regulable: the provision of an important service and the possession of unusually disproportionate bargaining power were sufficient to warrant price regulation. Far from being an invalid reason for state regulation of enterprise, grossly disproportionate bargaining power was the talisman that transformed an otherwise private enterprise into a public business subject to price regulation.

There are at least two likely explanations for the greater judicial hesitancy to uphold regulations of the employment contract on grounds of unequal bargaining power. First, the widespread cultural embrace of free labor ideology quite naturally produced a sentiment that labor was somehow "special," that the right to work on terms of one's own bargain was less susceptible to legislative regulation than other contractual prerogatives.[29] Second, low levels of unemployment and steadily rising real wages probably persuaded judges that the disparities in bargaining power between employer and employee were not so great as to justify rate regulation.[30] As Justice Sutherland remarked in *Adkins*, "We cannot close our eyes to the notorious fact that earnings everywhere in all occupations have increased—not alone in states where the minimum wage law obtains but in the country generally. . . ."[31] The unprecedented levels and duration of unemployment experienced in the 1930s, however, made it more likely that judges could see the differentials in bargaining power in the employment context—the disparity in market power between the providers of employment opportunity and the consumers of such opportunity—in the same way they had always viewed such exaggerated differentials between producers and consumers of certain other "indispensable" goods and services.[32] This is the point of Hughes' allusion to "the economic conditions which have supervened" since *Adkins*, "in light of which the reasonableness of the exercise of the protective power of the State must be considered."[33] Hughes' contention was not, as Justice Sutherland suggested in dissent, that the meaning of the Constitution changes with the ebb and flow of economic events.[34] It was instead that changes in economic conditions had made appropriate to the employment context the application of a principle that the Court had long recognized, and had reiterated in *Nebbia*, namely, that gross disparities in bargaining power between buyers and sellers may justify regulation of the price at which a good or service is sold.

The application of this principle to the employment context was of course facilitated by the Court's decision in *Nebbia*. While the Court throughout the 1920s had repeatedly invalidated regulations on the grounds that the business involved was purely private,[35] Roberts' opinion abandoned in favor of a criterion of reasonableness the public/private distinction that had constrained the range of permissible deviations from the neutrality principle. Just as the oversupply of milk had rendered dairy farmers vulnerable to the operations of the market (i.e., had left them with unequal bargaining power), so the oversupply of labor in the 1930s had left workers similarly vulnerable. And just as an unregulated milk market threatened the supply of wholesome milk to the public at large, so the employment of workers at subminimum wages threatened the public health and the public treasury. In both cases, circumstances giving rise to vulnerability and exploitation, coupled with attendant adverse ripple effects throughout society, were held to afford sufficient reason for regulation of the price of the exchange. In both cases, "the normal law of supply and demand was insufficient to correct maladjustments detrimental to the community."[36] *West Coast Hotel* was, as Richard Friedman has observed, "an application of *Nebbia*."[37]

Thomas Chapin, writing in the wake of the *Parrish* decision, noted that the *Adkins* opinion had "relied strongly" on the general rule against price-fixing that had obtained at that time: "the opinion described the wage-limiting law as 'simply a price-fixing law.'" When *Nebbia* abrogated the general rule against price-fixing, "the corollary rule as to wage-fixing was destined to follow it into limbo sooner or later." "It is vital to a proper appraisal of the *Parrish Decision*," Chapin contended, "to characterize it chiefly as a strong reinforcement of the new doctrine of price regulation under the police power. The case of *Nebbia v. New York* purported to sweep away the distinction between price regulation and other regulation of private business, thus obviating the 'public interest' formerly a prerequisite to regulation of rates in any field. Viewing wages as price, the instant case strengthens the doctrine." Alluding to the attempts of the Court to erect "a logically consistent system," Chapin concluded: "The interaction of the price-fixing cases and the wage-fixing cases suggests a concise outline of how the conclusion of the logical syllogism may set up such stresses as to help compel the revision of the major premise, the *Parrish*

Case being the logical outcome of this tedious process." In a footnote, Chapin laid out the constituent premises of this "logical syllogism."

> There can be no price-fixing save in a business affected with a public interest [citing *Munn*]; therefore, since wages are the price of labor, there can be no wage-fixing in private business [citing *Adkins*]. But now regulation of prices is permissible like any regulation [citing *Nebbia*]; therefore a minimum wage statute is valid [citing *Parrish*].

Roberts' "real change of heart was not in 1937, then," Chapin concluded, "but in 1934, with the *Nebbia Case*."38

Morehead v. Tipaldo and the Roberts Memorandum

The fly in this ointment, of course, is the Court's 1936 decision striking down New York's minimum wage law, *Morehead v. New York ex rel. Tipaldo*.39 If, as I have contended, the positions Roberts staked out in *O'Gorman* and *Nebbia* left him intellectually committed to the constitutionality of the minimum wage, then why did he not manifest this commitment when first given the opportunity?

In fact, it appears that he might have. Between the time that *Nebbia* was decided and the time that *Tipaldo* was handed down, the Court heard two other cases in which it was contended that a wage-fixing regulation violated liberty of contract. In each of these cases, Roberts joined a majority opinion that invalidated the statute in question on more than one constitutional ground. Yet in each case the Court refrained from invoking the doctrine of liberty of contract and the authority of *Adkins*.

Roberts joined the majority opinion in *A.L.A. Schechter Poultry Corp. v. United States*, which struck down the wage and hour provisions of the New York Poultry Code promulgated pursuant to the National Industrial Recovery Act. Chief Justice Hughes' opinion for the Court held that those provisions exceeded the grant of congressional authority to regulate interstate commerce, and also ran afoul of the nondelegation doctrine. This dual indictment of NIRA made clear that the Court was not averse to identifying more than the single constitutional defect necessary to render the statute void. Yet the Court pointedly refused to hold that the wage and hour provisions violated the due process clause of the Fifth Amendment.40

There might have been several reasons for this omission. Hughes, who thought *Adkins* had been wrongly decided, had assigned the majority opinion to himself and was not about to invoke a precedent he disliked. Brandeis, who was also in the majority, thought *Adkins* similarly distasteful41 and certainly would have refused to join an opinion reaffirming it. Yet if the Four Horsemen and Roberts had wished to reaffirm *Adkins*, they could have written a separate opinion doing so. With five votes behind it, this opinion would have been recent, binding precedent. The failure of the Four Horsemen to write separately on the due process issue suggests that Roberts might not have been prepared to join such an opinion affirming *Adkins*.

Less ambiguous, however, was a case decided the following term. Roberts' was the crucial fifth vote for Sutherland's majority opinion in *Carter v. Carter Coal Co.*, which struck down the wage and hour provisions of the Bituminous Coal Conservation Act on the grounds (a) that they exceeded the scope of federal power under the commerce clause, and (b) that insofar as the Act delegated to the majority of coal producers (rather than the government) the power to fix the hours and wages to be worked by employees of other coal producers, it was "clearly arbitrary" and therefore violated the due process clause of the Fifth Amendment. With these holdings Chief Justice Hughes concurred. The majority opinion did not, however, suggest that the due process clause would have prohibited state governments from regulating the wages of coal miners. Nor did the opinion suggest that wage-fixing in general infringed liberty of contract. The price regulation provisions of the Act were struck down not because coal was not a business affected with a public interest, as the Four Horsemen were presumably prepared to hold, but instead because the majority found those provisions not to be severable from the unconstitutional wage and hour provisions.[42] In light of the fact that both of these New Deal initiatives were declared unconstitutional on more than one ground, the failure of a majority of the Court to affirm counsels' contentions that the wage-fixing provisions also infringed liberty of contract was conspicuous.[43] This is particularly true in *Carter*, where everyone in the majority except Roberts had been in the *Adkins* majority. The remarkable failure of Justice Sutherland, who authored *Adkins*, to cite that precedent in his opinion for the majority in *Carter* gives rise to the inference that the failure to mobilize liberty of contract doctrine in *Carter* was a concession to Roberts.

Yet when the Court did again rule on the constitutionality of minimum wage regulation, Roberts joined the Four Horsemen in reaffirming *Adkins*. How, in light of the jurisprudential commitments he had manifested in *O'Gorman* and *Nebbia*, and perhaps in *Schechter* and *Carter*, could he have done this?

If Roberts had been merely giving stare decisis its due, voting in such a way as to reaffirm a precedent with which he disagreed, he would have been doing nothing at all unusual. In fact, he would not have been the first justice to disagree with *Adkins* and yet follow it—he would have been the fifth. In 1925 and again in 1927, minimum wage cases had come before the Court. In *Murphy v. Sardell*,[44] the Court affirmed per curiam a decision striking down Arizona's minimum wage statute. The Arizona attorney general sought to distinguish the state statute from the measure invalidated in *Adkins*, while counsel for the California minimum wage commission submitted an amicus brief in which he contended that *Adkins* was wrongly decided and ought to be overruled.[45] Yet only Justice Brandeis noted a dissent. Justice Holmes noted that he concurred solely because he considered himself bound by the authority of *Adkins*. Taft and Sanford, who had dissented in *Adkins*, and Stone, who would dissent in *Tipaldo*, all concurred silently.[46] In *Donham v. West-Nelson Mfg. Co.*,[47] the Court affirmed per curiam a decision striking down Arkansas' minimum wage statute. Attorneys for the state again contended that *Adkins* ought to be overruled.[48] But again, only Brandeis noted a dissent, while Taft, Holmes, Sanford, and Stone all silently concurred.[49] In both of these cases the Court was squarely asked to overrule *Adkins*, and had the four other justices who thought the case had been wrongly decided followed Brandeis' lead, *Adkins* could have been granted a deserved repose as early as 1925. As Charles Curtis noted, "Roberts had done no more by joining with the ex-majority [in *Tipaldo*] than to follow [*Adkins*] as a precedent that was binding on him. No more, indeed, than Holmes himself had done, when he accepted Adkins in the two cases that had come up from Arizona and Arkansas shortly afterwards."[50]

This practice of following precedents with which one disagreed was not confined to the 1920s. As Alpheus Thomas Mason reported, Stone himself continued to adhere to this practice throughout the late 1930s, especially in cases in which the governing precedent had not been frontally attacked.

> [W]hen the majority ducked reconsideration of the old doctrine of "reproduction cost" in ratemaking, {Frankfurter}, much to Stone's dismay, rushed out a concurrence to do battle with the devil. "I am satisfied," Stone wrote him, "that in the near future *Smyth v. Ames* [source of the "reproduction cost" rule] will be overruled. I think it is going to come naturally and more easily if we withhold our attack until we have a case where the issue is raised and unavoidable. After all, *Smyth v. Ames* isn't as old as *Collector v. Day*, and I have disagreed with the latter for a good many years, but I thought it wiser not to say so until the Graves case two weeks ago. . . ."

Indeed, in March of 1937 Stone and Cardozo concurred in an opinion holding the employee of a municipal water corporation immune from federal taxation on the authority of *Collector v. Day*. The federal government had sought to distinguish *Day* rather than to have it overruled. In explanation of their concurrence, the two justices wrote:

> We concur in the result upon the ground that the petitioner has brought himself within the terms of the exemption prescribed by Treasury Regulation 74, Article 643, which for purposes of this case may be accepted as valid, its validity not being challenged by counsel for the Government.
>
>   In the absence of such a challenge no opinion is expressed as to the need for revision of the doctrine of implied immunities declared in earlier opinions.[51]

Roberts always insisted, though he never had the poor taste to do so publicly, that his vote in *Tipaldo* was not a reflection of his views on the constitutional merits of the minimum wage. In 1945, at Felix Frankfurter's urging, Roberts drafted a memorandum explaining his behavior in the two minimum wage cases.[52] From this memorandum emerge two interrelated yet distinct explanations.

The first of these explanations, remarkably consonant with the views of Stone and Cardozo noted earlier, concerns the litigation strategy of the attorneys for the state of New York. In his memorandum Roberts wrote:

> Both in the petition for certiorari, in the brief on the merits, and in oral argument, counsel for the State of New York took the position that it was unnecessary to overrule the *Adkins* case in order to sustain the position of the State of New York. It was urged that further data and experience and additional facts distinguished the case at bar from the *Adkins* case. The argument seemed to me disingenuous and born of timidity. I could find nothing in the record to substantiate the alleged distinction. At conference I so stated, and stated further that I was for taking the State of New York at its word. The State had not asked that the *Adkins* case be overruled but that it be distinguished. I said I was unwilling to put a decision on any such ground.

The opinion was assigned to Justice Butler, to whom Roberts stated "that I would concur in any opinion which was based on the fact that the State had not asked us to overrule *Adkins* and that, as we found no material difference in the facts of the two cases, we should therefore follow the *Adkins* case." Butler originally drafted such a narrowly tailored opinion.[53] But after Stone had circulated a dissent impugning the *Adkins* precedent,[54] Butler "added matter to his opinion, seeking to sustain the *Adkins* case in principle." "My proper course," Roberts reflected, "would have been to concur specially on the narrow ground I had taken. I did not do so. But at conference in the Court I said that I did not propose to review and re-examine the *Adkins* case until a case should come to the Court requiring that this should be done."[55]

When the Court reconvened in October of 1936, Roberts voted to note probable jurisdiction in the appeal of the Washington Supreme Court's decision upholding the state's minimum wage statute. Roberts did so, he later wrote, because "in the appeal in the *Parrish* case the authority of *Adkins* was definitely assailed and the Court was asked to reconsider and overrule it. Thus, for the first time, I was confronted with the necessity of facing the soundness of the *Adkins* case."[56] Thus, in his first vote on the merits of minimum wage regulation, Roberts took a position consistent with those he had taken earlier.[57]

This explanation was not merely a post hoc rationalization. It was fully consistent with the opinions of the court in *Tipaldo* and *Parrish*.[58] "The *Adkins* case," wrote Justice Butler for the *Tipaldo* majority,

> unless distinguishable, requires affirmance of the judgment below. The petition for the writ sought review upon the ground that this case is distinguishable from that one. No application has been made for reconsideration of the constitutional question there decided. The validity of the principles upon which that decision rests is not challenged. This court confines itself to the ground upon which the writ was asked or granted. [citations omitted]. Here the review granted was no broader than that sought by the petitioner. [citation omitted]. He is not entitled and does not ask to be heard upon the question whether the *Adkins* case should be overruled. He maintains that it may be distinguished on the ground that the statutes are vitally dissimilar.

The majority held that the New York statute was not materially different from the statute declared unconstitutional in *Adkins*. And because the authority of *Adkins* had not been challenged, it required that the Court strike down the New York statute.[59] As one might have expected, and as events were to prove out, the Four Horsemen were more than ready to rest their decision on the broader ground that *Adkins* was correctly decided, that minimum wage statutes were per se unconstitutional, and that the New York statute was invalid irrespective of whether it was distinguishable from the statute struck down in *Adkins*.[60] The only possible reason for Butler to rest the majority opinion on such a narrow ground is that Roberts insisted on it as the price of his vote.[61]

In his majority opinion in *Parrish*, Hughes explained the *Tipaldo* decision in terms consistent with both Butler's opinion and Roberts' memorandum. In *Tipaldo*, he wrote, the Court of Appeals of New York had said that it found no material difference between the two statutes, and this Court held that the "meaning of the statute" as fixed by the decision of the state court "must be accepted here as if the meaning had been specifically expressed in the enactment." [citation omitted]. That view led to the affirmance by this Court of the judgment in the *Morehead* case, as the Court considered that the only question before it was whether the *Adkins* case was distinguishable and that reconsideration of that decision had not been sought. . . . We think that the question which was not deemed to be open in the *Morehead* case is open and is necessarily presented here.[62]

By 1936 it was a well-established rule of Supreme Court appellate practice that review upon certiorari was limited to the issues raised in the petition.[63] The petition filed by the state of New York did not explicitly request that *Adkins* be overruled. Indeed, the overwhelming bulk of the petition was devoted to identifying material legal and factual distinctions between the New York regulation and that struck down in *Adkins*. Of all of the "Questions Presented," "Reasons for Allowing This Writ," and "Assignments of Error" raised in the petition, only one might plausibly have been construed to request the Court to overrule *Adkins*. The sixth of the "Reasons for Allowing This Writ" stated: "The circumstances prevailing under which the New York law was enacted call for a reconsideration of the *Adkins* case in the light of the New York act and conditions aimed to be remedied thereby."[64] This was hardly an unequivocal call for a repudiation of *Adkins*. It might more easily have been understood as a restatement of New York's central argument: that material distinctions between the language of the two statutes and the intervention of an economic depression made the New York statute a reasonable exercise of the police power where the District of Columbia statute had not been.[65] Insofar as *Adkins* was the controlling precedent regarding the validity of minimum wage regulation, any case concerning the constitutionality of a minimum wage statute would necessarily involve the construction and consideration of that precedent to determine its scope and meaning.

The petition was certainly sufficiently ambiguous so that it was not unreasonable to construe it in light of the arguments advanced in the brief and at oral argument. And neither in the brief nor at the argument did attorneys for the state request or suggest that *Adkins* be overruled. The brief offered instead a detailed explanation of why the New York statute was consistent with and indeed supported by *Adkins*. Similarly, briefs of amici curiae contended that "The New York statute differs radically from that considered by this Court in the *Adkins* case," and "The New York Minimum Wage Law, passed in the light of the decision of Adkins v. Children's Hospital, 261 U.S. 525, is supported as to constitutionality by the opinion in that case."[66] Nowhere was it requested that *Adkins* be overruled.

The Washington minimum wage statute considered in *Parrish*, by contrast, had been enacted in 1913, before the *Adkins* decision was handed down. Like the District of Columbia statute, it did not require that the wages prescribed have any relation to the reasonable value of the services rendered.[67] There was accordingly no hope of distinguishing the Washington statute on the grounds that had been offered by attorneys for the state of New York. And as Chief Justice Hughes observed, the

Washington State Supreme Court, unlike the New York Court of Appeals, had effectively declared that *Adkins* had already been overruled. "The state court," Hughes noted, "has refused to regard the decision in the *Adkins* case as determinative and has pointed to our decisions both before and since that case as justifying its position. We are of the opinion that this ruling of the state court demands on our part a re-examination of the *Adkins* case." As Appellant's counsel observed, "the issue before this Court is simply whether the Adkins case is to be reconsidered and reversed or whether its authority is to be sustained."[68]

These explanations are admittedly not entirely satisfactory. To be sure, the party defending the Washington statute was this time the appellee rather than the appellant, and therefore, unlike the New York attorney general, did not frame the questions to be considered on appeal. Yet the attorneys for the state of Washington did not request that *Adkins* be overruled, and though the state supreme court had declared that *Adkins* was no longer good law, Roberts might conceivably have voted to strike down the statute on the grounds that the controlling authority had not been specifically challenged by the litigants. Several commentators have noted that Roberts voted to overrule the venerable case of *Swift v. Tyson* in 1938 even though the validity of that precedent had not been questioned by the parties. Edward Purcell plausibly suggests that Roberts might have acted as he did in *Erie* because he felt badly burned by criticism of his vote in *Tipaldo*, though it should be noted that Stone, who had earlier evinced similar procedural scruples, also joined the *Erie* majority without the prompting of such criticism.[69] Merlo Pusey and Richard Friedman have speculated that the public outcry following the *Tipaldo* decision might have prompted Roberts to face squarely the question of *Adkins*' continued vitality.[70] It may have been that Roberts thought that striking down a minimum wage statute on such a narrow, technical ground twice in less than one year was simply taking the niceties of appellate procedure too seriously, especially when the effect was to reaffirm a precedent he had no stake in preserving.

But these inconsistencies in approach to technical questions of appellate practice, in which Roberts was clearly not alone, should not distract us from the larger point. The fact that between 1936 and 1938 Roberts might have changed his approach in such matters is not what scholars mean when they refer to "the Constitutional Revolution of 1937" or the "switch in time." The question is whether Roberts' vote in *Tipaldo* signified his concurrence with the *Adkins* precedent. The technical reasons offered in his memorandum and supported by the opinions in *Tipaldo* and *Parrish* confirm that it did not. The fact that he may thereafter not have been so bashful about overruling precedents does not mean that the amply corroborated reasons offered to explain his behavior in 1936 were not sincere.

Yet the majority opinion did not confine itself to the technical rationale undergirding Roberts' vote. Eight pages into his majority opinion, Justice Butler wrote, "The state court rightly held that the *Adkins* case controls this one and requires that the relator be discharged upon the ground that the legislation under which he was indicted and imprisoned is repugnant to the due process clause of the Fourteenth Amendment."[71] All of the reasoning pertinent to the Court's holding had by this point been set out, and this last quoted statement would appear to have been one suitable to conclude the opinion. Indeed, it probably was the conclusion of Butler's draft opinion, before Stone circulated his dissent. The published opinion, however, went on for another eight pages, reaffirming in dicta the continued vitality of the *Adkins* precedent. In the course of this discussion Butler made some statements that it is hard to believe were concurred in by someone who had joined *O'Gorman* and written *Nebbia*.[72] *Adkins*, Butler wrote, "and the reasoning upon which it rests clearly show that the state is without power by any form of legislation to prohibit, change or nullify contracts between employers and adult women workers as to the amount of wages to be paid."[73] It is conceivable (though extremely unlikely) that *Nebbia*, taken alone, left intact the notion that the labor contract was somehow especially resistant to regulation. But taking *Nebbia* in conjunction with *O'Gorman*, which upheld over the Four Horsemen's dissent the regulation of compensation for services, it is difficult to understand how Roberts could have subscribed to a statement so reminiscent of Sutherland's extreme dictum in *Ribnik*. Nothing Roberts had written or subscribed to supported such an assessment of legislative power to fix compensation; on the contrary, as the Four Horsemen and contemporary commentators had observed, it all pointed in precisely the opposite direction. As Virginia Wood noted, "The majority views in [*Tipaldo*] must have come as quite a shock to those who thought that two years previously Justice Roberts had performed the last rites for the affected with a public interest concept."[74]

They certainly came as a shock to Justices Stone, Brandeis, and Cardozo, who filed a vigorous dissent. Throughout his opinion, Stone repeatedly adverted to *Nebbia*'s broad notion of the public interest. No one had ever denied, Stone wrote, that freedom of contract might be restrained "by a statute passed in the public interest." The Court had repeatedly held "that legislatures may curtail individual freedom in the public interest." "No one doubts that the presence in the community of a large number of those compelled by economic necessity to accept a wage less than is needful for subsistence is a matter of grave public concern, the more so when, as has been demonstrated here, it tends to produce ill health, immorality and deterioration of the race." It was clear that "a wage insufficient to support the worker does not visit its consequences upon him alone; that it may affect profoundly the entire economic structure of society and, in any case, that it casts on every taxpayer, and on government itself, the burden of solving the problems of poverty, subsistence, health and morals of large numbers in the community. Because of their nature and extent these are public problems." Indeed,

> In many cases this Court has sustained the power of legislatures to prohibit or restrict the terms of a contract, including the price term, in order to accomplish what the legislative body may reasonably consider a public purpose. They include cases, which have neither been overruled or discredited, in which the sole basis of regulation was the fact that circumstances, beyond the control of the parties, had so seriously curtailed the regulative power of competition as to place buyers or sellers at a disadvantage in the bargaining struggle, such that a legislature might reasonably have contemplated serious consequences to the community as a whole and have sought to avoid them by regulation of the terms of the contract.[75]

Here Stone cited predominantly price control cases: *Munn v. Illinois, Brass v. Stoeser, German Alliance Ins. Co. v. Lewis, Terminal Taxicab Co. v. District of*

Columbia, and the rent control cases; the time and manner of wage payment cases; and *Nebbia v. New York*.[76] No one had yet attempted "to say upon what theory the amount of a wage is any the less the subject of regulation in the public interest than that of insurance premiums [citing *German Alliance*], or of the commissions of insurance brokers [citing *O'Gorman*], or the charges of grain elevators [citing *Munn* and *Brass v. Stoeser*], or of the price which the farmer receives for his milk, or which the wage earner pays for it [citing *Nebbia*]."[77] The absence of such viable distinctions had formed the basis of decision in *O'Gorman*, *Nebbia*, and more recent cases following *Nebbia*.[78] Quoting at length from Roberts' opinion,[79] Stone contended, "That declaration and decision should control the present case. They are irreconcilable with the decision and most of what was said in the *Adkins* case. They have left the Court free of its restriction as a precedent. . . ." *Adkins* and *Nebbia* presented the Court with "conflicting precedents." It was Stone's view that "We should follow our decision in the *Nebbia* case. . . ."[80]

Contemporary scholars also expressed considerable surprise when the *Tipaldo* decision came down.[81] After quoting some of the expansive language of Roberts' *Nebbia* opinion, one commentator observed, "Bearing in mind these words, one would have felt confident that the New York Minimum Wage Law could successfully withstand charges of unconstitutionality." Reminding the reader of a similarly expansive passage from *Nebbia*, another observer remarked that "it seems very difficult to understand why prices can be fixed without violating due process, but wages cannot be. Both interfere with liberty to contract." Another commentator, after noting the Court's recent decision in *Nebbia*, opined that "the real reason for the holding in the *Morehead* case is the weight of *stare decisis* which slows down the never ending process of legal change." And in the wake of the Court's decision in *Parrish*, commentators expressed a gratified sense of doctrinal resolution. *Morehead* had sounded a dissonant, suspended chord; *Parrish* made sense. As a consequence, these observers were prepared to accept the technical explanation for Roberts' behavior that appeared on the face of the opinions. "It now seems clear," wrote one commentator, "that Mr. Justice Roberts' concurrence in an opinion so at variance with the principle of his own pronouncement in *Nebbia v. New York* was only obtained because of the supposed procedural bar to a re-examination of the Adkins case." Thomas Chapin, believing that *Nebbia* had logically entailed "a liberal ruling in the *Morehead Case*," concurred. *Morehead*, he wrote, "went off on a technicality." "Considering the ground of decision in the *Morehead* case," wrote another, "and considering also that it was Justice Roberts who wrote the opinion of the Court in the *Nebbia* case, his switch to the liberal side [in *Parrish*] can be sufficiently explained without resorting to political explanations."[82]

The Four Horsemen had recognized *Nebbia*'s inconsistency with *Adkins* in 1934; Stone, Brandeis, and Cardozo had remarked on the inconsistency of the two cases in their *Tipaldo* dissent; and numerous observers had noted the inconsistency in both 1934 and 1936. Could Roberts, the author of *Nebbia*, have been the only one who was oblivious to the logical consequences of his own opinion?

If Chief Justice Hughes recognized the implications of *Nebbia* for *Adkins*, he was not prepared to say so publicly in 1936. Hughes filed a dissenting opinion in which he summarized his view of the case: "In view of the difference between the statutes involved, I cannot agree that the case should be regarded as controlled by *Adkins*. . . ."[83] While Brandeis, Stone, and Cardozo joined this opinion voting to uphold the statute based on the distinctions Hughes identified, Hughes did not join Stone's broadside attack on *Adkins*. In other words, as Norman Macbeth had predicted,[84] Hughes was prepared to distinguish *Adkins* but not to overrule it. This brings us to the second explanation embedded in the Roberts memorandum.

Roberts reports that at the conference at which certiorari was granted in *Tipaldo*, he said he "saw no reason to grant the writ unless the Court were prepared to reexamine and overrule the *Adkins* case."[85] This recollection is odd, because the first half of the *Tipaldo* opinion gives as its reason for not addressing the issue of whether *Adkins* ought to be overruled the fact that the petition did not request such consideration. If the Court were confined to considering the issues presented in the petition, the fact that the justices were prepared to face an issue not raised in the petition would have been irrelevant. This passage in the memorandum suggests that Hughes, and perhaps Brandeis and Stone, all of whom spoke at conference before Roberts, had spoken in favor of the grant on the grounds that the New York statute was distinguishable from its District of Columbia predecessor. Roberts appears to have been informing his colleagues that he was prepared to consider the issue of whether *Adkins* should be overruled irrespective of what the petition asked, but that he would not join an opinion upholding the New York statute on the ground that it was distinguishable from the one struck down in *Adkins*.[86]

The memorandum's account of the conference following oral argument is consonant with this reading. Roberts characterized the argument of the attorneys for the state in terms that could as easily have been used to describe Chief Justice Hughes' dissent: "It was urged that further data and experience and additional facts distinguished the case at bar from the *Adkins* case. The argument seemed to me disingenuous and born of timidity. I could find nothing in the record to substantiate the alleged distinction. At conference I so stated. . . . The State had not asked that the *Adkins* case be overruled but that it be distinguished. I said I was unwilling to put a decision on any such ground."[87] Roberts' remarks at this conference again followed those of everyone except the junior Cardozo. Hughes, who spoke first, almost certainly expressed the views that later appeared in his dissent. Brandeis and Stone, who joined Hughes' dissent, probably expressed similar views. It is not clear that Brandeis, Stone, or Cardozo evinced at conference their preparedness to repudiate *Adkins*. It appears that Stone may not have decided to write his dissent until after Hughes had already circulated his.[88] But even if Brandeis, Stone, and Cardozo had all expressed at conference a willingness to overrule *Adkins*, it did not then (and indeed does not now) appear that Hughes was prepared to take that step. It very likely appeared to Roberts at the time that even were he to join Stone, Brandeis, and Cardozo, a splintered Court producing no majority opinion would uphold the New York statute without overruling *Adkins*. As Roberts' memorandum makes clear, he did not think that that could be done in good conscience.[89]

This is the interpretation suggested by Frankfurter, who must have had more than one conversation about these events with Roberts before requesting that Roberts reduce his account to writing. "[W]hen the *Tipaldo* case was before the Court in the spring of 1936," Frankfurter stated, Roberts "was prepared to overrule the *Adkins* decision. *Since a majority could not be had for overruling it,* he silently agreed with the Court in finding the New York statute under attack in the *Tipaldo* case not distinguishable from the statute which had been declared unconstitutional in the *Adkins* case."[90]

There are at least two possible explanations for Hughes' reluctance to overrule *Adkins.* The first is that offered by the Roberts memorandum and the *Tipaldo* opinion: the petition for certiorari had not requested such action. Though Hughes' dissent was critical of the majority opinion on a number of fronts, it did not assail the claim that the petition confined the justices to consideration of whether the case was distinguishable from *Adkins.* If this was the case, it may be that Hughes was the only one who took this position. The Four Horsemen were clearly prepared to reconsider *Adkins* and reaffirm it.[91] Brandeis, Stone, and Cardozo were prepared to reconsider *Adkins* and overrule it,[92] and Roberts' remarks suggest that he was prepared to join them. Hughes was prepared to distinguish *Adkins* but not to overrule it,[93] and Roberts was prepared to overrule it but not to distinguish it. There being no majority to overrule *Adkins,* Roberts may have sought to confine the majority opinion to the narrowest possible ground by grasping onto Hughes' reasoning for not reaching the issue of *Adkins'* status. By insisting that his vote come at the price of a narrow, technical holding with which he did not fully agree, Roberts may have sought both to avoid reaffirming *Adkins* and to avoid supporting an opinion that suggested that the New York statute could be upheld without overruling *Adkins.*

The second possible explanation concerns Hughes' jurisprudential style. Hughes is remembered for his inclination and capacity to distinguish away disfavored precedents rather than overruling them,[94] and his dissent in *Tipaldo* is one of his more celebrated performances in this regard.[95] It appears that Hughes' penchant for maintaining the ostensible stability of precedent may have prevented the formation of a majority to overrule *Adkins.* Yet one might reasonably wonder, especially in light of his opinion in *Parrish,* whether Hughes was so wedded to preserving the facade of stare decisis that he willingly sacrificed the New York statute on its altar. A simple five-minute conversation with Roberts could presumably have persuaded Hughes to vote to overrule *Adkins,* thereby sustaining the New York law and perhaps averting the constitutional confrontation of 1937.

Yet two characteristics of Hughes' style as chief justice suggest that it is quite possible that such a conversation never took place. First, Hughes was virtually obsessed with the prompt disposition of the cases on the Court's docket, and he sought to get through as many cases as possible at the judicial conference. The brevity of discussion of the cases at conference rankled some of his colleagues. "By employing the methods of a military commander," Justice Stone's biographer reported, "Hughes made his administration a model of efficiency. At judicial conferences discussion was rationed. . . . Rarely did anyone speak out of turn. . . . For him 'the conference was not a debating society but a place where nine men do solos.' Stone sometimes bitterly criticized such expeditious procedures. With so little opportunity for an exchange of ideas, constitutional interpretation seemed more like counting noses, the judicial conference an administrative voting device."[96] "In May 1932 John Bassett Moore passed along [to Stone] a comment by one of the Justices that 'under the present C.J. votes are taken practically without deliberation . . . and that the discrepancies sometimes exhibited are partly due to the lack of any previous general discussion which might have simplified the issue.'" Stone agreed, replying, "I have no hesitation in saying that I think discussion of our cases should be much fuller and freer."[97] Justice Brandeis once remarked wryly, "Sometimes our conferences would last six hours and the Chief Justice would do almost all the talking."[98] Brandeis later complained to his successor, William O. Douglas, that Hughes' insistence on keeping the docket current left inadequate time to "mull over" cases. "The Chief is certainly an efficient chief," Douglas agreed. "But as Brandeis says you sometimes pay a heavy price for that efficiency."[99] Stone appears to have been especially aggravated by Hughes' conduct of the conference during the 1935 term, when *Tipaldo* was decided. He complained of the conference in *United States v. Butler*, which in January of 1936 struck down the Agricultural Adjustment Act of 1933: "the main question in the case was decided practically without discussion and with no analysis or consideration of the relation of conditional gifts for a national purpose to the spending power conferred upon Congress." "The whole history of the case," Stone lamented, "was characterized by inadequate discussion and great haste in the production and circulation of the opinions."[100]

Roberts' memorandum suggests that something similar may have happened in *Tipaldo*. When Roberts indicated at conference that he saw no reason to grant certiorari unless the Court were prepared to overrule *Adkins*, "there was no response around the table."[101] There was at this conference apparently no discussion of whether a majority was willing to repudiate *Adkins*. At the conference following oral argument, Chief Justice Hughes presumably opened the discussion by stating that he thought the *Tipaldo* case distinguishable from *Adkins*. Roberts evidently presumed that the chief justice had either forgotten or disregarded Roberts' remarks at the earlier conference. By the time it was Roberts' turn to vote, it must have appeared that there was no majority for overruling *Adkins*. Roberts then stated that he was unwilling to rest the decision on the grounds proposed by Hughes; and so far as the documents available to us reveal, Hughes did not at that point express any willingness to overrule *Adkins*, nor did he inquire of Roberts whether that would make any difference in the way he voted. Roberts may quite understandably have left the conference believing that Hughes was unprepared to overrule *Adkins*.

Due to the second feature of Hughes' style, it is unlikely that this misunderstanding was cleared up by any conversation between the two outside of the conference. Hughes' sense of the proprieties of his office kept him from soliciting support for his views outside the conference. His biographer reports that he "had only contempt for the kind of chief who would take a judge aside and say, 'Can't you see the tight spot we're in; you've got to help us out.'"[102] "I am sure that it was part of a well thought out program," Justice Roberts later recounted, "that the Chief Justice, after the argument of the case and prior to the conference, did not discuss the merits of that case or the probable disposition of it with any of his brethren. . . . what his conclusion was, none of us knew until he announced it at conference. He neither leaned on anyone else for advice nor did he proffer advice or assistance to any of us, but left each of us to form his own conclusions. . . ."[103] Hughes' view that the positions of the justices ought only to be discussed at conference, where all were present,[104] probably kept him from approaching Roberts privately; and Roberts' respect for Hughes' sense of propriety probably kept him from approaching Hughes.[105]

This may be the meaning of Frankfurter's rather ambiguous marginalia in his copy of Pusey's biography of Hughes. "In *West Coast Hotel*," he wrote, "issue of overruling *Adkins* had to be faced and Roberts had been ready to do that, but wasn't asked in *Tipaldo*."[106] Just who it was that hadn't done the asking was left conspicuously unclear. But a letter to Paul Freund written in 1953 left little doubt where Frankfurter, who had obviously discussed the matter at length with Roberts, thought the fault lay. "The fact is," the letter stated, "that Roberts did not switch. He was prepared in *Tipaldo* to make a majority overruling *Adkins*. He was not prepared to distinguish *Adkins*. Because there was no majority for overruling *Adkins* he was in the majority in the *Morehead* case. . . ."[107]

Tipaldo was argued on April 28 and 29,[108] at the end of the difficult 1935 term. With the nerves of the justices frayed and with the press of business at the end of the term, an already uncommunicative Court was probably at its least communicative. The case was presumably voted on in conference within the week, and Butler set about writing the majority opinion along the lines specified by Roberts. Butler subsequently circulated his draft, and Hughes, whose dissent is clearly responsive to Butler's opinion, circulated his draft sometime before May 26. On May 26, Stone wrote Hughes informing him that "I am writing a brief memorandum stating my belief that I think the decision should rest on broader grounds."[109] Sometime between May 26 and May 29, Stone circulated his draft.[110] Butler's modified majority opinion was delivered June 1, the last day of the term.[111] Because the second half of Butler's final product was written in response to Stone's dissent, Butler must not have written the passages that Roberts found objectionable until the last week of the term. At that point Roberts had on his desk Stone's dissent, which Brandeis and Cardozo had joined but Hughes had not and apparently would not; Hughes' dissent distinguishing *Adkins* without overruling it; and Butler's opinion, which deviated from the limited rationale on which Roberts had initially agreed. His proper course would have been to concur specially, as he later said, or to have engaged Hughes privately on the issue of overruling *Adkins*. Doing the latter would have involved agreeing on a majority opinion substantially different from the opinion circulated by Hughes, and almost certainly extending the term. At the end of the most fractious and exhausting term of Hughes' tenure, the exasperated justice probably had neither the energy nor the inclination to pursue either course. He, like his colleagues, was most likely simply anxious for the term to end.[112] He probably threw up his hands; he certainly sat on them.

It must in retrospect have been an acute source of embarrassment to Hughes and Roberts that a simple failure to communicate might have caused the Court to reach such a disastrous decision. Both must have felt more than a little sheepish that an overly delicate sense of propriety or simple fatigue could have produced an opinion and a result with which neither agreed. It may be that this is why the usually restrained Hughes "almost hugged" Roberts when the latter indicated that he would vote as he did in *Parrish*.[113] And this may account for Roberts' reluctance to reduce to writing the memorandum he gave to Frankfurter.[114] Roberts had already been roundly criticized for his "switch," but Hughes' reputation had escaped relatively unscathed.[115] The memorandum corroborated the implications of the *Tipaldo* and *Parrish* opinions that the blame for the *Tipaldo* result lay with the timidity and disingenuousness of the New York attorney general. But between the lines it also suggested that part of the fault lay with Hughes, who was still alive in 1945 and for whom Roberts felt considerable regard and affection.[116] Roberts left it to Frankfurter's discretion when to make the contents of the memorandum public;[117] and to avoid embarrassing either of them, Frankfurter waited until both had died to do so.

There is therefore some irony in the suggestion that by including in the *Parrish* opinion an explanation of the technical nature of the *Tipaldo* holding, Hughes was graciously attempting to save face for Roberts.[118] For even when he capitulated to Frankfurter's request, Roberts wrote the memorandum in such a way that those who believed his explanation would lay the blame for *Tipaldo* at the feet of the New York attorney general, while those who didn't buy it would continue to blame Roberts himself. Roberts has thereby succeeded in shielding Hughes from what may have been the chief's share of the blame for the *Tipaldo* fiasco.

The Minimum Wage Cases in Perspective

Any attempt to reconstruct these events necessarily rests on a large degree of conjecture; the question of Roberts' true motivation is not susceptible of definitive resolution. Let us, therefore, assume the worst. Let us assume that in the spring of 1936 Roberts voted as he did not for the reasons just discussed but instead because he relished the prospect of employers exploiting women at starvation wages and found mobilization of the doctrine of "liberty of contract" a convenient means of maintaining his perverse vision of the social order. Let us assume further that he voted as he did in *Parrish* not for the reasons just discussed, but because he was a spineless hypocrite who folded at the first hint of public pressure. Assuming all of this to be true, what is the significance of *Parrish* in the sweep of the history of economic substantive due process?

When *Parrish* was handed down in 1937, the principal authorities constituting economic substantive due process had already been discarded. By 1917 it was clear that the Court would no longer hold that regulation of the hours of labor in ordinary trades was beyond the reach of the police power. Though *Lochner* was cited as authority in *Adkins*, it would never again be mobilized to invalidate an hours regulation. Insofar as hours regulation was concerned, Chief Justice Taft was correct when he remarked that *Bunting* had overruled *Lochner sub silentio*. In 1930, in the case of *Texas & New Orleans R.R. Co. v. Brotherhood of Railway and Steamship Clerks*, the Court effectively overruled *Adair v. United States*, which had held that anti-yellow-dog contract statutes violated substantive due process, and thereby cleared the way for national collective bargaining legislation.[119] And in 1934, *Nebbia* had abandoned the doctrine restricting price regulation to a narrow category of businesses affected with a public interest. Never again would the Court strike down a price regulation on the ground that the business regulated was private. By 1937, the prohibition against minimum wage legislation was about all that was left of economic substantive due process. A decision formally announcing the last breath of a moribund body of jurisprudence hardly deserves to be called a "constitutional revolution." It was instead the final phase of a long and unevenly staged judicial withdrawal. The empire of substantive due process was already in a state of collapse when the *Parrish* decision officially lowered the flag over its last colony.

PART III

THE TRAIL OF THE YELLOW DOG

The three decades spanning the years 1908 to 1937 saw a remarkable transformation of the Supreme Court's jurisprudence concerning the rights of workers to organize. In 1908, the Court held that a federal law prohibiting employers from discharging an employee because of his membership in a labor union violated the liberty of contract secured to the employer by the Fifth Amendment.[1] In 1915, the Court similarly declared a state statute prohibiting the use of "yellow-dog" contracts unconstitutional.[2] In 1937, by contrast, the Court upheld provisions of the Wagner Act prohibiting both discharges for union membership and the use of yellow-dog contracts.[3] In short, by 1937, the doctrine of "liberty of contract" no longer operated as a bar to legislation protecting the rights of workers to organize for purposes of collective bargaining.

Remarkably, the intellectual history of this transformation has been neglected. Historians writing about the Wagner Act cases, preoccupied by the more dramatic commerce clause issues, have tended to give only cursory treatment to the due process dimensions of the decisions.[4] Viewing the outcome of the cases as essentially political responses to external political pressures[5] has apparently obviated any sustained conceptual or doctrinal analysis.

The tale of the yellow-dog contract is naturally of interest because of its centrality to the development of American labor law and the decline of substantive due process. Beyond this, however, the story can be seen as a critical chapter in the development of American liberal legalism. The yellow-dog contract provoked something of a crisis in liberal discourse because it brought into conflict two time-honored liberal values: liberty of contract and freedom of association. Recent scholarship has shown how "liberty of contract" was forged from such diverse liberal resources as Adam Smith's liberal political economy, Jacksonian liberalism, and the Northern "free labor" ideology that animated the abolitionist movement.[6] Freedom of association enjoyed no less venerable liberal pedigree. Its protection against government infringement enshrined in the First Amendment,[7] the freedom to affiliate with the lawful organizations of one's choice had been a widely embraced feature of American culture since well before the Civil War.[8] The passion with which the American people celebrated this liberty had attracted the fascination of Alexis de Tocqueville during his journey to the United States in the 1830s.[9]

The yellow-dog contract exposed a tension between these two values of American liberalism. For with the yellow-dog contract, its opponents contended, the employer was using his constitutionally protected liberty of contract as a means to inhibit his employee's freedom to associate with his fellow workingmen. In characteristically liberal terms, the answer to this charge would turn on whether the employee was seen as having surrendered his freedom of association voluntarily, or as a product of coercion. The answer to this question would in turn depend upon assumptions about the structure of the labor market—assumptions that would change over time. Beneath this discourse, I believe, lay concerns about whether labor unions were properly analogized to the other sorts of voluntary associations celebrated by American liberalism. As those concerns became increasingly allayed over time, labor's advocates could more successfully appropriate the liberal rhetoric of associational freedom.

Yet the story of the yellow dog's demise cannot be adequately understood by looking at cultural context alone. In order to understand the voting patters of the various justices and the views they expressed in their opinions, one must pay close attention to the development of doctrine. A study of the doctrine pertaining to the yellow-dog contract reveals to us yet again the weblike, interconnected structure of laissez-faire constitutionalism. The doctrinal manifestations of commerce clause and due process jurisprudence were not simply free-floating rules that could be changed or abandoned without consequences extending beyond the particular doctrine involved. These areas of doctrine were developmentally intra- and interdependent. Modifications of one substantive due process doctrine entailed changes in another; developments in due process and commerce clause doctrine produced mutual, synergistic ramifications. In short, doctrinal commitments made by justices in one area of doctrine entailed corresponding commitments in another area. In order to follow the trail of the yellow dog, we must also trace these ripple effects across structurally related areas of doctrine.

6

The Liberal Dilemma

The idea of "liberty of contract" is generally thought to have first appeared in a Supreme Court decision in *Allgeyer v. Louisiana*, decided in 1897; to have entered American constitutional jurisprudence in 1886 with *Godcharles v. Wigeman*; and to have emerged in American social thought well before the Civil War.[1] It is curious, then, that when Congress enacted the Erdman Act in 1898, no one in either house suggested that its section 10 was unconstitutional.[2] That section prohibited interstate carriers from, inter alia, (1) requiring "any employee, or any person seeking employment, as a condition of such employment, to enter" into a so-called yellow-dog contract ("an agreement, either written or verbal, not to become or remain a member of any labor corporation, association, or organization"), and (2) "threaten[ing] any employee with loss of employment" or "unjustly discriminat[ing] against any employee" because of his union membership.[3] Why, in an era in which constitutional debate on the floor of both houses of Congress flourished,[4] did these legislators believe that such abrogations of an employer's common law contractual prerogatives were constitutional?

The opinion of the district court in *United States v. Adair*[5] suggests the unarticulated rationale on which many in Congress may have relied. The indictment charged that William Adair, master mechanic of the Louisville and Nashville Railroad Company, had discharged locomotive fireman O. B. Coppage because of the latter's membership in the Order of Locomotive Firemen. Adair's demurrer contended, inter alia, that section 10 of the Erdman Act violated the liberty of contract secured to him under the Fifth Amendment.

District Judge Andrew M. Cochran conceded that the Fifth Amendment constituted an independent limitation on the federal power to regulate interstate commerce. The liberty of contract secured to a lawful *private* business, however, was greater than that secured to a common carrier engaged in interstate commerce. Because the latter "exercises a public function," held the Court, "[t]he only possible ground for holding that [section 10] is in violation of the fifth amendment is that it has no real and substantial relation to the free course of interstate commerce." Because section 10's "tendency" was "to prevent an interruption to interstate commerce by reason of strikes, lockouts and boycotts,"[6] it constituted a legitimate regulation of the contractual relations of a business affected with a public interest. In other words, the common carrier's status as a business affected with a public interest rendered it subject to regulations to which a purely private business could not constitutionally be subjected; and the relationship between the company's contractual relations with its employees and the free flow of interstate commerce provided the rationale supporting the instant regulation.

A majority of the justices of the United States Supreme Court disagreed with Judge Cochran. The majority opinion, written by Justice John Marshall Harlan, took no notice of the fact that the company was a business traditionally regarded as affected with a public interest, and stated the parties' contractual rights in absolutist terms.

> While, as already suggested, the rights of liberty and property guaranteed by the Constitution against deprivation without due process of law, is [sic] subject to such reasonable restraints as the common good or general welfare may require, it is not within the functions of government—at least in the absence of contract between the parties—to compel any person in the course of his business and against his will to accept or retain the personal services of another, or to compel any person, against his will, to perform personal services for another.[7]

The common law prerogative of the employer to discharge his employee at will for any or no reason, Justice Harlan appeared to be saying, was insulated from government regulation by the due process clause of the Fifth Amendment.

Yet despite having held that the statute violated the Fifth Amendment, Harlan went on to entertain at length the suggestion that, the Fifth Amendment notwithstanding, section 10 might be a legitimate exercise of the federal power to regulate commerce among the states. At first blush, this seems a curious mode of analysis. The commerce power, after all, was conferred in Article I, Section 8 of the original Constitution of 1787. The Fifth Amendment is an amendment to that document, and accordingly trumps the commerce clause to the extent the two are in conflict. If the Fifth Amendment rendered section 10 of the Erdman Act unconstitutional, one is led to inquire, how could the statute have been independently sustained under the commerce power? It would seem that Harlan's Fifth Amendment analysis should have ended the inquiry into the statute's constitutionality.

The solution to this conundrum lies in recognizing that Harlan and his colleagues were, like Judge Cochran, reasoning by analogy to Fourteenth Amendment due process cases. The Court had recognized in *Holden v. Hardy*[8] and *Lochner v. New York*[9] that the Fourteenth Amendment's due process clause did not prohibit the state from regulating the labor contract if such regulation was reasonably related to the protection of public health, safety, or morals. Conventionally termed "police powers," these powers to protect public health, safety, and morals were held to be inherent in the sovereignty of the several states; and with these residuary police powers, the Court had held, "the Fourteenth Amendment was not designed to interfere."[10]

The federal government, as a government of enumerated powers, did not have residuary police powers. However, Congress did possess a power analogous to the police powers of the state legislatures. Just as the states were empowered to legislate to protect public health, safety, and morals, the federal government was empowered to legislate to protect the free flow of interstate commerce.[11] Harlan's mode of analysis thus suggests that a majority of the Court believed that the impact of employer-employee relations on interstate commerce might have provided a "commercial police power" rationale for the regulation of rights otherwise secured by the Fifth Amendment.

Yet unlike Judge Cochran, the majority could find no "real and substantial relation" between interstate commerce and the acts proscribed by section 10. "[W]hat possible legal or logical connection is there between an employee's membership in a labor organization and the carrying on of interstate commerce?" queried Justice Harlan. "Such relation to a labor organization cannot have, *in itself* and in the eye of the law, any bearing upon the commerce with which the employee is connected by his labor and services."

> One who engages in the service of an interstate carrier will, it must be assumed, faithfully perform his duty, whether he be a member or not a member of a labor organization. His fitness for the position in which he labors and his diligence in the discharge of his duties cannot in law or sound reason depend in any degree upon his being or not being a member of a labor organization. It cannot be assumed that his fitness is assured, or his diligence increased, by such membership, or that he is less fit or less diligent because of his not being a member of such an organization. It is the employee as a man and not as a member of a labor organization who labors in the service of an interstate carrier. Will it be said that the provision in question had its origin in the apprehension, on the part of Congress, that if it did not show more consideration for members of labor organizations than for wage-earners who were not members of such organizations, or if it did not insert in the statute some such provision as the one here in question, members of labor organizations would, by illegal or violent measures, interrupt or impair the freedom of commerce among the States? We will not indulge in any such conjectures. . . .[12]

Justice Joseph McKenna, writing in dissent, thought the majority was simply being dense. "[I]t is not necessary to suppose that labor organizations will violate the law," wrote the dissenting justice. "Their power may be effectively exercised without violence or illegality. . . ." The Senate committee had opined, McKenna noted, that "this bill, should it become law, would reduce to a minimum labor strikes which affect interstate commerce. . . ." "A provision of law which will prevent or tend to prevent the stoppage of every wheel in every car of an entire railroad system," wrote McKenna, certainly concerned practices having a "direct influence on interstate commerce."[13]

Yet McKenna was careful to note the limits of his disagreement with the majority.

> I would not be misunderstood. I grant that there are rights which can have no material measure. There are rights which, when exercised in a private business, may not be disturbed or limited. With them we are not concerned. We are dealing with rights exercised in a *quasi*-public business and therefore subject to control in the interest of the public.[14]

McKenna was thus thinking about section 10 in much the same way that Judge Cochran had. The common law contractual prerogatives of the employer were regulable at all only because the business concerned was affected with a public interest; the impact that the employer's exercise of those prerogatives exerted on interstate commerce provided the commercial police power rationale for their regulation.[15]

Despite the fact that the majority had disagreed with McKenna about the impact of an employer's labor policies on interstate commerce, both majority and minority had embraced a common analytical model. Though Harlan and his colleagues in the majority were almost willfully agnostic about the relationship between railroad labor relations and interstate commerce, they had forged an important connection between commerce clause jurisprudence and due process jurisprudence. The sphere of liberty of contract protected by the Fifth Amendment was now defined in terms of the impact that employer-employee relations exerted on interstate commerce. If the Court ever came to view those relations as exerting a direct effect on interstate commerce, the Fifth Amendment would no longer serve to insulate those relations from congressional regulation. Moreover, though the majority had expressed no opinion on the issue, McKenna had suggested that the employer's common law contractual prerogatives could be regulated only if his business was affected with a public interest. So as the category of businesses affected with a public interest expanded, the sphere of liberty protected by the Fifth Amendment would accordingly contract. Thus three areas of constitutional jurisprudence—liberty of contract, the concept of a business affected with a public interest, and the notion of what constituted a direct effect on interstate commerce—had become developmentally interdependent.

An issue similar to that presented in *Adair* was to appear before the Court in 1915. *Coppage v. Kansas*[16] concerned the constitutionality of a Kansas statute prohibiting employers from requiring their employees, as a condition of employment, to sign yellow-dog contracts. A Mr. Hedges, a switchman for the St. Louis and San Francisco Railway Company and a member of the Switchmen's Union of North America, had refused to sign a yellow-dog contract presented to him by his employer. Mr. T. B. Coppage, superintendent of the company (and apparently no relation to the O. B. Coppage of *Adair* fame), had accordingly discharged Mr. Hedges. Mr. Coppage was indicted and convicted under the Kansas statute, and appealed his conviction to the Supreme Court.

Justice Mahlon Pitney, who had voted for the Erdman Act in 1898 while a congressman from Morristown, New Jersey,[17] wrote the opinion of the Court declaring the statute unconstitutional. The Kansas statute, the Court held, was not distinguishable in principle from the federal statute reviewed in *Adair*. "Under constitutional freedom of contract," wrote Pitney, "whatever either party has the right to treat as sufficient ground for terminating the employment, where there is no stipulation on the subject, he has the right to provide against by insisting that a stipulation respecting it shall be a *sine qua non* of the inception of the employment, or of its continuance if it be terminable at will."[18]

Because *Coppage* concerned a state statute, the commerce power could not be invoked to provide a police power rationale. The regulatory justification would accordingly have to be found within the conventional categories of the state's police power. "[W]hat possible relation," asked Pitney, did the statute have "to the public health, safety, morals or general welfare? None is suggested, and we are unable to conceive of any." The primary object of the statute was that of "leveling inequalities of fortune,"[19] and this was not a recognized police power rationale.

Justice McKenna, who had dissented in *Adair*, demonstrated his fidelity to *Adair*'s analytical model by joining the *Coppage* majority. Both cases had involved regulations of a business affected with a public interest. But in *Coppage*, unlike in *Adair*, there had been no police power rationale on which to justify the regulation of the employment contract.

Dissenting for himself and Justice Hughes,[20] Justice Day chided the majority for not taking the associative rights of the workers seriously. "Would it be beyond the legitimate exercise of the police power," asked the dissenters, "to provide that an employee should not be required to agree, as a condition of employment, to forego affiliation with a particular political party, or the support of a particular candidate for office?" Might not the state prohibit an employer from requiring its employee to join or not to join a particular church? "It seems to me," wrote Justice Day, "that these questions answer themselves." "The law should be as zealous to protect the constitutional liberty of the employee as it is to guard that of the employer. A principal object of this statute is to protect the liberty of the citizen to make such lawful affiliations as he may desire with organizations of his choice. It should not be necessary to the protection of the liberty of one citizen that the same right in another citizen be abridged or destroyed."[21]

A defense of the right to join a union cast in the rhetoric of freedom of association was not novel in 1915. In *Commonwealth v. Hunt*, decided in 1842, Chief Justice Lemuel Shaw of the Supreme Judicial Court of Massachusetts had deployed similar associational rhetoric in his landmark opinion holding that labor unions were not per se criminal conspiracies.[22] In upholding the right of the Boston Journeymen Bootmakers' Society to organize, Shaw sought to analogize unions to other common societies formed for purposes of mutual aid and protection. "Such an association," he wrote, "might be used to afford each other assistance in times of poverty, sickness and distress; or to raise their intellectual, moral or social condition; or to make improvement in their art; or for other proper purposes." The association's objective of recruiting all bootmakers into the society was not unlawful, Shaw held, for it would give to the union "a power which might be exerted for [such] useful and honorable purposes. . . ."[23]

Following Shaw's opinion in *Hunt*, American courts generally adhered to the view that the formation of labor associations for mutual aid and protection was perfectly legal.[24] Indeed, throughout the balance of the nineteenth and twentieth centuries, American judges generally agreed that strikes to obtain higher wages, shorter hours, or better working conditions were lawful.[25] Shaw's view that strikes to obtain a closed shop were legal, however, was not so readily accepted by the American bench. Throughout the late nineteenth and early twentieth centuries, state and federal courts repeatedly held that strikes and boycotts designed to secure the employment of only union workers were unlawful.[26] Such union actions were enjoinable, the courts held, for two reasons: first, they constituted coercive interferences with the right of the employer to run his business as he saw fit; and second, they aimed to require the non-union workingman to surrender a portion of his associational liberty as the price of plying his lawful trade.

In *Plant v. Woods*, the Supreme Judicial Court of Massachusetts condemned the defendant union's threats to strike and boycott employers employing certain non-union plaintiffs. "The purpose of these defendants," the court found, "was to force the plaintiffs to join the defendant association, and to that end they injured the plaintiffs in their business, and molested and disturbed them in their efforts to work at their trade." The union men "had no right to force other persons to join them." The attempt by the defendants "to compel the [non-union men] against their will to join the association" was, the court held, "intolerable, and inconsistent with the spirit of our laws."[27]

Erdman v. Mitchell involved one closed-shop strike in a larger campaign "to drive every plumber in Philadelphia into the United Association of Journeyman Plumbers." In *Erdman*, the court found that the defendant union members, through a perfectly peaceful strike, "undertook, by intimidation of plaintiffs and their employers to coerce the plaintiffs into joining their organization." "By this conduct of defendants," the court noted, "plaintiffs have been unable to secure any steady employment at their trade, and will have to enter one of defendants' unions or leave the city." Condemning the union's actions, the court accepted the plaintiffs' contention that "an agreement by a number of persons that they will by threats of a strike deprive a mechanic of the right to work for others merely because he does not choose to join a particular union, is a conspiracy to commit an unlawful act, which conspiracy may be restrained." *Erdman* is of particular interest, because it was not a case of a court protecting the right of workers to remain non-union men. The plaintiffs in the case were actually members of another union, who wished to remain loyal to the association with which they had voluntarily affiliated.[28]

In *Casey v. Cincinnati Typographical Union*, the court decried the boycott of a non-union newspaper as "an organized effort to force printers to come into the union, or be driven from their calling for want of employment."[29] The court in *Old Dominion Steamship Co. v. McKenna* stated the rule succinctly: "All combinations and associations designed to coerce workmen to become members, or to interfere with, obstruct, vex, or annoy them in working, or in obtaining work, because they are not members . . . are *pro tanto* illegal combinations or associations."[30]

As these cases made clear, the rights of workers to associate together, even to strike, were legally protected; these rights simply could not be used as a means to coerce workers in the exercise of their right to freedom of association. In deploying associational rhetoric in the *Coppage* dissent, Day and Hughes were simply calling for symmetry in the protection of associational liberty. Granted that the employer's liberty of contract was generally constitutionally protected, the dissenters would have held, the state could constitutionally prohibit him from using his freedom of contract to coerce the employee into forgoing his associational liberty. "While this court should, within the limitations of the constitutional guaranty, protect the free right of contract, it is not less important that the State be given the right to exert its legislative authority, if it deems best to do so, for the protection of rights which inhere in the privileges of the citizen of every free country."[31]

At the core of the disagreement between the majority and the dissent lay a difference over whether the employee's agreement not to join a union was the product of coercion. The majority was able to resolve the tension between liberty of contract and freedom of association by finding simply that the employee had voluntarily contracted away this associational right. To the majority justices, there was no coercion involved. The dissenters could not accept this voluntary waiver theory; indeed, they seemed prepared to take judicial notice that such a waiver would always be the product of coercion. For Day and Hughes, the yellow-dog contract was coercive per se.[32]

Yet the majority was not taking the position that economic pressure exerted in the employment context could not constitute coercion. Less than three years following the *Coppage* decision, the Court would enjoin an effort by the United Mine Workers (UMW) to unionize a non-union mine.[33] All of the employees of the Hitchman Coal and Coke Company had signed yellow-dog contracts. An agent of the UMW proceeded secretly to persuade employees of the company to agree to join the union. The plan was that once a sufficient number of employees had agreed to do so, they would quit in a body, join the union, and refuse to return to work unless the company consented to a closed-shop agreement with the UMW.

The Court enjoined the UMW's actions as an unlawful attempt to induce the employees to breach their contracts with the company. The Court further made it clear that it was troubled by "misrepresentations, deceptive statements, and threats of pecuniary loss" made by the union representative to the company's employees, as well as by the history of violence associated with coal strikes. But the Court also repeatedly condemned threats to strike for a closed-shop agreement as "coercive" of the employer and of the employees who had chosen not to join the union. The objective of such a strike, the Court stated, would be "to coerce the employer and the remaining miners to 'organize the mine,' that is, to make an agreement that none but members of the Union should be employed. . . ." "The same liberty which enables men to form unions, and through the union to enter into agreements with employers willing to agree, entitles other men to remain independent of the union. . . ."[34]

In dissent, Justice Brandeis criticized the asymmetry presented by the *Coppage* and *Hitchman* decisions. "If it is coercion to threaten to strike unless [the employer] consents to a closed union shop, it is coercion also to threaten not to give one employment unless the [employee] will consent to a closed non-union shop. The employer may sign the union agreement for fear that *labor* may not be otherwise available; the workman may sign the individual agreement for fear that *employment* may not otherwise be obtainable."[35] As Brandeis was not-so-obliquely suggesting, the fact that the Court (and the American judiciary generally) simultaneously embraced the view that a strike for a closed shop was coercive while the exaction of a yellow-dog contract was not[36] seemed the rankest anti-union hypocrisy.

Perhaps it was. The majority may have remained troubled by the reputation for violence and syndicalism that had become associated with unionism as a result of the events of Haymarket Square, Homestead, the "Debs Rebellion," and other similar instances.[37] Yet the majority's view that yellow-dog contracts were not coercive may not have seemed as preposterous in 1915 as it appears from the vantage point of the late twentieth century. As Herbert Hovenkamp has recently noted, America suffered throughout the nineteenth century from severe shortages of labor. In part as results of such shortages, slavery persisted in the United States long after it had disappeared in other Western nations; American entrepreneurs led the world in the development of labor-saving technology; America maintained virtually an open immigration policy; and the United States experienced significantly less labor unrest than contemporary England. Wages in the United States rose steadily throughout the nineteenth and early twentieth centuries, and wages and working conditions for American laborers were generally far better than those obtained by European workers.[38]

In light of these historical consequences of the labor shortage, argues Hovenkamp, political economists writing in the early twentieth century "perceived the bargaining positions of capital and labor as more or less equal. Indeed, they felt that the advantage, if any, lay with labor. . . . They argued that it was labor and not employers that could make take-it-or-leave-it offers."[39]

Illustrative of the view that laborers could avail themselves of a veritable smorgasbord of employment options was the opinion of the Georgia Supreme Court in *Western & Atlantic R.R. Co. v. Bishop.*[40] In *Bishop*, an employee of the railroad had in his employment contract waived his statutory right to recover against the company for injuries occasioned by the negligence of his fellow servant. Subsequently injured by a fellow employee, Bishop sought to have the waiver set aside on the grounds that it violated public policy. Bishop relied heavily on the U.S. Supreme Court decision in *Railroad Company v. Lockwood,*[41] which had held void as against public policy a contract exempting a common carrier from liability for damage to freight or passengers caused by the negligence of the carrier or its servants. Distinguishing *Lockwood*, the Georgia court held that the carrier stood in a monopolistic relation to the passenger or shipper, and its contractual prerogatives could be regulated for that reason. In relation to its employee, however, the railroad held no such monopoly. Upholding the contractual waiver, the court held that the railroad was "only one of a million of employers with whom [Bishop] might have sought employment."[42]

The massive waves of immigration to the United States in the late nineteenth and early twentieth centuries may have helped somewhat to ameliorate the perception of labor shortage that undoubtedly lay behind the Georgia court's seemingly hyperbolic remarks. Between 1886 and 1916 nearly 19 million immigrants arrived in the United States.[43] Yet wage rates continued to rise significantly, especially in the years leading up to the *Coppage* decision. Despite nearly flat growth in the 1890s, real wages in the United States rose 37 percent between 1890 and 1914.[44] This occurred despite the fact that not even 8 percent of the American labor force was unionized at any time before 1914.[45] The productive capacity of the American economy appeared to be more than adequate to absorb the flood of new immigrants.[46] Indeed, the lot of the American worker seemed to be getting consistently better rather than worse.[47] The existence of some unemployment was acknowledged, but was frequently attributed to laziness or other defects of character.[48] In 1907, the year in which the *Hitchman* case was commenced, the nationwide unemployment rate was 2.8 percent;[49] in 1917, the year of the Court's decision, the national rate was only 4.6 percent.[50] The justices clearly doubted that the panhandle of West Virginia harbored a large untapped reservoir of labor. As Justice Pitney wrote for the majority, "[i]t was one thing for [the company] to find, from time to time, comparatively small numbers of men to take vacant places in a going mine, another and a much more difficult thing to find a complete gang of new men to start up a mine shut down by a strike. . . ."[51]

Though the Court probably did not have access to some of these specific statistics on wages and employment, the Justices undoubtedly entertained at least an impressionistic understanding of their import. In his opinion striking down the District of Columbia minimum wage law in *Adkins v. Children's Hospital,* Justice Sutherland remarked: "[w]e cannot close our eyes to the notorious fact that earnings everywhere in all occupations have increased—not alone in States where the minimum wage law obtains but in the country generally. . . ."[52] Reasoning in the idiom of Adam Smith, many legal minds must have continued to believe that the growth in demand for labor had exceeded the growth in supply. A judge who had grown to maturity in the labor-short nineteenth century might well have thought that the American laborer in 1915 was actually bargaining from a position of some strength.[53] To be sure, individual laborers and employers often did not bargain from equal positions of strength—even in times of low unemployment—and the *Coppage* majority recognized this.[54] But these disparities in bargaining power were not in the majority's view so great as to render the labor contract the product of coercion. As they saw it, the laborer wishing to retain his freedom to associate with a union could always find another employer to bargain with. Recognizing the structure of the labor market and the perceived ease of employee mobility,[55] an employer in a labor-hungry market was in no position to "coerce" his employee into contracting away his associational freedom. But an employer struck for a closed shop was frequently in no position to bargain with a non-union man.

If such a view was problematic in 1915,[56] it was to become increasingly implausible. The demobilization of the armed forces following World War I, coupled with the tremendous influx of European immigrants in 1919 and 1920, occasioned fears of widespread unemployment.[57] Indeed, 1921's unemployment rates of 21.2 percent in the manufacturing and transportation sectors marked the highest rate in decades.[58] President Harding brought together a Commission on Unemployment in 1921, and attempts to alleviate the problem through state unemployment insurance programs began in earnest.[59] The AFL again renewed its long-standing campaign for immigration restriction. Some business interests predictably contended that there was a labor shortage, but few were persuaded. In 1921 and again in 1924, a Republican-controlled Congress and White House enacted and signed legislation placing substantial restrictions on immigration.[60] Despite this contrived contraction of the labor market, the subsequent onset of the Great Depression brought sustained unemployment in numbers previously unimaginable.[61] By the depression decade of the 1930s, no one could seriously claim that the American worker stood before a cornucopia of employment opportunity.

The cases condemning strikes for a closed shop demonstrated that the courts were prepared to see coercion in economic pressure exerted by one of the parties to the employment relationship. As the *Hitchman* case illustrated, the meaning of the term "coercion" was not so constricted that the Court could not have found that an employee was coerced into signing a yellow-dog contract. There was no need for the Court to expand its notion of coercion to include pressure brought to bear from a superior bargaining position. In order to arrive at the conclusion that yellow-dog contracts were coercive, however, the Court would have to change its assumptions about the relative bargaining strengths of employers and employees. Changes in the structure of the labor market between 1915 and the 1930s would prompt a re-examination of those assumptions.

Yet in 1915, Day and Hughes were not contending that the employment relationship was inherently coercive and therefore regulable in all its aspects.[62] The dissenters were instead suggesting that there were certain valuable rights of association to which liberty of contract ought to give way. Indeed, it was the nature of the right compromised that appears to have led them to the conclusion that the bargain was coerced. Day's analogies between yellow-dog contracts and contracts promising not to join a particular church, political party, or other "such lawful affiliations" were of course designed to reduce the majority's position to absurdity. But by implying that the majority would have decided cases involving such hypothetical contracts differently, the dissenters were also accusing the majority of according labor unions second-class status as voluntary associations. As one historian has put it, "American labor organizations lived in a legal twilight zone, expressions of an associational impulse growing in society at large, yet differentiated from other expressions of that impulse by society's law. . . ."[63]

In 1915, only Day, Holmes, and Hughes were prepared to reach across that twilight zone to assimilate unionism to liberalism's traditional solicitude for voluntary association. In 1930, however, Hughes would return from a fourteen-year hiatus in his judicial career to lead a reconstituted Court. During his tenure as chief justice, the accommodation between contractual and associational liberty for which he and Justice Day had contended would be struck.

7

Associationalism Ascendant

Wartime Lessons and a New Profile for Organized Labor

As the country confronted the exigencies of domestic production, communication, and transportation brought on by World War I, it became clear that the *Adair* majority's professed agnosticism on the relationship between union-management relations and interstate commerce was no longer tenable. It was now "essential to the national safety that the volume of production be maintained at the highest possible level, and that the avenues of communication and transportation remain always open."[1] It was recognized that industrial strife would tend to frustrate the implementation of these critical objectives. Accordingly, the National War Labor Board was established in April of 1918 for the purpose of ensuring the peaceful and prompt settlement of labor disputes in vital war industries.[2]

President Wilson appointed to the co-chairmanship of the board former President William Howard Taft. Taft, a former judge on the United States Court of Appeals, a professor at Yale Law School, and a future chief justice of the United States, was perhaps the most prominent conservative lawyer of the day, and was widely expected to be a pro-employer member of the board. But, as Taft's biographer reports, the future chief justice found his experience on the board to be personally transformative. An extended trip to the munitions and textile mills of the South convinced Taft of the need for the establishment of minimum wages. This conviction was duly reflected in the orders of the board, and subsequently in Taft's dissent in *Adkins v. Children's Hospital*.[3]

Taft and his fellow board members also recognized that industrial peace was necessary to the uninterrupted production and transportation of the goods needed for the successful prosecution of the war. To this end the board announced that (1) "The right of workers to organize in trade unions and to bargain collectively, through chosen representatives, is recognized. This right shall not be denied, abridged, or interfered with by the employers in any manner whatsoever"; and (2) "Employers shall not discharge workers for membership in trade unions, nor for legitimate trade union activities."[4] The board ordered numerous reinstatements with back pay for employees discharged for engaging in legitimate union activities; prohibited employers from requiring employees to sign yellow-dog contracts; and forbade employers to require their employees to join company unions.[5] Indeed, the board ordered employers to discontinue the use of yellow-dog contracts in cases involving General Electric, Smith and Wesson, and the Omaha and Council Bluffs Street Railway Company.[6] The war had temporarily transformed businesses that were ordinarily purely private into businesses affected with a national public interest and consequently subject to a greater degree of regulation.[7] And the National War Labor Board, headed up by a leading conservative and the next chief justice, had taken judicial notice of the fact that an employer's interference with his employees' legitimate associational activities could impede the capacity of such a business to perform its crucial public function.[8]

The years following World War I also brought increasing solicitude for the associational rights of the nation's workers. This may well have been a by-product of changing perceptions about the nature of labor unions. At the turn of the century, Christopher Tomlins has noted, the leadership of the American labor movement had embraced trade unionism as a means to achieve larger, radical political goals. Through association, Samuel Gompers had explained, "the workers would come to know that 'the state is by rights theirs' and would thereupon take over the functions of government 'in the interests of all.'"[9] Collective bargaining was "an entering wedge toward industrial democracy and abolition of the profit system," the end result of which would be "full labor control" of industry.[10]

Over the course of the next twenty years, however, the AFL sloughed off "its old associational ideology for a redefined voluntarism which drastically downplayed the radical political connotations of associationalism." Instead of a means to "accomplish the transformation of prevailing political and social institutions," "[v]oluntary association and collective bargaining became mechanisms for the improvement of material conditions within the political and industrial framework of the new corporate economy."[11] By World War I, Tomlins argues, "this ideology was manifest in virtually all of the AFL leadership's actions."[12] Rather than conceptualizing themselves as corporative bodies seeking to absorb the functions of the state, AFL unions now saw themselves as individual entities pursuing their own legitimate self-interests within the state's common law contractualist paradigm. "Organized workers, they argued, were freely associating citizens who ought to enjoy the same freedoms of action and expression that individual workers and citizens enjoyed. . . . In Gompers's hands, the AFL model was a labor version of the kind of business-based associationalism that elite reformers like Herbert Hoover and organizations like the National Civic Federation advocated during the first decades of the new century."[13] In addition, the AFL sought to refurbish its public image "by providing a model of the good worker/citizen that was essentially the same as that to be found in the literature of the middle-class, Progressive movement. The worker was intelligent, responsible, civic-minded, thrifty, self-reliant, tolerant of other people's religions, and patriotic. . . ."[14]

The liberalization of the AFL was accompanied by two other major developments in the history of labor unions. First, as the result of a wave of prosecutions initiated during and in the wake of World War I, the syndicalist Industrial Workers of the World was virtually defunct by the early 1920s.[15] Second, the years following World War I also saw the relationship between the Socialist Party and the nation's workers grow increasingly attenuated. By 1921, membership in the party had dwindled to 13,000. By 1928, membership had fallen to under 8,000, and the party had become "increasingly an organization of ministers and intellectuals rather than industrial workers."[16] "The labor movement of the 1920s," Tomlins concludes, "was a loose and disaggregated combination of individual organizations, not the quasi-syndicalist association of self-governing trades established in 1886. As such, its reconciliation to the prevailing common law tradition was no longer problematic."[17] In other words, unions had come increasingly to be seen as liberal institutions.

These changes in the complexion of the labor movement made defenses of unions cast in the rhetoric of liberal rights discourse increasingly resonant. Indeed, the growing recognition of the associational legitimacy of unions was widely expressed in the critique of yellow-dog contracts that flourished in the 1920s and 1930s. Opponents of the contract "repeatedly depicted the agreement as an illiberal institution, which snatched from workers their rights of free association, speech, and thought." The yellow-dog contract, argued one Illinois labor leader, violated the workers' rights of free association, "the essential difference between the free man and the slave." Such contracts were "a plain denial of the right of association," wrote Felix Frankfurter and Nathan Greene. Echoing Justice Day's *Coppage* dissent, Edwin Witte wrote: "would anyone tolerate for a moment aid by the courts to employers in the enforcement . . . of promises which they may exact from their employees not to join the Methodist Church or the Masons, or any other religious or fraternal organization?" Cornelius Cochrane, a persistent critic of the contract for the *American Labor Legislation Review*, likewise echoed Justice Day's critique. "Union labor," he wrote, "is convinced that if employers insisted upon employees signing a contract that they would not vote the Republican or Democratic ticket, or attend the Protestant or Catholic Church, or join the Knights of Columbus or the Masons, there would be an immediate public outcry against this invasion of the right of voluntary association." "[U]nless we are permanently to overthrow the American principle that organization into voluntary societies is to be encouraged rather than strangled," Cochrane contended, "the 'yellow dog' contract must be declared illegal." "Voluntary Labor organization," wrote Donald Richberg, "is just as much a means of preserving freedom as voluntary management association. . . ." It was "necessary for the Government to prevent those abuses of economic power that compel men to give up their constitutional right of self-organization and association for mutual aid and protection." A study of labor relations in the coal industry undertaken by the United States Coal Commission in 1922 and 1923 resulted in a scathing denunciation of the contract. "A manager," stated the Commission's report, "who can mine coal only with the use of spies, intimidation, and forced contracts, which aim to destroy the freedom of will of his workers, is not much of a manager and less of a man."[18]

By the late 1920s the New York courts were refusing to enforce yellow-dog contracts on the grounds that they were void for lack of mutuality.[19] Emboldened by the trend, Wisconsin passed a statute in 1929 declaring yellow-dog contracts void and unenforceable because opposed to public policy; Arizona, Colorado, Ohio, and Oregon followed suit two years later.[20] And in 1930 the Senate rejected the nomination of John J. Parker to the Supreme Court largely because Parker had upheld the validity of yellow-dog contracts in the *Red Jacket Coal* case.[21] Even Parker's senate supporters vigorously denounced the yellow-dog contract and called for its statutory abolition.[22] Of the ten senators who spoke in defense of Parker's nomination, only one suggested that the contract was legitimate.[23]

The Railway Labor Act and *Texas & New Orleans Railroad Co. v. Brotherhood of Railway Clerks*

The Court was not again confronted with the kinds of constitutional issues presented in *Adair* and *Coppage* until Hughes returned to lead the Court in 1930. *Texas & New Orleans Railroad Co. v. Brotherhood of Railway and Steamship Clerks* concerned the constitutionality of section 2 of the Railway Labor Act of 1926. The provision in question provided in pertinent part: "Representatives, for the purposes of this Act, shall be designated by the respective parties . . . without interference, influence or coercion exercised by either party over the self-organization or designation of representatives by the other." The Railroad had previously recognized the Brotherhood but had, in the wake of a dispute over wages, sought to organize its own company union of railway clerks and "endeavored to intimidate members of the Brotherhood and to coerce them to withdraw from it and to make [the company union] their representative in dealing with the Railroad Company." The district court issued a temporary injunction ordering the Railroad and its agents to cease "interfering with, influencing, intimidating, or coercing" any of the clerks in their "free and untrammeled right of self-organization." The Railroad nevertheless proceeded to recognize the company union, and not the Brotherhood, as the legitimate representative of its clerical employees. The district court subsequently found the Railroad in contempt of its earlier order. The Court directed the Railroad to purge itself of contempt by (1) disestablishing the company union, (2) reinstating the Brotherhood as the representative of its clerical employees, and (3) reinstating certain employees who had been discharged by the Railroad for participating in lawful union activities.[24] The temporary injunction was subsequently made permanent, and a motion to vacate the order in the contempt proceedings was denied. The Circuit Court of Appeals affirmed the decree, and the Supreme Court granted a writ of certiorari.[25]

In the congressional debates over the Railway Labor Act, which had set up a system for the voluntary arbitration of disputes between the railroads and their employees, section 2 had been uncontroversial. Members of both houses of Congress had repeatedly justified the provisions of the bill by observing that railroads were businesses affected with a public interest and that the public had an interest in the continuous and uninterrupted flow of commerce.[26] *Adair* and *Coppage* had twice been cited in the context of a debate over whether the Interstate Commerce Commission (ICC) could constitutionally set aside a wage agreement between a railroad and a union.[27] No one, however, had suggested that those cases rendered section 2 constitutionally infirm.

Predictably, the brief for the Texas and New Orleans Railroad did. The Railroad contended that all of its actions, including the discharge of its employees, were constitutionally protected. Relying principally on *Adair* and *Coppage*, the Railroad asserted that its agents

> had an inherent constitutional right even *to make membership in [the company union] a condition to the continuation of employment.* Certainly this includes the lesser right to peaceably, without threats, influence employees to join [the company union], and to recognize [the company union] as the only organization through which they would confer and negotiate with their employees. . . . [T]he defendants had the constitutional right to refuse to confer or negotiate with any organization at all, which includes the right to confer and negotiate only in a particular manner.[28]

The federal government, the Railroad contended, could not constitutionally require an employer "to retain in his service an unwanted employee, or . . . to deal or not to deal with certain groups of his employees." Nor could the commerce power supply the police power rationale for regulating the employer's constitutional prerogatives. Railway labor organizations were not in 1930, any more than they had been when *Adair* was decided, "so definitely connected with interstate commerce that Congress may require the employer to deal or not to deal with them in certain ways." "If the evils existing in 1898 [the year of the Erdman Act's enactment] after the great strike [the Pullman strike of 1894] were not sufficient to authorize a much milder interference with the relations of employer and employee," argued the Railroad, "it is difficult to see how conditions have so changed as to authorize an even greater interference when conditions have changed, if at all, for the better."[29]

On the brief for the Brotherhood was the Chicago-based attorney for the Railway Employees' Department of the AFL, Donald Richberg. Richberg, who would one day replace Hugh Johnson as the head of the National Recovery Administration, was a co-author of what would become the Norris-LaGuardia Act and the principal architect of the Railway Labor Act.[30] Richberg's extensive experience dealing with the constitutional dimensions of labor law made him singularly qualified to defend the Act before the Court.[31]

Richberg's principal task was to provide the analytic link that the majority had found missing in *Adair*—the connection between membership in a labor organization and interstate commerce. Richberg's strategy was to recount the lessons learned during and in the wake of World War I. In *Wilson v. New*,[32] decided in 1917, the Court had held that it was within the emergency war power of the federal government to prescribe wages for railway employees in a case in which a railroad and its employees' union could not reach an agreement concerning wages. The Court had held that the government might "exert the legislative will for the purpose of settling the disputes, and bind both parties to the duty of acceptance and compliance, to the end that no individual dispute or difference might bring ruin to the vast interests concerned in the movement of interstate commerce." The government must have, the Court had held, the "power to remedy a situation created by a dispute between employers and employees as to rate of wages, which, if not remedied, would leave the public helpless." The extreme step of wage-fixing had admittedly been taken in a time of emergency which no longer obtained; but the Court had nevertheless recognized the impact that a dispute between management and organized labor might exert on interstate commerce.[33]

In the wake of World War I, Richberg noted, Congress had enacted Title III of the Transportation Act of 1920. The Act had created the Railroad Labor Board, which was designed to settle labor-management disputes that threatened to interrupt interstate commerce. The railway employees were to be represented before the board by representatives of their various labor organizations. Therefore, argued Richberg, the Act had "created an imperative legal recognition of a very definite legal connection between membership in a labor organization and the carrying on of interstate commerce."[34]

The Railway Labor Act similarly "expressed a public policy to adopt as the means of preventing interruptions of interstate commerce, and therefore, as the means of a most necessary regulation of interstate commerce, the encouragement of collective bargaining between carriers and their employees. . . ." "Thus," concluded Richberg, "the questioning of the majority opinion in the *Adair* case—as to the 'legal or logical connection * * * between an employee's membership in a labor organization and the carrying on of interstate commerce'—is completely answered. The connection is now both legal and logical."[35]

Having offered up the commercial police power rationale for the regulation, Richberg next sought to minimize the law's intrusion on the employer's liberty of contract, to emphasize its protection of the employees' freedom of association, and to note the public nature of the railroad's business. In making his argument, Richberg glossed over the fact that the Railroad had been found in contempt for discharging some of its union employees, and that in order to have purged itself of contempt it would have been required to reinstate them. Richberg rather contended that the Railway Labor Act, unlike the Erdman Act, did not "make it a crime for an employer to hire whom he pleases, or discharge whom he pleases. The Act does not attempt to limit his power of hiring or discharge. The Act provides only that those who *are* his employees shall have the right to designate their own representatives to negotiate with him concerning terms and conditions of employment. . . . It must be apparent that there is not in issue in the present case the basis of the decision in the *Adair* case, that is, the right of the employer to hire whom he pleases."[36]

The "minor restraint here sought upon the employer's liberty of contract," Richberg contended, ought to be indulged in order to protect the fundamental rights of its employees. "[T]he right of employees to associate themselves together (which is, of course, an inherent right under our form of government), should be protected as a 'legitimate object for the exercise of the police power.'" And why were the associational rights of these employees a fit subject for the protection of the police power? Because "[r]ailway employees are 'charged by law' with public duties, and by Act of Congress their *organizations* have been charged with most important public duties."[37]

Richberg had now pressed all of the requisite analytic buttons. The common law prerogatives of the employer were subject to police power regulation because the business in which he was engaged was affected with a public interest. The wartime experience had made clear that the connection between labor-management relations and interstate commerce was sufficiently close to provide the rationale for invocation of the commercial police power. And with respect to such businesses affected with a public interest, the legislature could constitutionally truncate the employer's common law prerogatives in order to protect employees in their exercise of legitimate rights of association.

A unanimous Supreme Court (Justice McReynolds did not participate) thought that the constitutionality of the Act was not even a close question.[38] "We entertain no doubt of the constitutional authority of Congress to enact the prohibition," wrote Chief Justice Charles Evans Hughes. Hughes gave short shrift to arguments that had carried the day in *Adair*. Indeed, the dismissal of *Adair's* contention that there was no nexus between membership in a labor organization and the free flow of interstate commerce merited no more than two sentences. "Congress," the Court held, "may facilitate the amicable settlement of disputes which threaten the service of the necessary agencies of interstate transportation. In shaping its legislation to this end, Congress was entitled to take cognizance of actual conditions and to address itself to practicable measures."[39]

The Court likewise demonstrated its willingness to take cognizance of actual conditions. The Railroad's promotion and subsidy of the company union and its discharge of the Brotherhood's leaders, the Court found, constituted "interference, influence or coercion" of its employees with respect to their rights to self-organization. Such terms were now held to mean "pressure, the use of the authority or power of either party to induce action by the other . . . the abuse of relation or opportunity so as to corrupt or override the will. . . ."[40] Because the threat of lost employment coerced the employees in their freedom to determine which (if any) labor association they might wish to join, their decision to join the company union could not be seen as a voluntary waiver of their right to associate with some other organization. The Railroad was using its contractual prerogatives as a means of depriving its employees of their freedom of association. Because the decision to join the company union was recharacterized as coerced rather than voluntary, the resolution of the conflict between liberty of contract and freedom of association effected by the *Coppage* majority was no longer available. Having abandoned Pitney's voluntary waiver theory, the Court would have to find some other reconciliation of the conflict between contractual and associational liberty.

For the first time, the Court resolved the conflict in favor of associational freedom. When these two competing liberal ideals came into conflict, the Court held, liberty of contract would have to recede so that freedom of association might be preserved. Accordingly, the Court held, section 2 of the Railway Labor Act constituted a legitimate protection of employees' right of free association.

The legality of collective action on the part of the employees in order to safeguard their proper interests is not to be disputed. It has long been recognized that employees are entitled to organize for the purpose of securing the redress of grievances and to promote agreements with employers relating to rates of pay and conditions of work. Congress was not required to ignore this right of the employees but could safeguard it. . . . Thus the prohibition by Congress of interference with the selection of representatives for the purpose of negotiation and conference between employers and employees, instead of being an invasion of the constitutional right of either, was based on the recognition of the rights of both.[41]

Such a characterization of the Court's reconciliation of the conflict of rights was less than forthcoming; and Hughes' prestidigital performance was far from over. Glossing over, as had Richberg, the fact that the district court's orders enforcing the Act had required the Railroad to reinstate employees it had discharged, Hughes dismissed *Adair* and *Coppage* as "inapplicable."

> The Railway Labor Act of 1926 does not interfere with the normal exercise of the right of the carrier to select its employees or to discharge them. The statute is not aimed at this right of the employers but at the interference with the right of employees to have representatives of their own choosing. As the carriers subject to the Act have no constitutional right to interfere with the freedom of the employees in making their selections, they cannot complain of the statute on constitutional grounds.[42]

This was a distinction that could be remembered just long enough to be stated once;[43] and there were at the time and have been since several commentators who wondered whether, after 1930, there was anything left of *Adair* and *Coppage*.[44] Just how much of those cases was left, to which of the Justices, and for what reasons, would not be clear until 1937.

The Luxuriation of the Associational Rationale

Congress was quickly alert to the possibilities offered by the *Texas & New Orleans* case, and was sensitive to the associational language employed in Hughes' opinion.[45] Section 3 of the Norris-LaGuardia Act, enacted in 1932, declared that yellow-dog contracts were contrary to the public policy of the United States and would henceforth be unenforceable in the federal courts.[46] Members of both houses repeatedly invoked the authority of the *Texas & New Orleans* case in support of this provision, and persistently declared that yellow-dog contracts deprived employees of their freedom of association.[47] "It would not be tolerated for a moment," argued Wisconsin's Senator Blaine, echoing the words of Justice Day's *Coppage* dissent, "if employers compelled all their employees to sign contracts that they would not belong to some lodge or to some particular church, or that they will vote the Republican ticket. . . ." But if employers could require employees to sign yellow-dog contracts, argued Blaine, they could prevent their employees from "doing anything, either in or out of working hours, that they do not like."[48]

The seriousness with which this associational rationale was taken was reflected in a disagreement between the House and Senate over the bill's declaration of policy. The version of the bill passed by the House provided in part

> Sec. 2. . . . Whereas . . . the individual unorganized worker is commonly helpless to exercise actual liberty of contract and to protect his freedom of labor . . . wherefore it is necessary that he have full freedom of association [to organize and select representatives, etc.][49]

The Senate version of the bill's declaration of policy inserted, between "wherefore" and "it is necessary," the phrase, "though he should be free to decline to associate with his fellows."[50] The House initially balked at the Senate's amendment; but the Senate, whose members nearly unanimously supported the anti-yellow-dog provision, insisted on its pristine formulation of the worker's associational liberty.[51] In the final version of the bill, the Senate's amendment prevailed.[52] As one commentator noted, "[t]he freedom of association of workers and of employers alike is held to be a necessity in order to foster freedom of contract."[53]

Senator Norris scored another victory for associational liberty the following year when Congress enacted the Bankruptcy Act of 1933.[54] Shortly before the close of the legislative session, Norris succeeded in persuading the Senate to amend the House version of the bill, adding what were to become sections 77(p) and (q).[55] Section 77(p) provided:

> No judge or trustee acting under this Act shall deny or in any way question the right of employees on the property under his jurisdiction to join the labor organization of their choice, and it shall be unlawful for any judge, trustee or receiver to interfere in any way with the organizations of employees, or to use the funds of the railroad under his jurisdiction, in maintaining so-called company unions, or to influence or coerce employees in an effort to induce them to join or remain members of such company unions.

Section 77(q) provided: "No judge, trustee, or receiver acting under this Act shall require any person seeking employment on the property under his jurisdiction to sign any contract or agreement promising to join or to refuse to join a labor organization," and required the judge, trustee, or receiver in question to discard any such contract in force before the subject property came under his jurisdiction.[56]

Defending his amendment on the Senate floor, Norris emphasized the fact that the worker's associational liberty would be thereby preserved. "It [the amendment] permits rather than compels men to join a so-called company union, to join whatever union they want to that they shall be free men, and that they shall not have that freedom taken away from them by any action of the receiver or by any order of the court."[57] As Irving Bernstein noted, Norris' amendment "outlawed both the yellow-dog contract and the closed shop."[58] This symmetrical protection of workers' associational liberty was again embraced by the Emergency Railroad Transportation Act of 1933, whose section 7(e) incorporated by reference sections 77(p) and (q) of the Bankruptcy Act.[59]

Similarly revealing were the debates over the 1934 amendments to the Railway Labor Act. The amendments created a new section 2, which set out the "general purposes" of the Act. Among these purposes was "to forbid any limitation upon freedom of association among employees or any denial, as a condition of employment or otherwise, of the right of employees to join a labor organization." And indeed, the backers of the bill mobilized associational rhetoric in its support. But the House and Senate differed on the form these associational protections should take. The original House bill prohibited employers from influencing, coercing, or requiring their employees to join company unions.[60] The Senate version prohibited employers from influencing, coercing, or requiring their employees to join any labor organization whatsoever. The Senate again insisted on its symmetrical formulation, and the House, adequately assured that the Senate's version prohibited company unions, again capitulated.[61] Once again, Congress had sought to safeguard workers' associational liberty by outlawing both the yellow-dog contract and the closed shop.[62]

Thus in four major pieces of legislation enacted in the early 1930s, Congress had evinced a preoccupation with symmetrical protections for the worker's freedom of association. The employer could not require the employee to agree not to join a union, nor could he discharge him for joining one. Neither could the employer seek to influence or coerce the employee into joining a company union. Finally, the employer could not, at his employee's union's behest or otherwise, seek to influence or coerce any of his employees into joining a noncompany union. In the discrete areas of industry covered by these acts, the asymmetry of the *Coppage* era appeared to be rectified. With the passage of the Wagner Act the next year, however, this preoccupation with symmetry would be abandoned, and the asymmetry of the yellow-dog period would be turned on its head.

Virginian Railway Co. v. System Federation, No. 40

The constitutionality of the amended Railway Labor Act was attacked before the Court in 1937. The dispute arose over attempts by the Railway to avoid collective bargaining with the Federation, which was the duly accredited representative of the Railway's mechanical department ("back-shop") employees. The district court's decree had directed the Railway (1) to "treat with" the Federation and to "exert every reasonable effort to make and maintain agreements concerning rates of pay, rules and working conditions . . ."; (2) not to enter into "any contract, undertaking, or agreement of whatsoever kind concerning rules, rates of pay or working conditions affecting its Mechanical Department employees, . . . except . . . with the Federation"; and (3) not to interfere with, influence, or coerce its employees with respect to their free choice of representatives, nor, for such purposes, to organize or foster any company union. As the Court's opinion noted, the Railway did not argue that the third part of the district court's order was unconstitutional. In view of the decision in the *Texas & New Orleans* case, noted the Court, "[t]hat contention is not open to it."[63]

The Railway did, however, challenge the other two portions of the lower court's order, and it did so on two fronts. The Railway clearly could not claim that it was not a business affected with a public interest—the business in which it was engaged was paradigmatically public. But the *Adair* case had also involved a business affected with a public interest, and the Railway could rely on the absolutist language in which Justice Harlan had described the employer's liberty of contract. Glossing over the fact that the Railway was engaged in a public business, attorney for the Railway James Piper told the Court that "the freedom of contract argument is that it is our right to refuse business negotiations with anyone." The Railway further argued that the back-shop employees were engaged in the purely intrastate activities of repair and manufacture, neither of which was sufficiently related to the interstate activities of the Railway to admit of federal regulation. Because the activities of the back-shop employees were beyond the reach of the federal commerce power, the impact of those activities on interstate commerce could not supply the commercial police power rationale for regulating the Railway's liberty of contract.[64]

The Act and the lower court's decree were defended by the Federation and by the United States, which filed a brief as amicus curiae. "The Railway Labor Act," argued the brief for the Federation, "does not require a carrier to enter into any contract, but merely that it shall negotiate with regard to the matter. . . . Negotiations are not contracts, and in and of themselves cannot have the effect of bringing into existence contractual rights or duties." "The petitioner is *not* placed under a duty to enter into a particular agreement, to agree upon particular terms, or to make any contract whatsoever," argued the brief for the United States. "One who confers, unlike one who contracts, is not bound as to any future conduct. His future freedom is not thereby restrained."[65]

This much was true. But the defenders of the Act also had to justify that portion of the lower court's order that had restrained the Railway from entering into any contract concerning rates of pay, rules, and conditions with anyone other than the Federation. That portion of the decree, noted the brief for the United States, did not restrain the Railway "in the normal exercise of its right to select or discharge its employees." But to the extent that the decree did impose limitations on the Railway's liberty of contract, observed the Federation's brief, it was important to bear in mind that the Railway was "a common carrier, a public utility, the operator of a business peculiarly charged with the public interest. Its business may, therefore, be regulated to a greater extend [sic] than is the case with other industries without infringing upon the constitutional guarantee of freedom of contract."[66]

There remained only the task of articulating the police power rationale for the regulation. The congressional power to regulate commerce could reach the activities of back-shop employees, argued the brief for the United States, even though such employees were not themselves engaged in interstate commerce. The *Texas & New Orleans* case had upheld the validity of the Act as applied to clerks, whose work was clearly intrastate in nature. A strike by the Railway's back-shop employees would "both endanger the safety of interstate transportation and directly obstruct its movement." Moreover, any dispute between the Railway and its back-shop employees would likely be communicated to Railway employees engaged in interstate commerce, thereby further threatening the continuity of interstate transportation. The purpose of the Act, argued the Federation, was "to aid and encourage the railroads and their employees to make and maintain agreements to the end that labor strife and discontent be allayed and labor harmony and good morale prevail; all to the end that there be no interruption of commerce in the public interest." The means employed by the Act were, the Federation contended, reasonably related to that legitimate end.[67]

The litigants were given a foreshadowing of the Court's decision when Justice Sutherland interrupted the Railway counsel's freedom of contract argument to inquire, "[d]o you attach any importance to the fact that the railroad company is engaged in a business charged with the public interest?" Piper's reply was a convoluted "no," and counsel for both the Federation and the United States were sure to emphasize the Railway's public nature in their presentations. "Does the fifth amendment," asked counsel for the United States, "prevent the Congress from infringing somewhat upon the absolute right to be perfectly free in the operation of your business and in your dealings with your employees in order to assure continuous operation of the railroad systems—a great public necessity . . . ?" Citing *Nebbia v. New York* for the proposition that due process requires "only that the law shall not be unreasonable, arbitrary, or capricious, and that the means selected shall have a real and substantial relation to the object sought to be obtained," counsel concluded that "the slight interference [here involved] with the personal liberty of the railroad management . . . seems a very minimum that they could be asked to relinquish in order that we may bring about industrial peace."[68]

The opinion of the Court, delivered March 29, was unanimous. Employing again the analytical model initially embraced in *Adair*, the Court noted that each of the doctrinal prerequisites to regulation of the employment relationship had been satisfied. First, the court noted, the business of the railroad was clearly affected with a public interest. "More is involved," wrote Justice Stone, "than the settlement of a private controversy without appreciable consequences to the public. The peaceable settlement of labor controversies, especially where they may impair the ability of an interstate carrier to perform its service to the public, is a matter of public concern."[69]

The Court nevertheless sought to minimize the extent of the intrusion on the employer's common law prerogatives. Neither the Act nor the decree required the Railway to enter into any agreement, held the Court—the Railway was merely required to "treat with" the Federation, not to contract with it. Moreover, the portion of the decree restraining the Railway from entering into a collective agreement with anyone other than the Federation did not prevent the Railway from refusing to enter into any collective contract and instead negotiating contracts with its employees on an individual basis. Because the provisions of the Act did not "'interfere with the normal exercise of the right of the carrier to select its employees or to discharge them,'" *Adair* and *Coppage* had "no present application."[70]

Finally, Justice Stone articulated the commercial police power rationale undergirding the instant application of the Act. A strike by the Railway's employees, he wrote, "if more than temporary, would seriously cripple [the Railway's] interstate transportation." The means prescribed by the Act were reasonably related to the legitimate end of preventing such interruptions of commerce. The Act was therefore a legitimate exercise of the federal government's commercial police power.[71]

Through early 1937, then, both Congress and the Court had shown increasing solicitude for the associational liberty of the American laborer. The Hughes Court had twice turned back substantive due process challenges to congressional statutes calculated to preserve the worker's right freely to associate with the labor organization of his choice. Thusfar, however, the Court had approved such legislation only as applied to businesses traditionally considered affected with a public interest. Whether the Court would approve such legislation if applied to businesses conventionally thought of as private remained to be seen. In other words, the justices had not yet clarified whether *Nebbia*'s declaration that "there is no closed class or category of businesses affected with a public interest" had modified *Adair*'s analytical model. The statute that would require the Court to address that question provided the blueprint for modern American labor relations.

8

Doctrinal Synergies

Capping off the flurry of labor legislation enacted in the 1930s was the National Labor Relations Act, otherwise known as the Wagner Act. Section 7 of the Act secured to employees "the right to self-organization, to form, join, or assist labor organizations, to bargain collectively through representatives of their own choosing, and to engage in concerted activities, for the purpose of collective bargaining or other mutual aid or protection."[1]

Section 8 described certain "unfair labor practices" in which employers were forbidden to engage. Sections 8(1) and 8(2) sought, as had their statutory predecessors, to preserve workers' freedom of association. Section 8(1) forbade the employer "to interfere with, restrain, or coerce employees in the exercise of the rights guaranteed in section 7." Section 8(2) sought to preserve employer neutrality among unions and to outlaw company unions by forbidding any employer "[t]o dominate or interfere with the formation or administration of any labor organization or contribute financial or other support to it." Section 8(3) constituted a frontal assault on *Adair* and *Coppage,* and a bet that the *Texas & New Orleans* case had overruled them. Resurrecting in substance section 10 of the Erdman Act, section 8(3) forbade any employer "[b]y discrimination in regard to hire or tenure of employment or any term or condition of employment to encourage or discourage membership in any labor organization." Section 8 thus clearly proscribed the nemeses of labor associationalism: anti-union discrimination in hiring and firing, company unions, and yellow-dog contracts.[2]

In the hearings and debates on the bill, opponents relied heavily on *Adair* and *Coppage* as precedents standing for the proposition that section 8 violated the Fifth Amendment.[3] Proponents of the bill, however, contended that those precedents were no longer applicable. "The power of Congress to guarantee freedom of organization, to prohibit the company-dominated union, and to prevent employers from requiring membership or nonmembership in any union has been upheld completely" in the *Texas & New Orleans* case, declared Senator Wagner. "[W]e cannot doubt that *Coppage v. Kansas* and *Adair v. United States* have been overruled."[4] Time would show that Wagner's proclamation of *Adair's* demise was, if not incorrect, at least exaggerated.

The Act's introductory "Findings and Policy" linked its commercial police power rationale to the rhetoric of associational liberty.

> The inequality of bargaining power between employees who do not possess full free-
> dom of association or actual liberty of contract, and employers who are organized in
> the corporate or other forms of ownership association substantially burdens and affects
> the flow of commerce. . . . It is hereby declared to be the policy of the United States
> to eliminate the causes of certain substantial obstructions to the free flow of com-
> merce and to mitigate and eliminate those obstructions when they have occurred by
> encouraging the practice and procedure of collective bargaining and by protecting
> the exercise by workers of full freedom of association. . . .[5]

In the floor debates, moreover, proponents defended the Act in associational terms.[6] But despite its evocation of associational rhetoric, the Wagner Act did not embrace the symmetrical protections for workers' associational freedom provided by earlier labor legislation. In the Senate debates on the bill, Senator Millard Tydings of Maryland sought to amend section 7 to read: "Employees shall have the right to self-organization, to form, join, or assist labor organizations, to bargain collectively through representatives of their own choosing, and to engage in concerted activities, for the purpose of collective bargaining or other mutual aid or protection *free from coercion or intimidation from any source.*"[7] The notion that workers ought to be entirely free from coercion in making associational decisions was a logical outgrowth of the associational paradigm embraced by Congress throughout the preceding decade; and the supporters of the amendment mixed associational rhetoric with citations to the Norris-LaGuardia Act in their remarks on the floor. "Is this not still the kind of country," Senator Tydings asked, "where a man can select, without coercion or intimidation, the kind of organization to which he shall belong?" "A laborer ought to be entitled without coercion from any side to say whether he wants to join this, that, or the other union, and if it is wrong for the employer, as it is wrong, to coerce labor or intimidate labor, it is equally wrong for somebody else to coerce laborers and intimidate them." Opponents of the amendment were hard put to disagree with the logic of Tydings' arguments; but fearful that judges hostile to labor might interpret "coercion" to include peaceful picketing and persuasion, even Senator Norris spoke against it.[8] The arguments of Wagner and Norris carried the day, and the amendment was defeated by a vote of 50 to 21.[9]

The rejection of the Tydings amendment was not the only evidence of the Senate's retreat from symmetrical associationalism. Section 9(a) of the Act provided that the representative selected by the majority of the employees in a unit would be the exclusive representative of all unit employees in negotiating the terms of employment: minority workers dissatisfied with the outcome of a certification election could not designate their own representatives to bargain on their behalf.[10] President Roosevelt himself had rejected the principles of majority rule and exclusive representation on the grounds that they interfered with freedom of association when he had mediated the automobile industry settlement in 1934.[11]

Moreover, section 8(3) broke with the policy of the Railway Labor Act by adopting a permissive posture toward the closed shop. The proviso to that section stipulated that "nothing in this Act . . . shall preclude an employer from making an agreement with a labor organization . . . to require as a condition of employment membership therein. . . ." In the debates over the Tydings amendment, Senator Daniel Hastings of Delaware condemned the asymmetry of the Act's protections for workers' associational liberty. The proviso, he argued, permitted "the reverse, as I understand, of the 'yellow dog' contract which has been so roundly and properly condemned in this body." "Does it not say, in so many words, that if the employer so desires, and the majority of the labor union so desires, they may make an agreement whereby no one may be employed in the establishment unless he belongs to that union, and will not that provision in this bill compel a minority of employees in that particular shop or that particular unit to join that union, whether they wish to or not, and pay all the fees which the union may desire to charge?"[12] But advocates of the proviso would not engage Hastings in associational terms. Associational rhetoric had carried them as far toward their goals as it could. At this juncture, the associational rationale was abandoned; as a result, the asymmetry of the *Coppage* era was revived in inverted form.

The attorneys at the NLRB were aware that these provisions of the Act did not square as neatly as had the Railway Labor Act with the associational ideology expressed in the *Texas & New Orleans* opinion, and they crafted their litigation strategy accordingly.[13] Preparing to defend the constitutionality of the Wagner Act before the Supreme Court, the NLRB lawyers sought out test cases that would not bring before the Court these more problematic provisions of the Act. Each of the test cases selected therefore involved an instance in which an employer had been found guilty of an unfair labor practice under section 8(3) because it had discharged one or more of its employees for engaging in legitimate union activities.[14] Such cases cleanly presented instances in which a worker's associational liberty had been compromised, and permitted the NLRB attorneys to mobilize associational rhetoric with the greatest effect.

The NLRB lawyers were also careful to select test cases in which an employer's labor relations could be said to have a direct effect on the flow of interstate commerce. Ultimately, they selected and prepared five cases (the so-called Wagner Act cases) through which to test the constitutionality of the Act. The Washington, Virginia and Maryland Coach Company was a small interstate transit company. The Associated Press was a national wire service utilizing interstate channels of communication. In each of these two cases, the nexus with interstate commerce was fairly clear. In addition to these cases, the NLRB also moved against three manufacturing operations: the Jones and Laughlin Steel Corporation in Aliquippa, Pennsylvania; the Fruehauf Trailer Company in Detroit, Michigan; and the Friedman-Harry Marks Clothing Company in Richmond, Virginia. In each of these manufacturing cases, the plant in question acquired its raw and semifinished materials from points outside its home state. After transforming these materials into a finished product, each plant shipped the bulk of its products to points outside its home state. These three cases had been carefully selected because they could be argued as current of commerce cases; and indeed, the NLRB lawyers briefed and argued the cases under that theory.[15]

The Wagner Act cases[16] were argued at the same time as the *Virginian Railway* case. The Washington, Virginia and Maryland Coach Company was admittedly a common carrier engaged in interstate commerce. Apparently recognizing that the *Texas & New Orleans* case was controlling, the company offered only a token due process argument.[17] None of the other businesses was so paradigmatically public, however, and each emphasized its essentially private nature in its briefs and arguments. The *Texas & New Orleans* case, argued counsel for Jones and Laughlin, was distinguishable from the instant case because the former involved "an interstate carrier, which is a public utility." Congress possessed broad powers to regulate the employment practices of such enterprises. Jones and Laughlin, however, was not a business affected with a public interest, and Congress was therefore without authority to regulate its common law prerogatives.[18]

The *Texas & New Orleans* case, contended counsel for the Friedman-Harry Marks Clothing Company, could not "be cited in any way as authority for the proposition that the Federal Government may place any limitation upon the right of an employer conducting a *private business*, to hire and fire with impunity. . . ." The Railway Labor Act, the company argued,

> applied only to common carriers engaged in the transportation of commerce between the several states, whose businesses are affected with a great national public interest. . . . (This difference is of the greatest significance and importance in a consideration of the National Labor Relations Act, which is applicable to inherently intrastate enterprises affected with no public interest, the internal regulation and continuance of which is admittedly of only private concern.)[19]

John W. Davis, arguing on behalf of the Associated Press, contended that "regulation of the right to contract in respect of a private business, is arbitrary and therefore void unless confined to the exigencies of a real emergency." The Wagner Act did "not even pretend to establish or follow a distinction between public and private business, [or] between public and private employment. . . ." On the contrary, the Act outlawed "all private and individual bargaining in respect of private enterprise in private industry." The Act as applied to the Associated Press was "an invasion of freedom of contract between an employer and an employee who are engaged in a wholly private occupation."[20]

The Act's defenders responded, of course, by mobilizing *Nebbia v. New York*. *Nebbia*, after all, had effectively retired the distinction between public and private enterprise. "[T]here is no closed class or category of businesses affected with a public interest," Justice Roberts had written for the majority. "The phrase, 'affected with a public interest' can, in the nature of things, mean no more than that an industry, for adequate reason, is subject to control for the public good." Regulation of enterprise was unconstitutional "only if arbitrary, discriminatory, or demonstrably irrelevant" to a policy that "may reasonably be deemed to promote public welfare." Attorneys defending the Act recognized that *Nebbia's* dismantling of the public/private distinction held dramatic implications for national collective bargaining legislation. After *Nebbia*, the category "business affected with a public interest" could no longer operate as an independent constraint on legislative power to regulate the employment relationship. So long as the legislation was not patently arbitrary or capricious, the legislature could regulate the employment relations of any business, irrespective of whether it had in the past been considered a business affected with a public interest. The distinction between public and private business was simply no longer pertinent, and the strand of due process doctrine from which that distinction had emerged no longer constituted a restraint on the exercise of governmental regulatory power. "The Fifth Amendment," argued the attorneys for the NLRB, "serves to invalidate legislation only so far as 'the means selected' are 'unreasonable, arbitrary or capricious', and have no 'real and substantial relation to the object sought to be attained.' [citing *Nebbia*]." The AFL cited *Nebbia* to the same effect in its amicus brief in *Washington, Virginia & Maryland Coach Co.* The purpose of the Act, argued Solicitor General Stanley Reed, was to prevent interruptions to the free flow of interstate commerce caused by labor disputes, and the means selected by the Act to achieve this end were "reasonable and proper in their character." The due process issue was accordingly completely controlled by the *Texas & New Orleans* case.[21]

The NLRB attorneys also mobilized associational rhetoric in defense of the Act. The Labor Board's brief in the *Associated Press* case contended that "the protection of employees in their freedom of association has been for a long time a recognized and fundamental part of the policy of the Federal Government in all aspects of labor relations subject to its control or legislative authority, and has been approved as just and reasonable."[22] The amicus brief filed by the American Newspaper Guild in the *Associated Press* case crystallized the defense of the Act in a single statement: "in the public interest, it is essential to enforce freedom of association for the purpose of negotiating the terms upon which labor is willing to sell its services to the end that there may be peace instead of war in matters affecting interstate commerce."[23]

The opinion in the *Washington, Virginia & Maryland Coach* case was, predictably, unanimous. The company was a common carrier engaged in interstate transportation, and its common law employment prerogatives were, like those of the Texas and New Orleans Railroad and the Virginian Railway, subject to reasonable regulation in the public interest. In the remaining cases, however, the justices split 5 to 4 on the due process issue. The rationales for each position were stated in the *Jones & Laughlin* majority opinion and dissent.[24]

Hughes' opinion for the majority drew extensively on the associational rhetoric he had employed seven years earlier. Citing *Texas & New Orleans* and *Virginian Railway*, Hughes held that the Act merely secured

> a fundamental right. Employees have as clear a right to organize and select their representatives as the respondent has to organize its business and select its own officers and agents. Discrimination and coercion to prevent the free exercise of [those employee rights] is a proper subject for condemnation by competent legislative authority.

The *Texas & New Orleans* decision had clearly established that an employer's discriminatory discharge of employees constituted a coercive interference with its employees' rights of association. And with the decision in *Nebbia*, it was clear that the Fifth Amendment did not limit governmental power to safeguard those rights from such coercion. Deploying the post-*Nebbia* language of due process, the Court found that restraint of the employer's common law prerogatives "for the purpose of preventing an unjust interference with that right cannot be considered arbitrary or capricious."[25] In the conflict between liberty of contract and freedom of association, the Court had again awarded victory to the latter.

Yet as it had in *Texas & New Orleans* and *Virginian Railway*, the Court minimized the Act's imposition on the employer's contractual liberty. The Act, wrote Hughes,

> imposes upon the respondent only the duty of conferring and negotiating with the authorized representatives of its employees for the purpose of settling a labor dispute. . . .
> The Act does not compel agreements between employers and employees. It does not compel any agreement whatever. It does not prevent the employer "from refusing to make a collective contract and hiring individuals on whatever terms" the employer "may by unilateral action determine." [citing *Virginian Railway*].

Accordingly, *Adair* and *Coppage* were again "inapplicable." The Act did not

> interfere with the normal exercise of the right of the employer to select its employees or to discharge them. The employer may not, under cover of that right, intimidate or coerce its employees with respect to their self-organization and representation, and, on the other hand, the Board is not entitled to make its authority a pretext for interference with the right of discharge when that right is exercised for other reasons than such intimidation and coercion.[26]

It was by now quite clear that "inapplicable" was a highly euphemistic way of describing the status of *Adair. Adair* and *Coppage* had embraced a thoroughgoing liberty of contract unchecked by a countervailing right to free association. The voluntary waiver theory of the *Coppage* Court had elided the conflict between these two liberal rights; and this elision was possible only against a backdrop of assumptions about the employment relationship that the Court no longer entertained. Changes in the structure of the labor market undoubtedly informed the Court's concept of coercion. But it is important to recognize that the distance from *Adair* to the Wagner Act cases was traversed within a framework of liberal rights discourse. Liberty of contract had not simply been abandoned as unworthy or anachronistic. It had instead been curtailed in order to safeguard the countervailing liberal right of free association.[27]

The Four Horsemen were not prepared to accept this accommodation in the three manufacturing cases, and we cannot understand their position without attention to doctrinal detail. Like the majority, the dissenters continued to work within the analytical model fashioned in *Adair*. Unlike the majority, however, the dissenting Justices did not see that model as having been modified by *Nebbia*. The Four Horsemen had balked at *Nebbia's* abandonment of the distinction between public and private enterprise. As a corollary, they were not committed to the consequences *Nebbia* implied for national collective bargaining legislation. Accordingly, the dissenters disagreed with the majority over the types of situations into which the federal government might project its authority in order to adjust the competing claims of contractual and associational freedom. The Four Horsemen thought that Congress might legitimately so project its authority in cases involving both a business affected with a public interest (as that concept had been understood before *Nebbia*) and a commercial police power rationale—this much the cases involving interstate common carriers made clear.[28] But in the absence of these two factors, Congress was in their view powerless to intervene in the competition. Thus, despite their concurrences in the *Texas & New Orleans, Virginian Railway,* and *Washington, Virginia & Maryland Coach* cases, the dissenters believed that *Adair* and *Coppage* still retained some vitality.

Justice McReynolds' lengthy discussion of the commerce power issue certainly would have sufficed as a front for a dissent motivated by crude anti-labor sentiment. Yet the dissenters went on in a separate section to condemn the application of the Wagner Act to the three manufacturing establishments as a violation of the Fifth Amendment. The manner in which they did so is eloquent testimony to the continuing vitality the *Adair* model held for them, and to the extent to which they continued to embrace pre-*Nebbian* notions of public and private.

As far as the Four Horsemen were concerned, the *Texas & New Orleans* case was "not controlling." There, Justice McReynolds wrote, the Court had been considering "an act definitely limited to common carriers engaged in interstate transportation over whose affairs Congress admittedly has wide power. . . ." That case had clearly dealt with a pre-*Nebbia* business affected with a public interest and an obvious commercial police power rationale. In the instant cases, however, the dissenters were not satisfied that the activities of the enterprises in question could directly affect interstate commerce. In their view, the enterprises in question were simply local manufacturing operations immune from federal regulation.[29] Accordingly, the impact of those employers' labor relations on interstate commerce could not provide the necessary rationale for federal police power regulation of contractual liberty.

Moreover, the businesses in which the various enterprises were engaged were not, the dissenters believed, affected with a public interest. Accordingly, the common law prerogatives of those employers to hire and fire at will were not subject to legislative abridgement. Citing *Adair* and *Coppage,* Justice McReynolds opined:

> The right to contract is fundamental and includes the privilege of selecting those with whom one is willing to assume contractual relations. This right is unduly abridged by the Act now upheld. A *private owner* is deprived of power to manage *his own property* by freely selecting those to whom *his manufacturing operations* are to be entrusted. We think this cannot lawfully be done in circumstances like those here disclosed.[30]

The disagreement between the majority and the dissent over whether the Wagner Act violated the Fifth Amendment thus was a disagreement over two basic issues. First, whether the businesses in which the enterprises were engaged were affected with a public interest; and second, whether the labor relations of the employers directly affected interstate commerce (the commercial police power issue). The disagreement over the first issue was essentially the disagreement expressed by the two sets of justices in *Nebbia v. New York.* As I shall argue in Part IV, the controversy over the second issue was likewise comprehended within that same *Nebbian* fracas. Thus, the fundamental issues that would divide the justices in the seminal labor cases of modern American constitutional law were decided not in response to the political pressures of 1937,[31] but in a 1934 dispute over the price of milk in upstate New York.

As the ultimate expositor of the Wagner Act, the Court would continue to define the extent of the Act's associational and contractual protections. The fundamental right of association was secure, but the legitimate concerted activities of labor associations were not without limits.[32] Similarly, the abandonment of *Adair* and *Coppage* did not signal a loss of all solicitude for employers' contractual prerogatives.[33] The Court's constitutional accommodation between associational and contractual rights had taken place within a framework of liberal rights discourse, and the terms of that discourse would continue to inform its construction of the statute. After 1937, however, the extent of the Court's protection of those rights was no longer a matter beyond congressional control. The constitutional revolution in labor law had been consolidated.

It is a commonplace that the Hughes Court era was the period during which the Supreme Court receded from its traditional solicitude for economic liberty and began to turn its attention instead to noneconomic forms of civil liberty. Yet the story is conventionally told as if the two forms of liberty were merely ships passing in the night: one on the ascendant, the other in decline.[34] In the context of the yellow-dog contract, however, the more appropriate image was the face-off. Assimilating unionism to other forms of voluntary association, labor's advocates successfully brought liberty of contract into a face-to-face conflict with freedom of association. Prefiguring and exemplifying the jurisprudential transformations for which it would become known, the Hughes Court from its inception consistently resolved this conflict in favor of associational liberty. The tale of the yellow dog thus was not just a sideshow in the demise of "laissez-faire" constitutionalism. It was emblematic of the Hughes Court's pivotal role in the recasting of American liberalism.

Yet before this resolution could be effected, the analytic prerequisites set out in the *Adair* model had to be satisfied. As we have seen, *Nebbia* effectively disposed of the model's requirement that the business regulated be affected with a public interest. But it was still necessary for the NLRB attorneys to demonstrate, and for the Court to agree, that labor conflict within the manufacturing enterprises in question posed a threat to the free flow of interstate commerce. To understand why such a contention was problematic, and how it became increasingly plausible, we must turn our attention to contemporaneous developments in commerce clause doctrine — developments in which *Nebbia* would again play a critical role.

PART IV

THE LEVEE BREAKS

The commerce clause dimensions of the Wagner Act cases,[1] unlike the due process dimensions, have received no shortage of attention from lawyers, historians, and political scientists. Instead, they have been central to the "switch in time" narrative. The claim that the Wagner Act cases marked a reversal of (or substantial departure from) the Court's earlier commerce clause jurisprudence has been received with near-unanimity by the scholarly community.[2] The conventional view is that the Court beat a "strategic retreat"[3] from its earlier jurisprudence.

This conventional wisdom has had a deleterious effect on our understanding of the development of commerce clause jurisprudence. The conceptualization of the Wagner Act cases as essentially political responses to political pressure has impoverished our understanding of commerce clause doctrine in two ways. First, the conventional learning ignores important conceptual and doctrinal continuities displayed both in Chief Justice Hughes' Wagner Act opinions and in decisions that followed in their wake. And second, the conventional wisdom understates the extent to which cases decided by the Roosevelt Court in the early 1940s were truly revolutionary.

This conventional wisdom is grounded in the potent combination of legal realism and Progressive historiography, critiqued in chapter 2, which has for decades served as the dominant paradigm for understanding the constitutional history of the late nineteenth and early twentieth centuries. On this view, dual federalism and substantive due process were merely convenient weapons in the arsenal of a reactionary Court devoted to maintaining the hegemony of corporate and financial elites at the expense of ordinary citizens. More recently, scholars have begun to challenge this view, persuasively contending that the doctrines of economic substantive due process were not simply spun out of thin air in order to protect the position of the robber barons of the Gilded Age. These doctrines, now understood as the juristic embodiments of such antebellum ideological commitments as Northern "free labor" ideology and the Jacksonian's egalitarian opposition to "class legislation," were in fact frequently deployed to the detriment of business interests.[4] Similarly, the roots of dual federalism may be seen in the ideological commitment to the preservation of liberty through the diffusion of power—a commitment that certainly antedated the Gilded Age, and can hardly be said to have been forged for the purpose of perpetuating elite hegemony.[5] In short, dual federalism and substantive due process were two conceptual manifestations of a well-established, integrated vision of civic liberty in the late-nineteenth- and early-twentieth-century- United States. We should not allow the fact that wealthy and powerful interests often manipulated these concepts to their advantage to cheapen our understanding.

This integrated vision of civic liberty was trenchantly set forth in a speech given by Chief Justice Melville Fuller before a joint session of Congress on the occasion of the centennial of George Washington's inauguration as president. Contemplating the future of the republic Washington had helped to create, Fuller spoke of two great dangers looming on the horizon.

> One was that "the drift toward the exertion of the national will" might ultimately result in "consolidation," which in turn would impair the "vital importance" of the states and undermine self-government by extending the sphere of legislative authority to such a degree that the people no longer controlled it. The other was "the drift . . . towards increased interference by the State in the attempt to alleviate inequality of conditions." Fuller admitted that "[S]o long as the interference is . . . protective only," it was not only legitimate but necessary. "But," he added, "the rights to life, to use one's faculties in all lawful ways, and to acquire and enjoy property, are morally fundamental rights antecedent to constitutions, which do not create, but secure and protect them."[6]

These concerns were of course to be manifested in the Fuller Court's commerce clause and due process jurisprudence. And just as the ideological commitments underlying these two areas of jurisprudence were part of an integrated vision of civic liberty for Fuller and many of his contemporaries, so during Fuller's tenure would the juridical manifestations of these commitments become integrated at the level of doctrine. As we saw in Part III, commerce clause jurisprudence was intimately entwined with substantive due process doctrine. A finding that a business's employment relations could have a direct effect on interstate commerce might provide the commercial police power rationale justifying federal labor regulations that would otherwise infringe liberty of contract. In this Part we find that this doctrinal cross-pollination flowed both ways. Not only did commerce clause jurisprudence inform due process jurisprudence; due process concepts informed commerce clause concepts as well. As a result, the two areas of doctrine became developmentally interdependent. Accordingly, just as developments in commerce clause jurisprudence implied transformations of due process doctrine, so changes in due process doctrine foretold modifications of commerce clause doctrine.

With this understanding, we can begin to trace the ways in which these constitutional conceptions evolved to the point that they could work a "constitutional revolution." We can see how these conceptions were forged and molded in the hands of the justices; how they were grasped, manipulated, and deployed by legislators framing statutes and lawyers selecting test cases and crafting legal arguments; how these legal arguments resonated with the doctrinal categories comprising the constitutional culture and consciousness of the Hughes Court justices; and how these categories ultimately became irrelevant in the hands of a new generation of men appointed to the Court by Franklin Roosevelt.

9

A Stream of Legal Consciousness

Categories and Images

In 1869, Chief Justice Salmon P. Chase used the opportunity presented by *Texas v. White* to adumbrate the contours of the postbellum constitutional order. "[T]he perpetuity and indissolubility of the Union," Chase declared, "by no means implies the loss of distinct and individual existence, or the right of self-government by the States." Each of the several state governments were, like the federal government, "'endowed with all of the functions essential to separate and independent existence.'" "The preservation of the States," Chase concluded,

> and the maintenance of their governments, are as much within the design and care of the Constitution as the preservation of the Union and the maintenance of the National Government. The Constitution, in all its provisions, looks to an indestructible Union, composed of indestructible States.[1]

The aphoristic quality of Chase's dictum disposed it to repetition; and indeed, "'an indestructible Union, composed of indestructible States' quickly supplanted *E pluribus unum* as the motto of choice for conveying the essence of American federalism." Moreover, because judicial review had been securely established by 1869, to say that the maintenance of such a Union was "within the design and care of the Constitution" was to appoint the federal judiciary as its conservator.[2]

Espousing the constitutional cosmology expounded by Chase in *Texas v. White*, Supreme Court justices of the late nineteenth century elaborated the theory of constitutional government that Edward Corwin dubbed "dual federalism." Because the federal government was one of enumerated powers, argued exponents of dual federalism, and because the Tenth Amendment reserved all unenumerated powers to the states, state and federal authorities were absolutely sovereign within their respective spheres of power. These respective spheres of state and federal authority were completely separate and distinct: there was no area in which state and federal authority overlapped. If an entity or activity was subject to federal regulation, it was immune to state regulation, and conversely. The boundaries and diameters of these spheres of federal and state authority were, moreover, immutable and timeless, the necessary implications of our constitutional system.[3]

In practice, the theory of dual federalism yielded a narrow construction of the scope of the federal government's power to regulate commerce. Two antitrust prosecutions from the 1890s will serve to illustrate this proposition. In *United States v. E. C. Knight Co.*, the American Sugar Refining Company had, through acquisition of four Pennsylvania refining companies, obtained control over 98 percent of the sugar refining capacity of the United States. The federal government brought an action under the Sherman Antitrust Act, seeking to void the transactions by which the Pennsylvania refineries had been acquired. In an opinion teeming with the language of dual federalism, the Supreme Court rejected the government's prayer. "That which belongs to commerce is within the jurisdiction of the United States," wrote Chief Justice Fuller, "but that which does not belong to commerce is within the jurisdiction of the police power of the State." The refinement of sugar was held to be a subject within the jurisdiction of the states. "Commerce succeeds to manufacture," the Court held, "and is not a part of it." "It is vital," explained Fuller, "that the independence of the commercial power and of the police power, and the delimitation between them, however sometimes perplexing, should always be recognized and observed, for while the one furnishes the strongest bond of union, the other is essential to the autonomy of the States as required by our dual form of government." Fuller found support for the Court's position in Justice Lamar's opinion in *Kidd v. Pearson:*

> Manufacture is transformation—the fashioning of raw materials into a change of form for use. The functions of commerce are different. . . . If it be held that the term [commerce] includes the regulation of all such manufactures as are intended to be the subject of commercial transactions in the future, it is impossible to deny that it would also include all productive industries that contemplate the same thing. The result would be that Congress would be invested, to the exclusion of the States, with the power to regulate, not only manufactures, but also agriculture, horticulture, stock raising, domestic fishing, mining—in short, every branch of human industry.

Combinations to control domestic enterprise in manufacturing, the Court held, affected interstate commerce only *indirectly*. To be subject to the federal commerce power, the impact of an activity was required to be *direct*.[4]

Hopkins v. United States further illustrates the restrictions placed upon the commerce power by dual federalism. *Hopkins* involved a prosection of members of the Kansas City Livestock Exchange under the Sherman Antitrust Act. The Exchange was an association of commission merchants doing business at the Kansas City Stock Yards. The Exchange had adopted certain governing rules which, the Justice Department contended, constituted agreements in restraint of trade. The objectionable rules prohibited members from buying livestock from any Kansas City commission merchant who was not a member of the exchange, and fixed the commissions for the sale of livestock. For a unanimous Court, Justice Rufus Peckham held that the transactions engaged in by the commission merchants were purely local in nature and therefore did not fall within the scope of the Sherman Act.

> The sale or purchase of livestock as commission merchants at Kansas City is the business done, and its character is not altered because the larger proportion of the purchases and sales may be of livestock sent into the State from other States or from the Territories. Where the stock came from or where it may ultimately go after a sale or purchase, procured through the services of one of the defendants at the Kansas City stock yards, is not the substantial factor in this case. The character of the business of the defendant must, in this case, be determined by the facts occurring at that city. . . . we regard the [commission merchant's] services as collateral to such [interstate] commerce and in the nature of a local aid or facility provided for the cattle owner towards the accomplishment of his purpose to sell them; and an agreement among those who render the services relating to the terms upon which they will render them is not a contract in restraint of interstate trade or commerce.[5]

Existing alongside of dual federalism as a restraint on governmental regulatory power was the distinction between public and private enterprise found in the Court's due process jurisprudence. At common law, the state was clothed with a general police power to regulate private business for the protection of public health, safety, and morals. Governmental regulation of prices charged for goods and services, however, was limited to "businesses affected with a public interest." The doctrine of a business affected with a public interest was first introduced into American constitutional law in *Munn v. Illinois*, a case involving the validity of an Illinois statute regulating rates for grain elevators. There a seven-man majority upheld the Illinois regulation against charges that it deprived the petitioner of his property without due process of law in violation of the Fourteenth Amendment. Holding that the grain elevator owned by Munn was a business affected with a public interest and therefore subject to reasonable regulation for the public good, Chief Justice Waite's majority opinion described the elevator as standing "in the very gateway of commerce, taking toll from all who pass."[6]

This language might seem more appropriate to the discussion of an issue concerning the commerce power than to discussion of a due process issue; and indeed, the common law doctrine from which Waite was borrowing had been developed in part to prevent exorbitant charges for necessary services from impeding the flow of commercial traffic. The image of a gateway of commerce was to be echoed in later commerce clause discourse, as the Court, while retaining the public interest doctrine as a due process restraint on state and federal regulatory authority, also sought to reunite the doctrine with its early commercial traffic rationale by transplanting it to the Court's commerce clause jurisprudence. Waite's invocation of commerce language in discussing a due process issue, then, foreshadowed the profound conceptual interrelation that later justices were to forge between those two areas of doctrine.[7]

Justice Field, joined by Justice Strong, filed a vigorous dissent. Envisioning an onslaught of business regulation and an end to property rights as he knew them, Field offered a generally applicable, bright-line distinction between public and private enterprise. Only where the owner enjoyed some special government-conferred privilege, Field contended, was his business affected with a public interest. The doctrine adopted by the majority, he lamented, would sanction price regulation of everything "from a calico gown to a city mansion."[8]

Yet despite the concerns of Justice Field, the class of businesses that the Court recognized as being affected with a public interest remained small for more than fifty years after *Munn*. In 1923, Chief Justice Taft identified three general classes of businesses affected with a public interest:

> (1) Those which are carried on under the authority of a public grant of privileges which either expressly or impliedly imposes the affirmative duty of rendering a public service demanded by any member of the public. Such are the railroads, other common carriers and public utilities.
>
> (2) Certain occupations, regarded as exceptional . . . Such are those of the keepers of inns, cabs and grist mills. . . .
>
> (3) Businesses which though not public at their inception may be fairly said to have risen to be such and have become subject in consequence to some government regulation. They have come to hold such a peculiar relation to the public that this is superimposed upon them. In the language of the cases, the owner by devoting his business to the public use, in effect grants the public an interest in that use and subjects himself to public regulation to the extent of that interest although the property continues to belong to its private owner and to be entitled to protection accordingly. . . .[9]

The select nature of membership in this third class of businesses affected with a public interest is illustrated by the fact that, *Munn* included, the Court cited only eight Supreme Court cases over a forty-six year period in which a statute had been upheld as a valid regulation of a business affected with a public interest.[10] Moreover, the Court's opinion evinced an intent to keep Taft's third class of businesses affected with a public interest narrow:

> It has never been supposed, since the adoption of the Constitution, that the business of the butcher, or the baker, the tailor, the wood chopper, the mining operator or the miner was clothed with such a public interest that the price of his product or his wages could be fixed by state regulation . . . nowadays one does not devote one's property or business to the public use or clothe it with a public interest merely because one makes commodities for, and sells to, the public in the common callings of which those above mentioned are instances.

Indeed, perhaps fearing the parade of horribles described by Field in his *Munn* dissent, Taft sought to define the contours of the third class of businesses affected with a public interest:

> In nearly all the businesses included under the third head above, the thing which gave the public interest was *the indispensable nature of the service and the exorbitant charges and arbitrary control to which the public might be subjected without regulation.*[11]

The concept of a business affected with a public interest became incorporated into commerce clause doctrine in an extremely important way in 1905. *Swift & Co.*

v. United States involved, in the words of Justice Holmes, a prosecution under the Sherman Act charging

> a combination of a dominant proportion of the dealers in fresh meat throughout the United States not to bid against each other in the live stock markets of the United States, to bid up prices for a few days in order to induce the cattle men to send their stock to the stock yards, to fix prices at which they will sell, and to that end to restrict shipments of meat when necessary, to establish a uniform rule of credit to dealers and to keep a black list, to make uniform and improper charges for cartage, and finally, to get less than lawful rates from the railroads to the exclusion of competitors.[12]

Holding the activities of the packers to be within the reach of the federal commerce power and thereby opening the first chink in the armor of dual federalism, Justice Holmes wrote:

> . . . commerce among the States is not a technical legal conception, but a practical one, drawn from the course of business. When cattle are sent for sale from a place in one State, with the expectation that they will end their transit, after purchase, in another, and when in effect they do so, with only the interruption necessary to find a purchaser at the stock yards, and when this is a typical, constantly recurring course, the current thus existing is a current of commerce among the States, and the purchase of the cattle is a part and incident of such commerce.[13]

This language could of course easily have been deployed to sustain the prosecution in *Hopkins.* Indeed, District Judge Cassius Foster had coined the term "current of commerce" in upholding the government's prosecution of the Kansas City Live Stock Exchange. When the current of commerce theory had been offered to the Supreme Court on appeal in 1898, however, the justices had unanimously rejected it.[14] In persuading those of his brethren who had so recently eschewed the current of commerce theory, therefore, Holmes was accordingly obliged to articulate a distinction between the facts of *Hopkins* and those of *Swift,* and mere location in a current of interstate commerce would not suffice. "All that was decided there," wrote Holmes,

> was that the local business of commission merchants was not commerce among the States, even if what the brokers were employed to sell was an object of such commerce. The brokers were not like the defendants before us, themselves the buyers and sellers. They only furnished certain facilities for the sales. Therefore, there again the effects of the combination of brokers upon the commerce was only indirect and not within the act. *Whether the case would have been different if the combination had resulted in exorbitant charges, was left open.*[15]

The clear implication of the highlighted language was noted by Chief Justice Taft in *Stafford v. Wallace:*

> . . . if the result of the combination of commission men in the *Hopkins Case* had been to impose exorbitant charges on the passage of livestock through the stockyards from

one State to another, the case would have been different . . . The effect on interstate commerce in such a case would have been direct.[16]

The language employed to distinguish *Hopkins* by Holmes in *Swift* and by Taft in *Stafford* is of course the language Taft used in *Wolff Packing* to describe the third class of businesses affected with a public interest. Indeed, between 1898, when *Hopkins* was handed down, and 1905, when *Swift* was decided, the Court had determined that stockyards were a business affected with a public interest.[17]

Holmes had made two significant conceptual moves here. First, by identifying the capacity to affect commerce directly with the capacity to exact exorbitant charges, Holmes effectively conflated the direct/indirect distinction of *Knight* with the public/private distinction of *Munn*. A business affected with a public interest had the capacity to affect commerce directly; a purely private business did not. Second, by accepting the concept of a current of commerce into the constitutional lexicon, Holmes threatened to bring business activities previously considered purely local within the reach of the federal commerce power.

Both of these moves were of course the stuff of a dual federalist's nightmare. If every business affected with a public interest had the capacity to affect interstate commerce directly, then every such business would be subject to federal regulation, and the police powers of the states would be greatly curtailed. Likewise, in an economy becoming increasingly integrated on a national scale, there was virtually no end to the list of business activities that could be conceived as existing in a current of commerce.

Holmes wrote *Swift* for a unanimous Court of justices reared on dual federalism, and the solution he implicitly proposed to this dilemma was simple yet ingenious: the two concepts, that of a current of commerce and that of a business affected with a public interest, would operate as reciprocal restraints on federal power and would, to an extent, become conflated. An intrastate business affected with a public interest could not be reached by the federal commerce power unless it could be located within a current of interstate commerce, and an intrastate business activity did not constitute part of a federally regulable current of commerce unless it was also a business affected with a public interest. In short, the current of commerce came to be understood as a sequence of interstate business activities connected by intrastate business activities affected with a public interest. Because the category of businesses affected with a public interest promised to remain small and select, the current of commerce promised to cut a narrow channel. The expansive potential of the fluid image of a current of commerce would be held in check by the inflexible, categorical distinction between public and private enterprise. The realities of a nationally integrated economy could thus be acknowledged by the Constitution without dismantling the categories of dual federalism or significantly altering the balance of intergovernmental authority. Holmes' current of commerce image accordingly did not threaten to undermine the values that underwrote the categorical distinctions of dual federalism.

This odd blend of image and category formed a neat compromise between the categorical, deductive, essentialist mode of judging often summed up in the term "formalism," and the more consequentialist or "realistic" style associated with sociological jurisprudence and its intellectual progeny. It was this conceptually hybrid understanding of the current of commerce that prevailed throughout the 1920s and, I shall argue, throughout the 1930s as well.[18]

The Current of Commerce, 1921–1930

Stafford v. Wallace brought to the Court the issue of the constitutionality of the Packers and Stockyards Act of 1921.[19] The Act authorized the secretary of agriculture to regulate the business of meat packers done in interstate commerce, and forbade the packers from engaging in any unfair, discriminatory, or deceptive practices in interstate commerce. Title III of the Act authorized the secretary to regulate transactions in the stockyards, including the rates to be charged for stockyard services and the fees to be charged by commission men making sales of stock in interstate commerce. The constitutionality of the Act was challenged by commission men doing business at the Union Stock Yards in Chicago.

The definition of commerce set forth in Title I betrayed the debt of the Act's draftsmen to Holmes. That definition provided in pertinent part:

> a transaction in respect to any article shall be considered to be in commerce if such article is part of that current of commerce usual in the live-stock and meat-packing industries, whereby live stock . . . are sent from one State with the expectation that they will end their transit, after purchase, in another. . . .

In its defense of the bill's constitutionality, the report of the House Committee on Agriculture relied heavily on *Swift*. Distinguishing *Hopkins*, the report stated that "Congress in treating this question is attempting to regulate evils which it had found to exist in respect to exorbitant charges and unreasonable practices in the stockyards, resulting in a direct burden on interstate commerce."[20]

Floor debate over the bill's constitutionality focused on two issues: first, whether the transactions taking place in the stockyards were in interstate commerce, opponents wielding *Hopkins* while proponents brandished *Swift*; and second, whether the stockyards were a business affected with a public interest. But the debates revealed more than merely a congressional desire to comply with the requirements of the commerce clause and the Fifth Amendment. Even as the legislators groped for analogies, humorously debating whether the Chicago stockyards were more like a railroad bridge or a hotel for pigs, a general understanding that only businesses affected with a public interest were part of a federally regulable stream of commerce informed the colloquy.[21] The Holmesian conflation of due process and commerce clause doctrines had become a working premise of congressional constitutional thought.

Holmes' formula had become received doctrine in the judicial branch as well, and the Act was accorded a warm reception before the High Court. "Whatever amounts to more or less constant practice," the Court declared in *Stafford*,

> and threatens to obstruct or unduly burden the freedom of interstate commerce is within the regulatory power of Congress under the commerce clause, and it is primar-

ily for Congress to consider and decide the fact of the danger and meet it. This Court will certainly not substitute its judgment for that of Congress in such a matter unless the relation of the subject to interstate commerce and its effect upon it are clearly non-existent.[22]

Taken at face value, this pronouncement would seem to have wrought a constitutional revolution beyond the wildest dreams of the most avid New Dealer; and, indeed, had it been so understood, the events of 1937 would lose some of their interest. Yet these words were not written by Holmes or Brandeis, but by Chief Justice William Howard Taft, a man who, though his health was failing badly in 1930, hesitated to resign from the Court because he distrusted Herbert Hoover as a "progressive."[23] The Court's deferential declaration must, therefore, be understood against the backdrop of Holmes' formulation, a formulation with which the *Stafford* analysis of the commerce power is suffused.

Taft initially identified as the goal of the Act the "unburdened flow" of livestock from West to East, unencumbered by "exorbitant charges."[24] The chief justice then proceeded to make his adoption of Holmes' formulation explicit:

> The stockyards are not a place of rest or final destination. Thousands of head of livestock arrive daily by carload and trainload lots, and must be promptly sold and disposed of and moved out to give place to the constantly flowing traffic that presses behind. The stockyards are but a throat through which the current flows, and the transactions which occur there are only incident to this current of commerce from the West to the East, and from one State to another. Such transactions can not be separated from the movement to which they contribute and necessarily take on its character. The commission men are *essential* in making the sales without which the flow of the current would be obstructed, and this, whether they are made to packers or dealers. The dealers are *essential* to the sales to the stock farmers and feeders. The sales are not in this aspect merely local transactions. They create a local change of title, it is true, but they do not stop the flow; they merely change the private interests in the subject of the current, not interfering with, but, on the contrary, being *indispensable* to its continuity. The origin of the live stock is in the West, its ultimate destination known to, and intended by, all engaged in the business is in the Middle West and East either as meat products or stock for feeding and fattening. This is the definite and well-understood course of business. The stockyards and the sales are *necessary factors* in the middle of this current of commerce.[25]

Having described the stockyards in the very language of "indispensability" he used to characterize his third class of businesses affected with a public interest in *Wolff Packing*, Taft drew his conclusion:

> The act, therefore, treats the various stockyards of the country as *great national public utilities* to promote the flow of commerce from the ranges and farms of the West to the consumers in the East. It assumes that they conduct a *business affected by a public use* of a national character and subject to national regulation. That it is a business within the power of regulation by legislative action needs no discussion. That has been settled since the case of *Munn v. Illinois*. . . . The only question here is whether the business done in the stockyards between the receipt of the live stock and the ship-

ment of them therefrom is a part of interstate commerce, or is so associated with it as to bring it within the power of national regulation.[26]

Applying the principles set forth in *Swift* to the findings of fact reproduced here, Taft answered the question posed in the affirmative, upholding the Act as a valid exercise of the federal commerce power. Justice McReynolds dissented without opinion, while Justice Day took no part in the decision of the case. Justice Van Devanter, later to be described, with Justice McReynolds, as one of the "Four Horsemen," voted with the majority.

A portion of Taft's discussion of *Swift* is worthy of some attention. "The application of the commerce clause of the Constitution in the *Swift Case*," wrote the chief justice,

> was the result of the natural development of interstate commerce under modern conditions. It was the inevitable recognition of the great central fact that such streams of commerce from one part of the country to another which are ever flowing are in their very essence the commerce among the States and with foreign nations which historically it was one of the chief purposes of the Constitution to bring under national protection and control. This court declined to defeat this purpose in respect of such a stream and take it out of complete national regulation by a nice and technical inquiry into the non-interstate character of some of its necessary incidents and facilities when considered alone and without reference to their association with the movement of which they were an essential but subordinate part.[27]

One can see Taft in this passage squinting in the direction of the commerce clause thought of New Dealers: the modern conditions of interstate commerce must be taken into account, and business activities should not be removed from the realm of federal power by nice and technical inquiries. Yet Taft's squinting was done through a set of conceptual lenses that limited the reach of his vision. In Taft's jurisprudential *Weltanschauung*, the distinction between public and private enterprise was not nice and technical, but true and immutable. Taft could speak expansively on judicial deference to congressional determinations and somewhat realistically about interstate commerce because he assumed the immutability of the jurisprudential backdrop against which he spoke. So long as the essential categories of substantive due process jurisprudence remained intact, so long as the public/private distinction informed commerce clause doctrine, the current of commerce doctrine posed no serious threat to the dual federalist order.

THE 1921 CONGRESS also enacted the Futures Trading Act, which sought to regulate sales of grain futures on boards of trade by taxing such sales at a prohibitive rate and then exempting from the tax all sales on boards of trade complying with federal regulations. The Act was declared an unconstitutional exercise of the taxing power in *Hill v. Wallace*.[28] Writing for a unanimous Court, Chief Justice Taft held that sales of grain futures on boards of trade were not per se interstate commerce, and that Congress therefore could not use its taxing power to regulate indirectly a business activity not within federal control. In dicta, however, the chief justice all but requested that Congress pass an act modeled on the Packers and Stockyards Act.[29]

Congress was not slow in responding to Taft's invitation. On September 21, 1922, the Grain Futures Act[30] became law. The Act adopted, mutatis mutandis, the definition of commerce set forth in the Packers and Stockyards Act.[31] Moreover, section 3 of the Act explicitly characterized the sale of grain futures on boards of trade as a business "affected with a national public interest."[32]

The report of the Senate Committee on Agriculture and Forestry defended the constitutionality of the bill on the authority of *Swift*, *Stafford*, and *New York and Chicago Grain & Stock Exchange v. Chicago Board of Trade*, wherein the Supreme Court of Illinois had held, invoking the language of *Munn*, that "the floors of this exchange hall stand in the gateway of commerce." Indeed, floor debate on the bill's constitutionality focused entirely on whether grain exchanges were located in a current of interstate commerce: even the bill's opponents conceded that boards of trade were businesses affected with a public interest and accordingly subject to regulation by the governments of the states in which they were located.[33]

The Grain Futures Act survived constitutional challenge in *Chicago Board of Trade v. Olsen*. Writing for a seven-man majority,[34] Chief Justice Taft immediately located the grain exchange in a current of interstate commerce.[35] Indeed, Taft noted, insofar as the case concerned "the cash grain, the sales to arrive, and the grain actually delivered in fulfillment of future contracts," it was indistinguishable from *Stafford*.[36] Addressing himself specifically to the effect of sales of grain futures on this current of commerce, Taft formulated the questions before the Court thus:

> The question is whether the conduct of such sales is subject to constantly recurring abuses which are a burden and obstruction to interstate commerce in grain? And further, are they such an incident of that commerce and so intermingled with it that the burden and obstruction caused therein by them can be said to be direct?[37]

Echoing the deferential posture the Court had struck in *Stafford*, Taft noted that Congress had specifically answered that question affirmatively in the text of the Act. Reviewing the evidence before the Court, Taft concluded that the justices would have been unwarranted in rejecting this finding of Congress as unreasonable. It was clear, he noted, that "manipulations of grain futures for speculative profit" exerted "a vicious influence and produce[d] abnormal and disturbing temporary fluctuations in prices" that "disturb[ed] the normal flow of actual consignments." By virtue of its singular capacity to exert such extraordinary influence on wheat prices, the Court held, following *Munn* and *Stafford*, that the Chicago Board of Trade was a business affected with a national public interest and was accordingly subject to federal regulation.[38]

Justice McReynolds again dissented without opinion, this time joined by Justice Sutherland, who had replaced Justice Clarke on October 2, 1922. Justice Van Devanter again voted with the majority, this time joined by the man destined to become the Fourth Horseman: Justice Pierce Butler, who replaced Justice Day on January 3, 1923.

THE PACKERS AND STOCKYARDS ACT came under attack again in *Tagg. Bros. & Moorhead v. United States*. There a group of commission agencies doing business in Omaha's Union Stockyards sought to enjoin the secretary of agriculture from regulating their fees. *Stafford* required the commission men to concede that they were engaged in interstate commerce at a public stockyards and were therefore subject to some Congressional regulation. They contended, however, that the rates charged for their services could not be regulated because their business was not affected with a public interest. The commission men argued essentially that only capital-intensive businesses could be affected with a public interest, that their business was labor- rather than capital-intensive, that rate-fixing for labor-intensive businesses constituted wage-fixing in violation of the Fifth Amendment, and that the commissions they charged for the sale of livestock therefore could not be regulated by Congress.[39]

The Court, in an opinion authored by Justice Brandeis, unanimously rejected the plaintiffs' contentions. "There is nothing in the nature of monopolistic personal services," wrote Brandeis,

> which makes it impossible to fix reasonable charges to be made therefor; and there is nothing in the Constitution which limits the Government's power of regulation to businesses which employ substantial capital. . . . Plaintiffs perform *an indispensable service in the interstate commerce in livestock.* They enjoy a substantial monopoly at the Omaha Stock Yards. . . . The purpose of the regulation attacked is to prevent their service from thus becoming an undue burden upon, and obstruction of, that commerce. [Citing *Stafford* and *Olsen.*][40]

Tagg Bros. reaffirmed Holmes' conflation of commerce clause and due process doctrines in an important way. The plaintiffs had sought to drive a wedge between the current of commerce doctrine and the public/private distinction, and the Court had unanimously rebuffed them. To be in the current of commerce, the Court said in effect, was to be a business affected with a public interest. In fact, the Court never once held that a business activity was located in a current of commerce but was beyond congressional rate regulation because it was not a business affected with a public interest.[41] Within the current of commerce doctrine, the conflation of the direct/indirect distinction with the public/private distinction was complete. When Edward Corwin argued that the Supreme Court had converted the direct/indirect distinction "into a sort of due process clause protective of state power,"[42] he wrote truer than he knew.

THE ROOT DISTINCTION of dual federalism opposed that which was local to that which was national. The dynamism of the current of commerce doctrine lay in its capacity to compromise this root distinction. A business activity that, when considered separately, was local, could nevertheless be rendered subject to national regulation if it could be characterized as a business affected with a public interest located in a current of interstate commerce. Yet despite its dynamic potential, current of commerce doctrine fit comfortably into the body of early-twentieth-century commerce clause jurisprudence, largely because it shared with that body of doctrine certain core assumptions about the nature of the federal commerce power.

Swift, Stafford, and *Olsen* could happily coexist in the minds of Taft Court justices with an array of cases in which a business activity was held to be beyond federal regulation or within the regulatory power of a state because it transpired at one of the *terminals* of a flow of interstate commerce. A few examples will suffice. In *United Mine Workers v. Coronado Coal Co.* and *United Leather Workers v. Herkert & Meisel Trunk Co.*, the Court held labor strikes at a coal mine and a trunk factory to be beyond the reach of federal jurisdiction under the Sherman Act. In the absence of a showing of a specific intent to restrain commerce, the Court held, strikes by the employees of enterprises engaged in production were local matters subject only to local regulation. Commerce succeeded to production, and was not a part of it.[43] In *Sonneborn Bros. v. Cureton*, the Court unanimously upheld a state wholesale sales tax on oil that included in its base local sales of oil shipped to Texas from outside the state. Rejecting the claim that the tax burdened interstate commerce in oil, the Court held that the oil had "come to rest" within the state in the company's warehouse, where it was held for local sale; and having thus become commingled with the general mass of property within the state, the oil was subject to state taxation. And in *Hygrade Provision Co. v. Sherman*, the Court upheld a New York statute regulating the sale of kosher meats against the contention that the regulation burdened interstate commerce. Once the meat had come to rest within the state and was held solely for local disposition and use, held the Court, it fell within the state's regulatory bailiwick, despite the fact that the regulation might "incidentally affect interstate commerce."[44]

In these cases, as in the current of commerce cases and other commerce cases of the period, commerce was "conceived of primarily as *transportation*."[45] "In light of the opinions of the United States Supreme Court," wrote Professor Ribble of the University of Virginia in 1934, "interstate commerce may be fairly described as movement, subject, at least in part, to human direction or control, which movement starts in one state and continues into another."[46] The commerce clause jurisprudence of the period, noted Edward Corwin a year later, betrayed "the Court's mental image of the interstate commerce process as a *physical movement merely* of goods from one state to another."[47] The current of commerce doctrine, noted Ribble, sought to deal with "practices which obstructed the flow of commerce among the states."[48] The existence of such "obstructions" to the interstate movement or transportation of goods, and the need for their removal, was the very focus of the doctrine.[49] The current of commerce doctrine could peacefully coexist with Taft Court commerce clause jurisprudence because it rested on this conception of commerce as physical movement.[50]

Yet despite this apparently cozy fit, the current of commerce doctrine contained within itself the potential for a terrific breach of interdoctrinal harmony. For the current of commerce doctrine was necessarily a slightly volatile exception to the pristine, symmetrical rules of dual federalism. And McReynolds in *Stafford*, joined by Sutherland in *Olsen*, had undoubtedly seen that it was an exception that could eventually swallow the rules. The public/private distinction helped to hold this volatility in check, but the fact remained that the current of commerce doctrine had the capacity to transform the local into the national. The production/commerce distinction was derived from the root local/national distinction, and the capacity to compromise the borders of the latter necessarily entailed the power to compromise those of the former. Indeed, both *Swift* and *Stafford* had suggested that the slaughter and packing of meat, both activities of production, occurred in the current of commerce.[51] The Court had never suggested that a production facility located in a current of interstate commerce caused a "break" in the current or was otherwise beyond federal regulation. The dicta in *Swift* and *Stafford* intimated that any tension between the current of commerce doctrine and the production/commerce distinction would be resolved in favor of the former. To borrow a metaphor from contract bridge, the current of commerce doctrine was trump.

The threat that the current of commerce doctrine posed to the production/commerce distinction was not lost on contemporary commentators.[52] In his 1931 presidential address before the American Political Science Association, Edward Corwin told his audience,

> in "the typical and actual course of events," even manufacturing becomes but a stage in the flow of the raw product to the mill and the out-flow of the finished product from the mill to the market; and while checking momentarily the current of interstate commerce, is at the same time, to adapt the words of Chief Justice Taft in *Stafford v. Wallace*, "indispensable to its continuity."

Discussing the current of commerce doctrine three years later, Corwin recapitulated this theme.

> What we are called upon to vision is a current which has its source in certain acts, or procedures, of production; which takes its way across the country with ever increasing volume and without interruption by, or even awareness of, state lines; which comes to pause now and again in an eddy, as it were, for certain further operations and transactions, including again acts of production (the preparation of meat products, fattening on the farms), but which ever resumes its flow to its diverse and nation-spread destination. . . .

And in 1936, writing for a lay audience on the eve of the CIO sit-down strikes in the automobile industry, Robert Carr noted that

> certain . . . enterprises, while not interstate in themselves, are nevertheless related to others that are, and for that reason become subject to federal control. What, for instance, of the manufacture of automobiles? The construction of a Ford in Detroit is not interstate commerce, but the steel and rubber and paint that make up the car are brought to Detroit from a dozen different states, and the finished Fords will be sent to every state in the Union, for sale. Clearly, the entire process from beginning to end involves interstate commerce at a good many points. Is this close relationship between the different steps that make up the complete process sufficient to enable Congress to regulate those steps that are not interstate along with those that are?[53]

Carr would not have long to wait for an answer.

Born in 1905 and nurtured through the 1920s, Holmes' formula was by the beginning of the New Deal decade a staple of American constitutional jurisprudence. In the decade to come it would undergo significant transformation, and by the decade's end it would be of little more than historical interest. Before its demise, however, it was to serve as the conceptual foundation of one of the more important events in the nation's legal history.

The Importance of *Nebbia v. New York*

In 1923, a group of the nation's most distinguished lawyers, jurists, and law professors formed the American Law Institute (ALI).[54] Among the founders were Charles Evans Hughes, former associate justice of the Supreme Court, Harlan Fiske Stone, dean of Columbia University School of Law, and Benjamin Cardozo, a judge on the New York Court of Appeals.[55] Troubled by the uncertainty and complexity of the common law in America, the founders of the ALI proposed to undertake the enormously ambitious task of "restating" it.[56] The inauguration of the National Reporter system in the 1870s had by the 1920s produced an avalanche of reported decisions "that made it impossible for judges and lawyers to stay properly informed."[57] The founders of the institute believed that "out of the overwhelming mass of law cases and legal literature clearer statements of the rules of the common law in effect in a great majority of the states could be made and expressed."[58] This would require that "the thousands upon thousands of decisions of courts be reduced to a systematic, concise statement of the law."[59] The institute's objective was "to promote the clarification and simplification of the law and its better adaptation to social needs."[60]

Many of the chief draftsmen on the Restatement projects, such as Samuel Williston and Austin Scott, were the authors of "massive treatises in the strict, conceptual, Langdell mold";[61] and the task of "restating" the law, while not necessarily a "formalist" exercise,[62] was of course a Langdellian enterprise.[63] The restaters would take a complex and unwieldy body of case law and extract from it its essential elements; from the thousands of reported cases on a given area of the law they would synthesize lean and clear rules of general application.[64] Beginning with the *Restatement of the Law of Contracts* in 1932, the institute published a series of Restatements of the principal areas of the common law: *Agency* in 1933, *Torts* and *Conflict of Laws* in 1934, and *Trusts* in 1935.[65] Between 1928 and 1935 the ALI also published tentative drafts of Restatements for the areas of business associations, property, and sales of land.[66] Just as the Supreme Court was confronting the issues of the constitutionality of the New Deal, the Langdellian task of restating the common law was proceeding apace.

By 1934, Hughes, Stone, and Cardozo, founders of the Restatement projects, had taken seats on the United States Supreme Court. And by that year it appears that these charter members of the Restatement movement, who came to legal maturity in the era of Langdellian hegemony, had begun to impress the Restatement methodology upon the nation's *constitutional* law.[67]

Nowhere was this impress more evident than in the case of *Nebbia v. New York*.[68] There, we recall, the Court turned back a substantive due process challenge to a New York agency's regulation of milk prices. In rejecting the contention that the price of milk could not be regulated because its production and sale were not businesses affected with a public interest, the Court retired the categorical distinction between public and private enterprise.[69] The Court declined to resolve the dispute by reference to abstract categories. Instead, Justice Roberts' opinion presented a lengthy survey of instances in which exercises of the police power had been sustained, both generally[70] and in the regulation of prices.[71] Price regulation had been upheld with respect to railroads,[72] grain elevators,[73] premiums for fire insurance,[74] interest rates,[75] compensation of insurance agents,[76] attorneys' contingent fees,[77] stockyards,[78] and private contract carriers.[79] From this array of exceptions to what was arguably a general rule against price regulation, Justice Roberts distilled a general principle. "It is clear," he wrote, "that there is no closed class or category of businesses affected with a public interest." "The phrase, 'affected with a public interest' can, in the nature of things, mean no more than that an industry, for adequate reason, is subject to control for the public good."[80]

The breakdown of the public/private distinction signaled by *Nebbia* held dramatic potential consequences for commerce clause doctrine. The current of commerce, we recall, was conceived as a sequence of interstate business activities connected by intrastate business activities affected with a public interest. As long as the class of business activities affected with a public interest remained small, the channel cut by the current of commerce promised to remain narrow. With *Nebbia*, however, the restraint that the public/private distinction had imposed upon the current of commerce image was removed. Because *Nebbia* threw the class of businesses affected with a public interest wide open, the internal logic of the current of commerce doctrine impelled the Court toward a recognition of a broader conception of the current of commerce. *Nebbia* made it possible to conceptualize what had previously been considered purely private enterprises as businesses affected with a public interest. This in turn made it possible to locate such business activities in a current of commerce subject to federal control.

Moreover, the Court's inclination to look to the effects exerted by a business activity rather than to the nature of the business considered in a vacuum, to examine the business pragmatically rather than metaphysically, prefigured the Court's retreat from the inflexible, categorical distinction between direct and indirect burdens on commerce. The impact of this abandonment of the old public/private distinction on the direct/indirect distinction would be realized, however, only within the framework of the doctrine within which the two distinctions had become conflated. Only within the context of a dispute which could be conceptualized as a current of commerce case would *Nebbia*'s ramifications for *Swift*'s internal logic be worked out. For want of such an appropriately tailored case, the impact of *Nebbia* on commerce clause doctrine remained latent for the next three years. But in 1937, the fallout from *Nebbia* was to be felt in a dramatic and often misunderstood way.

10

Catching the Current

Interlude: *Schechter Corp. v. United States*
and *Carter v. Carter Coal*

Schechter Corp. v. United States involved the conviction of a Brooklyn slaughter-house operator for several violations of the "Live Poultry Code."[1] The Live Poultry Code, promulgated pursuant to the National Industrial Recovery Act (NIRA),[2] contained provisions establishing, inter alia, minimum wages and maximum hours of labor.

The Schechter Corporation was a slaughterhouse operator that purchased live poultry from commission men in New York City and Philadelphia, slaughtered the purchased poultry at its Brooklyn slaughterhouse, and then sold the slaughtered poultry to local retail poultry dealers and butchers for direct sale to consumers. The corporation did not sell poultry in interstate commerce. The principals of the corporation were convicted of violating, inter alia, the provisions of the code pertaining to minimum wages and maximum hours.

The lawyers in the Justice Department had not intended for *Schechter* to be the case in which the Court would determine the constitutionality of the NIRA. The department had been preparing *United States v. Belcher*,[3] a prosecution for violation of the wage and hour provisions of the Lumber and Timber Code, to serve as the NIRA test case. As the April 8, 1935, date for Supreme Court oral argument approached, however, department lawyers began to doubt the prudence of using *Belcher* as the vehicle for a constitutional test. Due both to doubts concerning the Lumber Code's constitutionality and the lack of a full trial record, the department requested March 25 that the case be dismissed. The Court granted the department's motion to dismiss the following week.[4]

The failure of NRA and department lawyers to formulate "a coherent litigation strategy pointed toward a strong, well-prepared constitutional test case"[5] had now left the administration without any promising test vehicles on the horizon. The NIRA was due to expire of its own terms in June and, as the *New York Times* and numerous other anti-NIRA commentators observed, the administration was "now in the indefensible position of urging Congress to extend with slight modifications an act the constitutionality of which it is deliberately refusing to test."[6] Fortuitously, the Second Circuit upheld the Schechters' conviction on the very day that *Belcher* was dismissed.[7] Due to the lateness in the Court's term, however, the case would not be heard by the Court until the following autumn unless the government requested expedited review. The statute might in the meantime expire or be re-enacted in modified form, in which event the Court would be less likely to grant certiorari and the necessity for a constitutional test might be avoided.[8] Donald Richberg, however, was able to convince Roosevelt that "the morale of the [NRA], already at a low ebb in coping with the herculean task of enforcement and facing widespread noncompliance, could not endure any further temporizing."[9] And so, against the advice of Felix Frankfurter and Tommy Corcoran, Solicitor General Reed requested expedited appeal April 11.[10]

Justice Department lawyers doubted from the beginning that the Schechters' slaughterhouse operations fell within the federal regulatory bailiwick. In particular, department attorneys "were uneasy about the evidentiary underpinnings of the commerce clause argument. They recognized that reliance on the expansive line of Supreme Court precedent required a showing of some 'burden' on an uninter-rupted 'stream of commerce. . . . '"[11] Blackwell Smith, acting general counsel to the NRA, hoped to base the defense of the NIRA on the current of commerce doc-trine. "May it not be possible," he asked, "to show that poultry when processed in New York is reshipped to New Jersey, Connecticut, etc. . . . ? If such reshipment does occur we feel that the case can hardly be distinguished from the stockyards cases."[12] As Taft and his colleagues had in *Stafford*, Smith assumed that the fact that the poultry stopped at a local production facility to undergo a change in form did not take it out of a current of interstate commerce. Subsequent research, how-ever, revealed no evidence of subsequent interstate shipment to undergird a cur-rent of commerce argument.[13] A memorandum from Robert Stern outlined the weaknesses of the government's case and recommended against expediting the appeal. The relationship between local wages and interstate commerce was so attenuated, remarked Stern, that the Court would probably consider it "indirect."[14] Stern reported "that there was practically nothing in the record that supported the government's position under the Commerce clause," but he was told it was too late for the government to change its position.[15] Solicitor General Reed warned Roo-sevelt that *Schechter* involved "wages and hours of slaughter house employees after poultry has been received in New York. . . . This is the most difficult type of labor provision to maintain."[16] Eventually even Blackwell Smith came to view *Schechter* as "the weakest possible case."[17]

The nine justices of the Supreme Court could not have agreed more. In an opinion written by Hughes, the Court unanimously reversed the convictions. The Court first held that, because the NIRA was an unconstitutional delegation of authority, the code enacted pursuant to this authority was void. Second, the Court held that even were the code otherwise a valid regulation, it could not constitution-ally be applied to the defendants. Because the defendants were not engaged in interstate commerce, their activities were beyond the reach of federal regulation. "The undisputed facts," wrote Hughes, afford no warrant for the argument that the poultry handled by the defendants at their slaughterhouse markets was in a *"current"* or *"flow"* of interstate commerce and was thus subject to congressional regulation. The mere fact that there may be a constant flow of commodities into a State does not mean that the flow continues after the property has arrived and has become commingled with the mass of property within the State and is there held solely for local disposition and use. So far as the poultry here in question is concerned, the flow in interstate commerce had ceased. The poultry had come to a permanent rest within the State. It was not held, used, or sold by defendants in relation to any further transactions in interstate commerce and was not destined for transportation to other States. Hence, decisions which deal with a stream of interstate commerce—where goods come to rest within a State temporarily and are later to go forward in interstate commerce—and with the regulations of transactions involved in that practical continuity of movement, are not applicable here.[18]

Nor, the Court held, did the defendants' transactions exert a direct effect on interstate commerce. The government argued that a slaughterhouse operator paying lower wages or reducing his overhead through exacting long hours of work was enabled to cut his prices, and that such cuts in prices generated a demand for cheaper goods and demoralized the price structure, thereby affecting interstate commerce.[19] These effects on interstate commerce, the Court held, were merely indirect. Indeed, Hughes stated, were such effects considered direct, "the extent of the regulation of cost would be a question of discretion and not of power."[20]

Justice Cardozo filed a concurring opinion in which Justice Stone joined. Cardozo agreed that the NIRA constituted an unlawful delegation of authority; but he also registered "another objection, far-reaching and incurable." Regarding the power of Congress to regulate commerce, Cardozo wrote:

> I find no authority in that grant for the regulation of wages and hours of labor in the defendants' business. As to this feature of the case little can be added to the opinion of the court. There is a view of causation that would obliterate the distinction between what is national and what is local in the activities of commerce. . . . Activities local in their immediacy do not become interstate and national because of distant repercussions.

"To find immediacy or directness here," wrote Cardozo, "is to find it almost everywhere."[21]

The unanimity of the decision impressed contemporary commentators. Edward Corwin noted with some consternation that even the "liberal" members of the Court appeared to be thinking about the commerce power in rigidly categorical terms rather than in the more flexible, consequentialist terms of some younger legal thinkers. "In a word," wrote Corwin, "the conceptualism, the determination to resist the inrush of fact with the besom of formula, which pervades the Chief Justice's opinion for the Court, is not altogether absent from Justice Cardozo's opinion. . . ."[22] "When men like Stone, Cardozo, Brandeis and Hughes believe that the Constitution compels them to decide, as they did in this case," wrote the *New Republic*, "there is no point any longer in saying that the Constitution is infinitely flexible."[23] One might question the *New Republic's* conclusion without doubting its premise. The Constitution itself may or may not possess considerable elasticity; but in practice it is malleable only to the extent that its authoritative interpreters believe it to be so. Though Cardozo was beginning to offer a less rigidly formal way of thinking about commerce power issues,[24] he and his colleagues had inherited modes of thinking about such issues that were simply incompatible with the ways that government attorneys were (and subsequent Supreme Court justices would soon be) thinking about those issues.[25] Corwin and the editors at the *New Republic* were sensitive to the fact that the intellectual styles that these aging justices had inherited from an earlier era played a critical role in the New Deal saga.

Despite the unanimity of *Schechter*, proponents of federal regulation of the economy did not despair. Owen Nee, for example, commenting on the *Schechter* decision in the *Wisconsin Law Review*, still saw room for regulation of the nation's major industries under the current of commerce theory. "The major group of industries over which it would seem there was the greatest likelihood of a constitutional federal control," he wrote, "are those in which raw materials are brought in from out of state to be manufactured into articles to be sold out of state, for example, enterprises such as General Motors or the Ford Motor Company. This seems the exact situation which we find in the *Swift* case."[26] Like Corwin and Carr, Nee recognized that the *Swift* line of cases had provided a warrant for federal regulation of "local" activities of production.

In the wake of the *Schechter* decision, Congress enacted the Bituminous Coal Conservation Act of 1935 (the "Guffey Coal Act").[27] The statute's introductory section detailed the circumstances thought to justify the Act. That section declared, among other things, that the mining and distribution of bituminous coal throughout the United States were affected with a national public interest, that the production and distribution of coal by producers directly affected interstate commerce, and that the right of workers to organize and bargain collectively over terms of employment was necessary in order to avoid the recurring obstructions to interstate commerce in coal caused by labor disputes at the mines. Section 4 of the Act set out the substantive provisions in controversy. Part II of that section authorized a National Bituminous Coal Commission to regulate the price at which bituminous coal was sold in interstate commerce. Part III conferred upon the employees of coal producers the right to organize and to bargain collectively, and it created a labor board to adjudicate labor disputes in the coal industry.

The Wagner Act, which was also enacted in the wake of the *Schechter* decision, sailed through Congress with comparative ease and was passed by large majorities in both houses.[28] The Guffey Coal Act was not to have such an easy go of it. Hearings held before a subcommittee of the House Ways and Means Committee in June of 1935 focused primarily on the question of the bill's constitutionality. The subcommittee requested that Attorney General Cummings and Solicitor General Reed appear and offer their views concerning the bill's constitutional basis.[29] Lawyers in the Justice Department were convinced that the bill was unconstitutional in light of *Schechter*,[30] and, according to an unconfirmed report, had told Cummings as much before his appearance.[31] Cummings refused to opine concerning the bill's constitutionality, instead advising the subcommittee "to push it [the bill] through and leave the question to the courts."[32]

On July 5, the day of Cummings' appearance before the subcommittee, President Roosevelt sent a letter to the chairman of the subcommittee, Samuel B. Hill, pleading for a favorable recommendation. "Admitting that mining coal, considered separately and apart from its distribution in the flow of interstate commerce, is an intrastate transaction," wrote the president,

> the constitutionality of the provisions based on the commerce clause of the Constitution depends upon the final conclusion as to whether production conditions directly affect, promote, or obstruct interstate commerce in the commodity. Manifestly, no one is in a position to give assurance that the proposed act will withstand constitutional tests . . . [but] all doubts should be resolved in favor of the bill, leaving to the courts, in an orderly fashion, the ultimate question of constitutionality. . . . I hope your committee will not permit doubts as to constitutionality, however reasonable, to block the suggested legislation.[33]

Though four of the seven members of the subcommittee continued to believe the bill to be unconstitutional, the White House was able to get the bill reported to the full House Ways and Means Committee "without recommendation."[34]

The bill faced similar difficulties in the full committee. Eight of the committee's eighteen Democrats and six of its seven Republicans were known to oppose the bill. The Democratic members of the committee held a series of secret meetings throughout early August in an attempt to muster enough votes to secure a favorable report. On August 12, a meeting of the full committee was held, at which the bill was reported favorably by a vote of 12 to 11. As Representative Allen Treadway of North Carolina remarked, "[t]his was made possible by the simple expedient of having two members of the majority party withdraw their negative votes and answer 'Present.'"[35]

The report of the minority focused almost exclusively on the question of the bill's constitutionality. Representative Jere Cooper of Tennessee filed with the minority report a brief against the bill in which four of his colleagues concurred. Cooper contended that the current of commerce cases could offer no constitutional support for the bill. "In the *Schechter* case," Cooper argued, "it was pointed out that when the poultry was trucked to slaughterhouses in Brooklyn for local distribution, it became commingled with the mass of property within the State, and the flow of commerce ceased."[36] "In the case of mining or producing coal, interstate commerce has not even commenced, so the coal is still a part of the mass of property of the State of its production until it commences its final movement for transportation from the State of its origin to that of its destination."[37]

In the floor debates on the bill members of both houses repeatedly contested proponents' claims that the commerce clause authorized congressional regulation of coal mining.[38] Representative Allen Treadway of North Carolina produced a lengthy argument distinguishing the mining of coal from the activities regulated in the current of commerce cases. Like the local sale of poultry, coal mining occurred at one of the *terminals* of the current of commerce. Citing *Schechter's* dismissal of the current of commerce argument, Treadway contended that "[i]f decisions which deal with a stream of interstate commerce have no relevancy in a case where interstate commerce has ended, then it would seem that they would have no relevancy in a case where interstate commerce has not begun."[39] *Swift* provided no more authority for congressional regulation of the production of coal at the mine than it did for federal regulation of production of cattle on the farm. The current of commerce decisions authorized federal regulation of local activities only in instances in which such activities were located in a current of interstate commerce. Coal mining was not so situated.[40]

The closeness of the final votes on the bill reflected the seriousness of the legislators' constitutional doubts. Though Republicans now held fewer than 30 percent of the seats in the House,[41] the bill was passed by the comparatively narrow margin of 194 to 168.[42] And in the Senate, where Democrats now held sixty-nine of the ninety-six seats,[43] the bill squeaked through by a vote of 45 to 37.[44] Despite considerable administration pressure, both public and private, a substantial number of Democrats defied the president.[45] According to Congressman Bertrand Snell of New York, this was "the first time in the history of the country that the House passed a bill which was opposed by the subcommittee which wrote it, by the full committee which approved it, by the Rules committee which brought it out on the floor, and toward which the entire house organization was entirely indifferent."[46] In light of the comparatively large margins by which the Wagner Act was passed, it seems unlikely that the negative votes on the Guffey Act were motivated by any general animosity toward federal regulation of labor relations. Many members of Congress sincerely doubted the constitutionality of the Guffey Coal Act but not that of the Wagner Act.[47] The feelings of many were summed up by Senator Tydings' ominous forecast of the Act's future: "Like an autumn flower it will be blown away by the first winter blast of the court."[48]

As Tydings predicted, the Supreme Court would soon vindicate the doubts of the minority. In an opinion written by Justice Sutherland, the Court held that part III was an unconstitutional attempt by Congress to regulate labor relations in the purely local activity of coal production. Denying the applicability of *Swift* and *Stafford*, the Court remarked: "It was nowhere suggested in these cases that the interstate commerce power extended to the growth or production of the things which, after production, entered the flow."[49]

> The restricted field covered by the *Swift* and kindred cases is illustrated by the *Schechter* case. . . . There the commodity in question, although shipped from another state, had come to rest in the state of its destination, and, as the Court pointed out, was no longer in a current or flow of interstate commerce. The *Swift* doctrine was rejected as inapposite. In the Schechter case the flow had ceased. Here it had not begun. The difference is not one of substance. The applicable principle is the same.[50]

The local production of coal was neither itself interstate commerce, nor was it part of a current of commerce, nor, the Court held, did it directly affect interstate commerce. Despite the Act's severability clause, the Court held that part III was not separable from the price-regulation provisions of part II.[51] Accordingly, the majority struck down the Act in its entirety.

Chief Justice Hughes filed a separate opinion in which he agreed that production preceded commerce and was therefore a subject of state rather than federal control. Hughes believed that part II was separable from part III, however, and therefore would have affirmed the portion of the lower court's opinion upholding the price-regulation provisions of the Act.

Most interesting, however, was an aside tucked away in Hughes' discussion of the federal commerce power: "We are not at liberty," he wrote, "to deny to the Congress, with respect to interstate commerce, a power commensurate with that enjoyed by the States in the regulation of their internal commerce. See *Nebbia v. New York.*"[52] Hughes' prophetic citation of *Nebbia* in the context of a discussion of the commerce power indicated his recognition that *Nebbia* had expanded the class of businesses affected with a *national* public interest as well as that of businesses affected with the public interest of a state.

Justice Cardozo filed a dissenting opinion in which Justices Stone and Brandeis joined. Cardozo contended that part II was a proper regulation of interstate commerce, that part II was separable from part III, and that, insofar as no controversy between the coal producers and their employees had yet materialized with respect to the provisions of part III, the employers' suits sought a premature declaration regarding part III's validity. Cardozo did hint at one point in his opinion that there might have been limited circumstances in which federal regulation of the wages of miners might have been constitutional.[53] However, it is safe to say that as of the time the *Carter* decision was rendered, no member of the Court had gone on record positively stating that the federal government had the power to regulate the labor relations of local enterprises engaged in production.

After *Nebbia*, there could be little doubt that the enterprises regulated in *Schechter* and *Carter* were affected with a public interest. Yet in both cases the potentially revolutionary impact of *Nebbia* on commerce clause doctrine, hinted at in Hughes' *Carter* opinion, could not be realized because the business activities in question could not be located within a current of interstate commerce. The following year, however, the Court would hear three cases through which the potential of *Nebbia* could be tapped.

The Wagner Act Cases

Framing the Act

The drafting of earlier New Deal statutes, such as the NIRA and the AAA, had been dominated by politicians, bureaucrats, and lobbyists who had paid little attention to thorny questions of constitutionality. By contrast, each of the drafters of the Wagner Act was a lawyer,[54] and the legal training of the Act's framers revealed itself in the central role that constitutional concerns played in their shaping of the Act's provisions.

Introduced in the Senate by Wagner on February 21, 1935, S. 1958 reflected the influence exerted by the current of commerce cases on the thought of its drafters. The bill stated in its Declaration of Policy that denials of the right to bargain collectively led "to strikes and other manifestations of economic strife, which create further obstacles to the free flow of commerce. . . . It is hereby declared to be the policy of the United States to remove obstructions to the free flow of commerce and to provide for the general welfare by encouraging the practice of collective bargaining. . . ." The term "affecting commerce" was defined to mean "in commerce, or burdening or

affecting commerce, or obstructing the free flow of commerce, or having led or tending to lead to a labor dispute that might burden or affect commerce or obstruct the
free flow of commerce."[55] An accompanying memorandum comparing the bill to its
predecessor in the seventy-third Congress noted that "[d]enials of the right to bargain
collectively through freely chosen representatives lead to strikes and other economic
strife, thus creating physical and other obstructions to the flow of interstate commerce."[56] The same memorandum repeatedly cited the Packers and Stockyards Act
and the Grain Futures Act as models for the bill's provisions, and *Stafford* and *Olsen*
as precedents bolstering the bill's constitutionality.[57]

The current of commerce language in the bill's Declaration of Policy, however,
was preceded by a broader commerce power justification for the bill. The declaration also stated that inequality of bargaining power obtained in instances in which
employees were not free to organize and bargain collectively, and "the resultant
failure to maintain equilibrium between the rate of wages and the rate of industrial
expansion impairs economic stability and aggravates recurrent depressions, with
consequent detriment to the general welfare and to the free flow of commerce."[58]
The language of this purchasing power theory was revised in the Senate Committee on Education and Labor,[59] but the theory itself retained its primacy throughout
the bulk of the bill's legislative history. Indeed, the purchasing power theory
remained the emphasized constitutional basis of the bill when it passed the Senate
by a vote of 63 to 12 on May 16.[60]

On May 27, 1935, however, the Supreme Court handed down its *Schechter* decision. Senator Wagner, fearing that the opinion cast some doubt on the constitutionality of his bill, managed to have the bill recommitted to the House Labor Committee
for the purpose of redrafting the Declaration of Policy and the definitions of commerce.[61] Wagner lieutenants Leon Keyserling, Calvert Magruder, and Philip Levy
revised the Declaration of Policy "to emphasize the effect of labor disputes on interstate commerce and to de-emphasize the mere economic effects which had been
rejected by the Court."[62] And indeed, as reported back on June 10, the bill now gave
the current of commerce theory primacy over the purchasing power theory. The
Declaration of Policy was now replaced by a "Findings and Policy," which began:

> The denial by employers of the right of employees to organize and the refusal by
> employers to accept the procedure of collective bargaining lead to strikes and other
> forms of industrial strife or unrest, which have the intent or the necessary effect of
> burdening or obstructing interstate and foreign commerce by (a) impairing the effi-
> ciency, safety, or operation of the instrumentalities of commerce; (b) occurring in the
> current of commerce; (c) materially affecting, restraining, or controlling the flow of
> raw materials or manufactured or processed goods from or into the channels of com-
> merce, or the prices of such materials or goods in commerce. . . .[63]

There followed a statement of the purchasing power theory, which was in turn followed by the argument that protection of the right of collective bargaining "safeguards commerce from injury, impairment, or interruption, and promotes the flow
of interstate and foreign commerce by removing certain recognized sources of
industrial strife and unrest. . . ."[64]

The amended bill also contained a revised definition of "affecting commerce." Though it retained "affecting commerce" as the defined term, Congress no longer made any pretense to jurisdiction over practices that merely "affected" commerce. Instead, the term was now defined to mean "in commerce, or burdening or obstructing commerce or the free flow of commerce, or having led or tending to lead to a labor dispute burdening or obstructing commerce or the free flow of commerce."[65]

Defending the amended bill on the floor of the House, Representative Charles Truax of Ohio drew again on the most powerful constitutional metaphor in the arsenal of federal regulatory power:

> Whenever the normal flow of the river is obstructed and impeded by water-logged trees and stumps or refuse, the only effective remedy is to either shove, pry out, or blast these impediments and so put the same logic and process of reasoning when the natural flow of manufactured goods or raw materials which are the products of wage-workers, of men who earn their bread by the sweat of their brows, is impeded, restrained, and obstructed by reactionary, selfish, greedy water-logged employers, then it is high time that Congress should enact legislation to remove once and for all time the causes of the impediments to human progress and welfare.[66]

Truax's colleagues concurred, and on June 19 the same house that was to express such grave constitutional misgivings about the Guffey Coal Act passed the Wagner Act by a voice vote.[67] The Senate conferees readily acceded to the House's amendments,[68] and the Senate agreed to the conference report without debate. Signing the bill July 5, President Roosevelt emphasized the comparatively modest ambitions of the legislation. The Wagner Act, he declared, "must not be misinterpreted. It may eventually eliminate one major cause of labor disputes, but it will not stop all labor disputes. It does not cover all industry and labor, but is applicable only when violation of the legal right of independent self-organization would burden or obstruct interstate commerce."[69]

The *Schechter* decision had intervened in time to give the Act's framers guidance concerning the commerce power theory most likely to sustain the Act through judicial review. The timing of the decision had also afforded the sponsors of the Act an opportunity to shore up its constitutional foundation. As Richard Cortner has noted, the Act's proponents now "were essentially betting on the viability of the 'flow of commerce' cases."[70] It was now up to the lawyers of the NLRB to find test cases for which the current of commerce doctrine could serve as a vessel.

Selecting the Test Cases

Before the Wagner Act had even been signed, the NLRB lawyers were preparing a strategy for selecting promising cases through which the constitutionality of the Act might be sustained. The "master plan," set forth in a memorandum entitled "Selection of Test Cases Under the National Labor Relations Act," was crafted in the early summer of 1935 and adopted by Charles Fahy when he became general counsel in August of that year. Anxious to avoid the fumbling that had characterized the defense of the NIRA, and temperamentally unlike the litigation-averse lawyers of the AAA, the NLRB lawyers "were eager to press for court enforcement of the

Wagner Act and determined to outline a step-by-step strategy leading from case selection to the Supreme Court."[71]

The NLRB lawyers recognized from the start that the most common and legally challenging type of case they would encounter would involve the application of the Act to enterprises engaged in manufacturing or processing. Here the NLRB would have to face the line of Supreme Court precedent holding that manufacturing and commerce were distinct. They also recognized that the line of precedent under which the Act was most likely to be sustained in such cases was that which authorized Congress to remove obstructions from the stream of commerce. "The first job of the NLRB, then, would be to develop cases in which obstruction, particularly to the flow of goods from one state to another, could be demonstrated conclusively." The NLRB lawyers were instructed in this regard to keep an eye out for enterprises in which "a substantial part of the raw materials flow from other states into the manufacturing plant and a substantial part of the resulting products flow out from the plant to other states."[72]

As Peter Irons has noted, the NLRB's litigation strategy was "a logical outgrowth of the structure of the Wagner Act and a perceptive analysis of the conflicting lines of precedent."[73] NLRB general counsel Charles Fahy certainly agreed. In a 1963 conversation with Charles Leonard, Fahy contended that "the Wagner Act should have been sustained on the basis of precedents . . . and I am not inclined to attribute the fact that it was sustained to anything but that it was believed to be constitutional." No doubt reflecting on the fact that Van Devanter and Butler had joined in the Taft Court's current of commerce opinions, Fahy remarked, "[i]n fact, I thought it might be sustained by a vote other than Roberts'."[74] Fahy was utterly confident that Hughes and Roberts would vote to sustain the Act and "encouraged his staff to prepare their arguments on the assumption that an unfavorable decision in *Carter* would not invalidate the Wagner Act."[75]

When that unfavorable decision came, therefore, the NLRB lawyers were not fazed. As *The United States Law Week* reported in the wake of the *Carter* opinion,

> The Government . . . contends that the question of the validity of the Labor Act is not controlled by the decision in the Guffey Act case. . . . The situations are distinguishable, it is claimed, and the Government may continue to regulate labor relations under the Wagner Act on the ground that strikes of employees would affect the current and flow of interstate commerce and block the stream of such commerce.[76]

In a speech delivered before the Labor Institute in Pittsburgh, NLRB chairman Warren Madden had asserted that "'It is obvious that decisions which relate to work on a commodity before the commodity has begun to move on an interstate journey, or after it has reached the end of an interstate journey, do not justify a prediction that the court will apply the same rule to work on a commodity which is at a mid-point in a long interstate journey.° ° °'" *Stafford v. Wallace* had made it clear that "local" activities were subject to federal control if they were located in a current of interstate commerce. "If the Wagner Act were to be applied to the employees in the Chicago stockyards, Mr. Madden argued, the decision of such a case in favor of the federal power . . . would seem to be much more obvious than it was under the Packers and Stockyards Act."[77]

Taking his cue from Taft's dicta in *Stafford*, Madden further asserted that the Act could constitutionally be applied "to the workers in a great meat packing plant since the stream of commerce flows not only through the stockyards but also through the packing plants, where the animals are converted into all kinds of packing house products which are in turn shipped out to other states."[78] Of course, if stockyards employees engaged in the "agricultural," "productive" activity of tending, watering, and fattening livestock were amenable to such regulation, and if packing house employees engaged in the "manufacturing" enterprise of slaughtering livestock and packing meat were similarly susceptible to federal control, then other manufacturing concerns located in a current of interstate commerce were also within the Wagner Act's reach. Madden accordingly contended that "The same reasoning applies to the employees in a great steel mill or to a truck factory to which materials are sent from other states to be assembled and shipped on again. The Constitution and the statute give the Labor Board jurisdiction over these situations and the Board proposes to proceed along these general lines. . . ."[79]

And so it did. The NLRB master strategy called for the identification of test cases involving the manufacture of goods that were vital to the nation's economy, and autos, steel, textiles, and clothing were all singled out for particular attention. Throughout 1935 and 1936, the NLRB lawyers winnowed and selected promising test cases, carefully guiding them through the trial and appellate courts. By late 1936, they had three promising test cases before the Supreme Court. The Jones & Laughlin Company manufactured steel at its plant in Aliquippa, Pennsylvania; the Friedman-Harry Marks Clothing Company manufactured men's clothing in Richmond, Virginia; and the Fruehauf Trailer Company built trailers in the Motor City. Each plant received the bulk of its raw materials from out of state, and each plant shipped the bulk of its products to states other than the one in which it was located. And in each case the company had been found guilty of an unfair labor practice under the provisions of the National Labor Relations Act.[80]

Briefing and Arguing the Cases

The briefs in these three cases dutifully carried out the directives of the master memorandum. The government relied principally on *Stafford* and *Olsen*. In each case the plant in question was located in a current of interstate commerce, and in each the government contended that labor disturbances at the plants threatened to obstruct the free flow of interstate commerce. Because location in a current of commerce transformed the local into the national, "the fact that the injury actually arises from local activities is of no moment."[81] The purpose of the Act, the government emphasized, was "to prevent the direct physical obstruction to the stream of commerce caused by industrial strife."[82]

The two principal challenges faced by the government attorneys were that of breaching the production/commerce distinction and that of distinguishing *Carter Coal*. For the former task the government relied heavily on *Stafford*. Citing Taft's portrait of a current of commerce flowing through "slaughtering centers," the government contended that "[t]he Court thus recognized that stoppage for purposes of processing in the packing plant, involving a definite interruption in the physical movement and a very distinct transformation in the nature of the commodity, did not cause a break in the 'stream' or 'current' of commerce in the constitutional sense." "Moreover," continued the government's brief,

> operations in the meat packing plants are as essentially manufacturing as are the operations at Aliquippa. It is common knowledge that meat packing involves a very extensive transformation in the nature of the commodity; this is fully brought out in the authorities upon which the Court relied in the Stafford case. There, as here, the essential purpose of the processing operation is not merely to facilitate the flow of commerce, but also to halt it and to transform the commodities in question into things considerably different, by manufacturing or processing operations of varying degrees of complexity. Indeed, due to the seasonal character of the supply of raw materials and the stable demand for meat products, with a consequent necessity for much storage, and to the necessary slowness of many of the operations in the meat-packing industry, such as chilling, curing and smoking, the delays or stoppages of the flow of products in that industry are frequently much longer than those in the operations of respondent.[83]

The current of commerce doctrine was also the principal means by which the Wagner Act cases were to be distinguished from *Carter Coal*. "[T]he National Labor Relations Act as here applied is concerned with activities which occur under circumstances closely related to a flow of commerce, and which directly affect that flow. In the *Schechter* case the flow of goods had ceased; in the *Carter* case the flow had not yet begun. In both cases the Court was careful to restrict its decision to that state of facts, and to distinguish the facts of cases such as *Stafford v. Wallace* and the case at bar." Industrial strife in the cases at bar did "not, in the words of the *Carter* case, operate 'mediately, remotely or collaterally'; rather, it actually stops the movement of goods."[84]

The government's oral arguments echoed the themes sounded in its briefs. In each case the government attorneys described in elaborate detail the in-flow of raw materials and the out-flow of semi-finished and finished products from the manufacturing plants. Again citing Taft's *Stafford* dictum, Warren Madden contended that the Court had there found meatpacking plants to be part of a current of interstate commerce. "[T]he analogy which we draw of the flow of raw materials into and through and the flow of finished products out of the steel mills," he contended, "seems to be a logical one."[85]

Throughout the course of their arguments, the government attorneys were at pains to distinguish *Carter Coal*. Indeed, immediately after Madden's invocation of the *Stafford* dictum, Justice Sutherland sought to lead him into the mistake of claiming for Congress the authority to regulate productive activities transpiring at the terminals of the current of commerce.

> JUSTICE SUTHERLAND: So far as the cattle are concerned, how far could you go? You say that that is an analogous situation?
> MR. MADDEN: That is right.
> JUSTICE SUTHERLAND: Taking it back, for instance, to the herder; suppose the herders raising cattle organized a union. Could Congress regulate that?

MR. MADDEN: I should say not, Your Honor. . . . We no more assert that manufacturing is interstate commerce than did this Court in *Stafford v. Wallace* assert that meat packing or soap making or feeding hay to cows is interstate commerce. We merely assert that the Government, which has the responsibility, cannot have the factory gates slammed in its face and have it said to it, "Inside here you have lost your control, and whatever happens to your great stream of commerce is none of the National Government's business."[86]

Madden's parry of Sutherland's thrust was representative of the government's strategy in arguing the Wagner Act cases. As Richard Cortner has noted, "the government was not seeking a full retreat from the direct-indirect effects formula and the doctrine of dual federalism, but rather a shifting of emphasis by the Court from those principles to the principles embodied in the stream of commerce cases."[87]

In his peroration, Labor Department solicitor Charles Wyzanski alluded, in connection with the Fruehauf case, to the CIO sit-down strikes taking place in the automobile industry.

[T]here is a national public interest in this subject . . . and I contend that where two colossal forces are standing astride the stream of commerce threatening to disrupt it, it cannot be that this Government is without power to provide for the orderly procedure by which the dispute may be adjusted without interruption to the stream of commerce.[88]

Wyzanski's invocation of Holmes' formula was the last thing the justices heard before retiring to their chambers to consider their decision.

The Opinions

The craftsmanlike labors of the NLRB lawyers had presented Hughes and his colleagues with a well-established doctrinal theory on which the Wagner Act might be sustained. In each of the three test cases, raw materials flowed in to the enterprise from outside the state and, after a transformation in form, were shipped on to purchasers outside the state of manufacture. Chief Justice Taft had made clear in *Stafford* that the fact that the enterprise in question was engaged in production was not dispositive; and, as a general proposition, this point was amply supported by numerous cases not involving the current of commerce theory.[89] *Schechter* and *Carter Coal* could both easily be distinguished on the grounds that the enterprises in question there had been located at one of the terminals of, rather than *in*, a current of interstate commerce. Indeed, the Court in each of those two cases had explicitly rejected current of commerce arguments for precisely that reason.

No departure from existing commerce doctrine was necessary in order to sustain the Act. Indeed, the current of commerce doctrine would have appeared to require that the Act be upheld. Had Hughes and his colleagues wished simply to uphold the Wagner Act, whether out of fear of the Court-packing plan or in response to the 1936 election, yet at the same time wished to maintain the appearance of a strict doctrinal consistency so as to avoid charges of trimming principles for political convenience, they could easily have done so by simply accepting the current of commerce theory offered up by the government. Had they done so, a great deal of historical confusion about the New Deal Court might have been averted.

Rather than taking the safe, convenient route marked by the government attorneys, Hughes and his colleagues from the *Nebbia* majority again indulged themselves in an eminently Langdellian enterprise. Like Williston and his colleagues with the American Law Institute, Hughes used the opportunity occasioned by the Wagner Act cases to set forth a grand restatement of the law. Of the same age and intellectual generation as Williston (born 1861), Hughes (born 1862) in *Jones & Laughlin* applied the Restatement method to commerce clause jurisprudence. Drawing together all of the various exceptions to the local/national distinction that had accrued over the past three decades, Hughes sought to reformulate them into a single, synthetic principle. The current of commerce cases were "particular, and not exclusive, illustrations" of the instances in which the federal government might, under the aegis of the commerce power, regulate activities that were, when considered separately, purely local in nature. Several cases had authorized congressional regulation of the intrastate rates of common carriers in order to prevent unjust discrimination against interstate commerce.[90] The Safety Appliance Act and the Hours of Service Act had similarly been upheld as applied to instrumentalities and persons working solely in intrastate transportation.[91] Antitrust prosecutions against combinations of employers engaged in productive industry had been sustained in *Standard Oil v. United States* and *United States v. American Tobacco Co.*[92] Similarly, the Sherman Act had consistently been successfully applied to the conduct of employees engaged in production where it had been shown that such conduct was intended to restrain or control the supply of a product entering and moving in interstate commerce.[93]

From among these disparate exceptions to the local/national distinction of dual federalism, Hughes concluded, one could deduce a single synthetic principle of general application. "Although activities may be intrastate in character when separately considered," wrote Hughes, "if they have such a close and substantial relation to interstate commerce that their control is essential or appropriate to protect that commerce from burdens or obstructions, Congress cannot be denied the power to exercise that control."[94]

Hughes was undoubtedly aware that the principle he was articulating was rather amorphous, and he hastened to assure that the Court did not intend to tamper with the contours of dual federalism:

> Undoubtedly the scope of this power must be considered in the light of our dual system of government and may not be extended so as to embrace effects upon interstate commerce so indirect and remote that to embrace them, in view of our complex society, would effectually obliterate the distinction between what is national and what is local and create a completely centralized government. The question is necessarily one of degree.[95]

As this passage illustrates, the distinction between direct and indirect burdens on commerce was not completely obsolete; it was, however, no longer rigidly categorical.[96] As it had in *Nebbia*, the Court declined to decide an issue of constitutional law by recourse to an essentialist metaphysic. "We are asked to shut our eyes," Hughes exclaimed, "to the plainest facts of our national life and to deal with the question of direct and indirect in an intellectual vacuum. . . . We have often said that interstate commerce itself is a practical conception. It is equally true that interference with that commerce must be appraised by a judgment that does not ignore actual experience."[97] Of course, this deformalization of the direct/indirect distinction, which mirrored *Nebbia's* deformalization of the public/private distinction, occurred in cases that the government had argued on a current of commerce theory—the doctrine within which the two distinctions had become conflated. The logical consequences that *Nebbia's* deformalization held for commerce clause doctrine were thus realized in the first current of commerce case the Court saw in the post-*Nebbia* era.

The language Hughes used to adumbrate his formulation was clearly influenced by Cardozo. Cardozo had in his *Schechter* concurrence, after all, stated that the law was not indifferent to considerations of degree, but that "[t]o find immediacy or directness here is to find it almost everywhere." "There is a view of causation," Cardozo had written, "that would obliterate the distinction between what is national and what is local in the activities of commerce. . . . Activities local in their immediacy do not become interstate and national because of distant repercussions."[98]

We unfortunately have virtually no record of any intracurial discussion of this issue. But it does not seem at all improbable that Cardozo had convinced Hughes and Roberts of several things: first, that in light of the extent to which the economy had become integrated since the days of their youth, the categories of direct and indirect, which they had inherited from the nineteenth-century Court, were no longer satisfactory ways of describing the manner in which certain activities affected interstate commerce; second, that in light of the dissatisfaction they had expressed in *Nebbia* with rigidly categorical ways of interpreting the due process clause, it was incongruous to cling to such a manner of construing the commerce clause; third, that in light of the numerous cases carving out exceptions to the local/national distinction, many of which Hughes had either written or joined, categorical doctrinal expressions of that distinction no longer accurately stated the nation's constitutional law; and finally, that as the ultimate expositors of constitutional principles, it was incumbent upon the justices to distill from the various fragments of existing commerce clause doctrine a single, unifying principle.

This is precisely what had happened during the drafting of the Restatement of Contracts in the 1920s. Samuel Williston (born 1861) and Arthur Corbin (born 1874) had been engaged in a fundamental dispute over what should be the Restatement's definition of consideration. Williston was a devotee of the very strict, classical definition of consideration set forth in section 75. Corbin, a great admirer of the contract opinions written by Cardozo (born 1870) while on the New York Court of Appeals, argued for the broader, detrimental reliance definition set forth in section 90. Initially, Williston and his followers won out. But at the ensuing meeting of the Restatement group, Corbin presented a plethora of cases in which the courts had imposed contractual liability in the absence of consideration as defined by section 75. Gentlemen, he reportedly said to them, you are engaged in restating the common law of contracts. What do you intend to do about these cases? The restaters found Corbin's arguments unanswerable and, as a result, section 90 was included in the Restatement of Contracts.[99]

For Hughes and Roberts, the beauty of adopting Cardozo's formulation was that it did not commit them to results different from those they had voted for in

Schechter and *Carter Coal.* Cardozo had concurred in *Schechter*; and while he had dissented in *Carter Coal*, he had not contended that the provisions of the Guffey Coal Act regulating working conditions were constitutional—he had written instead that the question of the constitutionality of those provisions was not yet ripe. Cardozo's formulation thus permitted Hughes and Roberts to accede to the intellectual merits of their fellow justice's arguments without feeling the twinge of intellectual hypocrisy.

Yet Hughes and Roberts must have recognized that this subtlety would be lost on most, and they surely knew that the midst of the Court-packing crisis would be considered a suspicious time during which to restate commerce clause jurisprudence. Indeed, they must have been sorely tempted to accept the doctrinally consistent alternative so painstakingly prepared for them by the NLRB lawyers. Rather than choosing to travel either the comfortable path paved by the current of commerce doctrine or the formidable restatement path, therefore, the justices chose a middle course. The government had prepared for the Court a rationale with an impeccable pedigree; and while the majority declined specifically to rest its decision on that rationale, the opinion made clear that had it wished to do so, the Court could easily have reached the same result with the current of commerce theory. The availability of the current of commerce theory as a doctrinal backstop served not only to distinguish the Wagner Act cases from *Schechter* and *Carter Coal*; it also served to assure both the justices and their audience that the Court was not trimming its principles to achieve the politically expedient result. The availability of the current of commerce rationale gave the Court the liberty to concede the persuasiveness of Cardozo's position.

Accordingly, Hughes structured his opinions so that the availability of the current of commerce theory was apparent to anyone who read them. In describing Jones & Laughlin's enterprise, Hughes emphasized the far-flung nature of its holdings, the integrated, interstate nature of its operations,[100] and the importance of the business in which the corporation was engaged.[101] By selecting these features of the enterprise for emphasis, Hughes cast the Aliquippa plant as a business affected with a public interest located in a current of interstate commerce. Raw materials came to Aliquippa from points outside Pennsylvania; at Aliquippa those materials were transformed into steel; the steel was then shipped to purchasers at various locations around the country. The Labor Board, Hughes noted, had characterized the company's plants at Pittsburgh and Aliquippa as "the heart of a self-contained, highly integrated body. They draw in the raw materials from Michigan, Minnesota, West Virginia [and] Pennsylvania in part through arteries and by means controlled by the respondent; they transform the materials and then pump them out through the vast mechanism which the respondent has elaborated."[102] The objective and effect of the corporations' far-flung activities was the movement of ore from the Great Lakes in raw form to points around the country in finished form. The Aliquippa plant stood in the very gateway of that integrated, interstate movement.

Hughes' opinions in the two companion cases to *Jones & Laughlin, NLRB v. Fruehauf Trailer Co.* and *NLRB v. Friedman-Harry Marks Clothing Co.*,[103] also made clear the availability of the current of commerce rationale. In each case raw or semifinished materials were imported from out of state and were, after manufacture, exported to other states in semi-finished or finished form. In each case, labor strife threatened a significant disruption of this interstate flow.

In culling the facts from the Labor Board's findings, Hughes carefully placed Fruehauf's Detroit trailer manufacturing plant in a current of interstate commerce:

> Respondent maintains 31 branch sales offices in 12 different States and has distributors and dealers in the principal cities of the country. A wholly-owned subsidiary operates in Toronto, Canada, where sales are made and considerable assembly work is done with materials obtained from the Detroit plant and in Canada. More than 50 per cent in value of the materials used by the respondent in manufacture, assembly and shipping during the year 1934 were transported to its Detroit plant from Ohio, Illinois, Indiana, and other States. Most of the lumber was transported from Southern States and most of the finished parts were transported from States other than Michigan. . . . More than 80 per cent of its sales are of products shipped outside the State of Michigan through and to other States and foreign countries.[104]

Noting the importance of Fruehauf in the trailer industry and the indispensable nature of its manufacturing plant, Hughes observed:

> In 1934, respondent's sales amounted to $3,318,000. Its nearest competitor sold only 37 per cent of that amount. . . . The manufacturing and assembly operations at the Detroit plant are essentially connected with and dependent upon the purchase, sales and distribution operations without the State of Michigan.[105]

Hughes similarly culled facts from the Labor Board's findings placing Marks' clothing manufacturing plant in a current of interstate commerce:

> Respondent, a Virginia corporation, has its plant at Richmond, where it is engaged in the purchase of raw materials and the manufacture, sale and distribution of men's clothing. The principal materials are woolen and worsted goods. 99.57 per cent of these goods come from States other than Virginia, 75 per cent being purchased in New York and fabricated for the most part in other States. Cotton linings come from several southern States. . . . Of the garments manufactured by respondent, 82.8 per cent are purchased by customers outside the State.

Concerning the men's clothing industry generally, Hughes noted the following findings of the board:

> The men's clothing industry is thus an industry which is nearly entirely dependent in its operations upon purchases and sales in interstate commerce and upon interstate transportation. There is a constant flow of raw wool from the western States and foreign countries to the mills of New England where it is transformed into men's wear fabrics, then to the sponging and shrinking plants of New York and Philadelphia, then, joined by the other necessary raw materials, to the fabricating factories of the Middle Atlantic States for manufacture into clothing.[106]

Hughes also noted the significance of the clothing industry in American life, citing the board's finding that "[t]he men's clothing industry is among the twenty most important manufacturing industries in this country." With respect to the importance of labor relations within that significant industry, Hughes observed:

> The Amalgamated Clothing Workers of America is a labor organization composed of over 125,000 men and women employed in the men's and boys' clothing industry. . . . The periods before the recognition by the employers of the Amalgamated was marked by long and bitter strikes. In 1921 there had been a general strike in New York City which had lasted for eight months and caused losses of millions of dollars to employers and employees. A similar general strike in New York in 1924 lasted for six weeks and involved all of the 500 firms in that area and their 35,000 workers. The wage loss to the workers was nearly $6,000,000, the financial loss to the manufacturers ran into the millions. . . . Today the Amalgamated has collective agreements with clothing manufacturers and contractors employing the greater number of the clothing workers in the United States.[107]

In both *Fruehauf* and *Marks*, the Court simply set forth the facts and, in the final paragraph of the opinion, upheld the application of the Wagner Act to the enterprise in question, "[f]or the reasons set forth in our opinion in *National Labor Relations Board v. Jones & Laughlin Steel Corp.*"[108] The Court neither elaborated doctrine nor applied, in any detailed fashion, doctrine to facts. The facts set forth in the opinions were the facts deemed by the Court to be relevant, under *Jones & Laughlin*, to a determination of the validity of the Act's application to the respective enterprises.[109]

Thus, in each of these three companion cases, the Court carefully located the enterprise in a current of interstate commerce and then proceeded to characterize the enterprise or the industry of which it was a part in the broad language of a business affected with a public interest innovated by *Nebbia*. Like Lord Hale's port warehouses and *Munn's* grain elevator, each of the enterprises in the Wagner Act cases stood astride a current of commerce and was capable of halting its flow. If a business activity could be located in a current of interstate commerce, and the enterprise itself or the industry of which it was a part could be characterized as affected with a public interest (as almost any industry could in the wake of *Nebbia*), the fact that the enterprise was one of production did not preclude federal regulation. It was not necessary to overrule *Carter Coal* in order to embrace this proposition, and the Court did not do what was not required.[110]

Justice Roberts himself, writing years later, suggested that the current of commerce metaphor had in fact formed part of the basis of the Court's decision. Describing the theory on which the Wagner Act had been framed and upheld, the retired justice wrote:

> That act premises its provisions upon the proposition that industrial conflicts interfere with and limit interstate transportation and commerce. Albeit a strike is localized in a given community, the flow of goods to and from that community is interfered with. The interference may be so great as to be a matter of national concern. . . . even though the situations with which the statute deals are in their essence purely local.[111]

These remarks suggest yet another possibility: that while Hughes may have become persuaded of the merits of Cardozo's views,[112] perhaps convincing himself that they merely paraphrased views he himself had articulated years earlier as an associate justice,[113] Roberts was prepared to join the majority opinion only because he conceptualized the controversies as current of commerce cases. Hughes may therefore have eschewed specific reliance on the current of commerce doctrine in order to reflect the views of himself, Cardozo, Stone, and perhaps Brandeis, while including passages evoking the current of commerce image in order to secure the crucial fifth vote of Roberts. If so, then the lawyerly labors of the NLRB attorneys in selecting, briefing, and arguing the cases were not in vain. For under either of the two explanations I have suggested—whether Roberts was prepared to accede to Hughes' synthesis because the current of commerce doctrine served as a doctrinal backstop distinguishing previous cases and publicly refuting charges of unprincipled expedience, or whether he simply saw the case as governed by the *Swift* line of authority—the government could not have obtained his vote had the Wagner Act cases been a replay of *Schechter* or *Carter Coal*. This certainly was the view taken by many observers, who thought that the cases could not be properly understood without an appreciation of their current of commerce dimensions.[114] Not the least among these observers were Justices Sutherland, Butler, Van Devanter, and McReynolds.

The Four Horsemen, defenders of the formalist faith, could not accept Hughes' restatement. Moreover, because they viewed the enterprises in question as purely private businesses not affected with a public interest, they could not concede the applicability of the current of commerce theory.[115] But their dissents should not be taken as a paroxysm of crude anti-labor sentiment. In the companion case of *Washington, Virginia & Maryland Coach Co. v. NLRB*, the Horsemen joined in the Court's unanimous opinion upholding the application of the Wagner Act to an interstate common carrier. And just two weeks earlier, in *Virginian Railway Co. v. System Federation No. 40*, the Horsemen had joined in the Court's unanimous opinion upholding the collective bargaining provisions of the amended Railway Labor Act.[116] But these cases, unlike the Wagner Act cases in which the Horsemen dissented, involved a business affected with a public interest clearly engaged in interstate transportation.

The dissenters, who had the advantage of being present when the cases were discussed in conference (and perhaps of discussing them with Roberts outside the conference), clearly believed that the majority rested its decision on the current of commerce doctrine. "[I]t is ruled," wrote Justice McReynolds, "that to discharge an employee in a factory because he is a member of a labor organization (any kind) may create discontent which may lead to a strike and this may cause a block in the 'stream of commerce'; consequently the discharge may be inhibited."[117]

> We are told that Congress may protect the "stream of commerce" and that one who buys raw materials without the state, manufactures it therein, and ships the output to another state is in that stream. Therefore it is said that he may be prevented from doing anything which may interfere with its flow. . . . May a mill owner be prohibited from closing his factory or discontinuing his business because to do so would stop the flow of products to and from his plant in interstate commerce? May employees in a factory be restrained from quitting work in a body because this will close the factory and thereby stop the flow of commerce? May arson of a factory be made a federal

offense whenever this would interfere with such flow? If the ruling of the Court just announced is adhered to these questions suggest some of the problems certain to arise.[118]

McReynolds' choice of examples for his reductio ad absurdum is revealing. The arson example merely evinces a solicitude for the values of federalism. But the other two examples combine federalist concerns with a concern for the protection of the kinds of zones of private economic decision making safeguarded by such due process doctrines as liberty of contract and the business affected with a public interest. Federalism and due process were both sentinels standing guard over a vision of liberty. The current of commerce doctrine's use of a due process formula to constrain a deviation from federalist orthodoxy was a monument to the normative commonality of these two principal pillars of laissez-faire constitutionalism, and its most striking example of their conceptual interrelation. *Nebbia* had, by renouncing its strand of due process doctrine, sundered this relation. It was no accident, then, that the dissenters in *Nebbia* were also the dissenters in the Wagner Act cases.

A close study of the Wagner Act decisions thus suggests that the current of commerce doctrine, as implicitly modified by *Nebbia v. New York*, served either as the safety-valve theory that allowed the majority to synthesize existing commerce doctrine into a general principle while at the same time assuring themselves and the world that they were not succumbing to political pressure, or as the doctrinal theory upon which Justice Roberts based his vote in support of the Act. Had the current of commerce theory not existed, the case might well have gone the other way.

Had it not been for the dramatic political events surrounding the Court's decisions, it would have been difficult to contend that there was anything very revolutionary in the opinions. Doctrinal synthesis had been a dominant mode of legal reasoning and scholarship at least since Langdell, and it was warmly embraced by the contemporary Restatement projects. Moreover, it is clear that what troubled the Court in these cases was the physical obstruction to the interstate movement of goods that might be created by unresolved industrial strife. The opinions clearly illustrate the Court's continued conceptualization of interstate commerce as the transportation of goods and people across state lines, and its understanding of the commerce power as the power to remove physical obstructions to that movement. Finally, the Court chose to shore up the synthetic portion of its opinion with an established doctrinal buttress: the current of commerce doctrine. No doubt the channel cut by the current had never before been understood to be so wide. But neither the 1936 election nor the Court-packing plan was required to broaden the channel. The expansion was implicit in the internal logic of *Swift* and *Nebbia*.

Thus the Court deciding these cases continued to operate within dominant stylistic, conceptual, and doctrinal paradigms. This was not revolution; it was the kind of incremental evolution that Thomas Kuhn might have described as "normal science."[119] In the late 1930s and early 1940s, however, Franklin Roosevelt would have the opportunity to transform the Court by appointing men who had come to legal maturity not in the age of Cooley and Langdell, but rather in the era of Pound and Llewellyn. During the tenure of these men the obstruction-to-transportation theory of commerce undergirding cases like *Jones & Laughlin* would give way to a broader understanding of the federal commerce power. This new understanding, under which federal regulatory power would become truly plenary, would render the current of commerce doctrine obsolete. Such a new understanding, however, would not be necessary to decide the cases before the Court during the next three terms. In fact, that plenary view would emerge with far less alacrity, ease, and certainty than has conventionally been thought.

11

The Persistence of Memory

Wagner's Wake

Reaction to the Wagner Act decisions was mixed. Many sanguine New Dealers were confident that *Carter Coal* had been overruled and the gateway to national regulation thrown wide open. Others were more circumspect. Solicitor General Stanley Reed, for example, wrote: "I do not see any clear inconsistency between Wagner on the one hand and the Guffey or N.R.A. decision on the other. The Wagner decision is based on the right to remedy situations which obstruct or tend to obstruct interstate commerce. The Guffey and the Poultry Code were aimed directly at wages, hours and labor conditions." Writing twelve years later, Charles Fahy, mastermind of the Wagner Act litigation strategy, agreed. "My own view was at the time and is now that the *Labor Board Cases* constituted no departure from the past, unless the very recent past, and that indeed they were distinguishable from the *Carter Coal* case. The principles laid down in earlier cases, cited and quoted in detail in the *Labor Board Cases*, seemed directly applicable." Political scientist Robert Cushman concurred. "It is important to note," Cushman observed, "that in none [of the Wagner Act cases] does the Court generalize beyond the facts of the case. There is no broad holding that all labor relations in industries producing goods for the interstate market are to be regarded as directly connected with interstate commerce."[1] Indeed, though Hughes' opinion had made it clear that the Court was not strictly speaking relying specifically on the current of commerce doctrine, many readers of the opinion saw the stream of commerce analogy as central to the Court's disposition of the cases, and wondered how much further the Court would go.

Jane Alvies sounded this theme in an article published in the *Ohio State Law Journal* in May of 1937. "The channels of commerce became deeper last month," wrote Alvies, "when the stream of labor litigation emerged with the stamp of constitutionality."

> To characterize the decision as one gained under pressure and as a personal victory does great injustice to the Court; for such prejudice overlooks the fact that the basis of

decision in the steel, trailer, Associated Press, and clothing cases is not entirely new but has been supported and fostered by other similar phases of development under the commerce clause. For a number of years business whose life is movement, which draws raw products in to be processed and sent out through the channels of interstate commerce and which depends for its life upon that commerce has been properly subjected to federal protection.

This is the "current of commerce" doctrine, drawn upon to sustain the government in the case of *Stafford v. Wallace.*

"The decisions under the Wagner Act warrant government interference to support collective bargaining," Alvies continued, "because the unsatisfactory method of dealing with strikes has choked the flow of commerce. . . ."[2]

Other commentators echoed this theme. "In the *Jones & Laughlin* and companion cases," wrote one observer, "the intrastate activity held controllable was in the 'stream of commerce,' that is, the raw materials were received from, and the finished product sent into interstate commerce." "[T]he Labor Relations Act was held to be constitutional," noted Paul Douglas and Joseph Hackman, "in so far as it used the powers of the federal government over interstate commerce to reduce labor disputes at points which were in the 'flow' of interstate commerce." "Great weight was placed on the fact that the factories obtained most of their raw materials from out-of-state sources and disposed of most of their finished products in out-of-state markets," John Trenam observed in the *Georgetown Law Review*. D. J. Farage mused that the finding of a direct effect on interstate commerce in the Wagner Act cases may have been "predicated on the fact that both the raw materials as well as the finished product moved in interstate commerce." "The crux of the majority opinion," concluded Burton Finberg, "is that Congress may protect the 'stream of commerce,' and that where a concern engaged in the business of manufacture buys its raw materials outside the state, converts it into a manufactured product, and ships that product to points outside the state—that concern is within the 'stream of commerce.'" Another commentator, writing in 1941, characterized the Wagner Act opinions this way: "Labor trouble in a manufacturing plant which stood in the middle of the 'flow of commerce' was found to have a sufficient effect upon interstate commerce because of resulting burdens and obstructions to justify extension of federal regulation under the Commerce Clause." Only "subsequent decisions" demonstrated "that for the Act to apply, it is not necessary that the employer involved be in the middle of the 'flow of commerce.'"[3]

The Court's holding that the Fruehauf Trailer Company, and especially that the Friedman-Harry Marks Clothing Company, fell within the Labor Board's jurisdiction reinforced the interpretation of the decisions as based on the current of commerce metaphor. The effect on commerce of a strike at the Jones & Laughlin plant, or even at the Fruehauf factory, would of course be considerable. But federal jurisdiction over an enterprise as small as the Friedman-Harry Marks Clothing Company surely had to be based on something other than a "degree of impact" test.[4] Thus, advised Warren Woods and Altha Connor Wheatley, "it is important to bear in mind the emphasis placed in the decisions in the trailer and clothing company cases on the facts which indicated a 'stream of commerce.' In neither of these cases was the employer a corporate Gargantua of the size of the Jones & Laughlin Steel Company. . . . there is plenty of room in the *Wagner Act* opinions for insisting in future cases that some 'flow' be shown before regulation will be permitted."[5]

Writing in the *Boston University Law Review*, Walter Daykin agreed.

[T]he Supreme Court has sustained the Board's ruling that if industry is in a vertically integrated form, that is if it controls the raw material, means of transportation, and the manufacturing processes, these activities of the company form a stream of commerce. In the *Friedman-Harry Marks* case this flow of commerce notion was carried further by the Court when it argued that an industry making men's clothing, when viewed in connection with related industries, constituted an important part of the flow of commerce. Here in this case the flow of wool from the western states and foreign countries, the making of this wool into men's wear fabrics, the sponging and shrinking of these fabrics, and the making of men's clothing are all related and form a continuous process, and any interruption of any of these phases of the process would interfere with the free flow of commerce.

The interruption to the flow of *transportation*, these observers reasoned, must have been the key to the decisions. "A return to the opinion rendered by Hughes in the *Jones & Laughlin* case," wrote Dean Ribble of the University of Virginia, "will demonstrate existing deference to the idea that the commerce power must be related to humanly directed movement from state to state."[6]

Several observers therefore doubted that either *Schechter* or *Carter Coal* had been overruled. "The rationale of the Wagner Act cases," wrote one commentator, "seems to be that Congress can legislate to prevent the outbreak of industrial warfare, which would stop the flow of commerce." "The *Schechter* decision may be distinguished because the government relied principally upon the contention that an increase in purchasing power would revive the flow of commodities, and causation of this type may be considered too remote in order to avoid a complete obliteration of the powers of the states."[7] Joseph Mueller concurred. *Schechter* and *Carter*, he observed, had "invalidated the regulation of wages and hours in enterprises functioning respectively at the source and the terminus of the stream of commerce." Those two decisions, he asserted, "are not applicable here. They may be distinguished not only as to the type of regulation involved, but also with respect to the theory upon which a relationship to commerce was sought to be established." Arguments for federal regulation that relied on the demonstration of "a long chain of economic cause and effect between labor costs, prices, and ultimate supply and demand," he predicted, would continue to be rejected by the Court.[8] "The *Guffey* and *Schechter* cases," Jane Alvies agreed, "are perhaps to be distinguished."

If the current of commerce is a criterion, coal mining in Pennsylvania and wholesale disposition of chickens in New York may be characterized as outside this current since they exist at the beginning and the end of commerce respectively and do not represent an intermediate or temporary point of abeyance. But even if we depart from the current of commerce doctrine to the newly announced criterion, still the *Guffey* and *Schechter* cases may be distinguished. . . . The Codes attacked in the *Guffey* and *Schechter* cases were attempting to regulate details of working conditions—hours of labor and wages—and were not confined to the more general field of enforcement of collective bargaining.[9]

"[I]n view of the *Guffey* and *Schechter* decisions," she concluded, "one is not yet prepared to say that regulation of hours, wages, and other conditions of labor have become subject to federal control merely because collective bargaining, one aspect of a business, has been declared to 'affect' interstate commerce."[10]

Lloyd Garrison, a leading authority in labor law, did not read the Wagner Act cases as conferring plenary jurisdiction on the NLRB. On the contrary, he identified five types of enterprise with respect to which the jurisdiction of the Labor Board remained in doubt:

> establishments where (1) the raw materials are local in origin, but the products are shipped outside the state, (2) the raw materials come from outside the state, but the products are sold in the local market, (3) only a portion of the raw materials come from outside the state and only a portion of the products are shipped outside the state, (4) substantially all the raw materials come from outside the state and substantially all the products are shipped outside the state, but the plant employs relatively few men, or does a very small fraction of the total interstate business, (5) the establishment, though wholly local in materials and products, is the sole source of essential parts, or of light and power, used by a wholly interstate manufacturer.[11]

Garrison was thus uncertain whether the Court was prepared to allow regulation even of all of those enterprises that could be located in a current of interstate commerce, let alone those that could not. In short, Garrison, like many other observers, remained unsure whether the Court would permit application of the Wagner Act to the vast majority of American businesses.

Writing from the vantage of the mid-1950s, Alpheus Thomas Mason echoed the views of contemporary commentators: "The Carter Coal case had strengthened the impression that Congress could not, without unconstitutionally invading the reserved powers of the states, govern the relations of industrial employers and employees. That difficulty remained even after the Jones & Laughlin decision. The principal barrier against congressional regulations of the economy—that the relation of employer and employee is 'local', and therefore beyond the reach of national control—had yet to be expressly removed."[12]

The opinion's mixed signals similarly produced divergent interpretations among the lower courts. Several federal judges wrote or joined opinions either explicitly stating or implicitly suggesting that *Jones & Laughlin* had overruled *Carter Coal*.[13] Many others, however, both Republican and Democratic appointees, took the contrary view that the two cases were consistent and that *Carter* remained good law.[14] As late as June of 1939, a Roosevelt appointee[15] dismissed for lack of jurisdiction a petition to recover wages under the Fair Labor Standards Act. Relying on *Schechter* and *Carter* as well as on *Jones & Laughlin*, the court held that the petition did not "state any facts which would make the employment of the plaintiffs a part of the 'stream of commerce' as described in the Jones & Laughlin case."[16]

Similarly divergent readings appeared in the pages of the *Congressional Record*. Consider, for example, the debate between Senator William Borah and Senator

James Pope over the implications of *Jones & Laughlin* for the constitutionality of what were to become the acreage allotment provisions of the Agricultural Adjustment Act of 1938. "The Jones-Laughlin case," Borah asserted, "dealt with acts which took place after the commodity had been put into the channels of interstate trade."

> The Jones-Laughlin case did not undertake to deal with the question of production of ore prior to the time the ore was being produced, but with the complete program for shipment in interstate commerce. In that case we had a corporation which was engaged in interstate commerce, in production, in manufacture, in the sale and shipment of a manufactured product, and the Court, dealing with a particular instance at the time which was moving in interstate commerce, said they would treat the matter as a whole.

"I invite the Senator's attention," Pope responded, "to the fact that in the Jones-Laughlin case the Court dealt with individuals who were engaged in local employment so far as the company was concerned."

> One was a motor inspector and another was engaged in the manufacture of commodities in connection with the steel plants located entirely within the State. There were no orders to ship the particular goods in interstate commerce. They were simply there working, producing materials and piling them up for possible future shipment in interstate commerce. It seems to me quite clear that the majority of the Court, in discussing interstate commerce, considered acts which in themselves would be purely local acts.

"It seems to me," Pope concluded, "it was clear in that case that those acts were in the stream of interstate commerce."

This was precisely Borah's point, and his response to Pope drove it home. "What were the facts of the Jones-Laughlin case?" he inquired.

> The raw material was produced. There was no effort to limit production or to say in advance how much ore should be mined. It was put in the channels of interstate trade. It was in process of movement in interstate trade. It was stopped for the purpose of being processed into another condition. The Court held that it was all one transaction, that whatever took place at Aliquippa was part of the movement in interstate trade; that the commodity did not stop there, that it did not begin there, that it was simply halted for the purpose of being changed from one form of manufacture to another. The Court was careful to say that it in no sense modified the N.R.A. case or the cases with reference to production. But owing to the fact that it was all one transaction, all one movement, all designed to accomplish a certain purpose, and that was to get the manufactured material in such condition that it ultimately could be sold, the Court held that it came within the interstate commerce clause of the Constitution. In my opinion the Court in no sense laid down so broad a rule as to say that prior to the production of coal or prior to the production of iron ore we could say how much the corporation would be permitted to produce.[17]

As Borah saw it, there was still a constitutional difference between interstate movement and local production, between activities taking place in a current of interstate commerce and those transpiring at the terminals of such a current. Rather than abandoning those categories, *Jones & Laughlin* fit comfortably within their matrix. For Borah as for others, *Carter Coal* remained good law.

The commerce clause opinions delivered by the Court in the three years following the *Jones & Laughlin* opinion did little to alleviate these uncertainties. *Santa Cruz Fruit Packing Co. v. NLRB*, decided in March of 1938, concerned the jurisdiction of the Labor Board over the activities of a fruit packing concern in northern California. The company shipped only about 37 percent of its product in interstate or foreign commerce and received the bulk of the produce it canned from within the state of California. The company contended that the manufacturing and processing in which it was engaged were local activities beyond the board's jurisdiction.[18] The opinion holding that the company was subject to the Act was supported by a majority comprised by Hughes, Brandeis, Stone, Roberts, and Hugo Black, who had replaced Van Devanter in 1937.[19] Hughes' opinion again disclaimed any specific reliance on the current of commerce doctrine.[20] The "close and intimate" relationship of the company's labor relations to interstate commerce was sufficient to support federal jurisdiction. Robert Stern reflected the view of many when he remarked years later that *Santa Cruz Fruit* "made it clear that industries at the beginning of the flow, producing raw materials within a state for shipment outside, were subject to the Act."[21]

Upon closer examination, however, it appears that such a broad reading of the case is unwarranted. First of all, the company was not a *producer* of raw materials at all: it was a food processor. Hughes' opinion did not assert jurisdiction over the growers who cultivated the produce that the company canned, and neither did the Labor Board. The opinion instead held that the Act applied to a company that received and processed "raw materials" only after they had already been produced and had begun a journey that would eventuate in their transport outside the state.

Second, and more important, neither the Labor Board nor the Court asserted jurisdiction over those of the company's employees who were actually engaged in processing. The case arose out of a dispute between the company and its warehousemen, who loaded the overland trucks and rail cars that carried the product in interstate commerce, as well as those trucks that carried the product to the docks when shipment was to be by boat. Upon learning that many of these warehousemen had begun an effort to unionize, the company locked them out. As a result a picket line was formed, "with such effectiveness that eventually the movement of trucks from warehouses to wharves ceased entirely." The teamsters refused to haul the merchandise. The warehousemen at the dock warehouses, whose job it was to unload the merchandise from the trucks at the dock, similarly refused to handle the goods. The stevedores, who moved the goods from dock to ship, wouldn't touch the company's cargo, and the sailors aboard the steam schooners refused to stow it.[22] All of these workers were involved not in the *manufacture* of the company's product, but rather in the initial stages of its interstate *transportation*. The company's dispute with these laborers created not a shutdown of local production, but an obstruction to "the movement of canned products in interstate and foreign commerce."[23] "The test of jurisdiction laid down in the *Jones & Laughlin* case," the NLRB had contended, "is whether 'stoppage of ° ° ° operations by industrial strife' would result in substantial interruption to the flow of interstate commerce."[24] Ordinarily, observed Chief Justice Hughes, "'There is a constant stream of loading and shipping of products' out of petitioner's plants throughout the entire year."[25] As a consequence of this labor dispute, that stream had run dry. "It would be difficult to find a case," concluded Hughes, still employing the vocabulary of dual federalism, "in which unfair labor practices had a more direct effect upon interstate and foreign commerce."[26]

The significance of the nature of the work in which the employees concerned were involved was not lost on all contemporary commentators. As one observer remarked, in *Santa Cruz* "the Court dealt with unfair labor practices visited upon warehousemen, teamsters, and stevedores. The activities of these men were more nearly related to marketing than to production." There, agreed another, "the board was only seeking to regulate labor relations of the warehousemen, teamsters, and stevedores—employees most directly connected with the interstate commerce aspects of the business."[27]

Consolidated Edison Co. v. NLRB,[28] decided later in 1938, concerned the question of the board's jurisdiction over a power company selling its product locally in New York City and Westchester County, New York. The NLRB advanced three arguments in favor of jurisdiction. First, the company was itself engaged in interstate commerce because it purchased coal, oil, and other raw materials from sources outside the state.[29] Second, the company sold electrical power to innumerable commercial and manufacturing enterprises in New York City, which were "engaged to a greater or lesser degree in interstate commerce." The cessation of electrical power to those enterprises would have been "substantially equivalent, in its effect upon interstate commerce, to simultaneous labor disputes in all these businesses."[30] The Court explicitly disclaimed reliance on the first argument,[31] thereby avoiding the need to confront *Schechter*, and did not take up the second argument, thereby sidestepping *Carter Coal*. Instead, the Court seized upon the government's third argument, which stressed the effect that a strike at Con Ed would have had on interstate transportation and communication.[32]

"[T]here is undisputed and impressive evidence," wrote Chief Justice Hughes for the Court, "of the dependence of interstate and foreign commerce upon the continuity of the service of the petitioning companies." Here Hughes cited a lengthy list of public and private entities that were dependent on the utilities for power. Each of them was indisputably an instrumentality of interstate communication or transportation: railroad companies, the New York Port Authority, piers, lighthouses, beacons, harbor lights, airfields, telegraph and telephone companies, the Radio Corporation of America, post offices, the United States Barge Office, the Customs House, the appraisers' warehouse and various federal office buildings. Were industrial strife to interrupt service to these consumers, the result would be catastrophic. "'Instantly, the terminals and trains of three great interstate railroads would cease to operate; interstate communication by telegraph, telephone, and radio would stop; lights maintained as aids to navigation would go out; and the business of interstate ferries and of foreign steamships, whose docks are lighted and operated by electric energy, would be greatly impeded.'"[33] Nowhere did the Court discuss the enormous effect that such a shutdown would have had on industrial production or on purchasing power. It was the direct and immediate effect that such strife would have had on the interstate movement of people, goods, and information that rendered the company subject to the board's jurisdiction.

This selection of the narrowest available ground for sustaining the Board's jurisdiction again impressed contemporary observers. "It is interesting to note the heavy emphasis placed by the Court on the consumption of petitioner's power by instrumentalities of interstate commerce, since this was only a small part of its total output," remarked an editor of the *Pennsylvania Law Review*.[34] Editors at the *Harvard Law Review* saw the case as a direct descendant of the *Virginian Railway* case[35] upholding the application of the Railway Labor Act to back-shop employees of interstate carriers.[36] In the wake of the Wagner Act decisions, Joseph Mueller had noted a number of "local occupations which are subject to federal control" due to the effect that labor disturbances in those occupations might have on interstate commerce. Among these Mueller had included "clerical work," citing the *Texas & New Orleans Railroad* case upholding the application of the Railway Labor Act to railway clerks; "repair and maintenance," citing *Virginian Railway*; "and other activities necessary to the commencement or termination of interstate movement. The last mentioned category includes such employees as baggage and express men, telegraph messengers, dock workers, etc."[37] The government had emphasized this line of argument in its *Consolidated Edison* brief;[38] the brief submitted by the United Electrical and Radio Workers of America had as well. "It is clear," the union's brief had contended,

> that the *motive-power* which sets in motion the through train between New York City and Chicago is as much an instrumentality of interstate commerce as the switch which turns on this power; and that the worker who produces this power and controls its continued flow is as much an integral part of interstate commerce as the man who turns on the switch which connects it with the train. Now, it is undisputed that the Federal Government has the power to control the employer-employee relations of the man who turns on the switch which starts this train on its course. . . . Clearly, if the Federal Government has the power to legislate upon the rights of the switchman who turns on the switch at the Grand Central Station in New York City which sets in motion the instrumentality of interstate commerce . . . the Federal Government must have the power to legislate so as to *insure the continuance of the flow of power* which will make the operation of that switch possible. After all, both switch and switchman are there only for the purpose of providing the flow of this power.[39]

Such an interruption in the flow of power, Hughes concluded, would have a direct effect on interstate commerce. Quoting with approval the language of the lower court's decision, Hughes again persisted in his use of the distinction between direct and indirect effects. "'Such effects,'" he wrote, "'we cannot regard as indirect and remote.'"[40]

The last major Hughes Court commerce clause decision involving the jurisdiction of the Labor Board was *NLRB v. Fainblatt*,[41] handed down in April of 1939. Fainblatt was a New Jersey company engaged in processing materials into women's sports garments on a contract basis. The raw or semi-finished materials were sent to Fainblatt from points outside New Jersey, were finished by Fainblatt, and were then delivered to a representative of the Lee Sportswear Company, who shipped them to points outside New Jersey.

The facts of the case invited a current of commerce analysis, and that invitation did not go unaccepted. Judge John Biggs Jr. of the Third Circuit, a Roosevelt appointee[42] dissenting from the panel majority's decision denying the board's jurisdiction, clearly saw the case in such terms. The question presented in the case, in his view, was "Are the operations of the respondents a part of a continuous flow of commerce between the States and have the acts of the respondents complained of led and do they tend to lead to a labor dispute burdening and obstructing commerce and the free flow of goods in commerce between the States?" His answer to this question, emphatically affirmative, echoed the arguments of the NLRB attorneys in the Wagner Act cases:

> Material shipped through interstate commerce comes into the respondents' plant at Somerville, is there turned into a finished product and goes out again into the currents of interstate commerce. Can the work performed by the respondents' employees be isolated from the stream of commerce whence the unfinished material comes and into which the completed product goes? Can the stream of commerce be impounded temporarily so that for the time being it loses its identity and force and ceases to exist as part of the current between the States?
>
> . . . If the authority of Congress over the flow of commerce between the States may be circumvented by the device of passing raw material through one door of a manufacturing plant and withdrawing the completed product through another, the express purpose of the National Labor Relations Act, the protection of commerce from the burden of labor disputes, is frustrated.[43]

On appeal the briefs carried this theme forward. The NLRB's brief put the "Question Presented" thus: "Whether the National Labor Relations Act may be validly applied to respondents, employers whose business consists of the processing of materials belonging to others, where the major portion of such materials are delivered to such employers through the channels of interstate commerce and, after processing, are in large part distributed through the channels of interstate commerce."[44] Throughout the brief the government repeatedly evoked the image of a flow or stream of interstate commerce. "[T]here is a steady and almost daily stream of materials across State lines to respondents' plant and of finished products from that plant to various parts of the United States," counsel contended.[45] "There is a constant and substantial flow of materials and finished products to and from respondents' plant across state lines."[46] Relying on not only the Wagner Act cases and their progeny but also *Stafford v. Wallace* and *Chicago Board of Trade v. Olsen*,[47] the brief asserted that "Stoppage of operations as a result of industrial strife between respondents and their employees would, therefore, directly obstruct the movement of substantial quantities of goods in interstate commerce."[48]

The amicus brief filed by the International Ladies Garment Workers' Union followed suit. Point I of the brief's argument asserted that "Respondent's activities are an integral part of the continuous stream and flow of interstate commerce." "The facts in the instant case forcibly demonstrate," attorney Elias Lieberman contended, "that respondents' activities constitute a 'bottle neck' or 'throat' through which the raw materials flow from various states to the respondents' plant and through which 'bottle neck' the finished products flow back into the stream of interstate commerce." "It can thus be seen that the respondents' activities in processing the raw materials into finished products make possible the flow of raw materials in interstate commerce to the State of New Jersey and make possible the flow of finished products from the State of New Jersey to various states of the Union. The respondents' enterprise is as much a 'throat' through which the current of interstate commerce flows as existed in the case of *Stafford v. Wallace*."[49] In fact, Lieberman presumed that *Schechter* was still good law, and used the current of commerce doctrine to distinguish *Schechter* from the instant case.

> In the case at bar neither the raw materials shipped to respondents nor the finished product manufactured by the respondents came to a *permanent* rest in the state of New Jersey. On the contrary, the goods came to a *temporary* rest in respondents' plant for the purpose of enhancing their value and of continuing their movement in interstate commerce. A mere temporary rest of the goods in the respondents' plant for the purpose of processing does not cause such a break in the "stream" or "current" of commerce as to render the Act inapplicable. (See *Stafford v. Wallace, supra.*)[50]

Accordingly, Lieberman concluded, "the case at bar is easily distinguished from the case of *A. L. Schechter Poultry Co. v. U.S.*"[51]

Justice Stone's majority opinion upholding the Labor Board's jurisdiction relied principally on the authority of the Wagner Act cases and their progeny. Yet his presentation of the facts of the case clearly located the plant in a current of interstate commerce. He opened the opinion by reporting that

> This petition raises the question whether the National Labor Relations Act is applicable to employers, not themselves engaged in interstate commerce, who are engaged in a relatively small business of processing materials which are transmitted to them by the owners through the channels of interstate commerce and which after processing are distributed through those channels.[52]

"Throughout the year," he observed, "there is normally a continuous day-by-day flow of shipments of raw materials to respondents' factory from points without the state, and of finished garments from respondents' plant to New York City and other points outside of New Jersey." Moreover, Stone's opinion based the board's jurisdiction over Fainblatt on the immediate effect that a labor dispute at the plant would have had on interstate transportation. "Here interstate commerce was involved in the transportation of the materials to be processed across state lines to the factory of the respondents and in the transportation of the finished product to points outside the state for distribution to purchasers and ultimate consumers." "Transportation alone across state lines is commerce within the constitutional control of the national government and subject to the regulatory power of Congress."[53] Here Stone cited *Gibbons v. Ogden* and *Champion v. Ames*;[54] in an earlier draft of the opinion he had instead cited *Stafford v. Wallace* and *Chicago Board of Trade v. Olsen*.[55] "The Board's finding that respondents' unfair labor practices have led and tend to lead to labor disputes burdening interstate commerce and interfering with its free flow," Stone concluded, "is supported by the evidence."[56]

The original draft of Stone's opinion had contained two passages suggesting that *Schechter*, or at least Cardozo's *Schechter* concurrence, was still good authority. In the first passage, Stone wrote:

the enterprise of an employer-manufacturer may be so small as to preclude any reasonable expectation of strikes or labor disturbances affecting the commerce even
though all his product is shipped in interstate commerce; or such disturbances within
the enterprise, regardless of its size, may be so remote in their effect on interstate commerce that any attempted control of unfair labor practices could not fairly be said to
be a regulation of interstate commerce.

The second passage began the concluding paragraph of the opinion. "The effect
upon interstate commerce was not so tenuous, speculative or remote that the regulation of the practices can be said to be in reality only a regulation of local industry
rather than of commerce. See *Schechter Poultry Co. v. United States*, 295 U.S. 495."[57]

Hughes' opinion in *Santa Cruz Fruit* had contained a similar passage,[58] and
Stone presumably included this language in part to please Hughes and Roberts. In
March of 1939, however, the Roosevelt appointees rebelled against this view. On
March 16, Black wrote Stone a letter objecting to both passages. With respect to the
first, he wrote that it was

> susceptible of being considered inconsistent with the holding that "the operation of
> the Act does not depend on any particular volume of commerce affected more than
> that to which courts would apply the maxim de minimis." If volume is not the con-
> gressional test (except as to application of the maxim de minimis) when would an
> enterprise shipping all of its goods in interstate commerce be so small as to preclude
> the probability that a strike which might close the plant would affect interstate com-
> merce? And should we here suggest the idea that a large factory shipping all of its
> product in interstate commerce might be excluded from the Act because its effect on
> commerce might be too remote? After a decision that volume of commerce is not the
> test under the Labor Act, is it necessary to indicate reservations concerning possible
> future situations involving different conditions?

Neither low volume nor "remoteness" were in Black's view legitimate grounds
upon which to deny the board jurisdiction over an enterprise's labor relations. This
passage, he wrote to Felix Frankfurter, who had succeeded Cardozo earlier that
year, "seems to me to be unnecessary and a trouble generator."[59]

With respect to the second passage Black was characteristically blunt. "I am not
in accord with the conclusion reached in the *Schechter* case on this point or with
the language used in reaching that conclusion," he objected. "This sentence would
in my judgment imply an approval of that decision and I do not wish to approve it
even by implication." That sentence, he wrote to Frankfurter, "gives the implied
approval of the Court to Hammer vs. Dagenhart."[60]

Frankfurter had also objected to the second passage, but in a more conciliatory
manner. "I wish you would consider the omission of the first sentence of the final
paragraph concluding with the *Schechter* case," he had written Stone on March 15.

> You know what lawyers are like, and that sentence might encourage them to begin to
> argue before us that the effect of unfair practices is "tenuous, speculative, or remote."
> They will do so any way, I know, but I think we might as well await the event without
> stimulating it. Omission of that sentence in no wise affects your argument. . . .

> How I envy you the extraordinary speed with which you turn out so admirable an important opinion.[61]

Stone replied to Frankfurter that his "object was not to reveal that unfair practices, which are really remote from any affect on commerce, are not within the Act." Presumably referring to the first passage to which Black would object, but to which Frankfurter had not, Stone explained, "I think that appears elsewhere in the opinion and is already well understood." Instead, Stone's purpose in including the second passage had been

> to reveal the only real basis on which the Schechter case can be sustained and thus, if possible, prevent the eternal reliance on that case to accomplish results which are inadmissible in the case of an ordinary strike which actually and obviously prevents shipments of goods in interstate commerce. Perhaps I am a little tender, due to the fact that, remaining silent in the *Schechter* case, I have felt that the only tenable reason for supporting it has never been adequately expressed. Perhaps even this is not worth while, but at any rate I will give your point further consideration and let you know.[62]

How exactly Stone's position differed from the Cardozo concurrence in which he had joined is not clear. Presumably he wanted to jettison the vocabulary of direct and indirect effects that Cardozo had deployed in his *Schechter* concurrence:[63] those terms appear nowhere in Stone's opinion. Yet it is clear that Stone, like Cardozo, was not prepared to abdicate the Court's role of policing the boundary between the local and the national, of making the final determination of whether the activities of a particular enterprise fell within the domain of federal regulatory authority.

Black's letter echoing Frankfurter's objection and adding another arrived in Stone's chambers the next day. After reciting his reservations, Black implied that he might write separately. "In view of the fact that the Court is divided, I hope that you may find it possible to eliminate these features of the opinion. With these omissions I shall be most happy to agree to the Opinion."[64] McReynolds and Butler had presumably announced their dissents at conference,[65] and it appeared that Frankfurter might be inclined to join a separate opinion written by Black. Brandeis had retired the previous month, and Douglas had not yet replaced him. Stone thus faced the prospect of having only four votes for his opinion. At this point he apparently concluded that the inclusion of the two passages was "not worth while," and there is no record of anyone objecting to the omissions. There is a suggestion, however, that Stone was a little sore about excluding the points on which he had been so "tender." "Although you doubtless do not agree," Black wrote him March 17, "I believe your Opinion is actually strengthened by the changes. . . ."[66] The impact of the Roosevelt appointments on the Court's commerce clause jurisprudence was beginning to manifest itself.

The opinion that Black praised is not the one that appears in the official reports, however. Presumably as part of a compromise worked out with Hughes and Roberts, the published opinion deleting the passages objected to by Black and Frankfurter inserted the following passage not present in earlier drafts: "Long before the enactment of the National Labor Relations Act it had been many times held by this Court that the power of Congress extends to the protection of interstate commerce from interference or injury due to activities which are wholly intrastate." Following this sentence was a footnote citing many of the authorities relied on by Hughes in his *Jones & Laughlin* opinion. Among them was *Chicago Board of Trade v. Olsen*.[67]

Thus, although Black and Frankfurter had succeeded in removing from the opinion language reconciling the decision with *Schechter*, several constitutional commentators still saw *Fainblatt* as a current of commerce case. In *Fainblatt*, wrote Robert Cushman, "The Court held that what appeared to be a purely local manufacturing process was in reality a link in a chain of interstate transactions. The business of the defendant was integrally tied in with the stream of interstate commerce, and accordingly was subject to the jurisdiction of the act and the order of the board." Kansas Judge John Somers expressed a comparable conceptualization of the decision in an address before the Kansas Bar Association:

> Fainblatt was a clothing manufacturer in New Jersey. Cloth was imported across the river from New York, made into clothes by Fainblatt and the finished garments immediately re-entered the stream of interstate commerce, although Fainblatt neither purchased the raw materials nor sold the finished garments. Throughout the year there was normally a continuous day-by-day flow of shipments of raw materials to Fainblatt's factory from points without New Jersey and of finished garments from his plant to New York City and other points outside the state of New Jersey. While . . . Fainblatt neither purchased the raw materials nor sold the garments, yet he did manufacture them in the stream or flow of interstate commerce.

The case, another observer reported, had raised "the question whether an independent plant performing a service on goods involved in a continuous flow of such interstate commerce is subject to the act." "In the view of the Court," concluded a third, "the essential fact was that the free flow of commerce was obstructed. . . ."[68]

The Court that produced these opinions was an institution in transition. Some of the justices, especially the new Roosevelt appointees, embraced broader conceptions of the commerce power than did Hughes and Roberts; of the justices comprising these majorities, Roberts probably held the least expansive views. Roberts did not write any of these opinions, and the papers of the justices leave no trace of how he conceptualized the cases. He probably did not agree with everything that was said in the opinions, and his personal habit of refraining from writing concurring opinions, which has contributed to so much confusion concerning his vote in *Tipaldo*, likely kept him from expressing his differences with the majorities. Yet it is not difficult to understand how one who had voted as Roberts had in *Schechter* and *Carter Coal* could have gone along with these later decisions without having an experience akin to that of Paul on the road to Damascus. *Santa Cruz Fruit* involved employees engaged not in production, but in the initial stages of interstate transportation. The *Consolidated Edison* opinion emphasized that the controversy there involved employees of an enterprise intimately linked with interstate transportation. And *Fainblatt*, like the Wagner Act cases, involved a manufacturing concern situated in the middle of a current of interstate commerce.

Decisions rebuffing constitutional challenges to federal regulation of the marketing of coal and agricultural commodities would push the frontiers of commerce clause jurisprudence no further than these Labor Board cases. Indeed, the Second New Deal's efforts to alleviate distress in these sectors of the economy would be built upon precedents erected well before the passage of the Wagner Act. And throughout the framing, defense, and ultimate vindication of these initiatives, Roberts' opinion in *Nebbia* would again play a central role.

The Marketing Angle and the *Shreveport* Connection

Currin v. Wallace involved an attack on the Tobacco Inspection Act of 1935, which authorized the secretary of agriculture to identify auction markets at which tobacco was purchased for subsequent shipment in interstate commerce. The Act prohibited the sale at such markets of tobacco that had not been inspected, graded, and certified by an authorized representative of the secretary of agriculture.[69] As the government would subsequently point out in its brief on appeal, such a statute was hardly a novelty in 1935. Congress had "frequently exercised this power to require inspection and grading of commodities entering interstate and foreign commerce and has excluded from such commerce commodities which have not been inspected or which fail to meet the standards deemed essential to the welfare of such commerce."[70] Federal inspection of livestock had been upheld by the Court,[71] and the establishment and enforcement of federal standards for grain moving in interstate commerce had been "tacitly approved" as well. Still other such inspection and grading statutes had "been in effect for many years without question as to their constitutionality."[72]

Tobacco warehousemen and auctioneers in Oxford, North Carolina, nevertheless contended that "the transaction of offering tobacco for sale at auction on the warehouse floor is not a transaction in interstate commerce and hence is not subject to congressional regulation."[73] The Act had been passed in the wake of the *Schechter* decision, yet it had aroused similar objections from only two congressmen.[74] Representative John W. Flannagan of Virginia had responded to suggestions that the bill encroached upon state prerogatives with astonishment. "No one, so far as I know, has ever attacked the constitutionality of the legislation," he remarked. "[T]his is one piece of legislation against which I did not think constitutional objections would be raised. . . . We have held hearing after hearing and not a single constitutional objection has been raised until this late hour." "We regulate the sale of wheat and cotton and cattle; why can we not legislate with respect to the grading of tobacco?"[75] Representative Franklin Hancock of North Carolina simply could not understand the relevance of *Schechter*. "[U]nder the facts before the Court in the Schechter case," he explained, "everybody knows that the poultry had landed in New York and its further use would be intrastate. Under the provisions of this bill, however, when the farmer delivers his tobacco to the warehouseman for sale, it is the first step into the stream of interstate commerce, which presents an entirely different question in every respect, so far as constitutionality is concerned."[76]

In a decision rendered by a panel of Coolidge and Hoover appointees,[77] the Fourth Circuit unanimously upheld the Act, characterizing the Oxford auction market as "a throat through which all of the tobacco sold enters the stream of interstate commerce."[78] In fact, as the government pointed out in its brief on appeal, "A substantial portion of the tobacco sold on the Oxford market is grown in Virginia."[79] Yet neither the government, nor the Fourth Circuit, nor the Supreme Court needed to rely only on the current of commerce theory in order to sustain the Act.

As the government demonstrated in its brief, the Taft Court had handed down a raft of decisions in the 1920s holding that local sales for subsequent shipment across state lines were themselves interstate commerce subject to federal regulation. In *Shafer v. Farmer's Grain Co.* the Court had invalidated a North Dakota statute requiring the grading of wheat at country elevators, 90 percent of which was purchased for shipment across state lines. "Buying for shipment, and shipping, to markets in other States . . . constitutes interstate commerce—the buying being as much a part of it as the shipping," Justice Van Devanter had maintained.[80] "The right to buy it [grain] for shipment, and to ship it, in interstate commerce . . . is a common right, the regulation of which is committed to Congress and denied to the states by the commerce clause of the Constitution."[81] In *Lemke v. Farmer's Grain Co.*, the Court had struck down another North Dakota statute providing for the inspection and grading of grain, limiting the purchase of grain to those licensed by the state, and authorizing the establishment of reasonable margins to be paid to producers of grain. Such legislation might lawfully be enacted by Congress, the Court observed, but not by a state legislature. "It is alleged," Justice Day had written,

> that such legislation is in the interest of the grain growers and essential to protect them from fraudulent purchases and to secure payment to them of fair prices for the grain actually sold. This may be true, but Congress is amply authorized to pass measures to protect interstate commerce if legislation of that character is needed. The supposed inconveniences and wrongs are not to be redressed by sustaining the constitutionality of laws which clearly encroach upon the field of interstate commerce placed by the Constitution under federal control.[82]

In *Dahnke-Walker Co. v. Bondurant*,[83] the Court had invalidated a Kentucky statute prescribing the terms upon which a foreign corporation might purchase grain within the state for subsequent shipment in interstate commerce. Such transactions, the Court held, were themselves interstate commerce and therefore immune from state-imposed obstructions and burdens.[84] Similarly, *Swift* and *Stafford* had upheld federal regulation of local sales of livestock that were to be shipped in interstate commerce.[85]

Chief Justice Hughes' opinion for the Court in *Currin* remarked that the evidence showed that "the sales consummated on the Oxford auction market are predominantly sales in interstate and foreign commerce." "So far as the sales are for shipment to other States or to foreign countries," Hughes observed almost wearily, "it is idle to contend that they are not sales in interstate or foreign commerce and subject to federal regulation." Quoting directly from *Dahnke-Walker*, Hughes con-

cluded that "Where goods are purchased in one State for transportation to another
the commerce includes the purchase quite as much as it does the transportation."
"There is no permissible constitutional theory which would apply this principle to
purchases of livestock as in the *Swift* and *Stafford* cases, and of grain as in the
Lemke and *Shafer* cases, and deny its application to tobacco." "Having this authority to regulate the sales on the tobacco market, Congress could prescribe the conditions under which the sales should be made in order to give protections to sellers or
purchasers or both."[86] Hughes' opinion made no reference to *Jones & Laughlin*,
nor indeed to any other case sustaining the Wagner Act. Doctrinally, those cases
were quite beside the point.

This decision was so unremarkable that it attracted little attention in the scholarly
journals. What comment it did generate evinced little surprise. "The application of
the commerce clause to the marketing of tobacco is new, but the principles upon
which the case was decided are certainly as old as the Swift, Stafford and Lemke
cases," wrote Judge John Somers. "It is true," wrote Robert Jackson, "that these auction sales were held wholly within the state and for some purposes might be subject
to some degree of state regulation. But auction markets constitute the throat of a
great interstate commerce in tobacco, and the Court held that federal inspection
could be imposed at that point, notwithstanding the tobacco had not yet moved
across state lines." When the Court upheld federal regulation of interstate milk sales
later that year in *United States v. Rock-Royal Co-operative, Inc.*, Robert Stern cited
Dahnke-Walker, Lemke, and *Currin* in maintaining that the Court had simply "reaffirmed the holding in a number of earlier cases that 'where commodities are bought
for use beyond state lines, the sale is a part of interstate commerce.'"[87]

Yet not all of the tobacco sold on the Oxford auction market was bought for use
beyond state lines. Some of that tobacco would be manufactured within the state.
There was, however, no way to tell before the sale which tobacco would be shipped
outside the state and which would not.[88] The intrastate and interstate transactions
on the auction market were "commingled." This made it "necessary," the chief justice concluded, "if the congressional rule were to be applied, to make it govern all
of the tobacco thus offered for sale." Hughes found authority for this federal regulation of intrastate sales in a railroad decision he had written himself nearly a quarter
of a century earlier: "Wherever the interstate and intrastate transactions of carriers
are so related that the government of the one involves the control of the other," he
had written, "it is Congress, and not the State, that is entitled to prescribe the dominant rule...."[89]

The source of this quotation was *Houston, East and West Texas Railway Co. v.
United States,* better known as the *Shreveport Case.*[90] In *Shreveport* the Court had
upheld an order of the Interstate Commerce Commission directing certain railroad companies to stop charging lower rates for carriage between points within the
state of Texas than were charged for comparable distances between points in
Louisiana and Texas. The Court approved this regulation of intrastate rates on the
ground that it was necessary in order to prevent such rate discrimination in favor of
intrastate commerce from becoming a burden on interstate commerce. The justices elaborated the *Shreveport* doctrine in *Railroad Commission of Wisconsin v.
Chicago, B. & Q. R. Co.,* upholding an ICC order establishing rates for intrastate

carriage in Wisconsin, notwithstanding a contrary existing state tariff schedule. "[S]uch orders as to intrastate traffic are merely incidental to the regulation of interstate commerce, and necessary to its efficiency," wrote Chief Justice Taft. "Effective control of the one must embrace some control over the other, in view of the blending of both in actual operation."

> Commerce is a unit and does not regard state lines, and while, under the Constitution, interstate and intrastate commerce are ordinarily subject to regulation by different sovereignties, yet when they are so mingled together that the supreme authority, the nation, cannot exercise complete, effective control over interstate commerce without incidental regulation of intrastate commerce, such incidental regulation is not an invasion of state authority. . . .[91]

Shreveport and *Railroad Commission of Wisconsin* were followed in several cases throughout the 1920s and 1930s, but the doctrine's reach was always limited to the paradigmatic business affected with a public interest: rail carriage.[92] The power of the federal government to regulate rates for intrastate transactions was after all derivative of its power to regulate rates for interstate transactions. Before *Nebbia*, the power of the federal government to regulate interstate rates had been in turn limited by the due process clause to that category of businesses susceptible to price regulation. Here again, the due process limitation on federal power had functioned as a federalism limitation. Read against the backdrop of the public/private distinction in due process jurisprudence, *Shreveport* and its progeny had posed little threat to the existing federal structure.

Once *Nebbia* had removed this due process constraint, however, it could no longer perform its role in maintaining the federal equilibrium. The *Dahnke-Walker* line of cases permitted federal regulation of sales for subsequent shipment in interstate commerce; *Nebbia* presumably permitted that regulation to extend to the price at which those goods moved in that commerce;[93] and *Shreveport* and *Nebbia* combined permitted federal regulation of the price at which similar goods were sold in intrastate commerce if such control were necessary to prevent discrimination between interstate and intrastate products. The convergence of these three lines of doctrine, and specifically the decision in *Nebbia*, provided the authors of the Second New Deal with a new recipe for addressing the problems that had for so long plagued the nation's energy and agricultural sectors. Moreover, this successful recipe had been conceptualized and implemented before the "breakthrough" of the Wagner Act cases.

Carter Coal Revisited

Congressional reaction to the *Carter Coal* decision had been swift. Within two days Senator Guffey had introduced a revamped bill from which the offending labor provisions had been excised. The revised bill retained the price-fixing sections, upon the constitutionality of which the *Carter* majority had not passed. The House passed the bill by a vote of 161 to 90, but a Senate filibuster prevented its enactment during the Seventy-fourth Congress.[94]

Guffey nevertheless reintroduced the bill in the next Congress, where it enjoyed spectacular success. As Ralph Baker put it, "The question of constitutionality of the measure was not the storm center that it had been in 1935." The aid of the Department of Justice had been solicited in drafting the bill, and Solicitor General Reed had testified to his belief that the revised bill would pass constitutional muster. "The House Ways and Means Committee had devoted considerable time to a discussion of the constitutional features, but apparently there was almost complete harmony in these discussions."[95] The bill was shepherded through the House by Representative Fred Vinson of Kentucky, who assured his colleagues of the bill's constitutionality. "[A]s a Member of this House," said the future chief justice, "I know the genuine respect that my colleagues here have for the law and the courts. As a lawyer and a Member of this body, I say to you that we have tried to square the language of this bill with the decisions of the Supreme Court. . . . Our efforts have not been to circumvent any opinion of our highest Court, but we have worked in a bona-fide attempt to meet the law laid down by them in a proper, legal, constitutional manner."[96]

Vinson then proceeded to explain the reasons for his confidence in the bill's constitutionality. As Alben Barkley would remark in the Senate, the bill's sponsors had "predicated this bill very largely upon a combination of decisions. . . ."[97] The first set of cases relied upon were the Taft Court opinions concerning federal power to regulate interstate sales. Citing *Dahnke-Walker* and *Lemke*, Vinson contended that those cases showed "conclusively that the States have no power over sales in interstate commerce. The Supreme Court has held that where a state statute is invalid as an unconstitutional burden on interstate commerce, such a holding implies that Federal regulation of the same subject matter would be constitutional."[98]

For the proposition that this power extended to price regulation, Vinson and his colleagues cited repeatedly to *Nebbia*.[99] If the Fourteenth Amendment's due process clause permitted the states to regulate intrastate prices, then the Fifth Amendment's due process clause afforded Congress the same power with respect to interstate sales. Here Vinson made much of Roberts' authorship of *Nebbia* and of his apparent refusal to join the Four Horsemen in invalidating the price-regulation provisions of the 1935 Guffey Coal Act. "Mr. Justice Roberts wrote [the *Nebbia*] opinion about a year before the Carter case. If he had any change in mind relative to the power of Congress to regulate prices and unfair methods of competition within its sphere, it would have been an easy matter to have invalidated those points of the statute."[100] If there had been five votes to strike down the price regulation provisions of the Act, Vinson asked, would the majority justices "have strained themselves to hide behind the inseparability of the labor-relations features to invalidate the whole act? I say that if five votes could have been secured they would have invalidated the regulation of prices and of unfair methods of competition sections of the bill."[101]

The bill regulated the price of intrastate coal, as well as that of interstate coal, because effective control of the latter was thought to require regulation of the former. As Senator Wheeler remarked, "so much of the coal of this country is used only in intrastate commerce that if those who produce it could break the price and cut the price of coal in intrastate commerce, and coal could be regulated only in interstate commerce, the bill would be completely ineffective."[102] Relying on *Shreveport* and its progeny, the bill's sponsors thought such regulation of the price of intrastate coal clearly constitutional. "Direct analogy for the validity of the regulation of intrastate sales of coal is to be found in the regulation of intrastate railroad rates which affect interstate rates," Vinson explained.[103] "Assuming . . . the power of Congress to regulate the price of coal in interstate commerce," the House Report concluded, "it is clear that Congress may also regulate the price of coal in intrastate commerce in any case where such intrastate commerce directly affects interstate commerce, as, for example, where it appears that prices of coal in intrastate commerce cause any undue or unreasonable advantage, preference, or prejudice, as between persons and localities in intrastate commerce on the one hand and interstate commerce on the other hand, or cause any undue, unreasonable, or unjust discrimination against interstate commerce."[104]

Senators and representatives who had opposed the 1935 Act on constitutional grounds were fully prepared to support the bill in its revised form. "I opposed the original Guffey Coal Act because I considered that, as drawn, it was unconstitutional," reported Representative John W. McCormack of Massachusetts. "I am supporting this bill because not only do I believe it to be constitutional but because the circumstances surrounding this particular industry should bring any person to the realization that legislative action is necessary to assist this industry and those dependent upon it for a living."[105] "When the former Guffey coal bill was acted on by the Senate," reported Senator Kenneth McKellar of Tennessee, "I voted against it solely because I thought the measure unconstitutional. I favored the purposes of the bill then, but, under the decisions of the Supreme Court, there was no doubt in my mind that the bill would be declared unconstitutional. It was declared unconstitutional. The pending bill, in my opinion, conforms to the Constitution, and I shall give it my support and vote."[106] The 1935 Act had passed the House by a vote of only 194 to 168.[107] On March 11, the 1937 bill passed the House without a record vote, and the vote to recommit the bill was 39 in favor, 340 opposed.[108] Support from the Senate was comparably strong. Whereas the 1935 Act had passed by a narrow 45 to 37 margin,[109] the 1937 Act breezed to passage on April 5 with a vote of 58 to 15—only seven Republicans joined eight defecting Democrats in opposing the bill.[110] This was approximately the same measure of support shown for the Wagner Act when it had sailed to victory in the Senate by a vote of 63 to 12 during the same summer that the original Guffey Act had just squeaked through. Moreover, this constitutional rationale had been fully worked out, these debates fully conducted, and these votes completed, all before the Supreme Court handed down its decisions in the Wagner Act cases on April 12.[111]

The legislators who enacted the Bituminous Coal Conservation Act of 1937 took the view that the price regulation made possible by *Nebbia* was perfectly consistent with the Tenth Amendment limitations articulated in *Carter Coal*. "In the light of the decisions of the Supreme Court," the Senate Report lamented, "control of production is apparently beyond congressional power. Consequently price regulation appears to be the only remaining means by which the Congress can transform into order the chaos which for a generation has notoriously ruled the bituminous coal industry of the Nation."[112] This distinction, between regulation of production and regulation of marketing, would prove to be central not only to Congress' efforts to ease the woes of the coal business but to its attempt to solve the farm problem as well.

The AAA the Second Time Around

In the immediate wake of the 1936 *Butler* decision striking down the acreage reduction provisions of the Agricultural Adjustment Act of 1933, a note in the *Yale Law Journal* had predicted that the amended Act's provisions regulating the marketing of agricultural commodities would nevertheless survive constitutional scrutiny. Citing *Dahnke-Walker, Lemke*, and related cases, the note's author opined that

> The constitutional theories of congressional power over interstate commerce provide formulae broad enough to sustain the provisions of the marketing orders limiting the quantities and fixing the prices of commodities moving across state lines. Sales made in interstate transactions, whether preceding or following shipment across state lines, appear to constitute interstate commerce itself within all the definitions thus far suggested by the Supreme Court. To regulate the factors of price and quantity in such transactions is therefore to regulate interstate commerce, not merely circumstances antecedent to, or consequent upon interstate commerce.[113]

This theory was adopted by the sponsors of the Agricultural Adjustment Act of 1938, which permitted the secretary of agriculture to prescribe and allocate marketing quotas for tobacco and other staple crops.[114] The report of the House Committee on Agriculture, which stated that the bill was "to provide for an adequate and balanced flow of agricultural commodities in interstate and foreign commerce," detailed the deleterious effects on commerce that flowed from "the disorderly marketing of tobacco." Unregulated marketing caused overcrowding and congestion of tobacco warehouses, rendered lower grades of tobacco that were normally marketable in interstate commerce unsalable, and caused sharp declines in tobacco prices. Such declines had prompted a subsequent diminution in interstate commerce in tobacco. Accumulated supplies and plummeting prices prompted farmers to hold their tobacco off the market, and grower protests had resulted in the temporary closure of various auction markets, thereby bringing interstate trade in tobacco to a standstill.[115] If "a regular even flow of such commodities into interstate and foreign commerce could be secured, then the disastrous consequences following such irregularity in marketing could be avoided." "If the excessive surpluses can be kept off the interstate and foreign market in years of plenty and fed into it in years of low production," the report concluded, "stable orderly flow of interstate commerce will be assured."[116]

The floor managers sold the bill's marketing provisions as a regulation of sales rather than of production. "Marketing quotas," maintained Senator Pope, the bill's chief sponsor, "at most have a remote effect upon the actual production of agricultural commodities. They are directed at marketing itself, and marketing of these basic commodities is certainly a part of interstate commerce."[117] "In the pending bill there is no effort made to prevent the flow of wheat or corn in interstate commerce until it is actually produced and after it is determined that the surpluses are such that they will affect interstate commerce," claimed Senator Pope. "There is no attempt to prevent production. Farmers may produce what they desire. . . ."[118]

Even some of the bill's opponents agreed with this position. The bill would have been constitutional, submitted Senator Warren Austin of Vermont, had it "contained nothing else but a provision for the regulation of the marketing of goods that cross a State line or a National line, or contracts for marketing, sale, or negotiation for marketing among the several States or between nations; there is, as implied, ample authority in the Constitution for Congress to take hold of that matter and regulate it, even to the point of fixing a quota upon every farm in the United States. . . ."[119] Austin's views are particularly interesting because he believed that *Butler, Schechter,* and *Carter Coal* were, even after *Jones & Laughlin,* still good law.[120] Over the objections of the Act's sponsors, however, several of its opponents denounced it as an unconstitutional effort to regulate the level of agricultural production. Restricting the amount of a commodity that could be marketed in interstate commerce was in their view a transparent attempt to accomplish what the Supreme Court had said in *Butler* could not be done.[121]

This line of argument was predictably embraced in *Mulford v. Smith*[122] by several Georgia and Florida tobacco growers who had been penalized for marketing more than their allotted quotas on a Georgia auction market in 1938.[123] The brief for the United States, which offered an extended refutation of this claim, leaned heavily on the line of authority the Court had used to sustain the Tobacco Inspection Act of 1935. "The question of federal power in this case," the government contended, "is fundamentally the same and just as simple as that before this Court in *Currin v. Wallace.*" "As this Court declared in the *Currin* case, sales of tobacco by growers through warehousemen to purchasers taking the tobacco outside the state *are* interstate commerce." Citing *Swift, Stafford, Currin, Dahnke-Walker,* and *Shafer,* the brief noted that "This Court has pointed out repeatedly that interstate commerce consists of buying and selling as well as of transportation." "Thus, the sale of tobacco at the warehouses when the buyer immediately thereafter transports the tobacco out of the State is itself interstate or foreign commerce and subject to Federal regulation."[124]

Butler was accordingly inapposite.[125] "The previous federal programs," the brief explained, "sought to assist farmers through adjustment of the quantity produced. This Act seeks to aid them by limiting merely the amount offered for sale, irrespective of what the production may have been or may be. . . ." The AAA of 1938 "in establishing marketing quotas does no more than limit the amount which may be sold and shipped in commerce." The Act regulated "only *sales* of tobacco. . . . To the extent that the Act is applied to interstate selling, it regulates interstate commerce itself, and clearly falls within the federal commerce power." A regulation of the amount of tobacco sold "regulates nothing that precedes or follows interstate commerce; it regulates only such commerce itself."[126]

"The Act regulates marketing, not production," the brief insisted. "It authorizes the setting of quotas for the amount to be marketed or sold, not the amount to be produced. It imposes no penalties on a grower because of the amount he produces nor does it attempt to control any of his conduct prior to the act of marketing."[127] The marketing quotas may have influenced the amount produced, but "the fact that a regulation of marketing may have such a collateral effect on production does not make it a regulation of production. Congress has power to regulate interstate commerce. If a law regulates such commerce, it is within the power of Congress, regardless of what effect upon other matters it may have."[128]

Here the attorneys for the United States offered numerous examples of statutes that had been upheld despite comparable collateral effects:

> Destruction of a monopoly in distribution may inevitably break up a monopoly in manufacture as well. . . . A state may prorate the production of oil without conflict with the commerce power, although the necessary and inevitable effect of the limitation of production upon the amount of oil shipped in interstate commerce cannot be gainsaid. . . . Conversely, Congress may limit the amount of oil distributed in interstate commerce, with an equally inevitable effect upon production, without thereby invading the field of state sovereignty. . . . Congress, on the other hand, by prohibiting the shipment of intoxicating liquor or of prison made goods to states whose laws prohibit their manufacture and sale inevitably discourages and restricts manufacture.[129]

"The protective tariff directly (and designedly) affects the amount of goods manufactured domestically," the argument continued, "yet it is not a regulation of manufacture."[130] The federal government had no power to suppress lotteries, yet the Court had upheld the Lottery Act in *Champion v. Ames*; it had no power to promote health, but the Pure Food and Drugs Act had been upheld in *Hipolite Egg Co. v. United States*; it had no power to promote morality, but the Mann White Slave Act had been upheld in *Hoke v. United States*; it had no power to prevent theft, but the Motor Vehicle Theft Act had been upheld in *Brooks v. United States*; it had no power to prevent kidnapping, but the Federal Kidnapping Act had been upheld in *Gooch v. United States*.[131] In all these cases, "the Acts were sustained because, irrespective of their various objectives, what was regulated was interstate commerce. The fact that the objective of each was, in one way or another, to promote the general welfare did not invalidate them as regulations of commerce, but served rather to justify them under the due process clause."[132]

If the statutes upheld in these cases were constitutional, the brief surmised, then surely the tobacco marketing provisions of the AAA passed muster. The prevention of the disruptions to interstate commerce brought about by disorderly tobacco marketing were "much more closely related to the underlying objectives of the commerce clause than protection of the public against immorality, crime, and disease." "The original purpose of the commerce clause was primarily economic, and the objectives of the most important commerce legislation enacted by Congress, like those of this Act, were to improve the economic well-being of the nation."[133] Moreover, many of these cases had upheld absolute prohibitions on the interstate shipment of particular items. "If such complete prohibitions are commerce regulations, a partial prohibition—which is what the quota system amounts to—must also be within the commerce power."[134]

The one exception to this line of authority was the 1918 decision in *Hammer v. Dagenhart*, in which the Court had by a 5 to 4 vote struck down a federal statute prohibiting interstate shipment of goods made by child labor. That case, the United States argued, had "been treated in later decisions as holding that the Child

Labor Act was invalid 'because it was not really a regulation of interstate commerce but a Congressional attempt to regulate labor in the state of origin, by an embargo upon its external trade.' Since in the act here under consideration Congress is not controlling production, but regulating interstate commerce in order to further orderly marketing and insure reasonable prices in such commerce itself, the same comment cannot legitimately be made. For this reason *Hammer v. Dagenhart* is distinguishable."[135] As the note in the 1936 *Yale Law Journal* had put it, in *Hammer* "the evil sought to be regulated was part of the productive process with no apparent relation to the movement of goods. But in this case the regulation is designed to solve a serious marketing problem in which the movement of commodities in interstate commerce plays a significant part; it may realistically be contended that any effect the regulation may have upon production is incidental."[136]

If the Child Labor Act had been invalid because of its aim, the brief continued, the same could not be said of the AAA of 1938. The latter Act employed a regulation of commerce to achieve a legitimate commerce purpose: "stabilization of the flow of commodities in interstate commerce and of the prices at which such goods are marketed for the benefit of producers and consumers."[137] "In numerous antitrust cases this Court has recognized that the supply of a commodity in interstate commerce was a proper concern of Congress under the commerce power." "The *Stafford* and *Olsen* cases demonstrate that stabilizing the market through the removal of undesirable fluctuations in price and in the amount moved is an appropriate exercise of the commerce power even if applied to intrastate transactions. All the more so when interstate commerce itself is regulated as it is here."[138] Most important legislation enacted and upheld under the commerce clause had similarly involved regulation designed to influence prices: the tariff, the Interstate Commerce Act, the Sherman Act, the Packers and Stockyards Act, the Grain Futures Act, and the Tobacco Inspection Act. The objective of the AAA of 1938 was "fundamentally the same."[139]

The production and sale of tobacco had never been considered a business affected with a public interest. Before 1934, the Fifth and Fourteenth Amendments would have proscribed regulation of tobacco prices. After *Nebbia*, however, this was no longer the case, and the removal of the due process limitation made available an additional rationale for the Act's validity under the commerce clause. Regulation of the price at which tobacco was sold in interstate commerce, the government contended, would have been "to regulate commerce itself." Congress had regulated the amount of tobacco marketed in order to influence the price at which it was sold. Thus, "A statute with an objective more legitimately or closely related to the regulation of interstate commerce would be difficult to find."[140]

"The lower federal courts," the brief observed, "have with one exception upheld the validity of marketing quotas established for fruits and vegetables under the [AAA of 1933] . . . later re-enacted as the Agricultural Marketing Agreement Act of 1937."[141] When *Mulford* came before the District Court for the Middle District of Georgia, a three-judge panel composed of two Hoover appointees and a Coolidge appointee[142] followed suit. More important, it did so, as one commentator would later say of the Supreme Court's affirming opinion, while "apparently adhering to the old concept[s]."[143] "We may concede," wrote Circuit Judge Sibley, that agriculture, mining, manufacture and the like are in themselves local activities, the regulation of which generally belongs to the States and not to Congress. . . . But the law in controversy does not directly regulate the production of tobacco. It does not penalize or forbid the production of any amount the grower pleases. He may do what he likes with it except to market it. Since most tobacco is grown only to be sold, the inability to sell the excess of a quota except at a loss at least of all profit would tend to and probably would result in the non-production of the excess so far as the grower can prevent it. But the Act directly deals only with the marketing, and not with the planting or production of tobacco. Since marketing is an act of commerce, like transportation, if marketing in interstate and foreign commerce alone had been regulated, there would be no fair doubt of the power generally to regulate.[144]

A commentator reporting the district court's opinion in the *Georgetown Law Journal* predicted a government victory before the Supreme Court. "The sections of the 1938 Act applying to the marketing of tobacco undoubtedly provide the most favorable test of the law for the United States," he wrote. "There is no attempt made to restrict or control crops by means of acreage allotments or to use acreage allotments even as a means to arrive at the marketing quota." "The 1938 Act is clearly distinguishable from the Agricultural Adjustment Act of 1933."[145]

Justice Roberts' majority opinion affirming the lower court bore this prediction out. "The statute does not purport to control production," Roberts wrote. "It sets no limit upon the acreage which may be planted or produced and imposes no penalty for the planting and producing of tobacco in excess of the marketing quota." "The Act did not prevent any producer from holding over the excess tobacco produced, or processing and storing it for sale in a later year."[146]

In its brief the government had supported its contention that the Act was not intended to operate as a regulation of production by observing that Congress had "contemplated that under certain conditions marketing quotas were to be established after the harvesting of the crop but before marketing." "Internal evidence in the statute of intention to regulate marketing rather than production may be found," the brief pointed out, "in the fact that Congress contemplated that some tobacco marketing quotas might become effective after the planting and growth of the crop." One section of the Act contemplated the imposition of marketing quotas more than two months after the tobacco in question had been harvested. Such quotas "could not possibly have been intended to limit production."[147]

This insight was particularly pertinent with respect to the growers before the Court in *Mulford*. As Justice Roberts observed for the Court, tobacco growers in southern Georgia and northern Florida had begun to arrange for the planting of their 1938 crop in December 1937 by preparing seed beds for planting. By the time the Act had been approved in February of 1938, each of the plaintiffs had already planted his seeds. Indeed, most if not all of the production of the tobacco had taken place before the marketing quotas were announced. "The marketing season for flue-cured tobacco in Georgia and Florida," Roberts reported, "commences about August 1st of each year. Each of the appellants was notified of the quota of his farm shortly before the opening of the auction markets. Prior to the receipt of notice each of them had largely, if not wholly, completed planting, cultivating, harvesting, curing and grading his tobacco. Until receipt of notice none knew, or could have known, the exact amount of his quota. . . ."[148] Under these circumstances, the government had argued, "Congress must have realized that the quota provisions for flue-cured tobacco for 1938 would become operative in time to control the amount marketed but not in time to control the amount produced."[149]

"[T]he statute," Roberts surmised after recounting the chronology of the 1938 tobacco season, "operates not on farm production, as the appellants insist, but upon the marketing of their tobacco in interstate commerce."[150] "It purports to be solely a regulation of interstate commerce," he observed, citing *Currin*, "which it reaches and affects at the throat where tobacco enters the stream of commerce,—the marketing warehouse."[151] This invocation of the current of commerce metaphor had been foreseen by the bill's floor manager in 1938. "It is well settled in the law," Senator Pope had argued, "that terminal warehouses are in interstate commerce."

> The Supreme Court has described them as the "bottle neck" through which the stream of commerce must flow. In the past disorderly marketing practices . . . have completely clogged those terminals, which are an integral part of interstate commerce. Not theoretically, but in fact, terminal warehouses have been so filled that there was no longer physical room for a bushel of wheat. That, Mr. President, is even more directly an obstruction to the orderly flow of interstate commerce than an industrial strike.[152]

As the government had argued, "Substantial quantities of the tobacco brought to the warehouses comes from outside the state."[153] With respect to the tobacco brought to the Georgia warehouse from Florida, the current of commerce doctrine was clearly apposite.

Some of the tobacco, however, had been grown within the state of Georgia, and to this the current of commerce rationale was inapplicable. Rather than treating the in-state and out-of-state tobacco separately, therefore, Roberts found support for the imposition of marketing quotas on all of the tobacco sold on the Georgia auction market in the line of cases stretching from *Dahnke-Walker* to *Currin*. Citing this line of authority Roberts stated that "This court has recently declared that sales of tobacco by growers through warehousemen to purchasers for removal outside the state constitute interstate commerce." Finding that the tobacco marketing provisions had a valid commerce purpose, Roberts continued, "Any rule, such as that embodied in the Act, which is intended to foster, protect and conserve that commerce, or to prevent the flow of commerce from working harm to the people of the nation, is within the competence of Congress."[154] "Within these limits the exercise of the power, the grant being unlimited in its terms, may lawfully extend to the absolute prohibition of such commerce," he continued, citing *Ames, Hipolite Egg, Hoke, Brooks,* and *Gooch*, "and *a fortiori* to limitation of the amount of a given commodity which may be transported in such commerce."[155]

By imposing limits on the amount of tobacco that a grower could market, the Act necessarily reached both interstate and intrastate tobacco sales. To the objection that such regulation exceeded congressional power, Roberts responded with citations to *Currin* and *Shreveport*. "The record discloses that at least two-thirds of all flue-cured tobacco sold at auction warehouses is sold for immediate shipment to an interstate or foreign destination," he reported. "In Georgia nearly one hundred per cent of the tobacco so sold is purchased by extrastate purchasers. In markets where tobacco is sold to both interstate and intrastate purchasers it is not known, when the grower places his tobacco on the warehouse floor for sale, whether it is destined for interstate or intrastate commerce. Regulation to be effective, must, and therefore may constitutionally, apply to all sales."[156] Again, the majority opinion was bereft of any citation to *Jones & Laughlin* or its Wagner Act progeny.

Justices Butler and McReynolds filed a dissent based on *Butler* and *Hammer*[157] and, as Solicitor General Robert Jackson later reported, "The decision was followed by a good deal of uninformed comment to the effect that Mr. Justice Roberts had reversed his position and that the Court had reversed itself on the subject of control of agricultural production by the Federal Government."[158] "This," Jackson asserted, "was certainly untrue."

> The first Agricultural Adjustment Act rested on the power to tax for the "general welfare." The latter Act rested on the power to regulate interstate commerce. The regulation of marketing was all that the latter Act attempted, and while regulation of marketing undoubtedly would have the effect of regulating production, nothing in the Constitution requires Congress to avoid such effects; were this not so, many a tax and tariff would be unconstitutional. The two opinions by Mr. Justice Roberts are not legally inconsistent, since they are not concerned with the same power of Congress.[159]

This distinction between the scope of the commerce power and the scope of the power to tax and spend was not a post-*Mulford* discovery. It had been explicitly relied on by the Act's floor manager, who had deployed in his defense of the Act the following remarks from Justice Roberts' *Butler* opinion:

> Despite a reference in its first section to a burden upon, and an obstruction to the normal currents of commerce, the act under review does not purport to regulate transactions in interstate or foreign commerce. Its stated purpose is the control of agricultural production, a purely local activity, in an effort to raise the prices paid the farmer. Indeed, the Government does not attempt to uphold the validity of the act on the basis of the commerce clause, which, for the purpose of the present case, may be put aside as irrelevant.[160]

The *Butler* opinion was thus limited to the federal power to tax and spend and cast no doubt on "the proper regulation by Congress of the interstate and foreign commerce pursuant to the provisions of this bill," Senator Pope had concluded.[161] Jackson himself had made the same argument in the government's *Mulford* brief. "It is clear from *Hill v. Wallace* and *Chicago Board of Trade v. Olsen*," he had written, "that Congress may utilize the commerce power to regulate subjects which it may not reach under the taxing power. The former case held invalid the Futures Trading Act, which imposed prohibitive taxes on certain types of dealing in grain futures. The latter case sustained the constitutionality of the Grain Futures Act, which contained an identical system of regulation under the commerce clause."[162] The idea that Congress could not address the farm problem by employing its fiscal powers to regulate production, but might do so by regulating marketing through its commerce power, no doubt perplexed many observers. But to the "Tenth Justice,"[163] steeped in the Court's federalism jurisprudence, it came as no surprise.

Nationalizing *Nebbia*

The series of cases that most trenchantly demonstrated *Nebbia's* impact on commerce clause jurisprudence involved, appropriately, federal regulation of milk sales. In the wake of the *Schechter* decision in 1935, Congress had sought to shore up the constitutional foundations of the Agricultural Adjustment Act with various amendments.[164] The Act's new section 8c authorized the secretary of agriculture to set minimum prices for sales between producers and processors of certain basic agricultural commodities, including milk, where the handling of the commodity took place "in the current of interstate commerce, or so as to directly burden, obstruct, or affect, interstate or foreign commerce in such commodity."[165]

The bill's backers defended its constitutionality by mobilizing the same triad of authorities they would later deploy in the debates over the Bituminous Coal Conservation Act of 1937. Sponsors relied on *Lemke, Shafer,* and *Dahnke-Walker* for the proposition that Congress had power to regulate interstate sales.[166] To support the claim that this power included the power to regulate interstate prices, and particularly milk prices, proponents repeatedly cited *Nebbia.*[167] Of course, several major metropolitan milk markets included both interstate and intrastate milk. It was "obvious," contended Representative Harold Cooley of North Carolina, "that in these interstate milk markets the fixing of minimum producer prices for interstate milk could not be effective without fixing equivalent prices for intrastate milk which is in direct competition with interstate milk, and the fixing of minimum producer prices for interstate milk alone would clearly discriminate against such milk."[168] Regulation of the price of such competing intrastate milk was therefore constitutional, Cooley and others argued, under the *Shreveport* doctrine.[169] The amendments passed the House by a vote of 168 to 52,[170] and the Senate, where only six Republicans joined nine Democrats in opposition, by a 64 to 15 margin.[171] After the *Butler* case was decided, the marketing provisions of the amended AAA were reenacted, with only minor modifications, as the Agricultural Marketing Agreement Act of 1937.[172]

United States v. Rock Royal Co-operative and its companion case, *H. P. Hood & Sons v. United States,*[173] involved a challenge to orders issued by the secretary of agriculture fixing minimum prices for the sale of milk in the New York and Boston metropolitan areas. The brief for the United States followed the line of argument adumbrated in the 1935 debates. It was settled that Congress could regulate contracts for the sale of commodities for subsequent shipment in interstate commerce, and that price was a term of such contracts that the due process clause no longer insulated from federal control.[174]

The majority opinion upholding the Act was written by Justice Stanley Reed, who had succeeded Sutherland the preceding year. The milk handlers had urged that "the sale by a dairy farmer who delivers his milk to some country plant"[175] was "a local transaction," "fully completed before any interstate commerce begins" and thus immune from federal regulation under the Tenth Amendment.[176] To this Reed had a ready response: "where commodities are bought for use beyond state lines," he wrote, citing *Lemke* and *Dahnke-Walker*, "the sale is a part of interstate commerce." *Nebbia* had recognized the authority of the states to regulate the price of intrastate milk sales,[177] and "The authority of the Federal Government over interstate commerce does not differ in extent or character from that retained by the states over intrastate commerce."[178] A fortiori, federal regulation of interstate milk sales was constitutional.[179]

Justice Roberts dissented in both *Hood* and *Rock Royal*. In *Hood* Roberts objected to certain provisions of the Act on nondelegation grounds;[180] in *Rock Royal* he was joined by Hughes in objecting to provisions of the marketing order there at issue, which he claimed worked an unreasonable discrimination against smaller handlers, thereby denying them due process of law.[181] Both Hughes and Roberts pointedly refrained from joining the *Rock Royal* dissent of McReynolds and Butler, which attacked the statute on Tenth Amendment grounds,[182] and of course neither Hughes nor Roberts suggested that the Fifth Amendment disabled Congress from regulating the price of milk.

By the time a challenge to the Bituminous Coal Conservation Act of 1937 came to the Court in 1940, at least one justice thought the statute so obviously constitutional that the Court ought not bother to hear the case. William O. Douglas, who had succeeded Brandeis the preceding year, wrote that "this court has probably upheld enough such regulatory acts that the decision can be said to be so clearly correct under this Court's decisions that the appeal presents no substantial question. . . . Appeal should be dismissed."[183] The appeal was heard, however, with the result that Douglas had anticipated. The brief for the appellee relied on *Rock Royal, Mulford, Currin, Lemke,* and *Nebbia*.[184]

Douglas' opinion for the majority made short work of the company's claims that the Act exceeded the scope of the commerce power and ran afoul of the Fifth Amendment's due process clause. "The regulatory provisions," wrote Douglas, "are clearly within the power of Congress under the commerce clause of the Constitution."

> The provisions are applicable only to sales or transactions in, or directly affecting, interstate commerce. The fixing of prices, the proscription of unfair trade practices, the establishment of marketing rules respecting such sales of bituminous coal constitute regulations within the competence of Congress under the commerce clause. As stated by Mr. Justice Cardozo in his dissent in *Carter v. Carter Coal*, "To regulate the price for such transactions is to regulate commerce itself, and not alone its antecedent conditions or its ultimate consequences." See *Tagg Bros. & Moorhead v. United States*. What is true of prices is true of the attachment of other conditions to the flow of a commodity in interstate channels. *Mulford v. Smith*. . . . See *United States v. Rock Royal Co-operative*.[185]

"Nor does the Act violate the Fifth Amendment," Douglas continued. "Price control is one of the means available to the states [citing *Nebbia*] and to the Congress [citing *Rock Royal*] in their respective domains for the protection and promotion of the welfare of the economy."[186] In a broad gesture to Hughes and Roberts, Douglas reminded his readers that "There is nothing in the *Carter* case which stands in the way. The majority of the Court in that case did not pass on the price-fixing features of the earlier Act. The Chief Justice and Mr. Justice Cardozo in separate minority opinions expressed the view that the price-fixing features of the earlier Act were constitutional. We rest on their conclusions for sustaining the present Act."[187] Cases upholding the Wagner Act went unmentioned yet again. The sole dissenter was Justice McReynolds, the lone remaining Horseman.[188]

Neither *Rock Royal* nor *Sunshine* had required the Court to reach the *Shreveport* issue in order to decide the case.[189] Reed's *Rock Royal* opinion, however, left little doubt where the Court stood. There was no question raised, he noted, "as to the power of the Congress to regulate the distribution in the area of the wholly intrastate milk. It is recognized that the federal authority covers the sales of this milk, as its marketing is inextricably intermingled with and directly affects the marketing in the area of the milk which moves across state lines."[190] The Court had held in *Currin* "that where sales for interstate transportation were commingled with intrastate transactions, the existence of the local activity did not interfere with the federal power to regulate inspection of the whole." In *Mulford* the Court had decided that "Power to establish quotas for interstate marketing gives power to name quotas for that which is to be left within the state of production." "Where local and foreign milk alike are drawn into a general plan for protecting the interstate commerce in the commodity from interferences, burdens and obstructions, arising from the excessive surplus and the social and sanitary evils of low values," Reed had concluded, "the power of the Congress extends also to the local sales."[191]

It therefore came as something of a surprise when a Seventh Circuit panel including two Roosevelt appointees[192] unanimously held that an order regulating milk sales in the Chicago area could not be applied to a handler that purchased and sold only intrastate milk.[193] The Wrightwood Dairy bought all of its milk from producers located in the state of Illinois, processed that milk at its Chicago plant, never intermingled it with any interstate milk, and sold and distributed its product solely within the state. Wrightwood's intrastate milk competed in the Chicago market with milk produced in Wisconsin, Indiana, and Michigan, however, and the United States contended that by virtue of this competition with interstate milk it was subject to federal regulation under the *Shreveport* doctrine.[194]

The Seventh Circuit recognized that the consequence of exempting Wrightwood from the order "may well be that the effective sanction of the order will wither before the force of competition, the morale of the market will disintegrate, and this attempt at solution of the problem by the National Government will fail." Nevertheless, the panel concluded that "a commodity wholly intrastate in character and handling does not directly burden, obstruct, or affect interstate commerce where the point of impingement of the intrastate transaction upon the interstate transaction is one of competition only." The court recognized that *Shreveport, Railroad Commission of Wisconsin, Currin,* and *Mulford* "permit the regulation of intrastate transactions which are closely commingled with or related to the interstate commerce regulated." "However," the panel maintained, "these cases do not extend to the facts before us."[195]

The Seventh Circuit explained this cryptic remark not by identifying any difference in fact or principle between *Wrightwood* and *Shreveport,* but instead by referring to the Court's more recent pronouncements in *Schechter*. "The effect upon commerce in the case now before us," wrote Judge Otto Kerner, "is no more direct than in the Schechter case." To accept the Government's *Shreveport* argument "would be to subscribe to a view of causation which, as Justice Cardozo said in the Schechter case . . . 'would obliterate the distinction between what is national and what is local in the activities of commerce.'"[196]

The government's brief on appeal evinced the shock that the decision had provoked. "Every district court which has passed upon the question, apart from the instant case, has also come to the conclusion that intrastate milk competing with interstate is subject to milk orders issued under the Agricultural Marketing Agreement Act," the brief pointed out.[197] Citing *Shreveport*, *Railroad Commission of Wisconsin*, *Currin*, and *Mulford*, the Petition for a Writ of Certiorari contended that "The decision below conflicts with the fundamental constitutional doctrine that the power of Congress extends to the control of intrastate acts when necessary to the effective regulation or protection of interstate commerce. A program for the establishment of minimum prices for interstate milk cannot be effective if intrastate milk can be sold competitively without restriction."[198] "The existence of competition between interstate and intrastate commerce, such as in the case at bar, has been regarded as presenting the typical, as well as perhaps the simplest, situation to which the doctrine is applicable."[199] "[I]n the *Shreveport Case* itself the federal regulation of intrastate railroad rates was upheld precisely because of competitive discrimination against interstate rates. The ruling below is thus inconsistent not only with the familiar principle for which the *Shreveport Case* stands, but also with the decision on its facts."[200]

The dairy responded with a parade of horribles:

> . . . it is petitioner's contention that a commodity wholly intrastate in character and handling, *directly* burdens, obstructs or affects interstate commerce where the point of impingement is *one of competition only*. This contention presents a dangerous and revolutionary construction of the Commerce Clause of the Federal Constitution which would enable the Federal Government to control every enterprise, every occupation and every activity of the people merely by showing that the product thereof is in competition with similar products which cross state lines. Such a restriction would reach all enterprises and transactions which were in competition with those of other states. The authority of the Federal Government would embrace all activities of the people, and the authority of the state over its domestic affairs would exist only by sufferance of the Federal Government. There would be no limit to Federal power, and the States and the people would be effectively deprived of their rights theretofore reserved to themselves and guaranteed to them under Article X of the Amendments to the Constitution of the United States.[201]

"There is hardly a single article produced or manufactured in common use," the company warned, "which can be said not to be in competition with a similar article produced or manufactured across state lines."[202]

Chief Justice Stone's opinion reversing the Seventh Circuit for a unanimous Court confirmed Reed's remarks in *Rock Royal*, relentlessly pursuing the logic of the *Nebbia/Shreveport* conjunction.[203] "Congress plainly has power to regulate the price of milk distributed through the medium of interstate commerce, *United States v.*

Rock Royal Co-operative," wrote Stone, "and it possesses every power needed to make that regulation effective."[204] "[T]he marketing of a local product in competition with a like commodity moving interstate may so interfere with interstate commerce or its regulation as to afford a basis for Congressional regulation of the intrastate activity. It is the effect upon its interstate commerce or its regulation, regardless of the particular form which the competition may take, which is the test of federal power. Cf. *Shreveport Case, supra; Railroad Commission of Wisconsin v. Chicago, B. & Q. R. Co., supra*."[205] "[T]he marketing of intrastate milk which competes with that shipped interstate would tend seriously to break down price regulation in the latter," Stone continued. "Under the conditions prevailing in the milk industry, as the record shows, the unregulated sale of the intrastate milk tends to reduce the sales price received by handlers and the amount which they in turn pay to producers." "We conclude that the national power to regulate the price of milk moving interstate into the Chicago, Illinois marketing area, extends to such control over intrastate transactions there as is necessary and appropriate to make the regulation of the interstate commerce effective; and that it includes authority to make like regulations for the marketing of intrastate milk whose sale and competition with the interstate milk affects its price structure so as in turn to affect adversely the Congressional regulation."[206]

The decision in *Wrightwood* awakened commentators to the possibility that the mixture of *Nebbia* with *Shreveport* was sufficiently potent to work a radical transformation of the federal system. "The remaining question to be decided by the federal courts," remarked one observer, "will be: What degree of competition is necessary to bring intrastate activity within the grasp of federal power. Conceivably *any* wholly intrastate activity competes with a similar interstate activity."[207] An editor at the *Columbia Law Review* agreed. "Since, theoretically, the standard of the instant case could make interstate and intrastate commerce coextensive, as every product on the market competes with every other for a portion of the total demand, the obvious problem in applying the new concept is to discover within what bounds the effects of actual competition will be given legal significance."[208] "[I]t would appear," an editor of the *Minnesota Law Review* suggested, "that a liberal application of the doctrine of the instant case could present some threat to the continued existence of the federal system."[209] "The implications of the 'competition' doctrine, if carried to their logical extreme," the *Columbia Law Review* observed, "would result in a complete withdrawal of the Supreme Court from its position as a check upon Congressional action under the commerce clause."[210]

These commentators were of course correct. The continued existence of the federal system they had known was threatened, and the Supreme Court would the very next term withdraw from its role as the umpire of that system. Moreover, as we shall see, *Nebbia* and *Shreveport* would have a further role to play in the demise of constitutional federalism. Yet those keeping vigil for the old order would not be forced to watch the Court slowly work out *Nebbia*'s implications for commerce clause jurisprudence. The justices would not permit the old federal system to linger while *Nebbia* dismantled it piece by piece and eventually swallowed it from within. For even as these commentators wrote, the Court was preparing with a single blow to demolish what was left of the doctrinal edifice that *Nebbia* had already done so much to erode.

12

The Struggle with
Judicial Supremacy

In the summer of 1937, the Four Horsemen began to put themselves out to pasture. Justice Van Devanter retired June 2, 1937; Justice Sutherland followed him on January 18, 1938. Due to illness Justice Butler did not participate in any of the cases heard during the 1939 term; he died in Washington on November 16, 1939. Justice McReynolds, dissenting to the end, retired February 1, 1941. Frustrated during his first term by his lack of opportunity to make any appointments to the Court, Roosevelt placed five justices on the High Bench during his second term. By the time the Court handed down its opinion in *United States v. Darby*[1] in 1941, the only justices remaining from the 1937 Court were Hughes, Roberts, and Stone.

The case concerned provisions of the Fair Labor Standards Act of 1938 that prohibited the employment of workers engaged in "production for interstate commerce" at substandard wages or for excessive hours, as well as the interstate shipment of goods made by employees working under such substandard conditions. The case presented a golden opportunity for the Court to overrule *Hammer v. Dagenhart*,[2] which had struck down the nation's first federal law regulating child labor[3] and had long been a black mark on the Supreme Court's record. Indeed, *Hammer* and a later case striking down a subsequent child labor law[4] had spawned a movement to add a Child Labor Amendment to the Constitution, a movement that had come near to success.[5] A justice sensitive to the public's passion for social reform and concerned about his place in history almost certainly would have relished the opportunity to pen the decision overturning such an odious precedent. Hughes had taken the lead in writing such controversial commerce clause decisions as *Schechter* and *Jones & Laughlin*, and one might well have expected the chief to take the lead in *Darby*.[6]

Yet he did not. Instead, he ceded the limelight and assigned the opinion to Stone. At the *Darby* conference, Hughes expressed substantial reservations about the power of Congress to regulate all "production for commerce." "The transportation counts stand on a different footing from the production counts," Hughes asserted. "The latter are not a part of interstate commerce." Indeed, Hughes' remarks at conference suggest that he did not believe that the Court had yet sanctioned federal regulation of production per se. The old categories had not been discarded. This case, Hughes thought, differed from the cases the Court had previously decided under the Wagner Act. "The present act," he stated, "is unique in that it reaches into the field of production." "It is an unusual statute in its application." Production was not in itself commerce, Hughes argued; and Congress had in the Act provided "no machinery for determining whether" "in a particular case" the requisite "close and substantial relationship" between the act of production and interstate commerce existed. If the regulatory power of Congress were extended to local acts having only "remote relationships" to interstate commerce, Hughes argued, "our dual system of government would be at an end." And here, Hughes noted, the report of the Labor Committee had indicated that the Act was intended to reach "every act no matter how trivial which has a relationship to commerce." "Congress would thus provide for minimum wages without any regard to [the] relation [to interstate commerce] of some little man with [a] mill." After an extended presentation Hughes reiterated the question for which he still had no answer: "Is this act within [the] power of Congress[?]" His concluding remark conveyed the gravity and difficulty of the central question of the case: "This is the most important case we have had by far in connection with the commerce power."[7] *Darby* was not, in Hughes' view, merely a footnote to *Jones & Laughlin*, a foregone conclusion entailed by a revolutionary decision taken in 1937. On the contrary, *Darby* was more important "by far." The author of *Jones & Laughlin* believed that the Court had as yet neither settled the scope of the federal commerce power nor abdicated responsibility for policing the power's exercise.

When the vote on the case was taken, seven of the justices voted to uphold the Act; but Hughes, who as chief voted only after listening to the opinions and votes of his colleagues, did not. Instead, he passed.[8] Hughes' reservations over the commerce clause issue were compounded by his concerns that the statute provided notice insufficient to support imposition of criminal penalties, and this apparently brought him to the brink of dissent. "Even with the best possible test," he wrote Stone privately, "the statute is a highly unsatisfactory one, but as it is a border line case I should prefer not to write."[9] And in place of his usually cheerful "I agree," he wrote grudgingly on the back of the circulated draft of Stone's opinion, "I will go along with this."[10]

The surviving *Darby* records curiously do not portray a Justice Roberts similarly struggling with the constitutional issue that so troubled Hughes. One can certainly detect remnants of dual federalist vocabulary in his conceptualization of the case. At conference he remarked, "With respect to control of goods I think we have to give credence to what Congress says—stop discrimination between states. I think we have to uphold it as having a *direct effect* on interstate commerce."[11] In all likelihood these remarks reflect Roberts' views only with respect to the transportation counts; Roberts may well have shared some of Hughes' reservations concerning the production counts. This inference is supported, as we shall see, by Roberts' subsequent public and private behavior in commerce clause cases that came before the Court after Hughes' retirement in 1941.

A. B. Kirschbaum v. Walling[12] concerned the applicability of the Fair Labor Standards Act to employees engaged in the operation and maintenance of buildings in Philadelphia and New York in which tenants produced large quantities of clothing for interstate commerce. An engineer and firemen produced heat, hot water, and steam necessary to the manufacturing operations and kept elevators, radiators, and fire sprinkler systems in repair. An electrician maintained light and power systems. Elevator operators ran freight elevators carrying goods received through and destined for the channels of interstate commerce, as well as passenger elevators carrying employees, customers, salesmen, and visitors. Watchmen protected the building from fire and theft. Carpenters kept halls, stairways, and other parts of the building used by the tenants in good repair. Porters kept the buildings clean and habitable. The question was whether these employees were engaged "in any process or occupation necessary to the production" of goods for commerce within the meaning of the Act.[13]

For the majority, the case involved solely a question of statutory construction, not one of constitutional power. Yet the majority's approach to the former type of question was permeated by the very categories and concerns that had guided earlier Courts in addressing questions of the latter type. The task, as Justice Frankfurter's opinion for the Court put it, was to determine "where boundaries must be drawn, under a federal enactment, between what it has taken over for administration by the central Government and what it has left to the States. The expansion of our industrial economy has inevitably been reflected in the extension of federal authority over economic enterprise and its absorption of the authority previously possessed by the States. Federal legislation of this character cannot therefore be construed without regard to the implications of our dual system of government." "We cannot," Frankfurter cautioned,

> indulge in the loose assumption that, when Congress adopts a new scheme for federal industrial regulation, it thereby deals with all situations falling within the general mischief which gave rise to the legislation. Such an assumption might be valid where remedy of the mischief is the concern of only a single unitary government. It cannot be accepted where the practicalities of federalism—or, more precisely, the underlying assumptions of our dual form of government and the consequent presuppositions of legislative draftsmanship which are expressive of our history and habits—cut across what might otherwise be the implied range of the legislation. Congress may choose, as it has chosen frequently in the past, to regulate only part of what it constitutionally can regulate, leaving to the States activities which, if isolated, are only local. . . . The history of Congressional legislation regulating not only interstate commerce as such but also activities intertwined with it, justifies the generalization that, when the Federal Government takes over such local radiations in the vast network of our national economic enterprise and thereby radically readjusts the balance of state and national authority, those charged with the duty of legislating are reasonably explicit and do not entrust its attainment to that retrospective expansion of meaning which properly deserves the stigma of judicial legislation.[14]

"Our dual system of government," "our history and habits," the distinction between "local" and "national" activities, and "the balance of state and national authority" were all desiderata to be preserved; but now they were to be preserved not by judicial review, but by judicial construction.

Surveying the legislative history of the Act, the Court was left in this case with "no doubt that Congress chose not to enter areas which it might have occupied." The House bill had applied to employers engaged in "any industry affecting commerce," while the Act in its final form had dropped the "affecting commerce" language and had instead purported to reach only employees "engaged in commerce or in the production of goods for commerce." The scope of the Act, Frankfurter concluded, "is not coextensive with the limits of the power of Congress over commerce." The Court nevertheless concluded that these employees "were engaged in occupations 'necessary to the production' of goods for commerce by the tenants. Without light and heat and power the tenants could not engage, as they do, in the production of goods for interstate commerce," Frankfurter reasoned. "The maintenance of a safe, habitable building is indispensable to that activity."[15]

Frankfurter hastened to add, however, that "some employees may not be within the Act even though their activities are in an ultimate sense 'necessary' to the production of goods for commerce. . . . 'Necessary' is colored by the context not only of the terms of this legislation but of its implications in the relation between state and national authority." As Cardozo and Hughes had put it in *Schechter* and *Jones & Laughlin*, the question was one of degree, of remoteness or proximity, of indirectness or immediacy. Employees whose work had "only the most tenuous relation to, and [was] not in any fitting sense 'necessary'" to the production of goods for commerce were not covered by the Act. In *Kirschbaum*, however, the work of the employees "had such a *close and immediate* tie with the process of production for commerce" that the employees fell within the terms of the Act.[16]

In his peroration Frankfurter observed more explicitly that the canons of construction the Court had just embraced in the statutory context had not long ago guided the Court's interpretation of the commerce clause: "What was said about a related problem is not inapposite here: 'Whatever terminology is used, the criterion is necessarily one of degree and must be so defined. . . . In maintaining the balance of the constitutional grants and limitations, it is inevitable that we should define their applications in the gradual process of inclusion and exclusion.'"[17] The source of this quotation was Hughes' majority opinion in *Santa Cruz Fruit*, written only four years earlier. If Frankfurter meant to draw a parallel, he perhaps inadvertently succeeded only in pointing up a distinction. For all of the opinion's ritual obeisances to "our dual form of government," it was nevertheless clear that what had once been principles of constitutional law were now little more than rules of statutory interpretation. The "related problem" to which Frankfurter alluded was quickly becoming a problem of the past.

This "problem" was of more than merely antiquarian interest to Justice Roberts, however. He agreed with the majority that the case presented a question of statutory interpretation,[18] but he adamantly insisted that it also raised an issue of federal power. "I think the power of Congress does not reach the purely local activities in question," he wrote in his lone dissent. "If it did, the commerce power alone would support regulation of any local action, since it is conceivable that such activity, however remotely, 'affects' commerce or is 'necessary' to the production of goods for commerce."[19] Roberts' little-noted dissent in *Kirschbaum* reveals that he had not capitulated to a plenary theory of federal power in *Jones & Laughlin*. Indeed, it makes clear that he had not done so even in *Darby*.

Roberts' response to a better-known case argued that same term further illustrates his continued solicitude for constitutional federalism. An Ohio farmer named Roscoe Filburn had been penalized for planting twice as many acres of wheat as he had been allotted by Secretary of Agriculture Claude Wickard under the amended Agricultural Adjustment Act of 1938. Filburn had marketed the harvest from his allotted acreage, and had reserved all of his surplus wheat for use and consumption on his own farm. Writing for a unanimous Court now dominated by Roosevelt appointees, Justice Robert Jackson upheld federal regulation of the growth of wheat that was never to enter the channels of commerce. The forcefulness and unanimity of Justice Jackson's opinion, however, belie the intellectual struggle that preceded delivery of this landmark decision.

The case was initially docketed for the 1941 term and was argued May 4, 1942.[20] At the initial conference, every participating justice except Roberts agreed with Stone's view that "this is a regulation of commerce." Justice Roberts passed, however, saying he was "in doubt" over whether the commerce clause authorized such a far-reaching regulation.[21] Yet eventually a majority of the Court came to share Roberts' reservations with respect to the commerce power issue the case presented. The growth of wheat for home consumption was not itself interstate commerce, nor was it intended for interstate commerce. Only if the activity produced a substantial effect on interstate commerce, therefore, was it properly subject to federal regulation. In the spring of 1942, the Court was not prepared to find such an effect. Justice Jackson produced two drafts of an opinion, in each of which the Court refused to reach the commerce clause issue. In each he remanded the case to the district court for additional factual findings that might better enable the Court to determine whether such an effect on commerce existed.[22]

In the first, shorter draft, Jackson only briefly adverted to the difficulty he and his colleagues were having in resolving the issue. "The constitutional issue involved is of the greatest magnitude, and we are of opinion that we should not pass upon it in the present state of the record, without the benefit of findings and consideration by the court below or a full presentation of the controlling economic facts relied upon."[23] The second draft, however, provides greater insight into the state of Jackson's thought in the spring of 1942.

In reviewing the applicable precedents, Jackson quoted liberally from *Jones & Laughlin's* encomium to federalism. There Hughes had written that the congressional power to regulate commerce

> must be considered in the light of our dual system of government, and may not be extended to embrace effects upon interstate commerce so indirect and remote that to embrace them, in view of our complex society, would effectually obliterate the distinction between what is national and what is local and create a completely centralized government. The question is necessarily one of degree.[24]

Against this backdrop, Jackson elaborated the troubling features of the Act.

> We cannot blink the fact that if this Act as amended and construed is to be sustained it regulates intrastate, in fact intra-farm, activities beyond any statute sustained by any former decision of this Court. If the courts are to adopt what appears to be its adminis-

trative construction, it would penalize a farmer for sowing his own seed on his own land and using the increase to sustain himself or his livestock. No distinction seems to be made between what is produced in the course of ordinary diversified or dairy farming in which the sale of animals is occasional or incidental and farming which consistently and as a business produces a major crop or livestock for the interstate market. The regulation appears to extend to matters which would not be thought of as commerce at all, for the penalty appears to be applied although the wheat sought to be regulated never leaves the farm on which it was produced and is never the subject of a sale of any kind or in any form.[25]

In other words, as he wrote Chief Justice Stone three days after circulating this draft, the activities regulated by the Act were "neither interstate nor commerce."[26]

This alone did not dispose of the issue of whether such control was within federal power, a question whose importance Jackson viewed as "obviously of first magnitude." Congress' power to regulate interstate commerce was plenary: "Its own will to act" was in such instances "sufficient justification." The power to regulate intrastate commerce, however, was a different matter. "The power to enter upon the state domain is justified only by a state of facts showing that the intrastate activities sought to be reached are of such a quality and substantiality that what would otherwise be an intrusion is proper for the protection and effective exercise of a granted federal power." The homage to "our dual system of government" implicit in this reference to an "intrusion" was corroborated elsewhere in the draft. "[I]n reaching into the reserved power of the States," Jackson wrote, "Congress may not act by its will alone, for it was not given to one of the parties to the federal compact to expand its own functions at will." Instead, "it is the function of the courts to determine whether the particular activity regulated or prohibited is within the reach of federal power."[27] Like Hughes, Jackson still saw the Court as the umpire of the federal system.

The legislative history and the facts on the record did not demonstrate to Jackson's satisfaction that the growth of wheat for home consumption exerted a substantial effect on interstate commerce, and he and his colleagues were unprepared to assume without proof that it did. The legislative findings had merely declared the necessity of the Act's provisions for effective regulation of interstate commerce in wheat. This, Jackson wrote, was clearly an inadequate constitutional foundation. "A mere finding of convenience will not sustain federal invasion of the intrastate field. Undivided power is usually exercised more conveniently than divided power, but our federal system is not to be disposed of for the convenience of federal administrators."[28]

The absence of factual findings bearing on the effect of Filburn's activity on interstate commerce, Jackson concluded, "have left us without adequate materials for confident judgment that an affirmative answer to the question of power would not 'effectively obliterate the distinction between what is national [and what is local] and create a completely centralized government.'"[29] The source of this quotation was, of course, Hughes' opinion in *Jones & Laughlin*.

Justices Roberts, Frankfurter, Murphy, and Byrnes each agreed to this draft.[30] This opinion, however, never saw the light of day. At a subsequent conference the justices reached a tentative agreement that the case be set for reargument rather than remanded.[31] In subsequent memoranda Chief Justice Stone and Justice Douglas argued in favor of disposing of the case promptly rather than hearing reargument, and Justice Black agreed with them.[32] Frankfurter wrote Stone in favor of reargument, noting "the far-reaching implications of the substantive constitutional question." "If the Act is to be sustained," wrote Frankfurter, "it would be far healthier to have a decision so far-reaching in its practical application made after adequate argument and after the kind of reflection by members of the Court upon the issues that simply could not be achieved in these last hurried days of the term."[33] Jackson, Roberts, Murphy, and Byrnes also favored reargument,[34] and Jackson prepared an order restoring the case to the docket for reargument the following October. The order directed counsel "to discuss the question whether the Act in question in so far as it deals with wheat consumed on the farm of the producer is within the power of Congress to regulate interstate commerce."[35]

The shift from a decision to remand to a decision to order reargument was substantial. Neither Frankfurter's letter to Stone nor Jackson's order said anything about adducing additional facts to support the contention that Filburn's activities affected interstate commerce substantially. Frankfurter instead emphasized the need for unhurried reflection, suggesting that the Court was on the verge of opening a new frontier in commerce clause jurisprudence rather than merely adjudicating a particularized issue of constitutional fact. And Jackson's order rather vaguely requested only that counsel discuss the scope of the commerce power. The decision to remand in Jackson's draft opinion had been based on the proposition that a factually detailed analysis of the effects on interstate commerce of production of wheat for home consumption was required in order to decide the case. Now no such analysis was requested or even mentioned. By the end of the term it was apparent that what the justices wanted was more time to think, not more facts to think about. The earlier decision to remand may have been in reality a device to buy the time the justices thought they needed. In any event, the decision to order reargument testifies to the uncertainty that a majority of the justices felt in the spring of 1942 concerning the scope of the commerce power.

This uncertainty is nicely captured in a letter that Jackson wrote to Stone on May 25, 1942. Jackson was apparently responding to a letter Stone had sent him citing cases in which governmental regulation had been upheld in the face of due process challenges. Jackson's response is worth quoting at length.

> In such cases if a rational basis is perceived it of course is not the Court's function to balance the reasons.
>
> And so it would be under the commerce clause if *the subject of the regulation were interstate commerce*. But here, admittedly, it is not. Activities that are neither interstate nor commerce are regulated because of their *effect on commerce*.
>
> The Constitution drew a line between state and federal power and here the Congress wants to cross that line admittedly. I suppose that before we give it our approval there must be some finding that it is warranted by facts and conditions. Otherwise the federal compact was pretty meaningless if Congress is to be sole judge of the extent of its own commerce power. As you have well pointed out in the *Darby* case, sometimes the Court has been required to determine the facts that carry federal power across the

line; sometimes administrative bodies do it; sometimes Congress has done it—but only, I think, where the effect was obvious to the naked judicial eye.[36]

This passage suggests that Jackson still believed that a fact-based inquiry was appropriate to determine the "reasonableness" of an exercise of the commerce power. But his explanation of why he favored reargument rather than remand suggests that he needed time and intellectual help, not more facts.

> The performance of the Court below and of the plaintiff's counsel gives little hope that they would much sharpen the real issue, and I am afraid that most of the Government men feel too sure of the Court to bother with enlightening it.
>
> So I would . . . with such meagre help as we will get from reargument settle down in the fall to deciding the merits.

It was issue-sharpening and enlightenment, not fact-finding, that was needed. This was confirmed by Jackson's concluding sentence, in which he confessed not factual ignorance, but conceptual confusion: "If a completely baffled mind can be called an open one, mine is."[37]

Still another passage in the letter further illuminates the state of Jackson's thought in May 1942.

> If I am wrong about the proposition that whereas regulation of commerce itself requires no justification beyond the will of Congress, but regulation of what is neither interstate nor commerce does depend upon a reasonably probable effect of some kind, not too indirect, remote or trivial, then we have no function but to stamp this Act O.K.[38]

The suggestion that the test of whether an activity was subject to federal regulation was whether it exerted an effect on commerce that was not "too indirect, remote or trivial" shows that Jackson was still thinking about commerce clause issues in the vocabulary employed by Cardozo and Hughes.

Jackson's posture in the spring of 1942 was not without irony. Only the year before, while attorney general of the United States, he had published *The Struggle for Judicial Supremacy*. Writing as an avowedly partisan New Dealer, Jackson had lambasted the Hughes Court's federalism jurisprudence of the mid-1930s.[39] He had ridiculed the *Butler* opinion's treatment of the national agricultural crisis as a "local" problem, and he had castigated the Court for holding in *Carter Coal* that the effect of wages and hours on interstate commerce in coal was "indirect." The words "direct" and "indirect," he had written dismissively, "are not in the Constitution." Whether the effect was direct or indirect was a "non-constitutional question."[40] Yet in his first year as a justice, Jackson was struggling with the prospect that he might have to hold that small-scale agricultural production for home use was a "local" matter exerting too "indirect" an effect on interstate commerce to be regulated by the national government.

Donning the ermine seems to have had some effect on the way that Jackson looked at commerce power issues, and it is an effect that he foresaw himself. In *The Struggle for Judicial Supremacy* he had written:

> our history shows repeated disappointment of liberal Presidents in their efforts to effect a permanent or even long-standing change of attitude or philosophy of the

Court by additions to its personnel. Why is it that the Court influences appointees more consistently than appointees influence the Court? I point out certain sustained institutional and procedural pressures towards conservatism which only the most alert Justices will sense and only the most hardy will overcome. Because of these constant pressures I would underwrite no futures even now.[41]

Among these "institutional and procedural pressures" was the justices' lawyerly cast of thought.

Justices are drawn only from the legal profession. The entire philosophy, interest, and training of the legal profession tend toward conservatism. . . . it is much concerned with precedents, authorities, existing customs, usages, vested rights, and established relationships. Its method of thinking, accepted by no other profession, cultivates a supreme respect for the past, and its order. Justice Cardozo has well said that the "power of precedent, when analyzed, is the power of the beaten track." No lawyer sufficiently devoted to the law to know our existing rules, the history of them, and the justification for them, will depart from them lightly.[42]

One hears in these passages echoes again of Maitland and Pound. Yet the tenacity of the categories and vocabulary of dual federalism was not, in Jackson's case, a simple instance of mindless inertia. Even so avid a New Dealer as Jackson was not prepared to deny that federalism was a *constitutional* as well as a political value. The vocabulary of dual federalism was so tenacious because, for Jackson as well as for Hughes and Cardozo, it served to safeguard that underlying constitutional value.

Yet Jackson's suggestion in his note to Stone that this vocabulary might be inappropriate, and that the alternative was to rubber-stamp congressional legislation, suggested that Jackson was beginning to flirt with this latter conception of the Court's function in supervising congressional exercises of the commerce power.

And, indeed, he was. During the summer of '42 Jackson wrote two memoranda to his law clerk in which he attempted to think his way through the commerce clause issue. Jackson confessed at the outset that the question in *Filburn* "presents a good deal of a problem to me. It seems idle to disguise it, for it appears to be a regulation of production and of production not for commerce either actually or in contemplation."[43] Such a regulation penetrated "the domain ordinarily reserved to the states to an extent not sustained by any prior precedent of this Court."[44] Under these circumstances, wrote Jackson, there were three possible holdings. First, the Court might hold that "production and consumption not for commerce is exclusively within the control of the state." Such a holding would be consistent with the line of cases descending from *Knight,* which held that local activities of production were presumptively subject solely to state control. Second, the Court might hold that such production "is normally within the control of the state but is transferred to federal control upon judicial findings that it is necessary to protect exercises of the commerce power." This holding would have been consistent with the line of cases descending from *Swift* and *Shreveport,* which stood for the proposition that particular facts could transform what was otherwise a local activity into a national one subject to federal control. But Jackson's third alternative was without precedent: "That it is normally within the control of the state but that it is transferred to federal control upon a mere Congressional assumption of control."[45]

Before the *Shreveport* case was decided, Jackson thought, there would have been no doubt that the first holding was appropriate to the resolution of the instant case.[46] Before that decision, questions concerning the scope of the commerce power had been decided using "legalistic rather than economic tests," legal formulae that tried to "classify economic processes in political terms."[47] Thus "navigation" and "commerce" (understood as transit) were federal, while "manufacturing, mining and production" were state matters.[48] *Shreveport* had introduced a new approach, "a break with localistic and legalistic thinking," admitting economic data as a factor in determining the scope of the commerce power.[49] *Shreveport* and its progeny had adopted the doctrine that "matters normally within the political domain of the states might be transferred to federal control because of their economic relationships."[50]

The difficulty with this approach was that "[e]conomic effects are exceedingly difficult to trace beyond immediate effects. . . ."[51] "The same economic forces which made the political pattern of a subdivided nation inept for regulatory purposes made all boundaries based on economic facts vague and blurred."[52] Nevertheless, the Court had attempted "to ascertain legal standards for weighing economic effects and for applying them to the commerce power." These standards, however, had been "neither consistent nor well defined."[53] The direct/indirect distinction employed in *Schechter* and "again emphasized" in *Jones & Laughlin* was a "legal phrase of limitation" having "almost no value in weighing economic effects," one among many unsatisfactory "judicial shibboleths."[54] Even *Darby's* statement that Congress may regulate what is "appropriate" for regulation in connection with interstate commerce, Jackson wrote, had as a test "no real value."[55]

This history of failure to frame an adequate standard caused Jackson to despair of the enterprise. Like Cardozo and Hughes, he recognized the complexity of interaction in an integrated economy;[56] unlike them, he saw no hope of formulating any meaningful criterion for distinguishing "local" from "national" economic activity.[57] "In such a state of affairs," he remarked, "the determination of the limit is not a matter of legal principle, but of personal opinion; not one of constitutional law, but one of economic policy."[58]

It was this realization that led Jackson to turn from his second possible holding to his third.[59] "We have all but reached an era in the interpretation of the commerce clause of candid recognition that we have no legal judgment upon economic effects which we can oppose to the policy judgment made by Congress in legislation,"[60] he wrote. In Jackson's view, that recognition had been implicit in the Roosevelt Court's recent decisions.[61] The "pretense of review," he observed, was "a shadow without substance."[62] "Under present standards, as presently applied, no law that has a conceivable chance of enactment in Congress can be held unconstitutional." "While a case might be conceived in which the relation and effect of that which was regulated to interstate commerce was non-existent or so remote as to make its regulation inappropriate, none occurs to me."[63] Yet Jackson recognized that it was *this* case that had brought the Court to a jurisprudential Rubicon. "If we sustain the present Act, I don't see how we can ever sustain states' rights again as against a Congressional exercise of the commerce power."[64] "If we sustain the present case, the judicial shibboleths as to limitation of the commerce power are without practical meaning, and that is within the commerce power which Congress desires to regulate."[65]

That summer, Jackson was ready to cross that Rubicon at high noon. "It is perhaps time that we recognize that the introduction of economic determinism into constitutional law of interstate commerce marked the end of judicial control of the scope of federal activity," he wrote.

> A frank holding that the interstate commerce power has no limits except those which Congress sees fit to observe might serve a wholesome purpose. In order to be unconstitutional by the judicial process if this Act is sustained, the relation between interstate commerce and the regulated activity would have to be so absurd that it would be laughed out of Congress.[66]

Jackson saw several policy reasons supporting such a frank recognition. First, he thought that maintaining a pretense of review brought disrespect on the judiciary. "To keep up the pretense means that we must more and more engage in pure quibbling as to what is appropriate, making the judicial process disrespectable for its quibbling."[67] Second, he thought that the prospect of judicial review forced Congress to frame legislation that was unnecessarily complex and indirect.[68] These statutes were "difficult to administer, difficult to obey, and difficult to adjudicate."[69] Finally, Jackson thought that the Court "should not stand as a symbol of a protection of states rights when in fact its power has vanished."[70] "[T]he judicial standards or legal standards for determining the limit of Congressional power are so tenuous and vague that they constitute no protection to the states in any event." Accordingly, it was "far better to place responsibility for intelligent and moderate use of this power on Congress than to keep up a pretense of sharing the responsibility which we have no standards for measuring."[71]

Adopting the third alternative made the case simple rather than troubling. No additional factual information was necessary.

> Congress has seen fit to regulate small and casual wheat growers in the interest of large and specialized ones. It has seen fit to extend its regulation to the grower of wheat for home consumption. Whether this is necessary, whether it is just, whether it is wise, is not for us to say. We cannot say that there is no economic relationship between the growth of wheat for home consumption and interstate commerce in wheat. As to the weight to be given the effects, we have no legal standards by which to set our own judgment against the policy judgment of Congress.[72]

Paraphrasing Hughes' oft-quoted remark about the judges and the Constitution, Jackson concluded that the growth of wheat for home consumption "is within the federal power to regulate interstate commerce, if for no better reason than the commerce clause is what the Congress says it is."[73]

In Jackson's view, "[a] candid recognition that the extent of the commerce power depends upon the facts of each case and that Congress is the primary and final judge of the meaning of those facts can be objectionable only because of its candor, and not because of its result."[74] Jackson's colleagues were apparently prepared for the result, but not for the candor.[75] For while the published opinion repudiated the first of Jackson's proposed alternative holdings, and refrained from a clear embrace of the second, it similarly avoided the frank recognition he had called for in his memoranda. Nevertheless, it appears that the justices in fact selected the third alternative.

The portion of Jackson's opinion dealing with the effect of Filburn's activities on interstate commerce contained nearly three pages of data on the economics of the wheat industry.[76] These were not new economic data adduced in response to the order for reargument, however. These data were drawn from a stipulation of facts that the parties had filed with the district court in January of 1942, and they were contained in the record that Jackson's May draft opinion had found so unsatisfying. Moreover, for all of their inherent interest, these data were almost entirely irrelevant to the issue facing the Court: the effect of growth of wheat for home consumption on interstate commerce in wheat. In fact, the mode of analysis Jackson employed in resolving that issue had been urged by the government in its first brief,[77] was outlined in Jackson's May draft opinion as a possible theory lacking adequate empirical support in the record,[78] and was almost fully developed in a memorandum he wrote to his law clerk more than two months before the government filed its second brief in September.[79]

Growth of wheat for home consumption, Jackson reasoned, reduced the demand for wheat sold in interstate commerce and thereby reduced the price at which such wheat was sold. Because Congress was empowered to regulate the prices at which goods were sold in interstate commerce, it could regulate those activities that affected such prices. Though Filburn's wheat-growing activities taken alone might exert little or no effect on the price of wheat, his activities, "taken together with that of many others similarly situated,"[80] might exert a substantial effect. Here again the shadow of *Nebbia* loomed large. The power of Congress to regulate growth of wheat for home consumption was derivative of its power to regulate the price at which wheat moved in interstate commerce. And it could not have had the power to regulate that price had the due process clause still limited price regulation to a narrow category of businesses affected with a public interest. Without *Nebbia*, the theory on which *Wickard* was decided would have been unavailable.

Yet *Nebbia* by no means decided the issue presented in *Wickard*. In *Wickard*, the kinds of attenuated economic arguments that had in *Schechter* been greeted with a skeptical eye even by Cardozo carried a unanimous Court only seven years later. Economic effects upon commerce that had in 1935 seemed to a unanimous Court too remote and indirect to subject local activities to congressional regulation were now sufficient to justify federal legislation. To embrace this proposition, it was necessary for Jackson and his colleagues to *reject* much of what Cardozo had written in *Schechter* and what Hughes had written in *Jones & Laughlin*. Jackson's opinion dismissed as irrelevant the question of whether the effect on commerce was direct or indirect, remote or proximate; the sole relevant issue was whether the effect exerted was in the aggregate "substantial."[81] Indeed, Stone's comments on Jackson's November 11, 1942, draft of the *Wickard* opinion testify to the intellectual distance the Court had traversed. "I like very much," Stone wrote, "what you say about 'direct' and 'indirect.' I had hoped for something like that when I remained silent and left it to Cardozo to write the concurring opinion in the Schechter Case. But he did not see the matter as you and I do."[82]

Jackson's opinion left no doubt that the Court had discarded the commerce clause vocabulary employed in the mid-1930s. But the opinion did appear to suggest that the effect of an activity on commerce must be in the aggregate substantial before it was subject to federal regulation; and at first blush it appears that it was the Court that was applying the substantiality test. Yet a closer reading of the text, informed by Jackson's private memoranda and correspondence, impels a different conclusion.

Much of Jackson's doctrinal discussion was devoted not to articulating the terms of a test, but to identifying tests that the justices would no longer employ. "[Q]uestions of federal power," he asserted, "cannot be decided simply by finding the activity in question to be 'production,' nor can consideration of its economic effects be foreclosed by calling them 'indirect.'" "Whether the subject of the regulation in question was 'production,' 'consumption,' or 'marketing' is, therefore, not material for deciding the question of federal power before us." The closest the opinion came to setting out a test was the following passage: "even if appellee's activity be local and though it may not be regarded as commerce, it may still, whatever its nature, be reached by Congress if it exerts a substantial economic effect on interstate commerce, and this irrespective of whether such effect is what might at some earlier time have been defined as 'direct' or 'indirect.'"[83]

The phrasing of this last sentence may have been deliberately lawyerly. The exertion of a substantial economic effect is framed as a sufficient rather than a necessary condition. Rather than saying that the effect *must* be substantial, the opinion provides that Congress *may* reach the activity *if* (but not only if) the effect is substantial. If this seems like a semantic quibble, consider the sentence with which Jackson concluded his discussion of the commerce power issue: "This record leaves us in no doubt that Congress may properly have considered that wheat consumed on the farm where grown, if wholly outside the scheme of regulation, would have a substantial effect in defeating and obstructing its purpose to stimulate trade therein at increased prices."[84] The record did not leave the Court in no doubt that wheat consumed on the farm *would* or *did* have such an effect; it left the justices in no doubt that "Congress may properly have considered" that it would have such an effect. The record that Jackson and his colleagues had considered utterly inadequate for a *judicial* determination of the substantiality of the effect was perfectly adequate for a *legislative* determination of the substantiality of that effect. The Court was not passing on whether Congress' determination was correct; it was merely finding that what Congress had "considered" was "proper." The opinion made no attempt to articulate any standard of propriety. Nor did it suggest what the Court would do in the event it found such consideration improper.[85]

A memorandum that Jackson circulated among his colleagues sheds further light. There Jackson adverted to "the presumption of constitutionality which is raised by Congressional action," before holding:

> We cannot say from anything in this record that the effect on commerce from the multiplication of individually trifling concerns of wheat for home consumption is not

substantial. . . . we ground our decision on the realities disclosed, which afford no basis for judicial denial to Congress of the power to extend its regulation to the production of wheat not intended for commerce or sale.[86]

Again, it is not clear what *would* have afforded a basis for such a judicial denial. Here Jackson seems to have been embracing a particularly robust presumption of constitutionality. The burden was on the statute's challenger to prove that the activity regulated produced in the aggregate no substantial effect on interstate commerce. Proof of such a negative would of course be virtually impossible, making the presumption of constitutionality for all practical purposes conclusive. Congress was clearly the *primary* judge of the statute's constitutionality; it was in reality the *final* judge as well.

Any doubt about what these elusive phrases meant to Jackson is removed by a glance at his private correspondence, in which he disavowed any further role for the Court in maintaining what Hughes had called "our dual system of government." In a letter to then-Circuit Judge Sherman Minton explaining his *Wickard* opinion, Jackson wrote: "If we were to be brutally frank, as you suggest, I suspect what we would say is that in any case where Congress thinks there is an effect on interstate commerce, the Court will accept that judgment. All of the efforts to set up formulae to confine the commerce power have failed. When we admit that it is an economic matter, we pretty nearly admit that it is not a matter which courts may judge."[87]

It appears that Jackson was attempting in *Wickard* to ground commerce clause jurisprudence in the political process theory that Stone had introduced into due process jurisprudence in *Carolene Products*.[88] Stone himself had transplanted the political process rationale to the intergovernmental tax immunity context in *Helvering v. Gerhardt*,[89] and to the dormant commerce clause arena in *South Carolina Highway Dept. v. Barnwell Bros.*[90] Perhaps in order to secure the vote of Hughes and thus a unanimous Court, Stone had not used his *Darby* opinion as an occasion to effect a similar transplant to commerce clause jurisprudence. Yet with his accession to the chief justiceship, Stone did not hesitate to press his views on the matter. The letter he wrote to Jackson in May 1942 citing due process cases had included a reference to *Carolene Products*. Jackson had responded, "I agree with [the cases Stone had cited] wholeheartedly and would not depart from them. I especially like your statement in *Carolene Products* of the principle."[91] And while at the time Jackson rejected the applicability of mere rationality review in the commerce clause context where intrastate activities were concerned, he was soon to come around. In June he wrote in a memorandum to his law clerk,

> The same people elect the state and the federal officers. The interests represented by the two are the same. The people can punish excess or irresponsibility in the use of the commerce power by Congressmen. It does not seem likely that the people would send men to Washington to take away powers which they elect state officers to exercise. . . . Federal power can, of course, discredit itself by attempting more than is just or can break down attempting more than it has capacity to organize or administer. Its excesses and irresponsibilities it must answer for at the polls.[92]

And in the *Wickard* opinion Jackson remarked briefly that effective restraints on the exercise of the commerce power "must proceed from political rather than from judicial processes."[93]

In *Swift* and *Adair,* the justices of the Fuller Court had integrated commerce clause and due process jurisprudence at the level of doctrine.[94] The dialectical relationship created by these integrations had by 1937 resulted in the unraveling of the doctrinal connections forged by earlier courts.[95] In the late 1930s, due process cases were governed by the rationality review of political process theory,[96] while commerce clause cases were governed by Hughes' "close and substantial relationship" test, the last gasp of moribund dual federalist theory.[97] By adopting the political process rationale in *Wickard,* Jackson reintegrated due process and commerce clause jurisprudence within the matrix of political process theory, thereby completing the dialectic of integration, disintegration, and reintegration.[98]

Though Roberts apparently eventually overcame enough of his doubts to join Jackson's opinion, even *Wickard* did not mark his acceptance of a plenary conception of the commerce power. For the very day that *Wickard* was decided, Roberts again published a lone dissent from an application of the Fair Labor Standards Act to employees engaged in "local" activities. *Warren-Bradshaw Drilling Co. v. Hall* concerned an independent contractor whose employees had partially drilled oil and gas wells owned by others in the state of Texas. Some of the oil and gas from those wells had subsequently moved in interstate commerce. Justice Murphy's opinion for the Court, which noted that the case presented "a problem of statutory delineation, not constitutional power" held that the employees fell within the terms of the Act. Again employing the constitutional vocabulary of Hughes and Cardozo in the service of statutory construction, the Court reasoned that the activities of the employees were "intimately related" to and bore a "substantial," "close and immediate tie" to the production of oil.[99]

Justice Roberts ridiculed the majority's refusal to acknowledge "the practical, as distinguished from a theoretical, distinction between what is national and what is local,—between what, in fact, touches interstate commerce and what, in truth, is intrastate." The majority opinion rested on a kind of house-that-Jack-built reasoning that would utterly obscure this distinction. Roberts' responsive reductio betrayed his continued allegiance, both conceptually and metaphorically, to the views expressed by Cardozo in his *Schechter* concurrence.

> The reasoning seems to be as follows: The oil will pass into commerce if it is mined. But it cannot be mined unless somebody drills a well. An independent contractor's men do part of the drilling. Their work is "necessary" to the mining and the transportation of the oil. So they fall within the Act.
>
> This is to ignore all practical distinction between what is parochial and what is national. It is but the application to the practical affairs of life of a philosophic and impractical test. It is but to repeat, in another form, the old story of the pebble thrown into the pool, and the theoretically infinite extent of the resulting waves, albeit too tiny to be seen or felt by the exercise of one's senses.
>
> The labor of the man who made the tools which drilled the well, that of the sawyer who cut the wood incidentally used, that of him who mined the iron of which

the tools were made, are all just as necessary to the ultimate extraction of oil as the labor of the respondents. Each is an antecedent of the consequent,—the production of goods for commerce. Indeed, if the respondents were not fed, they could not have drilled the well, and the oil would not have gone into commerce. Is the cook's work "necessary" to the production of the oil, and within the Act?

"I think," he concluded, "that Congress could not and did not intend to exert its granted power over interstate commerce upon what in practice and common understanding is purely local activity, on the pretext that everything everybody does is a contributing cause to the existence of commerce between the States, and in that sense necessary to its existence."[100] Congress had not sought to regulate such paradigmatically "local" activities; but more important, on Roberts' view, Congress *could not* reach such activities even if it wanted to.

Hall was Roberts' last stand for constitutional limits on the commerce power. In *Walton v. Southern Packaging Corp.*, where the Court upheld application of the Act to a night watchman for a manufacturing plant that shipped a substantial portion of its product in interstate commerce, Roberts concurred in the result, "considering himself bound by the decision in *Kirschbaum v. Walling.*"[101] Yet he continued to dissent from opinions construing the Act to apply to what he saw as affairs of purely local concern,[102] occasionally bringing with him one of his brethren.[103] And on more than one occasion Roberts was able to persuade a majority of his colleagues that the Act was not intended to apply to matters he thought reserved to the states.[104]

This was all perfectly consistent with the political process approach—though arguably at odds with the "unworkable standards" rationale—undergirding Jackson's opinion in *Wickard*. After all, if Congress disagreed with the Court's construction of the Act, it could clarify its intentions and secure its objectives through simple statutory amendment. These opinions erected no constitutional obstacle to federal regulation. But there was no doubt that the statutory construction avenue of attack opened by Frankfurter in *Kirschbaum* was now the only remaining means by which Roberts might seek to preserve "our dual system of government." Arguments that had commanded unanimity on the *Schechter* Court—and by which Roberts was apparently still persuaded—were now received about as warmly as the government's macroeconomic arguments had been in the sick chicken case.

This transformation was highlighted by the Roosevelt Court's treatment of *Jones & Laughlin* itself. *Darby* cited the case only once in passing;[105] the published *Wickard* opinion, unlike Jackson's earlier drafts, didn't cite it at all. Such short shrift leads one to wonder whether the justices of 1941–42 regarded *Jones & Laughlin* as a particularly important or revolutionary case.[106] They certainly recognized that much of what Hughes had written was in tension with their broader conceptions of federal power: Jackson clearly saw Hughes' opinion as only one among many inadequate judicial attempts to articulate a formula that would salvage the role of the Court in supervising exercises of the commerce power. And while Hughes had taken care to draw a portrait of interstate movement of goods being physically impeded, to locate Jones & Laughlin's plant in a current of interstate commerce that could be envisioned in the mind's eye, the authors of *Darby* and *Wickard* believed that it was simply no longer necessary to bother. The current of commerce doctrine, once the most promising doctrinal escape hatch from the strictures of dual federalism, had in a very short time become little more than a quaint artifact of a bygone era.[107]

The intracurial struggles in *Darby* and *Wickard* underscore the point that the Court's commerce clause decisions between 1937 and 1940 were not revolutionary. The development of doctrine had remained slow, subtle, careful, lawyerly. As Fred Vinson and his congressional colleagues recognized, the coupling of *Nebbia* with longstanding commerce clause doctrine provided Congress with a constitutional foundation adequate to support properly crafted programs of national economic regulation. Once the legislators had grasped the relationship between due process and commerce clause doctrine, they had little difficulty in enacting federal programs that could weather judicial review. Again and again between 1937 and 1940, the doctrinal apparatus assembled by the Second New Deal Congresses provided the basis for judicial decisions upholding federal power.

As the internal records of the *Darby* and *Wickard* decisions demonstrate, however, that doctrinal apparatus was not sufficient to sustain the far-reaching regulations of production presented in those cases. Unlike the commerce clause decisions that had preceded them, *Darby* and *Wickard* required the Court to repudiate existing jurisprudential commitments. By the end of 1942, the Court was thinking about the federal commerce power (and the role of the Court in policing exercises of that power) in ways that were fundamentally at odds with the ways the Court had treated such issues only five years before. Indeed, *Jones & Laughlin* bears in many respects a far greater resemblance to the commerce cases that preceded it than it does to *Darby* and *Wickard*. To be sure, it was only after overcoming severe personal doubts that even four of the Roosevelt appointees were prepared to reach the result in *Wickard*. But as Stone's report of even Cardozo's views in *Schechter* suggests, one may reasonably doubt that the justices of the 1937 Court would have reached the same conclusions had death and retirement not spared them such dilemmas.[108]

The fact that such a transformation of commerce clause jurisprudence coincided with Roosevelt's bevy of new appointments to the Court brings to mind Max Planck's remark in his *Scientific Autobiography:* "a new scientific truth does not triumph by convincing its opponents and making them see the light, but rather because its opponents eventually die, and a new generation grows up that is familiar with it."[109] It was the replacement of the Nine Old Men with younger men who had more recently come to legal maturity—men who, though not without difficulty, were able to break free of an older constitutional vocabulary and embrace a new conception of the judicial function—that brought forth a new paradigm for commerce clause jurisprudence. *This*—not the plot of the conventional story of capitulation to external political pressure—was the "structure" of the constitutional revolution. Ironically, then, the proponents of the electoral theory of the revolution in commerce clause jurisprudence are correct—not because the results of the 1936 election persuaded the Nine Old Men to ratify the New Deal, but because the Democratic victory enabled Franklin Roosevelt, through the power of appointment, to refashion the High Court in his own image.

FOR THE REVOLUTION in due process doctrine, however, Roosevelt can claim no credit. The centerpiece of substantive due process during the Taft Court years had been the public/private distinction. The Court had deployed this distinction not only to strike down workplace regulation, as it did in *Adkins* and *Wolff Packing*, but also in several cases to invalidate price regulation on the ground that the business involved was not affected with a public interest.[110] In the late 1920s, however, Taft began to fear that new appointments to the Court might produce the collapse of this bulwark against illegitimate redistribution. Resisting the temptation to resign brought on by advancing age and declining mental powers, Taft wrote: "I must stay on the court in order to prevent the Bolsheviki from getting control."[111] Taft's fear of "the Bolsheviki" gaining control of the Court was brought on by his distrust of President Hoover as a "Progressive." "[T]he only hope we have of keeping a consistent declaration of constitutional law," he wrote his brother in December of 1929, "is for us to live as long as we can."[112] Yet the state of his health that autumn must have caused Taft to doubt whether he could outlast Hoover's term. In September he wrote to Justice Pierce Butler:

> With Van and Mac and Sutherland and you and Sanford, there will be five to steady the boat, and while the appointment of Stone to be Chief Justice would give a great advantage to the minority, there would be a good deal of difficulty in working through reversals of present positions, even if I either had to retire or were gathered to my fathers, so that we must not give up at once.[113]

But after the collapse of his health prompted Taft to resign in February 1930, there would not be five to steady the boat. Justice Sanford died unexpectedly in March, giving Hoover two vacancies to fill. The appointments of Hughes and Roberts produced precisely the results that Taft had feared. Joining Brandeis, Stone, and Holmes, these two new justices provided the margin of victory in *O'Gorman*, whose result and implications alarmed the Four Horsemen. In 1932 Hoover filled the vacancy created by Holmes' departure with Benjamin Cardozo, who embraced his predecessor's views on substantive due process, and the influence of whose commerce clause views is manifest in Hughes' *Jones & Laughlin* opinion. And in 1934 Roberts wrote the opinion with which the narrowest possible majority discarded the linchpin of substantive due process jurisprudence.[114] *Apres ça, le déluge.* The presidential author of "the Constitutional Revolution of 1937," then, was not the man the people had overwhelmingly returned to office the preceding November. It was instead, ironically, the man the electorate had repudiated in Roosevelt's favor in 1932: Herbert Hoover.[115]

Notes

Introduction

1. For citations to a sample of the many instances of this conventional view, see Barry Cushman, "Rethinking the New Deal Court," *Va. L. Rev.* 80 (1994): 201, 202–3, n.1, and notes, infra, 8, 9, and 17. For its most recent expression, see William E. Leuchtenburg, *The Supreme Court Reborn* (New York, 1995).

2. See, e.g., Michel Les Benedict, "Laissez-faire and Liberty: A Re-Evaluation of the Meaning and Origins of Laissez-Faire Constitutionalism," *Law and Hist. Rev.* 3 (1985): 293; William Forbath, "The Ambiguities of Free Labor: Labor and the Law in the Gilded Age," *Wisc. L. Rev.* 1985 (1985): 767; Charles W. McCurdy, "Justice Field and the Jurisprudence of Government-Business Relations: Some Parameters of 'Laissez-faire' Constitutionalism, 1863–1897," *J. Am. Hist.* 61 (1975): 970; McCurdy, "The Roots of 'Liberty of Contract' Reconsidered: Major Premises in the Law of Employment, 1867–1937," *Y.B. Sup. Ct. Hist. Soc.* 1984 (1984): 20; McCurdy, "The *Knight* Sugar Decision of 1895 and the Modernization of American Corporation Law, 1869–1903," *Bus. Hist. Rev.* 53 (1979): 304; William E. Nelson, "The Impact of the Antislavery Movement upon Styles of Judicial Reasoning in Nineteenth Century America," *Harv. L. Rev.* 87 (1974): 513; Melvin Urofsky, "Myth and Reality: The Supreme Court and Protective Legislation in the Progressive Era," *Y.B. Sup. Ct. Hist. Soc.* 1983 (1983): 53; Howard Gillman, *The Constitution Besieged: The Rise and Demise of Lochner Era Police Powers Jurisprudence* (Durham, N.C., 1993).

3. Until very recently, Michael Parrish had been virtually the only scholar in the past twenty years to focus serious attention on the Hughes Court; see Parrish, "The Hughes Court, the Great Depression, and the Historians," *The Historian* 40 (1978): 286, and Parrish, "The Great Depression, the New Deal, and the American Legal Order," *Washington L. Rev.* 59 (1984): 723, and even he appeared to have abandoned his solitary vigil. More recent years have witnessed a revival of interest in the period. See, e.g., Michael Ariens, "A Thrice-Told Tale, or Felix the Cat," *Harv. L. Rev.* 107 (1994): 620; Richard D. Friedman, "A Reaffirmation: The Authenticity of the Roberts Memorandum, or Felix the Non-Forger," *U. Pa. L. Rev.* 142 (1994): 1985; Friedman, "Switching Time and Other Thought Experiments: The Hughes Court and Constitutional Transformation," *U. Pa. L. Rev.* 142 (1994): 1891.

4. Bruce Ackerman, "Constitutional Politics/Constitutional Law," *Yale L. J.* 99 (1989): 453, 510, n. 121. Ackerman continues, with admirable candor, "I have no doubt that my own understanding has been greatly disadvantaged as a result." Ibid.

5. *West Coast Hotel v. Parrish,* 300 U.S. 379 (1937).

6. *Washington, Virginia & Maryland Coach Co. v. NLRB,* 301 U.S. 142 (1937); *Associated Press Co. v. NLRB,* 301 U.S. 103 (1937); *NLRB v. Friedman-Harry Marks Clothing Co.,* 301 U.S. 58 (1937); *NLRB v. Fruehauf Trailer Co.,* 301 U.S. 49 (1937); *NLRB v. Jones & Laughlin Steel Corp.,* 301 U.S. 1 (1937).

7. *Helvering v. Davis,* 301 U.S. 619 (1937); *Steward Mach. Co. v. Davis,* 301 U.S. 548 (1937); *Carmichael v. Southern Coal & Coke Co.,* 301 U.S. 495 (1937).

8. See, e.g., Edward Corwin, *Court Over Constitution* (Princeton, N.J., 1938); Corwin, *Constitutional Revolution, Ltd.* (Claremont, Calif., 1941); Robert H. Jackson, *The Struggle for Judicial Supremacy* (New York, 1941); Benjamin F. Wright, *The Growth of American Constitutional Law* (New York, 1942); Carl B. Swisher, *American Constitutional Development* (Boston, 1943); Joseph Alsop and Turner Catledge, *The 168 Days* (Garden City, N.Y., 1938).

9. See, e.g., Richard Cortner, *The Wagner Act Cases* (Knoxville, Tenn., 1964); Alfred Kelly and Winfred Harbison, *The American Constitution: Its Origins and Development* (New York, 1948); Alpheus Thomas Mason, *Harlan Fiske Stone: Pillar of the Law* (New York, 1956); Robert McCloskey, *The American Supreme Court* (Chicago, 1960); Paul Murphy, *The Constitution in Crisis Times, 1918–1969* (New York, 1972); Walter F. Murphy, *Congress and the Court* (Chicago, 1962); Leo Pfeffer, *This Honorable Court* (Boston, 1965); Fred Rodell, *Nine Men: A Political History of the Supreme Court from 1790 to 1955* (New York, 1955); Bernard Schwartz, *The Supreme Court: Constitutional Revolution in Retrospect* (New York, 1957).

10. See Parrish, "The Hughes Court, the Great Depression," 286, 302–3.

11. Merlo J. Pusey, *Charles Evans Hughes* (New York, 1951); Samuel Hendel, *Charles Evans Hughes and the Supreme Court* (New York, 1951), 264–65; Dexter Perkins, *Charles Evans Hughes and American Democratic Statesmanship* (Boston, 1956), 182; Paul Freund, "Charles Evans Hughes as Chief Justice," *Harv. L. Rev.* 81 (1967): 4.

12. See, e.g., the reviews of Pusey's biography of Hughes by Edward Corwin, *Am. Pol. Sci. Rev.* 46 (1952): 1167; Samuel J. Konefsky, *Yale L. J.* 61 (1952): 765; and Alpheus Thomas Mason, "Charles Evans Hughes: An Appeal to the Bar of History," *Vand. L. Rev.* 6 (1952): 1.

13. Ackerman, *We the People: Foundations* (Cambridge, Mass., 1991), 49.

14. Kelly and Harbison, *The American Constitution,* 754.

15. Ackerman, *We the People,* 49.

16. I do not mean to suggest here that law and politics are not deeply related. I do assert, however, that the relationship between law and politics is far more complex than a simple function. See infra, ch. 2.

17. Hendel, *Charles Evans Hughes and the Supreme Court,* 255; Jackson, *The Struggle for Judicial Supremacy,* 191–92, 218, 235; Mason, *Harlan Fiske Stone,* 455, 458; Wright, *The Growth of American Constitutional Law,* 179; Murphy, *The Constitution in Crisis Times,* 153–54; Corwin, *Constitutional Revolution, Ltd.,* 53, 72; Schwartz, *The Supreme Court,* 16, 35; William F. Swindler, *Court and Constitution in the Twentieth Century* (Indianapolis, Ind., 1969), II:79, 90, 99–100, 137; Corwin, *Court Over Constitution,* 156 and n. 60; Cortner, *The Wagner Act Cases,* pp. vi, 176–77; McCloskey, *The American Supreme Court,* 176–77; William Leuchtenburg, "Franklin D. Roosevelt's Supreme Court 'Packing' Plan," in Harold M. Hollingsworth and William F. Holmes, eds., *Essays on the New Deal* (Austin, Tex., 1969), 94; Rodell, *Nine Men,* 249–50; Alsop and Catledge, *The 168 Days,* 143, 146; Charles Leonard, *A Search for a Judicial Philosophy: Mr. Justice Roberts and the Constitutional Revolution of 1937* (Port Washington, N.Y., 1971), 3; Carl B. Swisher, *American Constitutional Development.* 2d. ed. (Boston, 1954), 955; Charles P. Curtis Jr., *Lions Under the Throne* (Boston, 1947), 29.

18. See ch. 1, infra.

19. *Nebbia v. New York*, 291 U.S. 502 (1934).

20. Justice McReynolds wrote despairingly to former Solicitor General James M. Beck that *Nebbia*, in tandem with *Home Bldg. & Loan Assn. v. Blaisdell*, 290 U.S. 398 (1934), marked "the end of the constitution as you and I regarded it. An alien influence has prevailed." J. C. McReynolds to James M. Beck, April 10, 1934, quoted in Morton Keller, *In Defense of Yesterday: James M. Beck and the Politics of Conservatism, 1861–1936* (New York, 1958), 254.

21. Because the public/private distinction did not play a comparably central role in the Court's jurisprudence concerning the federal power to tax and spend for the general welfare, I have treated those cases only briefly in chapter 1. For recent scholarship reconciling the Social Security Act cases with *United States v. Butler*, 297 U.S. 1 (1936), see Thomas R. McCoy and Barry Friedman, "Conditional Spending: Federalism's Trojan Horse," *Sup. Ct. Rev.* 1988 (1988): 85, 105–16; Friedman, "Switching Time," 1953–60.

1. Roosevelt's Shadow

1. The text of the bill and accompanying messages from Roosevelt and Attorney General Homer Cummings are printed at 81 Cong. Rec. 877–81 (75-1) (1937).

2. Alpheus Mason and William Beaney, *The Supreme Court in a Free Society* (New York, 1968), 184.

3. Wright, *The Growth of American Constitutional Law*, 200–202, 205, 222; Murphy, *The Constitution in Crisis Times*, 115; Alsop and Catledge, *The 168 Days*, 141; Rodell, *Nine Men*, 247, 249; Pfeffer, *This Honorable Court*; Alpheus Thomas Mason, *The Supreme Court: Palladium of Freedom* (Ann Arbor, Mich., 1963), 137; Leuchtenburg, "Franklin D. Roosevelt's Supreme Court 'Packing' Plan."

4. Ibid., 95; Hendel, *Charles Evans Hughes and the Supreme Court*, 131, 253; Murphy, *Congress and the Court*, 65; Schwartz, *The Supreme Court*, 16–17; Swindler, *Court and Constitution*, II:81; McCloskey, *The American Supreme Court*, 175; Corwin, *Court Over Constitution*, 127; Corwin, *Constitutional Revolution, Ltd.*, 74–75; Mario Einaudi, *The Roosevelt Revolution* (New York, 1959), 219–21; Mason, *Harlan Fiske Stone*, 463; Swisher, *American Constitutional Development*, 944, 954; Cortner, *The Wagner Act Cases*, 188; Peter Irons, *The New Deal Lawyers* (Princeton, N.J., 1982), 272–73; Paul R. Benson Jr., *The Supreme Court and the Commerce Clause, 1937–1970* (New York, 1970), 75; Parrish, "The Great Depression, the New Deal, and the American Legal Order," 723, 731, 734; Parrish, "The Hughes Court, the Great Depression," 286; Robert Stern, "The Commerce Clause and the National Economy, 1933–1946," *Harv. L. Rev.* 59 (1946): 645, 677.

5. William G. Ross, *A Muted Fury: Populists, Progressives and Labor Unions Confront the Courts, 1890–1937* (Princeton, N.J., 1994), 93–103, 163–65, 169–70.

6. *Bailey v. Drexel Furniture Co.*, 259 U.S. 20 (1922) (striking down a federal tax on goods made with child labor).

7. *Adkins v. Children's Hospital*, 261 U.S. 525 (1923) (striking down a District of Columbia law prescribing minimum wages for women).

8. Murphy, *Congress and the Court*, 49–52; Ross, *A Muted Fury*, chs. 9–10, pp. 290–91.

9. Ibid., 295–97; Leuchtenburg, *The Supreme Court Reborn*, 94.

10. William Leuchtenburg, "The Origins of Franklin D. Roosevelt's 'Court-Packing' Plan," *Sup. Ct. Rev.* 1966 (1966): 347; Mason, *Harlan Fiske Stone*, 426.

11. Ross, *A Muted Fury*, 298; Ronald Feinman, *Twilight of Progressivism* (Baltimore, Md., 1981), 121.

12. See, e.g., *Jones v. SEC*, 298 U.S. 1 (1936) (denying the authority of the Securities Exchange Commission to investigate for fraud the contents of a registration statement after it

had been withdrawn, and characterizing the commission's behavior as arbitrary, unreasonable, autocratic, obnoxious, offensive, inquisitorial, odious, pernicious, and reminiscent of the intolerable abuses of the Star Chamber); *Carter v. Carter Coal*, 298 U.S. 238 (1936) (striking down the Guffey Coal Act). See also *State ex rel. Morehead v. Tipaldo*, 298 U.S. 587 (1936) (striking down a New York minimum wage law for women).

13. Indeed, rumors of a presidential plan to pack the Court had circulated as early as January of 1934. That month the *Literary Digest* reported: "In the intimate Presidential circle the idea of reconstituting the Supreme Court has been considered. . . . In the conversation within the Roosevelt circle, a court of fifteen, instead of the present nine, has been mentioned." "News and Comment from the National Capital," *Literary Digest*, January 20, 1934, p. 10, quoted in Leuchtenburg, *The Supreme Court Reborn*, 85.

14. Alsop and Catledge, *The 168 Days*, 71–74, 123, 128; Pusey, *Charles Evans Hughes*, 753; James T. Patterson, *Congressional Conservatism and the New Deal: The Growth of the Conservative Coalition in Congress, 1933–1939* (Lexington, Ky., 1967), 87, 89–90.

15. Pusey, *Charles Evans Hughes*, 753; Alsop and Catledge, *The 168 Days*, 59, 115–17, 164–76, 181; Leonard Baker, *Back to Back: The Duel Between FDR and the Supreme Court* (New York, 1967), 86–88.

16. Patterson, *Congressional Conservatism and the New Deal*, 87–88.

17. E. Kimbark MacColl, "The Supreme Court and Public Opinion: A Study of the Court Fight of 1937" (unpublished Ph.D. dissertation, University of California, Los Angeles, 1953), 223–25, cited in Patterson, *Congressional Conservatism and the New Deal*, 88, n. 34. Wrote Senator Arthur Capper, "The protests reaching Washington from all sections have been overwhelming. We have seen nothing like it in years." Arthur Capper to William Allen White, February 27, 1937, W. A. White MSS, Box 186, cited in Patterson, *Congressional Conservatism and the New Deal*, 88.

18. Alsop and Catledge, *The 168 Days*, 71–72.

19. Murphy, *Congress and the Court*, 61, 62.

20. Pusey, *Charles Evans Hughes*, 753–54; Alpheus T. Mason, *Brandeis: A Free Man's Life* (New York, 1946), 624; Alsop and Catledge, *The 168 Days*, 73.

21. Ibid., 51.

22. Ibid., 70, 71, 88, 96.

23. Pusey, *Charles Evans Hughes*, 753; Patterson, *Congressional Conservatism and the New Deal*, 90–91.

24. Alsop and Catledge, *The 168 Days*, 69–70, 95.

25. Ibid., 67.

26. Pusey, *Charles Evans Hughes*, 760; David J. Danelski and Joseph S. Tulchin, *The Autobiographical Notes of Charles Evans Hughes* (Cambridge, Mass., 1973), 302; Baker, *Back to Back*, 67–68; Freund, "Charles Evans Hughes as Chief Justice," 4, 23, n. 64.

27. Swindler, *Court and Constitution*, II:38.

28. Alsop and Catledge, *The 168 Days*, 77.

29. Act of March 1, 1937, Ch. 21, 50 Stat. 24; Swindler, *Court and Constitution*, II:69.

30. In fact, both Van Devanter and Sutherland decided to retire shortly after the Sumners bill was enacted. Danelski and Tulchin, *Autobiographical Notes*, 303. Told of this by Justice Stone, Representative Emanuel Celler delivered a radio speech in early March in which he informed the public that the president's plan was unnecessary because two of the justices planned to retire within the next six months to one year. Baker, *Back to Back*, 169–70. Indeed, Justice Sutherland later informed several correspondents that he would have left the bench shortly after the passage of the Sumners bill had the Court-packing plan not been pending. George Sutherland to Nicholas Murray Butler, January 12, 1938; GS to a Mr. Preston (initials unknown), January 18, 1938; GS to Richard R. Lyman, January 21, 1938, Sutherland MSS, Box 6,

Library of Congress. The Court bill was also the only thing keeping Van Devanter from retirement. Baker, *Back to Back,* 229. The remarkable capacity of New Deal Democrats to find ways to keep their judicial opponents on the high bench is one of the great comic ironies of the era.

31. Alsop and Catledge, *The 168 Days,* 88–89.

32. Ibid., 96, 101.

33. Ibid., 87–88, 103.

34. Among those present were Wheeler, Tydings, Walter George of Georgia, Fredrick Van Nuys of Indiana, Edward Burke of Nebraska, Peter Gerry of Rhode Island, Harry Byrd of Virginia, Josiah Bailey of North Carolina, Bennett Champ Clark of Missouri, Tom Connally of Texas, William King of Utah, Kenneth McKellar of Tennessee, and Royal Copeland of New York. Baker, *Back to Back,* 99; Alsop and Catledge, *The 168 Days,* 103–4; Pusey, *Charles Evans Hughes,* 754; Burton K. Wheeler, *Yankee from the West* (Garden City, N.Y., 1962), 322.

35. Leuchtenburg, "Franklin D. Roosevelt's Supreme Court 'Packing' Plan," 88.

36. Leon Keyserling, "The Wagner Act: Its Origins and Current Significance," *G.W. L. Rev.* 20 (1960): 199, 210–11.

37. Henry S. Morgenthau Jr., "Diaries" (microfilm), The Franklin D. Roosevelt Library, Hyde Park, New York, Book 55, p. 95, quoted in Baker, *Back to Back,* 47.

38. Alsop and Catledge, *The 168 Days,* 92, 93.

39. Baker, *Back to Back,* 195; Alsop and Catledge, *The 168 Days,* 130–32; Swindler, *Court and Constitution,* II:71.

40. Chairman Henry Ashurst of Arizona, Matthew Neely of West Virginia, M. M. Logan of Kentucky, William Dietrich of Illinois, Key Pittman of Nevada, James Hughes of Delaware, George Norris of Nebraska, and George McGill of Kansas. Alsop and Catledge, *The 168 Days,* 120.

41. William King of Utah, Frederick Van Nuys of Indiana, Edward Burke of Nebraska, Tom Connally of Texas, William Borah of Idaho, Warren Austin of Vermont, Frederick Steiwer of Oregon, and Joseph O'Mahoney of Wyoming. Ibid.

42. Carl Hatch of New Mexico and Patrick McCarran of Nevada. Ibid. In fact, Hatch had confided to Senator Vandenberg on February 6 that he was inclined to oppose the bill. Vandenberg Notes, February 6, 1937, in Scrapbook 1937, Vandenberg MSS, cited in Patterson, *Congressional Conservatism and the New Deal,* 107–8.

43. Baker, *Back to Back,* 149; Alsop and Catledge, *The 168 Days,* 122–24.

44. Ibid., 124.

45. Baker, *Back to Back,* 153–56; Alsop and Catledge, *The 168 Days,* 124–26.

46. Hearings on S. 1392, Senate Judiciary Committee, (75–1), 488–91.

47. Baker, *Back to Back,* 159.

48. Ibid., 159–60; Wheeler, *Yankee from the West,* 333.

49. *New York Times,* June 24, 1943, quoted in Pusey, *Charles Evans Hughes,* 766.

50. Melvin Urofsky, *Louis D. Brandeis and the Progressive Tradition* (Boston, 1981), 166.

51. *West Coast Hotel v. Parrish* was handed down March 29, 1937, 300 U.S. 379; the Wagner Act cases were handed down April 12, 1937, 301 U.S. 1, 49, 58, 103, 142; the Social Security cases were argued April 7–9, 301 U.S. 495, 548 and May 5, 1937, 301 U.S. 619.

52. *West Coast Hotel,* 300 U.S. at 379.

53. *Morehead v. New York ex rel. Tipaldo,* 298 U.S. 587 (1936).

54. Owen J. Roberts to Felix Frankfurter, Memorandum dated November 9, 1945, printed in Felix Frankfurter, "Mr. Justice Roberts," *U. Pa. L. Rev.* 104 (1955): 311, 314–15; Pusey, *Charles Evans Hughes,* 757; Alfred Kelly, Winfred Harbison and Herman Belz, *The American Constitution: Its Origins and Development,* 7th ed. (New York, 1991), 488.

55. Alsop and Catledge were aware as early as 1938 that the *Parrish* vote had taken place before the announcement of the Court-packing plan, though they believed that the vote had

taken place in January rather than December. Alsop and Catledge, *The 168 Days*, 140. The persistence of the view that *Parrish* was at least partially influenced by the Court-packing plan is therefore something of a mystery. See, e.g., Murphy, *The Constitution in Crisis Times*, 115.

56. Baker, *Back to Back*, 179, 191.

57. James MacGregor Burns, *Roosevelt: The Lion and the Fox* (New York, 1956), 303.

58. Alsop and Catledge, *The 168 Days*, 92.

59. Ibid., 186–87. James Patterson reports that during the Court fight only thirty-five Democratic senators were dependable supporters of the Roosevelt initiative. Patterson, *Congressional Conservatism and the New Deal*, 126.

60. Baker, *Back to Back*, 68, 151–52, 233; Patterson, *Congressional Conservatism and the New Deal*, 94–95; Murphy, *Congress and the Court*, 59.

61. Feinman, *Twilight of Progressivism*, 128, 131.

62. John Callan O'Laughlin to William Allen White, March 8, 1937, "The Papers of William Allen White," Library of Congress, Box 186, quoted in Baker, *Back to Back*, 151.

63. Senator Arthur Capper to William Allen White, February 26, 1937, "The Papers of William Allen White," Library of Congress, Box 186, quoted in Baker, *Back to Back*, 191–92.

64. Alsop and Catledge, *The 168 Days*, 186–87, 206.

65. Baker, *Back to Back*, 93–94.

66. *Washington, Virginia & Maryland Coach Co. v. NLRB*, 301 U.S. 142 (1937); *Associated Press Co. v. NLRB*, 301 U.S. 103 (1937); *NLRB v. Friedman-Harry Marks Clothing Co.*, 301 U.S. 58 (1937); *NLRB v. Fruehauf Trailer Co.*, 301 U.S. 49 (1937); *NLRB v. Jones & Laughlin Steel Corp.*, 301 U.S. 1 (1937). For a critical examination of the view that these cases were decided as they were due to the pendency of the Court-packing bill, see infra, parts III and IV.

67. Friedman, "Switching Time," 1972.

68. See infra, ch. 10.

69. *Washington, Virginia & Maryland Coach Co.*, 301 U.S. at 142.

70. *Parrish*, 300 U.S. at 379, 400; *Associated Press Co.*, 301 U.S. at 103, 133; *Labor Board Cases*, 300 U.S. 1, 76 (1937).

71. Several observers doubted that the minimum wage and Wagner Act decisions would have any impact on the plan's chances for passage; others concluded that the decisions actually increased those chances. See Friedman, "Switching Time," 1970–71.

72. *Wickard v. Filburn*, 317 U.S. 111 (1942). The case was initially argued May 4, 1942, was reargued October 13, 1942, and was decided November 9, 1942.

73. *Brown v. Board of Education*, 347 U.S. 483 (1954). The case was initially argued December 9, 1952, was reargued December 8, 1953, and was decided May 17, 1954.

74. Alsop and Catledge, *The 168 Days*, 163.

75. Baker, *Back to Back*, 193.

76. "Court Bill Faces a Committee Veto, Ashurst Concedes," *New York Times*, April 25, 1937, p. 1.

77. Henry Fountain Ashurst, *A Many-Colored Toga: The Diary of Henry Fountain Ashurst*, ed. George Sparks (Tucson, Ariz., 1962), 571–72.

78. Baker, *Back to Back*, 195; Alsop and Catledge, *The 168 Days*, 195.

79. Ibid., 201.

80. Leuchtenburg, "Franklin D. Roosevelt's Supreme Court 'Packing' Plan," 97.

81. Alsop and Catledge, *The 168 Days*, 201.

82. Leuchtenburg, "Franklin D. Roosevelt's Supreme Court 'Packing' Plan," 100–101, citing Lindsay Warren to A. D. McLean, May 23, 1937, Warren MSS, Box 17.

83. Richard C. Cortner, *The Jones & Laughlin Case* (New York, 1970), 172.

84. Alsop and Catledge, *The 168 Days*, 209.

85. Ibid., 206; Pusey, *Charles Evans Hughes*, 760.

86. Alsop and Catledge, *The 168 Days*, 209–15.

87. *Carmichael v. Southern Coal & Coke Co.*, 301 U.S. 495, 527–31 (1937).

88. *Steward Machine Co. v. Davis*, 301 U.S. 548, 609–16 (1937).

89. *Helvering v. Davis*, 301 U.S. 619 (1937).

90. *Carmichael*, 301 U.S. at 527, 531.

91. *Chamberlin v. Andrews*, 299 U.S. 515 (1936).

92. For example, Senator Norris was sponsoring legislation requiring a majority vote of 7 to 2 to invalidate an act of Congress, to limit judicial tenure, and to permit direct popular vote on constitutional amendments. Alsop and Catledge, *The 168 Days*, 94; Ross, *A Muted Fury*, 307–8. Senator O'Mahoney backed a constitutional amendment to the same effect. Senator Wheeler offered a constitutional amendment that would have permitted a supermajority of Congress to reenact legislation declared unconstitutional. Senator Borah's amendment would have conferred upon the states broad regulatory powers. Senator Burke's amendment proposed a mandatory judicial retirement age. Alsop and Catledge, *The 168 Days*, 113; Ross, *A Muted Fury*, 308. Senate Majority Leader Robinson, Speaker of the House Bankhead and Senate Judiciary Committee Chairman Ashurst also each sponsored constitutional amendments. Alsop and Catledge, *The 168 Days*, 41. See also Leuchtenburg, "The Origins of Franklin D. Roosevelt's 'Court-Packing' Plan," 359. Numerous variations on these proposals were also embodied in bills introduced early in 1937. Ross, *A Muted Fury*, 309.

93. Alsop and Catledge, *The 168 Days*, 28–29. The administration considered amendments of several types. One type would have required a supermajority of the Court to invalidate acts of Congress and state legislatures. Another would have permitted a supermajority of Congress to reenact an invalidated statute. A third type would have enlarged federal and/or state regulatory authority. Leuchtenburg, "Franklin D. Roosevelt's Supreme Court 'Packing' Plan," 73; Alsop and Catledge, *The 168 Days*, 28; Baker, *Back to Back*, 130.

94. Alsop and Catledge, *The 168 Days*, 28.

95. Leuchtenburg, "The Origins of Franklin D. Roosevelt's 'Court-Packing' Plan," 386.

96. Leuchtenburg, "The Origins of Franklin D. Roosevelt's 'Court-Packing' Plan," 384; Baker, *Back to Back*, 130; Patterson, *Congressional Conservatism and the New Deal*, 89. See Benjamin V. Cohen to Stanley Reed, January 7, 1937, and Edward S. Corwin to Lucy R. Mason, September 24, 1936, Cohen MSS, Box 7, Library of Congress.

97. Alsop and Catledge, *The 168 Days*, 28–29; Leuchtenburg, "Franklin D. Roosevelt's Supreme Court 'Packing' Plan," 73; Baker, *Back to Back*, 130–31; Roosevelt to Felix Frankfurter, February 9, 1937, in Max Freedman, ed., *Roosevelt and Frankfurter: Their Correspondence, 1928–1945* (Boston, 1967), 381–82; Benjamin V. Cohen to Louis D. Brandeis (undated), Cohen MSS, Box 13, Library of Congress. Roosevelt believed that state legislatures were dominated by conservative interests and lawyers, both of whom would be resistant to the types of constitutional amendment he was considering. The president was especially mindful of the long and unsuccessful attempt to ratify the child-labor amendment. Roosevelt wanted to capitalize on the momentum from his electoral victory before the movement for reform ran out of steam. Leuchtenburg, "The Origins of Franklin D. Roosevelt's 'Court-Packing' Plan," 360, 384–85.

98. Leuchtenburg, "Franklin D. Roosevelt's Supreme Court 'Packing' Plan," 73; Leuchtenburg, "The Origins of Franklin D. Roosevelt's 'Court-Packing' Plan," 386; Baker, *Back to Back*, 131.

99. Roosevelt to Felix Frankfurter, February 9, 1937, in Freedman, ed., *Roosevelt and Frankfurter: Their Correspondence, 1928–1945*, 382; Leuchtenburg, "The Origins of Franklin D. Roosevelt's 'Court-Packing' Plan," 386; Alsop and Catledge, *The 168 Days*, 29.

100. Leuchtenburg, "The Origins of Franklin D. Roosevelt's 'Court-Packing' Plan," 386.

101. Alsop and Catledge, *The 168 Days*, 29; Leuchtenburg, "The Origins of Franklin D. Roosevelt's 'Court-Packing' Plan," 386–87.

102. Alsop and Catledge, *The 168 Days*, 29, 78, 95, 109–13, 152–53, 158–59, 161, 196–97, 206–7, 216; Leuchtenburg, "Franklin D. Roosevelt's Supreme Court 'Packing' Plan," 98–99; Baker, *Back to Back*, 182, 190, 198–99, 232–33; Patterson, *Congressional Conservatism and the New Deal*, 94.

103. Alsop and Catledge, *The 168 Days*, 154, 156–58; Baker, *Back to Back*, 182, 184; Leuchtenburg, "Franklin D. Roosevelt's Supreme Court 'Packing' Plan," 100.

104. Baker, *Back to Back*, 233–34; Leuchtenburg, "FDR's Court-Packing Plan: A Second Life, a Second Death," *Duke L. J.* 1985 (1985): 673, 681–83; Leuchtenburg, *The Supreme Court Reborn*, 150–51; Alsop and Catledge, *The 168 Days*, 246, 248.

105. Ibid., 246, 248, 250; Baker, *Back to Back*, 246–47. Senator McCarran threatened publicly to stand in the Senate until he dropped in order to prevent a vote on the bill. Ibid., 233.

106. Alsop and Catledge, *The 168 Days*, 250. See Baker, *Back to Back*, 233–35, 239, 246–47.

107. Alsop and Catledge, *The 168 Days*, 264–65; Baker, *Back to Back*, 243.

108. Ibid., 218.

109. James MacGregor Burns reached the same conclusion four decades ago:

> That the court bill probably never had a chance of passing seems now quite clear. Roosevelt's original proposal never commanded a majority in the Senate. In the House it would have run up against the unyielding Sumners, and then against a conservative Rules Committee capable of blocking the bill for weeks. From the start Democratic leaders were worried about the bill's prospects in that chamber. Robinson's compromise plan might have gone through the Senate if he had lived. More likely, though, it would have failed in the face of a dogged Senate filibuster, or later in the House.
>
> Any kind of court reform would have had hard going. The popular reverence for the Constitution, the conception of the Supreme Court as its guardian, the ability of judges—especially Hughes—to counterattack in their own way, the deep-seated legal tradition in a Congress composed of a large number of lawyers—all these were obstacles. (Burns, *Roosevelt: The Lion and the Fox*, 314.)

See also Lionel V. Patenaude, "Garner, Sumners, and Connally: The Defeat of the Roosevelt Court Bill in 1937," *Southwestern Historical Quarterly* 74 (1970): 36, 51, arguing that "Sumners' opposition was probably enough to ensure [the bill's] defeat."

110. For examples of this view, see Irons, *The New Deal Lawyers*, 277; McCloskey, *The American Supreme Court*, 175, 224; Baker, *Back to Back*, 176; Mason, *Harlan Fiske Stone*, 456, 463; C. H. Pritchett, *The Roosevelt Court: A Study in Judicial Politics and Values, 1937–1947* (New York, 1963), 8–9; Curtis, *Lions Under the Throne*, 160; Einaudi, *The Roosevelt Revolution*, 219–21; Hendel, *Charles Evans Hughes and the Supreme Court*, 131, 253; Corwin, *Constitutional Revolution, Ltd.*, 73; Cortner, *The Wagner Act Cases*, 188; J. W. Chambers, "The Big Switch: Justice Roberts and the Minimum-Wage Cases," *Labor History* 10 (1969): 44; Parrish, "The Great Depression, the New Deal, and the American Legal Order," 723, 728–34; Parrish, "The Hughes Court, The Great Depression," 286, 297–301; Stern, "The Commerce Clause and the National Economy," 645, 677.

111. Leuchtenburg, *Franklin D. Roosevelt and the New Deal* (New York, 1963), 196. Yet Leuchtenburg notes that "Landon did not do quite so badly as first impressions suggested. . . . Landon polled nearly a million more votes than Hoover had," and carried eighty-seven more counties; he carried a greater percentage of the popular vote than Cox had in 1920 or Davis had in 1924; and FDR's percentage of the popular vote, though great, "roughly approx-

imated Harding's in 1920." Leuchtenburg, "Election of 1936," in Arthur Schlesinger, ed., *History of American Presidential Elections, 1789–1968* (New York, 1971), 2843.

112. U.S. Constitution, Art. III, Sec. 1.

113. "Most economic indexes in 1934 remained as low as in 1931." Paul K. Conkin, *The New Deal*, 2d ed. (New York, 1975), 48; see also, Arthur M. Schlesinger, Jr., *The Politics of Upheaval* (Cambridge, Mass., 1960), 2.

114. Leuchtenburg, *Franklin D. Roosevelt and the New Deal*, 116. Perhaps in light of the Democrats' success in 1934, Professor Leuchtenburg has suggested that the 1936 election should be seen not as a "critical election" but as "the capstone of a 'critical period,'" which began in 1932 "when Franklin D. Roosevelt became the first Democratic candidate to win election with a majority of the vote since Franklin Pierce's triumph in 1852." Leuchtenburg, "Election of 1936," 2845.

115. Leuchtenburg, *Franklin D. Roosevelt and the New Deal*, 116–17.

116. Quoted in Schlesinger, *The Politics of Upheaval*, 1.

117. Swindler, *Court and Constitution*, II:19; Arthur M. Schlesinger, *The Coming of the New Deal* (Boston, 1988), 507.

118. Leuchtenburg, *Franklin D. Roosevelt and the New Deal*, 117.

119. Swindler, *Court and Constitution*, II:30.

120. See, e.g., *Carter v. Carter Coal Co.*, 298 U.S. 238 (1936); *United States v. Butler*, 297 U.S. 1 (1936); *Louisville Bank v. Radford*, 295 U.S. 555 (1935); *Schechter Poultry Co. v. United States*, 295 U.S. 495 (1935); *Retirement Board v. Alton Railroad Co.*, 295 U.S. 330 (1935); *Panama Refining Co. v. Ryan*, 293 U.S. 388 (1935).

121. Leuchtenburg, "Election of 1936," 2812–2815; Donald R. McCoy, *Landon of Kansas* (Lincoln, Nebr., 1966), 128, 167–68, 210–11, 228–29, 241, 271–75, 286, 302–5, 313–24, 328–38; Schlesinger, *The Politics of Upheaval*, 524–33, 540, 603.

122. Alsop and Catledge, *The 168 Days*, 19–20; Mason, *Harlan Fiske Stone*, 439; Pusey, *Charles Evans Hughes*, 750; Swisher, *American Constitutional Development*, 941.

123. D. Johnson and K. Porter, *National Party Platforms, 1840–1972* (Urbana, Ill., 1973), 362.

124. Murphy, *The Constitution in Crisis Times*, 151 and n. 74; Johnson and Porter, *National Party Platforms*, 365–70.

125. Ibid., 367; Curtis, *Lions Under the Throne*, 154; Murphy, *The Constitution in Crisis Times*, 151 and n. 74.

126. Leuchtenburg, *Franklin D. Roosevelt and the New Deal*, 151; Dexter Perkins, *The New Age of Franklin Roosevelt 1932–1945* (Chicago, 1957), 219.

127. 79 Cong. Rec. 7681 (74–1) (1935). The bill passed by a voice vote in the House. 79 Cong. Rec. 9731 (74–1) (1935).

128. Johnson and Porter, *National Party Platforms*, 367.

129. See McCoy, *Landon of Kansas*, 331.

130. Ibid., 272.

131. McCoy, *Landon of Kansas*, 227–28, 232–33, 241, 249, 268; Schlesinger, *The Politics of Upheaval*, 613–14; Clyde A. Weed, *Nemesis of Reform: The Republican Party During the New Deal* (New York, 1994), 101, 243, n. 58, citing *New York Times*, July 24, 1936, p. 1.

132. McCoy, *Landon of Kansas*, 305–6; Schlesinger, *The Politics of Upheaval*, 613–14; Wilbur J. Cohen, "The Advent of Social Security," in Katie Louchheim, ed., *The Making of the New Deal: The Insiders Speak* (Cambridge, Mass., 1983), 156.

133. Edwin Witte notes that "many of the staunch advocates of social security" shared several of Landon's reservations concerning the old-age pension provisions of the Act, and that as a consequence "there had been little popular support for this program." Edwin E. Witte, "Organized Labor and Social Security," in Milton Derber and Edwin Young, eds., *Labor and the New Deal* (New York, 1972), 257.

134. McCoy, *Landon of Kansas*, 331, 334, 336; Schlesinger, *The Politics of Upheaval*, 636; Leuchtenburg, "Election of 1936," 2820.

135. See, e.g., Schlesinger, *The Politics of Upheaval*, 635–36.

136. 79 Cong. Rec. 6070, 9650 (74–1) (1935). The Act "passed the House of Representatives by the crushing vote of 372 to 33 and the Senate by 76 to 6. No measure of the New Deal period received more emphatic approval." Perkins, *The New Age of Franklin Roosevelt*, 33. Several members shared Landon's reservations concerning the old-age provisions of the Act but ultimately voted in favor of it. Thomas H. Eliot, "The Advent of Social Security," in Louchheim, ed., *The Making of the New Deal*, 165; Witte, "Organized Labor and Social Security," in Derber and Young, eds., *Labor and the New Deal*, 257; Weed, *Nemesis of Reform*, 160–63.

137. Johnson and Porter, *National Party Platforms*, 366–67. For example, the platform criticized the Act for denying benefits to nearly two-thirds of the adult population, including domestic and agricultural workers. Years later, New Dealer Thomas Eliot explained why these workers were excluded: "Then there was the problem of domestic servants. Henry Morgenthau was absolutely insistent that they not be covered, and they weren't in the original act. This whole thing was so colossally new to us that we thought it would just be too much for the poor ignorant housewife to figure out the Social Security coverage. Having seen housewives struggle with their cook's Social Security, I'm not sure he was wrong." Thomas H. Eliot, "The Advent of Social Security," in Louchheim, ed., *The Making of the New Deal*, 165.

138. Not the least of which was the steadily improving state of the economy throughout 1936. See Perkins, *The New Age of Franklin Roosevelt*, 51; Leuchtenburg, "Election of 1936," 2811, 2849.

139. Witte, "Organized Labor and Social Security," in Derber and Young, eds., *Labor and the New Deal*, 256. Witte asserts that Landon "took a position of outright opposition to almost the entire program." Ibid.

140. Because Roosevelt had offered few specific proposals for his second term, Henry Breckenridge deprecated the notion that much meaning could be taken from the election. "The people have spoken," he wrote, "and in the fullness of time Roosevelt will tell us what they have said." "To be sure," notes William Leuchtenburg, "many ballots must have been cast for FDR by voters who admired his personality and cared not a hoot about his principles. . . ." Leuchtenburg, "Election of 1936," 2849.

141. Witte, "Organized Labor and Social Security," in Derber and Young, eds. *Labor and the New Deal*, 243, 247, 250; Johnson and Porter, *National Party Platforms*, 331.

142. *Carmichael*, 301 U.S. at 495, 527–31.

143. *Steward Machine Co. v. Davis*, 301 U.S. 548, 609–16 (1937).

144. *Helvering v. Davis*, 301 U.S. at 619.

145. Leuchtenburg, *Franklin D. Roosevelt and the New Deal*, 238, 243, 250; Robert McElvaine, *The Great Depression* (New York, 1984), 294; Patterson, *Congressional Conservatism and the New Deal*, 126–337; Feinman, *Twilight of Progressivism*, 136–44.

146. Roosevelt-backed agricultural legislation, fair labor standards legislation, conservation legislation, and adminsitrative reorganization all foundered both in the 1937 general session and in the special session called by the president in November of that year. Perkins, *The New Age of Franklin Roosevelt*, 63.

147. Leuchtenburg, *Franklin D. Roosevelt and the New Deal*, 250–51.

148. Ibid., 265–68, 271–73, 279,; Leuchtenburg, "Franklin D. Roosevelt's Supreme Court 'Packing' Plan," 110; Baker, *Back to Back*, 280; see also Patterson, *Congressional Conservatism and the New Deal*, 128–337.

149. See, e.g., *Wickard v. Filburn*, 317 U.S. 111 (1942) (upholding Agricultural Adjustment Act of 1938); *Phelps-Dodge Co. v. NLRB*, 313 U.S. 177 (1941) (upholding Wagner Act against

Fifth Amendment challenge); *United States v. Darby*, 312 U.S. 100 (1941) (upholding Fair Labor Standards Act of 1938); *Sunshine Anthracite Coal v. Adkins*, 310 U.S. 381 (1940) (upholding Bituminous Coal Conservation Act of 1937); *NLRB v. Fainblatt*, 306 U.S. 601 (1939) (upholding Wagner Act against commerce clause challenge); *Tennessee Power Co. v. TVA*, 306 U.S. 118 (1939) (upholding right of TVA to sell electric power in competition with private power companies); *Mulford v. Smith*, 307 U.S. 38 (1939) (upholding Agricultural Adjustment Act of 1938); *Currin v. Wallace*, 306 U.S. 1 (1939) (upholding Tobacco Inspection Act of 1935); *Alabama Power Co. v. Ickes*, 302 U.S. 464 (1938) (holding that privately owned power companies had no standing to challenge the constitutionality of federal loans and grants to aid in the construction of municipally owned power plants); *Electric Bond Co. v. SEC*, 303 U.S. 419 (1938) (upholding Public Utility Holding Company Act of 1935); *NLRB v. Santa Cruz Fruit Packing Co.*, 303 U.S. 453 (1938) (upholding Wagner Act against commerce clause challenge); *Consolidated Edison v. NLRB*, 305 U.S. 197 (1938) (upholding Wagner Act against commerce clause challenge); *United States v. Bekins*, 304 U.S. 27 (1938) (upholding Municipal Bankruptcy Act of 1937).

150. Swindler, *Court and Constitution*, II:122.

151. See, e.g., *Borden Co. v. Borella*, 325 U.S. 678 (1945) (Roberts joins Stone dissent); *10 East 40th Street Building, Inc. v. Callus*, 325 U.S. 578 (1945); *Kirschbaum Co. v. Walling*, 316 U.S. 517 (1942) (Roberts, J., dissenting); *Warren-Bradshaw Co. v. Hall*, 317 U.S. 88, 93 (1942) (Roberts, J., dissenting); *United States v. Hutcheson*, 312 U.S. 219, 243 (1941) (Hughes joins Roberts' dissent); *Apex Hosiery Co. v. Leader*, 310 U.S. 469 (1940); *NLRB v. Fansteel Metallurgical Corp.*, 306 U.S. 240 (1939).

152. *H. P. Hood & Sons v. United States*, 307 U.S. 588, 603 (1939) (Roberts, J., dissenting); *United States v. Rock-Royal Co-operative*, 307 U.S. 533, 583 (1939) (Hughes joins Roberts' dissent).

153. See, e.g., *Bowles v. Willingham*, 321 U.S. 503, 529 (1944) (Roberts, J., dissenting); *Yakus v. United States*, 321 U.S. 414, 448 (1944) (Roberts, J., dissenting); *H. P. Hood & Sons v. United States*, 307 U.S. 588, 603 (1939) (Roberts, J., dissenting).

154. Pritchett, *The Roosevelt Court*, 208, 191.

155. See, e.g., Urofsky, *Louis D. Brandeis and the Progressive Tradition*, 167; Baker, *Back to Back*, 31–32; Jackson, *The Struggle for Judicial Supremacy*, 235; Murphy, *The Constitution in Crisis Times*, 153; Mason, *Harlan Fiske Stone*, 456; Cortner, *The Jones & Laughlin Case*, 159; Swisher, *American Constitutional Development*, 954.

156. See, e.g., Leonard, *A Search for a Judicial Philosophy*, 109; Mason, *Harlan Fiske Stone*, 457, 463; McCloskey, *The American Supreme Court*, 175; Cortner, *The Wagner Act Cases*, 175, 188; Corwin, *Constitutional Revolution, Ltd.*, 73; Irons, *The New Deal Lawyers*, 272–73; Einaudi, *The Roosevelt Revolution*, 219–21. It is worthy of note, however, that the largest and most serious set of sit-down strikes, those waged by the United Auto Workers (UAW) at General Motors plants in Flint, Michigan, and elsewhere, were settled *before* the *Jones & Laughlin* decision was handed down, and without the intervention of the National Labor Relations Board. The UAW's Flint strike was settled February 11, 1937—more than two months before the Court upheld the National Labor Relations Act. See Sidney Fine, *Sit-Down: The General Motors Strike of 1936–37* (Ann Arbor, Mich., 1969), 303–12. Similarly, the UAW strikers at the Chrysler plant in Detroit withdrew from their sit-down strike March 24, 1937, nearly three weeks before the Court's opinion was rendered. J. Woodford Howard Jr., *Mr. Justice Murphy* (Princeton, N.J., 1968), 151–52. Indeed, the UAW sought to employ the sit-down tactic as a means of obtaining recognition as the exclusive representative of auto workers precisely because they doubted (quite reasonably, it appears) that they had sufficient votes to win recognition elections held under the provisions of the Wagner Act. Fine, *Sit-Down*, 111, 118–19, 144, 181–82, 185–88, 255–56; Howard, *Mr. Justice Murphy*, 125–26, 137;

Melvyn Dubofsky, "Not So 'Turbulent Years': Another Look at the American 1930's," *Amerikastudien* 24 (1979): 5, 16.

Moreover, as Melvyn Dubofsky has observed, the scale of industrial unrest in 1937 was hardly historically singular. "[O]nly 7.2 per cent of employed workers were involved in walkouts . . . and their absence from work represented only 0.0043 per cent of all time worked." These percentages were approximately the same as those experienced during the strike wave of 1934, which Commissioner of Labor Statistics Isadore Lubin had concluded "could not match 1919 in intensity, duration, or number of workers involved." For the statistical basis of Dubofsky's and Lubin's conclusions, see Ibid., 5, 12–13.

Even if the sit-down epidemic did influence the Court's disposition of the Wagner Act cases, however, the conclusion that the strike wave prompted decisions precipitating a constitutional revolution is hardly warranted. It seems quite likely that such events would persuade the justices of the accuracy of the Government's theory of the cases: that a labor disturbance at a manufacturing plant could cause a blockage in a flow of interstate commerce, and that the federal government was empowered to employ reasonable means to prevent such blockages from occurring, and to dislodge them once they had formed. See part IV, infra.

157. Corwin, *Constitutional Revolution, Ltd.*, 74–75. Why this concern was not manifest in Hughes' positions in *Schechter, Butler,* and *Carter Coal* is not explained.

158. See Frankfurter, "Mr. Justice Roberts," 311, 314–15.

159. Ibid.; Danelski and Tulchin, eds., 767–68. Stone wrote that he thought *Jones & Laughlin* represented a shift on the part of Hughes and Roberts. Mason, *Harlan Fiske Stone,* 459. Cardozo clerk Joseph Rauh Jr. reported that Cardozo, who had dissented with Stone in *Carter Coal,* took a similar view. Louchheim, ed., *The Making of the New Deal,* 58; Joseph Rauh, "Historical Perspectives: An Unabashed Liberal Looks at a Half-Century of the Supreme Court," *N.C. L. Rev.* 69 (1990): 213, 217–18. Neither Stone nor Cardozo, however, accused Hughes or Roberts of succumbing to political pressure. Indeed, it appears that in later years, after the initial thrill of vindication had passed and he had had time for sober reflection and further conversation with his colleagues, Stone may have changed his view of what happened in *Jones & Laughlin.* See infra, ch. 5, n. 51, ch. 12, n. 106.

2. Judging the Image of New Deal Court Judging

1. See, e.g., Irons, *The New Deal Lawyers,* 46–47; Benson, *The Supreme Court,* 64; Hendel, *Charles Evans Hughes and the Supreme Court,* 63; McCloskey, *The American Supreme Court,* 149–50; Wright, *The Growth of American Constitutional Law,* 197–99; Corwin, *Constitutional Revolution, Ltd.,* 34; Schlesinger, *The Politics of Upheaval,* 458–467; Kelly and Harbison, *The American Constitution,* 736, 744–45; Cortner, *The Jones & Laughlin Case,* 48; Alpheus Thomas Mason, *The Supreme Court from Taft to Warren* (Baton Rouge, La., 1958), vii–ix, 38, 123; Parrish, "The Great Depression, the New Deal, and the American Legal Order," 729.

2. See, e.g., Leuchtenburg, *Franklin D. Roosevelt and the New Deal,* 143; Swisher, *American Constitutional Development,* 920; Kelly and Harbison, *The American Constitution,* 736–37; Cortner, *The Wagner Act Cases,* 142–46; Irons, *The New Deal Lawyers,* 13; Schlesinger, *The Politics of Upheaval,* 458–467; Pfeffer, *This Honorable Court;* Mason, *The Supreme Court from Taft to Warren,* 52, 64; Parrish, "The Great Depression, the New Deal, and the American Legal Order," 729–30; Parrish, "The Hughes Court, the Great Depression," 286.

3. See, e.g., Rodell, *Nine Men,* 217; Irving Brant, *Storm over the Constitution* (New York, 1936), 240; Baker, *Back to Back,* 105; Wright, *The Growth of American Constitutional Law,* 127; Alsop and Catledge, *The 168 Days,* 6; Mason, *Harlan Fiske Stone,* 425; Kelly and Harbi-

son, *The American Constitution*, 756–57; Irons, *The New Deal Lawyers*, 102; Parrish, "The Hughes Court, the Great Depression," 288, 295. This view has been briefly criticized in Conkin, *The New Deal*, 69.

4. *Texas & New Orleans R.R. Co. v. Brotherhood of Railway & Steamship Clerks*, 281 U.S. 548 (1930); *Nortz v. United States*, 294 U.S. 317 (1935); *Norman v. Baltimore & Ohio R.R. Co.*, 294 U.S. 240 (1935); *Home Bldg. & Loan Assn. v. Blaisdell*, 290 U.S. 398 (1934); *Nebbia v. New York*, 291 U.S. 502 (1934); *Ashwander v. Tennessee Valley Authority*, 297 U.S. 288 (1936); Lilienthal to Felix Frankfurter, February 17, 1936, Lilienthal MSS, Princeton University Library, quoted in Leuchtenburg, "The Origins of Franklin D. Roosevelt's 'Court-Packing' Plan," 375; Swisher, *American Constitutional Development*, 938.

5. See, e.g., Bernard Bellush, *The Failure of the NRA* (New York, 1975).

6. See, e.g., Conkin, *The New Deal*, 38–40; Irons, *The New Deal Lawyers*, ch. 8; Venkataramani, "Norman Thomas, Sharecroppers, and the Roosevelt Agricultural Policies, 1933–37," *Mississippi Valley Historical Review* 47 (1960): 225.

7. William Leuchtenburg, "The Origins of Franklin D. Roosevelt's 'Court-Packing' Plan," 368, citing *Washington Post*, January 8, 1936.

8. Leuchtenburg, *The Supreme Court Reborn*, 98.

9. Raymond Moley, *The First New Deal* (New York, 1966), 261.

10. HFS to Herbert Hoover, March 27, 1934, quoted in Mason, *Harlan Fiske Stone*, 370–71; HFS to Charles C. Burlingham, January 9, 1936, quoted in Mason, *Harlan Fiske Stone*, 416; HFS to his sister, June 2, 1936, quoted in Mason, *Harlan Fiske Stone*, 426; Allison Dunham, "Mr. Justice Stone," in Allison Dunham and Phillip Kurland, eds., *Mr. Justice* (Chicago, 1964), 231; Lewis Paper, *Brandeis* (Englewood Cliffs, N.J., 1983), 345–47; Bruce Murphy, *The Brandeis/Frankfurter Connection* (New York, 1982), 139–43.

11. *United States v. Butler*, 297 U.S. 1 (1936); *Schechter Poultry Corp. v. United States*, 295 U.S. 495 (1935).

12. Dunham, "Mr. Justice Stone," in Dunham and Kurland, eds., *Mr. Justice*, 231; HFS to Felix Frankfurter, May 9, 1935, quoted in Mason, *Harlan Fiske Stone*, 393; Mason, *Harlan Fiske Stone*, 390; *Railroad Retirement Board v. Alton Railroad Co.*, 295 U.S. 330 (1935); *Nortz*, 294 U.S. at 317; *Norman*, 294 U.S. at 240.

13. Paper, *Brandeis*, 346; Interview with Paul Freund, October 18, 1982, Stanley Reed Oral History Project, Univ. of Kentucky, 17.

14. Paper, *Brandeis*, 350; *Louisville Joint Stock Land Bank v. Radford*, 295 U.S. 555 (1935).

15. *Panama Refining Co. v. Ryan*, 293 U.S. 388 (1935). Harold Ickes, *Secret Diary* (New York, 1954), I:273.

16. *United States v. Butler*, 297 U.S. 1 (1936).

17. *Carter*, 298 U.S. at 238.

18. *Morehead v. New York ex rel. Tipaldo*, 298 U.S. 587 (1936).

19. *Schechter Poultry Corp.*, 295 U.S. at 495.

20. *Louisville Bank v. Radford*, 295 U.S. 555 (1935).

21. *Morehead*, 298 U.S. at 587.

22. *Butler*, 297 U.S. at 1.

23. *Nebbia*, 291 U.S. at 502.

24. *Texas & New Orleans R.R. Co.*, 281 U.S. at 548.

25. *Ashwander*, 297 U.S. at 288.

26. *Helvering v. Davis*, 301 U.S. at 619.

27. HFS to G. R. Farnum, October 31, 1941, quoted in Mason, *Harlan Fiske Stone*, 417.

28. Paul Freund, "Mr. Justice Brandeis," in Dunham and Kurland, eds., *Mr. Justice*, 185.

29. See Barry Cushman, "The Secret Lives of the Four Horsemen," *Va. L. Rev.* 83 (1997): 559; Conkin, *The New Deal*, 90. Former Stone clerk Herbert Wechsler reports that the "lib-

eral" Stone thought Butler was "too soft in dealing with criminal matters." Louchheim, ed., *The Making of the New Deal*, 53.

30. Joseph Paschal, "Mr. Justice Sutherland," in Dunham and Kurland, eds., *Mr. Justice*, 222; Paschal, *Mr. Justice Sutherland: A Man Against the State* (Princeton, N.J., 1951), 36, 41, 56, 63, 65–73, 235; Harold M. Stephens, "Mr. Justice Sutherland," *ABA Journal* 31 (1945): 446. See also Hadley Arkes, *The Return of George Sutherland* (Princeton, N.J., 1994).

31. "Compulsory Workmen's Compensation Law," S. Doc. 131 (63–1), p. 11 (1913). See Paschal, *Mr. Justice Sutherland*, 70.

32. Speech to Conference of Federal Judges of the Fourth Circuit, Asheville, N.C., June 9, 1932, quoted in Pusey, *Charles Evans Hughes*, 691.

33. Wheeler, *Yankee from the West*, 329; Swindler, *Court and Constitution*, II:72–73.

34. For a recent deprecation of this view, see Leuchtenburg, *The Supreme Court Reborn*, 231–32.

35. Ashurst, *The Diary of Henry Fountain Ashurst*, 503–4, quoted in Baker, *Back to Back*, 14–15.

36. Irons, *The New Deal Lawyers*, 23–24; Joseph P. Lash, *Dealers and Dreamers* (Garden City, N.Y., 1988), 123. Wyzanski wrote to Frankfurter that "the codemaking process went 'so far beyond the bounds of constitutionality that it would be useless' to test it in the Courts." Ronen Shamir, *Managing Legal Uncertainty: Elite Lawyers in the New Deal* (New York, 1995), 16. Secretary of Labor Frances Perkins also harbored doubts that federal regulation of wages and hours could pass constitutional muster. Robert F. Himmelberg, *The Origins of the National Recovery Administration* (New York, 1976), 191. Jerome Frank harbored similar doubts with respect to the validity of the codes under the commerce clause. Lash, *Dealers and Dreamers*, 122–23.

37. Shamir, *Managing Legal Uncertainty*, 15–16. These misgivings were shared by Felix Frankfurter, who "also harbored grave doubts about the ability of the NIRA to successfully pass the Court's judicial review. . . . and urged the NRA to avoid tests on constitutionality." Ibid. Milton Handler remarked in August of 1933 that "Candor demands the admission that for the statute . . . to be sustained . . . requires a change of attitude on the part of the Supreme Court no less revolutionary than the law itself." Ibid., quoting Milton Handler, "The National Industrial Recovery Act," *A.B.A. J.* 19 (1933): 440, 482. These doubts concerning the Act's constitutionality were of course widely echoed by members of the private bar. See Shamir, *Managing Legal Uncertainty*, 18–35.

38. Schlesinger, *The Coming of the New Deal*, 108; Ickes, *Secret Diary*, 101; Nathan Miller, *FDR: An Intimate History* (New York, 1983), 328–29. "Those who drafted the NIRA, those who administered it, and those who defended it were well aware that the law was unconstitutional by traditional legalistic standards. . . . The NIRA, in this respect, was the first in a series of laws whose constitutionality had not been firmly situated within the body of existing judicial precedents; rather, it was based on an instrumental philosophy and on the belief that, if necessary, it would be possible to push the Supreme Court to uphold the law as an emergency measure, or, at best, to accommodate it within a new constitutional framework." Shamir, *Managing Legal Uncertainty*, 32–33.

39. Stone to John Bassett Moore, May 30, 1935, quoted in Mason, *Harlan Fiske Stone*, 395.

40. Irons, *The New Deal Lawyers*, 155.

41. Burns, *Roosevelt: The Lion and the Fox*, 168–69.

42. Irons, *The New Deal Lawyers*, 147; Lash, *Dealers and Dreamers*, 220–21.

43. Senate Report 711, 75th Cong., 1st. Sess., 18, 45.

44. Gene M. Gressley, "Joseph C. O'Mahoney, FDR, and the Supreme Court," *Pacific Hist. Rev.* 40 (1971): 183, 197. See also, Pusey, *Charles Evans Hughes*, 747; Pusey, *The Supreme Court Crisis* (New York, 1937), 44; Swindler, *Court and Constitution*, II:33.

45. FDR Press Conference #173, January 9, 1935, quoted in Schlesinger, *The Politics of Upheaval*, 255.

46. Irons, *The New Deal Lawyers*, 227.

47. Ibid., 227, 229.

48. Ibid., 252, quoting from author interview with Charles Fahy, June 22, 1978.

49. *Carter*, 298 U.S. at 278; Irons, *The New Deal Lawyers*, 252–53. On the drafting of the Wagner Act, see chs. 8 and 10, infra.

50. Frances Perkins, *The Roosevelt I Knew* (New York, 1946), 286–87.

51. Murphy, *The Brandeis/Frankfurter Connection*, 165–78; Paper, *Brandeis*, 354–57; Philippa Strum, *Louis D. Brandeis: Justice for the People* (Cambridge, Mass., 1984), 381–87; LDB to Elizabeth Brandeis Raushenbush, September 16, 1933, September 30, 1933, November 17, 1933, April 20, 1934, and June 8, 1934, in Melvin Urofsky and David Levy, eds., *Letters of Louis D. Brandeis* (Albany, N.Y., 1978), V:520, 523, 526–27, 536, 539–40; Elizabeth Brandeis Raushenbush to LDB, September 20, 1933, September 24, 1933, February 5, 1934, February 12, 1934, and February 15, 1934, *The Papers of Louis Dembitz Brandeis*, University of Louisville (microfilm), Reel 64.

52. Thomas Emerson, *Young Lawyer for the New Deal: An Insider's Memoir of the Roosevelt Years* (Savage, Md., 1991), 23–24.

53. Irons, *The New Deal Lawyers*, 75–82, 85–86, 91. Donald Richberg later wrote in his autobiography that he "had expressed my grave doubts of our success to everyone with whom the case had been privately discussed." Richberg, *My Hero* (New York, 1954), 190–91. Paul Freund reports that the *Schechter* case most likely would not have been heard by the Court before the NIRA expired by its own terms in June of 1935, and might not have been heard at all, had the Justice Department not requested that the case be expedited. The decision to expedite was taken not because of the merits of the case, but because NRA administrators complained that the morale of the organization could not withstand further temporizing. Freund, "Charles Evans Hughes as Chief Justice," 31–32. See also Interview with Paul Freund, October 18, 1982, Stanley Reed Oral History Project, Univ. of Kentucky, 25–26.

54. Irons, *The New Deal Lawyers*, ch. 12; James A. Gross, *The Making of the National Labor Relations Board* (Albany, N.Y., 1974), chs. 5–6; Thomas I. Emerson, "The National Labor Relations Board," in Louchheim, ed., *The Making of the New Deal*, 210; Ralph F. Fuchs and Walter Freedman, "The Wagner Act Decisions and Factual Technique in Public Law Cases," *Wash. U. L. Q.* 22 (1937): 510, 512–13. See chs. 8 and 10, infra.

55. See, e.g., Lash, *Dealers and Dreamers*, 220.

56. Irons, *The New Deal Lawyers*, 11.

57. Freedman, ed., *Roosevelt and Frankfurter: Their Correspondence, 1928–1945*, 260.

58. Cortner, *The Wagner Act Cases*, 67; Emerson, *Young Lawyer for the New Deal*, 34. Paul Freund observed: "[T]he Solicitor Generalship is in many ways like the tenth Justice of the Supreme Court. The Supreme Court Justices expect the Solicitor General to help them. To be not simply an advocate for the government, but a resource, whose briefs will develop the background of the law, all of the relevant authorities, and whose briefs can be relied on implicitly for accuracy and integrity. And they expect a Solicitor General to have a staff that is . . . is devoted to . . . to the same end. When . . . when a new Solicitor General is appointed, he makes the rounds of the . . . justices making a courtesy call on each. And he comes back from those calls deeply impressed with the expectations that the justices have of him and his staff. During the early New Deal days with J. Crawford Biggs as Solicitor General, I . . . I think it's fair to say that the Court did not have that same confidence. Mr. . . . Mr. Biggs was by experience a trial lawyer, [or] really a jury lawyer, and he would make rather emotional arguments but he had not had experience with Federal law including constitutional law, nor was his strength in appellate advocacy. And I think the Court felt that

government was not getting that kind of representation that it needed, nor was the Court getting the kind of help that it needed." Interview with Paul Freund, October 18, 1982, Stanley Reed Oral History Project, Univ. of Kentucky, 21.

59. Ickes, *Secret Diary*, 243. Felix Frankfurter contemporaneously informed Ickes that Roosevelt "now thoroughly understands the weakness" of the Department of Justice. Ickes expressed agreement in his diary: "It is indeed weak. It is full of political appointees. It has some hardworking, earnest lawyers, but no outstanding ones." Ibid., 247.

60. Ibid.

61. Irons, *The New Deal Lawyers*, 155.

62. Baker, *Back to Back*, 27.

63. Schlesinger, *The Politics of Upheaval*, 261. "Cummings was an able man," reported Paul Freund, "but not a hard worker. He loved to go off on golfing holidays." Interview with Paul Freund, October 18, 1982, Stanley Reed Oral History Project, Univ. of Kentucky, 20.

64. Irons, *The New Deal Lawyers*, 235–36.

65. Schlesinger, *The Politics of Upheaval*, 393–395.

66. Irons, *The New Deal Lawyers*, 288–89. See Fuchs and Freedman, "The Wagner Act Decisions," 510, 512–13, 531.

67. Freund, "The Solicitor General," in Louchheim, ed., *The Making of the New Deal*, 96.

68. Frankfurter to Roosevelt, May 29, 1935, in Freedman, ed., *Roosevelt and Frankfurter: Their Correspondence, 1928–1945*, 272–73.

69. Eugene D. Genovese, *Roll, Jordan, Roll: The World the Slaves Made* (New York, 1974), 25; Robert Gordon, "Critical Legal Histories," *Stan. L. Rev.* 36 (1984): 57, 101. On the "relative autonomy" of law generally, see also Ibid., 88–90, 98–101, 109–113; Mark Kelman, *A Guide to Critical Legal Studies* (Cambridge, Mass., 1987), 249–51; Morton Horwitz, *The Transformation of American Law, 1780–1860* (Cambridge, Mass., 1977), xiii; Mark Tushnet, "Perspectives on the Development of American Law: A Critical Review of Friedman's 'A History of American Law,'" *Wisc. L. Rev.* 1977 (1977): 81.

70. Duncan Kennedy, "Toward an Historical Understanding of Legal Consciousness: The Case of Classical Legal Thought in America, 1850–1940," *Research in Law and Sociology* 3 (1980): 4–5.

71. Roscoe Pound, *The Formative Era of American Law* (Boston, 1938), 82; Frederic W. Maitland, *English Law and the Renaissance* (Cambridge, Mass., 1901), 18; Curtis, *Lions Under the Throne*, 190–91. For an analysis of the shortcomings of Pound's conception of the relative autonomy of law, see Gordon, "Introduction: J. Willard Hurst and the Common Law Tradition in American Legal Historiography," *Law & Soc. Rev.* 10 (1975): 9, 38–41.

72. Gordon, "Historicism in Legal Scholarship," *Yale L. J.* 90 (1981): 1017, 1044.

73. McCurdy, "Justice Field, " 970.

74. *Wolff Packing v. Industrial Ct.*, 262 U.S. 522 (1923); *Williams v. Standard Oil Co.*, 278 U.S. 235 (1929); *Nebbia*, 291 U.S. at 502; *Hopkins v. United States*, 171 U.S. 578 (1898); *Swift v. United States*, 196 U.S. 375 (1905); *Stafford v. Wallace*, 258 U.S. 495 (1922); *Adair v. United States*, 208 U.S. 161 (1908); *Texas & New Orleans R.R. Co.*, 281 U.S. at 548. It is worthy of note that all of these reassessments and revisions occurred before 1937.

75. *Champion v. Ames*, 188 U.S. 321 (1903).

76. *Hipolite Egg Co. v. United States*, 220 U.S. 45 (1911).

77. *Hoke v. United States*, 227 U.S. 308 (1913).

78. *Brooks v. United States*, 267 U.S. 432 (1925).

79. *Hammer v. Dagenhart*, 247 U.S. 251 (1918).

80. *McCray v. United States*, 195 U.S. 27 (1904).

81. *United States v. Doremus*, 249 U.S. 86 (1919).

82. *Bailey v. Drexel Furniture*, 259 U.S. 20 (1922).

83. *Hill v. Wallace*, 259 U.S. 44 (1922).

84. See, e.g., Corwin, *Twilight of the Supreme Court*, (New Haven, Conn., 1934); Thomas Reed Powell, "The Child Labor Law, the Tenth Amendment, and the Commerce Clause," *So. L. Q.* 3 (1918): 175; H. E. Willis, *Constitutional Law of the United States* (Bloomington, Ind., 1936), 287–88.

85. See chs. 9 and 10, infra.

86. See chs. 3–10.

Part II. A New Trial for Justice Roberts

1. *Morehead v. New York ex rel. Tipaldo*, 298 U.S. 587 (1936); *Parrish*; 300 U.S. at 379. See, e.g., Cortner, *The Jones & Laughlin Case*, 159; Curtis, *Lions Under the Throne*, 160–61; Hendel, *Charles Evans Hughes and the Supreme Court*, 131, 253; Irons, *The New Deal Lawyers*, 277; Mason, *The Supreme Court from Taft to Warren*, at 108; Mason, *Harlan Fiske Stone*, 456, 463; McCloskey, *The American Supreme Court*, 175, 224; Pritchett, *The Roosevelt Court*, 8–9; Ariens, "A Thrice-Told Tale," 620; Chambers, "The Big Switch," 44; Parrish, "The Great Depression, the New Deal, and the American Legal Order," 731–34; Parrish, "The Hughes Court, the Great Depression," 297–301.

2. *Morehead*, 298 U.S. at 587; *Parrish*, 300 U.S. at 379. See Alsop and Catledge, *The 168 Days*, 135; Chambers, "The Big Switch," 73; Mason, "Harlan Fiske Stone and FDR's Court Plan," *Yale L. J.* 61 (1952): 791, 809.

3. See, e.g., Alsop and Cataledge, *The 168 Days*, 140; Pusey, *Charles Evans Hughes*, 757; Baker, *Back to Back*, 175–76.

4. See, e.g., Cortner, *The Jones & Laughlin Case*, 159; Curtis, *Lions Under the Throne*, 160–61; Hendel, *Charles Evans Hughes and the Supreme Court*, 131, 253; Irons, *The New Deal Lawyers*, 277; Mason, *The Supreme Court from Taft to Warren*, 108; Mason *Harlan Fiske Stone*, 456, 463; McCloskey, *The American Supreme Court*, 175, 224; Pritchett, *The Roosevelt Court*, 8–9; Chambers, "The Big Switch," 44; Parrish, "The Great Depression, the New Deal, and the American Legal Order," 731–34; Parrish, "The Hughes Court, th Great Depression," 297–301.

5. See ch. 1, supra.

6. See, e.g., Baker, *Back to Back*, 31–32; Cortner, *The Jones & Laughlin Case*, 159; Jackson, *The Struggle for Judicial Supremacy*, 234–35; Mason, *Harlan Fiske Stone*, 456; Murphy, *The Constitution in Crisis Times*, 153–54; Swisher, *American Constitutional Development*, 2d ed., 954; Urofsky, *Louis D. Brandeis and the Progressive Tradition*, 167.

7. *Adkins v. Children's Hospital*, 261 U.S. 525 (1923); Frankfurter, "Mr. Justice Roberts," 311, 314–15. Michael Ariens' recent intimation that Frankfurter may have manufactured the memorandum for his own pupuses, see Ariens, "A Thrice-Told Tale," has been effectively refuted in Friedman, "A Reaffirmation," 1985.

8. See, e.g., Erwin Griswold, "Owen J. Roberts as a Judge," *U. Pa. L. Rev.* 104 (1955): 332, 340–44; Leuchtenburg, *Franklin D. Roosevelt and the New Deal*, 232, n. 5; Thomas Reed Powell, *Vagaries and Varieties in Constitutional Interpretation* (New York, 1956), 81, n. 89; Pusey, *Charles Evans Hughes*, 701; Schlesinger, *The Politics of Upheaval*, 479. See also Ariens, "A Thrice-Told Tale," 653–64; Freund, "Charles Evans Hughes as Chief Justice," 29–30: Pusey, *The Supreme Court Crisis*, 49. Pusey reiterated his defense of Roberts in "Justice Roberts' 1937 Turnaround," *Y.B. Sup. Ct. Hist. Soc.* 1983 (1983): 102, 106–7.

9. See, e.g., Ariens, "A Thrice-Told Tale"; Chambers, "The Big Switch"; Irons, *The New Deal Lawyers*, 279; Parrish, "The Hughes Court, the Great Depression," 296–97; Parrish, "The Great Depression, the New Deal, and the American Legal Order," 732. A notable exception is Friedman, "Switching Time," 1891.

10. *Nebbia*, 291 U.S. at 502.

11. See, e.g., Curtis, *Lions Under the Throne*, 159; Frankfurter, "Mr. Justice Roberts," 316–17; Friedman, "Switching Time," 1939–40, 1952–53; Pusey, *Charles Evans Hughes*, 700–702; Pusey, "Justice Roberts' 1937 Turnaround," 106.

12. *Parrish*, 300 U.S. at 379.

3. *The Public/Private Distinction and the Minimum Wage*

1. On the significance of the public/private distinction in the history of American law generally, see Morton Horwitz, "The History of the Public/Private Distinction," *U. Pa. L. Rev.* 130 (1982): 1423; Elizabeth Mensch, "The History of Mainstream Legal Thought," in David Kairys, ed., *The Politics of Law: A Progressive Critique*, rev. ed. (New York, 1990), 13–37.

2. See, e.g., H.G. Wood, *A Practical Treatise on the Law of Nuisances in Their Various Forms, Including Remedies Therefor at Law and in Equity*, 3d. ed. (San Francisco, Calif., 1893).

3. Charles McCurdy, "Justice Field and the Jurisprudence of Government-Business Relations: Some Parameters of Laissez-Faire Constitutionalism, 1863–1897," in Lawrence Friedman and Harry Scheiber, eds., *American Law and the Constitutional Order* (Cambridge, Mass., 1988), 246, 255–59.

4. See, e.g., Michael Les Benedict, "Preserving Federalism: Reconstruction and the Waite Court," *Sup. Ct. Rev.* 1978 (1979): 39.

5. Harry Scheiber, "The Road to *Munn*: Eminent Domain and the Concept of Public Purpose in the State Courts," in Donald Fleming and Bernard Bailyn, eds., *Law in American History* (Cambridge, Mass., 1971), 329–402.

6. Ibid.; Corwin, "The Basic Doctrine of American Constitutional Law," *Mich. L. Rev.* 12 (1914): 247, 261–71; Clyde Jacobs, *Law Writers and the Courts* (Berkeley, Calif. 1954); McCurdy, "Justice Field"; Glynn S. Lunney, Jr., "A Critical Reexamination of the Takings Jurisprudence," *Mich. L. Rev.* 90 (1992): 1892, 1906–24. See also Charles Fairman, *Reconstruction and Reunion, 1864–1868, Part One* (New York, 1971), 918–1116; Morton Horwitz, *The Transformation of American Law, 1870–1960: The Crisis of Legal Orthodoxy* (New York, 1992), 10–11, 22–27.

7. Gillman, *The Constitution Besieged*; see also Horwitz, *The Transformation of American Law*, 19–31 (discussing the idea of the neutral state and the consequences of the principle of neutrality).

8. See Benedict, "Laissez-Faire and Liberty," 293, 298, 304–31; Owen Fiss, *Troubled Beginnings of the Modern State, 1888–1910* (New York, 1993), 156, 160; Gillman, *The Constitution Besieged*; Horwitz, *The Transformation of American Law*, 4–5, 9, 11, 16, 19–30; Jacobs, *Law Writers and the Courts*; McCurdy, "Justice Field," (1988) 251; Stephen A. Siegel, "Understanding the *Lochner* Era: Lessons from the Controversy over Railroad and Utility Rate Regulation," *Va. L. Rev.* 70 (1984): 187, 189–92; Aviam Soifer, "The Paradox of Paternalism and Laissez-Faire Constitutionalism: United States Supreme Court, 1888–1921," *Law & Hist. Rev.* 5 (1987): 249, 278; Cass Sunstein, "Lochner's Legacy," *Colum. L. Rev.* 87 (1987): 873, 878–89.

9. *Calder v. Bull*, 3 U.S. 386, 388 (1798).

10. U.S. Constitution, Am. V (emphasis added).

11. See *Cole v. La Grange*, 113 U.S. 1 (1885); *Parkersburg v. Brown*, 106 U.S. 487 (1882); *Loan Assn. v. Topeka*, 20 Wall. 655 (1874); Gillman, *The Constitution Besieged*; Jacobs, *Law Writers and the Courts*, 98–159; Lunney, "A Critical Reexamination of the Takings Jurisprudence," 1906–24.

12. *Munn v. Illinois*, 94 U.S. 113, 119–20 (1877).

13. Id. at 121.

14. On the origins of the "public interest" concept in English legal thought and its adoption in *Munn*, see Charles Fairman, "The So-Called Granger Cases, Lord Hale, and Justice Bradley," *Stan. L. Rev.* 5 (1953): 587, 588; Walter H. Hamilton, "Affectation with Public Interest," *Yale L. J.* 39 (1930): 1089, 1092–99; Breck P. McAllister, "Lord Hale and Business Affected with a Public Interest," *Harv. L. Rev.* 43 (1930): 759, 768–69.

15. *Munn*, 94 U.S. at 126.

16. See Francis Hargrave, *A Collection of Tracts Relative to the Law of England from Manuscripts* (London, 1787).

17. *Munn*, 94 U.S. at 127.

18. *Aldnutt v. Inglis*, 12 East. 527, 537 (1810).

19. *Munn*, 94 U.S. 127–28, 130.

20. Waite to J. Sheldon, March 30, 1877, quoted in C. Peter Magrath, *Morrison R. Waite: The Triumph of Character* (New York, 1963), 187.

21. See McCurdy, "Justice Field" (1988), 259–61.

22. *Munn*, 94 U.S. at 142–45.

23. Id. at 146–47.

24. Id. at 148–54.

25. *German Alliance Ins. Co. v. Kansas*, 233 U.S. 389, 432 (1914) (Lamar, J., dissenting).

26. *Budd v. New York*, 143 U.S. 517 (1892).

27. *Brass v. Stoeser*, 153 U.S. 391 (1894).

28. *Chicago, Burlington & Quincy R.R. Co. v. Iowa*, 94 U.S. 155, 161 (1877).

29. See *Chicago & Grand Trunk Ry. Co. v. Wellman*, 143 U.S. 339 (1892); *Railroad Commission Cases*, 116 U.S. 307 (1886); *Dow v. Beidelman*, 125 U.S. 680 (1888); *Winona & St. Peter R.R. Co. v. Blake*, 94 U.S. 180 (1877); *Chicago, Milwaukee & St. Paul R.R. Co. v. Ackley*, 94 U.S. 179 (1877); *Peik v. Chicago & Northwestern Ry. Co.*, 94 U.S. 164 (1877); Charles Warren, "The Progressiveness of the United States Supreme Court," *Colum. L. Rev.* 13 (1913): 294, 301, n. 16, and cases there cited.

30. *Van Dyke v. Geary*, 244 U.S. 39, 48 (1917); see also *Spring Valley Water Works v. Schottler*, 110 U.S. 347, 354 (1884).

31. *Producers Transp. Co. v. R.R. Comm.*, 251 U.S. 228, 231 (1920); see also *Pipe Line Cases*, 234 U.S. 548, 561 (1914).

32. *Cotting v. Kansas City Stock Yards Co.*, 183 U.S. 79, 85 (1901); see also *Stafford v. Wallace*, 258 U.S. 495, 516 (1922).

33. *Chicago Board of Trade v. Olsen*, 262 U.S. 1, 40–41 (1923).

34. *German Alliance Ins. Co. v. Kansas*, 233 U.S. 389, 415 (1914).

35. *Tyson v. Banton*, 273 U.S. 418, 445–47 (1927) (Holmes, J., dissenting).

36. *Terminal Taxicab Co. v. Kutz*, 241 U.S. 252 (1916); *Tyson v. Banton*, 273 U.S. 418, 445–47 (1927); *Nebbia v. New York*, 291 U.S. 502 (1934).

37. The opinion appears to assume that those two meanings were coextensive. *Munn*, 241 U.S. at 254–56.

38. Id. at 254–55.

39. Id. at 256.

40. *Block v. Hirsh*, 256 U.S. 135, 155–56 (1921); 41 Stat. 297 (1919).

41. E.g., *German Alliance Insurance Co. v. Lewis*, 233 U.S. 239 (upholding regulation of rates charged for fire insurance).

42. *Block*, 256 U.S. at 155. Similar statutes were upheld in *Levy Leasing Co. v. Siegel*, 258 U.S. 242 (1922) and *Marcus Brown Holding Co. v. Feldman*, 256 U.S. 170 (1921).

43. Compare Justice Field's assertion that the "line of division" between the spheres of federal and state authority was as clear as if it were "traced by landmarks and monuments visible to the eye." *Tarble's Case*, 80 U.S. 397, 406 (1871).

44. *Highland v. Russell Car & Snow Plow Co.*, 279 U.S. 253, 255, 260–62 (1929). On the "public purpose" doctrine and its significance in the law of eminent domain and taxation, see McCurdy, "Justice Field"; Scheiber, "The Road to *Munn.*"

45. *Stephenson v. Binford*, 287 U.S. 251, 264 (1932). "Here the circumstance which justifies what otherwise might be an unconstitutional interference with the freedom of private contract is that the contract calls for a service, the performance of which contemplates the use of facilities belonging to the State; and it would be strange doctrine which, while recognizing the power of the state to regulate the use itself, would deny its power to regulate the contract so far as it contemplates the use. 'Contracts which relate to the use of the highways must be deemed to have been made in contemplation of the regulatory authority of the State.'" Id. at 274.

46. *Munn*, 94 U.S. at 146–47.

47. 15 Stat. 77 (1868); *United States v. Martin*, 94 U.S. 400 (1876).

48. *Atkin v. Kansas*, 191 U.S. 207, 218–19, 222, 224 (1903). "[W]e can imagine no possible ground to dispute the power of the State to declare that no one undertaking work *for it or for one of its municipal agencies*, should permit or require an employee on such work to labor in excess of eight hours each day, and to inflict punishment upon those who are embraced by such regulations and yet disregard them. It cannot be deemed a part of the liberty of any contractor that *he* be allowed to do public work in any mode he may choose to adopt, without regard to the wishes of the State. On the contrary, it belongs to the State, as the guardian and trustee for its people, and having control of its affairs, to prescribe the conditions upon which it will permit public work to be done on its behalf, or on behalf of its municipalities" (emphasis in original). Id. at 222–23.

49. *Ellis v. United States*, 206 U.S. 246 (1907); see also *United States v. Garbish*, 222 U.S. 257 (1911).

50. *Balt. & Ohio R.R. Co. v. I.C.C.*, 221 U.S. 612 (1911).

51. *Holden v. Hardy*, 169 U.S. 366 (1898); *State v. Holden*, 14 Utah 71, 94–95 (1896); Brief for the Plaintiff in Error, 12, 22, 46.

52. In *Smyth v. Ames*, 169 U.S. 466 (1898), the Court held that a rate regulation that deprived a business affected with a public interest of a reasonable rate of return on its investment constituted a taking of private property without just compensation in violation of the Fourteenth Amendment's due process clause. If, however, the regulated rate afforded the business such a reasonable rate of return, the deprivation of the business's opportunity to enjoy greater profits by charging a higher rate did not amount to a taking of private property. Such rate regulation was permissible at all, of course, only if the business in question was affected with a public interest.

53. The notion that restrictions on work constituted not only deprivations of liberty but also takings of property, derived from the Lockean/Smithean view that labor was the source of all property, was a recurrent theme in the legal literature of the period. See, e.g., *Butler v. Perry*, 240 U.S. 328, 333 (1916); *Coppage v. Kansas*, 236 U.S. 1, 14 (1915); *Riley v. Massachusetts*, 232 U.S. 671 (1914); *Holden v. Hardy*, 169 U.S. 366, 378 (1898) (Argument for Plaintiff in Error); *Butcher's Union Co. v. Crescent City Co.*, 111 U.S. 746, 757 (1884) (Field, J., concurring); *Slaughterhouse Cases*, 83 U.S. 36, 122 (1873) (Bradley, J., dissenting); *Slaughterhouse Cases*, 83 U.S. 36, 110 (1873) (Field, J., dissenting); *Slaughterhouse Cases*, 83 U.S. 36, 56 (1873) (Argument against the monopoly); Jacobs, *Law Writers and the Courts*, 36–37; Paul Kens, *Judicial Power and Reform Politics: The Anatomy of Lochner v. New York* (Lawrence, Kans., 1990), 62, 104–5; T. R. Powell, "Due Process and the Adamson Law," *Colum. L. Rev.* 17 (1917): 114.

54. This point was made by counsel attacking the constitutionality of Oregon's ten-hour law for female employees of laundries in *Muller v. Oregon*, 208 U.S. 412 (1908): "Nor do the princi-

ples declared in *Atkin*, 191 U.S. at 207, support the statute under consideration. There was no question in that case involving the power of a state to make it a criminal offense for an employer to contract with his employees in *private work* in excess of a limited number of hours. The statute there under review related to *public work*, and the state may properly limit the terms under which its work may be done." Brief for the Plaintiff in Error, p. 30 (emphasis in original).

55. "The common law of nuisance deals with nearly all the more serious or flagrant violations of the interests which the police power protects, but it deals with evils only after they have come into existence, and it leaves the determination of what is evil largely to the peculiar circumstances of each case.

"The police power endeavors to prevent evil by placing a margin of safety between that which is permitted and that which is sure to lead to injury or loss." Ernst Freund, *The Police Power, Public Policy, and Constitutional Rights* (Chicago, 1904), 25. See also Horwitz, *The Transformation of American Law*, 27–28; 2 Kent, Comm. 340 and notes, quoted in Corwin, "The Basic Doctrine of American Constitutional Law," 264.

56. See, e.g., *Hadacheck v. Sebastian*, 239 U.S. 394 (1915); *Reinman v. City of Little Rock*, 237 U.S. 171 (1915); *N.Y. & N.E. R.R. Co. v. Bristol*, 151 U.S. 556 (1894); *Mugler v. Kansas*, 123 U.S. 623, 658, 664–69 (1887); *Pacific Ry. Co. v. Humes*, 115 U.S. 512 (1885). See generally, McCurdy, "Justice Field," 250–51; Joseph Sax, "Takings and the Police Power," *Yale L. J.* 74 (1964): 36–40.

57. See *Munn*, 94 U.S. at 124 (Government may require "each citizen to so conduct himself, and so use his own property, as not unnecessarily to injure another."); *Crowley v. Christensen*, 137 U.S. 86 (1890) (sale of intoxicating liquors may be prohibited under state's police power); *Barbier v. Connolly*, 113 U.S. 27 (1885) (ordinance prohibiting laundries from operating between 10 P.M. and 6 A.M. a valid exercise of the police power). Christopher G. Tiedeman, in his influential treatise on the police power, argued that "The police power of the government is shown to be confined to the detailed enforcement of the legal maxim, *sic utere tuo ut alienum non laedas.*" Christopher G. Tiedeman, *Limitations of Police Power*, vii–viii, quoted in Jacobs, *Law Writers and the Courts*, 60. Thomas Cooley had endorsed the same view in his *Constitutional Limitations*, 1st ed. (Boston, 1868), 577. See also 2 Kent, Comm. 340 and notes, quoted in Corwin, "The Basic Doctrine of American Constitutional Law," 247, 264; Lunney, "A Critical Reexamination of the Takings Jurisprudence," 1906–12. As Jacobs points out, "This was but one way of saying that the police power was to be exercised for public, as distinguished from private, purposes." Jacobs, *Law Writers and the Courts*, 100.

58. *Holden*, 169 U.S. at 366, 395–97. See also *Cantwell v. Missouri*, 199 U.S. 602 (1905) (upholding a similar Missouri statute).

59. *Muller v. Oregon*, 208 U.S. 412, 421–22 (1908). Similar maximum hours statutes for women were upheld on the authority of *Muller* in *Bosley v. McLaughlin*, 236 U.S. 385 (1915); *Miller v. Wilson*, 236 U.S. 373 (1915); *Hawley v. Walker*, 232 U.S. 718 (1914); and *Riley v. Massachusetts*, 232 U.S. 671 (1914).

60. Horwitz, *The Transformation of American Law*, 29; Fiss, *Troubled Beginnings*, 156.

61. *Lochner v. New York*, 198 U.S. 45, 64 (1905).

62. Fiss, *Troubled Beginnings*, 161.

63. Benedict, "Laissez-faire and Liberty," 308.

64. *Lochner*, 198 U.S. at 57.

65. "Clean and wholesome bread does not depend upon whether the baker works but ten hours per day or only sixty hours a week." Id.

66. Id. at 59.

67. Id. at 56, 61. See Horwitz, *The Transformation of American Law*, 30.

68. *Lochner*, 198 U.S. at 64.

69. "Speaking generally, the State in the exercise of its powers may not unduly interfere with the right of the citizen to enter into contracts that may be necessary and essential in the enjoyment of the inherent rights belonging to everyone, among which rights is the right 'to be free in the enjoyment of all his faculties; to be free to use them in all lawful ways; to live and work where he will; to earn his livelihood by any lawful calling; to pursue any livelihood or vocation.'" *Lochner*, 198 U.S. at 65; "there is a liberty of contract which cannot be violated even under the sanction of direct legislative enactment." Id. at 68.

70. Id. at 66–67.

71. "[T]he police power cannot be put forward as an excuse for oppressive and unjust legislation." *Lochner*, 198 U.S. at 66. Harlan had expressed this view eighteen years earlier in *Mugler v. Kansas*, 123 U.S. 623, 661 (1887):

> The courts are not bound by mere forms, nor are they to be misled by mere pretences. They are at liberty—indeed, are under a solemn duty—to look at the substance of things, whenever they enter upon the inquiry whether the legislature has transcended the limits of its authority. If, therefore, a statute purporting to have been enacted to protect the public health, the public morals, or the public safety, has no real or substantial relation to those objects, or is a palpable invasion of rights secured by the fundamental law, it is the duty of the courts to so adjudge, and thereby give effect to the Constitution.

> Nevertheless, "every possible presumption is to be indulged in favor of the validity of a statute. . . ."

72. *Lochner*, 198 U.S. at 68. "[A] large discretion 'is necessarily vested in the legislature to determine not only what the interests of the public require, but what measures are necessary for the protection of such interests.'" Id. at 66.

73. Id. at 68–72.

74. Id. at 72–73. See Sunstein, "Lochner's Legacy," 877–78.

75. *Lochner*, 198 U.S. at 76 (emphasis mine). See Fiss, *Troubled Beginnings*, 180–81; Sunstein, "Lochner's Legacy," 877–79.

76. For a discussion of the operation of these three modes in the minimum wage context, see Peter Caldwell, "Minimum Wage Laws," *J.B.A. Kan.* 5 (1937): 256, 257.

77. *Lochner*, 198 U.S. at 55, 64 (emphasis mine).

78. Brief for Plaintiff in Error, at 34–38.

79. *Knoxville Iron Co. v. Harbison*, 183 U.S. 13 (1901). See also *Keokee Consolidated Coke Co. v. Taylor*, 234 U.S. 224 (1914); *Dayton Coal Co. v. Barton*, 183 U.S. 23 (1901).

80. *Rail & River Coal Co. v. Yaple*, 236 U.S. 338 (1915); *McLean v. Arkansas*, 211 U.S. 539 (1909).

81. *Patterson v. Bark Eudora*, 190 U.S. 169 (1903). See also *Strathearn Steamship Co. v. Dillon*, 252 U.S. 348 (1920).

82. *Erie Railroad Co. v. Williams*, 233 U.S. 685 (1914); *St. Louis, Iron Mountain & St. Paul Railway Co. v. Paul*, 173 U.S. 404, 407, 409 (1899).

83. Ernst Freund had observed this in his 1904 treatise on the police power. In a section entitled "Rate of Wages," he wrote: "Considerations of health and safety which complicate the question of hours of labor do not enter into the question of rates. The regulation would be purely of an economic character. It would be closely analogous to the regulation of the price of other commodities or services." E. Freund, *The Police Power, Public Policy, and Constitutional Rights*, 303.

84. *Munn*, 94 U.S. at 152–53.

85. Id. at 125.

86. *Frisbie v. United States*, 157 U.S. 160, 166 (1895). "No man has a legal right to a pension, and no man has a legal right to interfere in the matter of obtaining pensions for himself or others."

87. *Ball v. Halsell*, 161 U.S. 72, 83–84 (1896); Act of March 3, 1891, c. 538, 26 Stat. 851; *Beers v. Arkansas*, 61 U.S. 527 (1857). See also *Margolin v. United States*, 269 U.S. 93 (1925); *Newman v. Moyers*, 253 U.S. 182 (1920); *Calhoun v. Massie*, 253 U.S. 170 (1920); *Capital Trust Co. v. Calhoun*, 250 U.S. 208, 218–19 (1919).

88. *Yeiser v. Dysart*, 267 U.S. 540, 541 (1925).

89. *Atkin*, 191 U.S. at 208–10.

90. The Court upheld per curiam a virtually identical Maryland statute in 1915. *Elkan v. State*, 90 A. 183 (1914), *aff'd*, 239 U.S. 634 (1915).

91. *Atkin*, 191 U.S. at 224. The Court's permissive posture toward minimum wage regulation for work falling within the public sphere, recognized by Justice Sutherland in his majority opinion in *Adkins v. Children's Hospital*, 261 U.S. 525, 547 (1923), suggests that wage-fund theory was not the dominant factor in the Court's minimum wage jurisprudence. See Herbert Hovenkamp, *Enterprise and American Law, 1836–1937*, 193–98 (Cambridge, Mass., 1991).

92. *Atkin*, 191 U.S. at 219. In fact, the brief for the Plaintiff in Error in *Holden v. Hardy* suggested that the application of such a statute to a purely private business would have been beyond the pale: "If this act had attempted to regulate the *price* to be paid for labor in mines and smelters—for instance, if it had provided that the laborer, although his hours of labor should be reduced to eight, should be paid what he had formerly received for ten, there could be no question as to its unconstitutionality . . ." Brief for Plaintiff in Error at 20 (emphasis in original). The brief went on to contend that Utah's eight-hour law for miners was unconstitutional because it was, indirectly, a regulation of wages.

> . . . yet as by the act the period of employment is, without the consent of the laborer, limited to eight hours per day, it would be only fair to the laborer that the act should further provide that he should lose nothing pecuniarily by reason of such reduction or limitation of his earning capacity, other laborers in similar and equally dangerous and unwholesome occupations . . . being permitted by the act to work and be paid for as many hours per day as they please or can contract for. (Id.)

The Court did not address this argument in its *Holden* opinion.

93. *Bunting v. Oregon*, 243 U.S. 426, 428–30 (1917).

94. *Holden v. Hardy*, supra; *Muller v. Oregon*, supra; *Miller v. Wilson*, supra; *Riley v. Massachusetts*, supra; *Hawley v. Walker*, supra; *Bosley v. McLaughlin*, supra.

95. See, e.g., *Street v. Varney Electrical Supply Co.*, 160 Indiana 338 (1903); *People v. Coler*, 166 N.Y. 1 (1901); *Low v. Rees Printing Co.*, 41 Nebraska 127 (1894); *Wheeling Bridge & Terminal Ry. Co. v. Gilmore*, 8 Ohio Cir. Ct. Rep. 858.

96. *Bunting*, 243 U.S. at 431–33.

97. Id. at 435–38. Because Chief Justice White and Justices Van Devanter and McReynolds dissented without opinion, it was left unclear whether they objected to the statute as a wage regulation, an hours regulation, or both. See Id. at 439.

98. Id. at 438. There was no discussion of "natural effects" or "common understandings." See *Lochner*, 198 U.S. at 59, 64.

99. Compare *Bunting*, 243 U.S. at 438–39 with *Lochner*, 198 U.S. at 71.

100. *Adkins v. Children's Hospital*, 261 U.S. at 525, 564 (Taft, C. J., dissenting). Taft pointed out that the Oregon statute upheld in *Bunting* "covered the whole field of industrial employment and certainly covered the case of persons employed in bakeries." Id. at 563. For this reason, Taft believed that *Bunting* must have overruled *Lochner*. Taft failed to see, however, that a law covering the whole field of industrial employment was far more likely to be seen as general welfare legislation (and thus not special legislation) than a law limiting its scope to bakeries. See *Bunting*, 243 U.S. at 439.

101. "Of course, mere declaration cannot give character to a law nor turn illegal into legal operation, and when such attempt is palpable this court necessarily has the power of review." Id. at 435.

102. Laws of Oregon, 1913, p. 92; *Stettler*, 139 P. at 743, 744. The measure was clearly couched as an exercise of the police power. The statute's preamble provided in part: "Whereas, the welfare of the state of Oregon requires that women and minors should be protected from conditions of labor which have a pernicious effect on their health and morals, and inadequate wages and unduly long hours and unsanitary conditions of labor have such a pernicious effect. . . ." Ibid.

103. *Stettler v. O'Hara*, 69 Ore. 519, 139 P. 743 (1914); *Simpson v. O'Hara*, 70 Ore. 261, 141 P. 158 (1914).

104. See Alexander Bickel and Benno Schmidt, *The Judiciary and Responsible Government, 1910–1921* (New York, 1984), 592–603.

105. Bickel and Schmidt, *The Judiciary and Responsible Government*, 602. Holmes, of course, believed that reliance on the police power was "superfluous." Ibid.

106. *Stettler v. O'Hara*, 243 U.S. 629 (1917).

107. *Wilson v. New*, 243 U.S. 332 (1917); 39 Stat. 761 (1916).

108. *Wilson*, 243 U.S. at 337. See also id. at 338.

109. Id. at 334–35. The government went on to contend, quite unnecessarily, that the public interest in railway transport would also justify the imposition of *maximum* wages: "On the other hand, the public is interested in preventing the payment of wages which are too high, since they constitute the largest element in the cost of transportation and necessarily affect rates. An unreasonably high wage means an unjust rate or impaired service. In either event it is the public that pays, and the public has the right to demand regulation of wages to the end that it may enjoy reasonable and just rates." *Wilson*, 243 U.S. at 335. The Court would accept a very similar argument fourteen years later in *O'Gorman & Young v. Hartford Fire Ins. Co.*, 282 U.S. 251 (1931). See infra. The appellees in *Wilson* were quick to point out that this rationale was not available to sustain the Adamson Act's minimum wage provisions: "It cannot be upheld by analogy to the ratemaking power. It does not purport to protect the public or interstate commerce against improper wages. On the contrary, it requires a heavy increase in wages. . . . It cannot be upheld on any theory of a power in Congress to control railroad expenses so as to promote reasonable rates. . . ." *Wilson*, 243 U.S. at 339.

110. Id. at 334–35 (emphasis mine).

111. "That the business of common carriers by rail is in a sense a *public* business because of the interest of society in the continued operation and rightful conduct of such business and that the *public* interest begets a *public* right of regulation to the full extent necessary to secure and protect it, is settled by so many decisions, state and federal, and is illustrated by such a continuous exertion of state and federal legislative power as to leave no room for question on the subject." Id. at 347 (emphasis mine).

112. Id. at 349, citing the Hours of Service Act, the Safety Appliance Act, the Employers' Liability Act, and cases upholding those acts.

113. "It is also equally true that as the right to fix by agreement between the carrier and its employees a standard of wages to control their relations is primarily *private*, the establishment and giving effect to such agreed on standard is not subject to be controlled or prevented by public authority." Id. at 347 (emphasis mine).

114. Id. at 349.

115. Id. at 347–48, 350–52.

116. ". . . an obligation rests upon a carrier to carry on its business and . . . conditions of cost or other obstacles afford no excuse and exempt from no responsibility which arises from

a failure to do so and . . . government possesses the full regulatory power to compel performance of such duty." Id. at 350.

117. As engaging in the business of interstate commerce carriage subjects the carrier to the lawful power of Congress to regulate irrespective of the source whence the carrier draws its existence, and as also by engaging in a *business charged with a public interest* all the vast property and every right of the carrier become subject to the authority to regulate possessed by Congress to the extent that regulation may be exerted considering the subject regulated and what is appropriate and relevant thereto, it follows that the very absence of the scale of wages by agreement and the impediment and destruction of interstate commerce which was threatened called for the appropriate and relevant remedy, the creation of a standard by operation of law binding upon the carrier. (Id. at 352 [emphasis mine].)

118. ". . . whatever would be the right of an employee engaged in a *private* business to demand such wages as he desires, to leave the employment if he does not get them and by concert of action to agree with others to leave upon the same condition, such rights are necessarily subject to limitation when employment is accepted in a *business charged with a public interest* and as to which the power to regulate commerce possessed by Congress applied and the resulting right to fix in case of disagreement and dispute a standard of wages as we have seen necessarily obtained." Id. at 352–53 (emphasis mine).

119. Id. at 353 (emphasis mine).

120. Id. at 353–54 (emphasis mine).

121. Id. at 364 (emphasis mine).

122. O. W. Holmes to F. Frankfurter, March 27, 1917, reprinted in Bickel and Schmidt, *The Judiciary and Responsible Government*, 473.

123. See Bickel and Schmidt, *The Judiciary and Responsible Government*, 467.

124. See Ibid., 461–62, 467, 473. Justice Clarke, unlike White, both joined the *Bunting* majority and voted to sustain Oregon's minimum wage statute in *Stettler*. He also voted to uphold the postwar rent control statutes challenged in *Levy Leasing Co. v. Siegel*, 258 U.S. 242 (1922), *Marcus Brown Holding Co. v. Feldman*, 256 U.S. 170 (1921), and *Block v. Hirsh*, 256 U.S. 135 (1921). It is therefore unlikely that he shared White's rather restrictive views on the power to regulate wages.

125. *Wilson*, 243 U.S. at 365–72.

126. Id. at 364–65 (emphasis mine).

127. Id. at 387.

128. Id. at 389.

4. *From* Adkins *to* Nebbia

1. 40 Stat. 960, c. 174 (1918); *Adkins*, 261 U.S. at 525.

2. Id. at 528–32, 535.

3. Id. at 535, citing *Coppage v. Kansas*, 236 U.S. 1 (1915) and *Adair v. United States*, 208 U.S. 161 (1908).

4. *Adkins*, 261 U.S. at 534.

5. Id. at 528, 532.

6. The practice of using revenue from public taxation for the support of the indigent was well established in the colonies in 1776, remained intact during the era of state and national constitution-making, and persisted throughout the nineteenth and early twentieth centuries. Despite numerous instances in which taxation was subjected to successful constitutional attack for violating the public purpose doctrine, "there was no attack at all on the universally

recognized power of government to tax its citizens to provide the basic needs of the poor," and "no court and no commentator invoked the public purpose doctrine to attack the basic structure of public relief." Constitutional conservatives from Brewer to Cooley concurred that poor relief was "among the unquestionably legitimate functions of government." Thomas C. Grey, "The Malthusian Constitution," *U. Miami L. Rev.* 41 (1986): 21, 42–44. Indeed, the U.S. Supreme Court adopted this position in *Kelly v. Pittsburgh*, 104 U.S. 78, 81 (1881), where it held that "the support of the poor. . . . [is a] public purpose in which the whole community have an interest, and for which, by common consent, property owners everywhere in this country are taxed."

7. This argument had been suggested by C. K. Burdick in the 1922 edition of his *The Law of the American Constitution*. On the subject of minimum wage regulation, he wrote: "It would seem that such legislation can not only be supported as an exercise of the police power for the protection of the physical and moral well-being of the workers involved, and so through them for the protection of the general welfare of the community, but also for the protection of the community against the burden of making up the deficit between the living wage and the wage received." Burdick, *The Law of the American Constitution* (New York, 1922), 582. T. R. Powell had sketched a similar defense of the minimum wage in 1917: "The theory of the legislation is that there is a public interest in having those who give their whole strength to an employer receive enough from the employer to maintain that strength, that there is a public interest in having an industry support itself instead of relying on outside subsidies." Powell, "The Constitutional Issue in Minimum Wage Legislation," *Minn. L. Rev.* 2 (1917): 1, 16.

8. *Adkins*, 261 U.S. at 535, 538; Brief for Appellees at 9–10, 13–15, 18–19, 29, 33–34; Argument of Wade Ellis at 29.

9. Brief for Appellees at 23–29 (similarly analyzing *Block v. Hirsh*); Oral Argument of Wade Ellis at 30.

10. Brief for Appellees at 23; *Adkins*, 261 U.S. at 536–37.

11. Id. at 546–47, 554–55, 558.

12. Id. 551. *Block v. Hirsh* was distinguished on the same ground. Id. at 552.

13. Cases upholding statutes regulating the time and manner of wage payment were brushed aside as inapplicable. Such statutes' "tendency and purpose was to prevent unfair and perhaps fraudulent methods in the payment of wages and in no sense can they be said to be, or to furnish a precedent for, wage-fixing statutes." Id. at 547.

14. The price fixed by the board need have no relation to the capacity or earning power of the employee . . . and, while it has no other basis to support its validity than the assumed necessities of the employee, it takes no account of any independent resources she may have. . . . What is sufficient to supply the necessary cost of living for a woman worker and maintain her in good health and protect her morals is obviously not a precise or unvarying sum—not even approximately so. The amount will depend upon a variety of circumstances: the individual temperament, habits of thrift, care, ability to buy necessaries intelligently, and whether the woman live alone or with her family. To those who practice economy, a given sum will afford comfort, while to those of contrary habit the same sum will be wholly inadequate. The cooperative economies of the family group are not taken into account though they constitute an important consideration in estimating the cost of living, for it is obvious that the individual expense will be less in the case of a member of a family than in the case of one living alone. (Id. at 555–56.)

15. The relation between earnings and morals is not capable of standardization. It cannot be shown that well paid women safeguard their morals more carefully than

those who are poorly paid. Morality rests upon other considerations than wages; and there is, certainly, no such prevalent connection between the two as to justify a broad attempt to adjust the latter with reference to the former. As a means of safeguarding morals the attempted classification, in our opinion, is without reasonable basis. No distinction can be made between women who work for others and those who do not; nor is there ground for distinction between women and men, for, certainly, if women require a minimum wage to preserve their morals men require it to preserve their honesty. (Id. at 556.)

16. Id.

17. Id. at 557–58.

18. "A statute requiring an employer to pay in money, to pay at prescribed and regular intervals, to pay the value of the services rendered, even to pay with fair relation to the extent of the benefit obtained from the service, would be understandable." Id. at 559.

19. Id. at 560.

20. Id. at 563–64.

21. Id. at 567–68.

22. *Wolff Packing Co. v. Industrial Court*, 262 U.S. 522, 524, 534, 540 (1923).

23. Id. at 523–24; Brief for Plaintiff in Error at 29–30, 42–43, 45, 51, 57; Supplemental Brief on Behalf of Defendant in Error at 12–13.

24. *Wolff Packing Co.*, 262 U.S. at 535.

25. Id. at 537–38.

26. Id. at 539–40.

27. Id. at 540–41 (emphasis in original).

28. [W]ithout saying that such limitations upon both [employer and employee] may not be sometimes justified, it must be where the obligation to the public of continuous service is direct, clear and mandatory and arises as a contractual condition express or implied of entering the business either as owner or worker. It can only arise when investment by the owner and entering the employment by the worker create a conventional relation to the public somewhat equivalent to the appointment of officers and the enlistment of soldiers and sailors in military service. (Id. at 541.)

29. Id. at 543.

The minutely detailed government supervision, including that of their relations to their employees, to which the railroads of the country have been gradually subjected by Congress through its power over interstate commerce, furnishes no precedent for regulation of the business of the plaintiff in error whose classification as public is at best doubtful. It is not too much to say that the ruling in *Wilson v. New* went to the border line, although it concerned an interstate common carrier in the presence of a nation-wide emergency and the possibility of great disaster. Certainly there is nothing to justify extending the drastic regulation sustained in that exceptional case to the one before us. (Id. at 543–44.)

See also *Dorchy v. Kansas*, 264 U.S. 286 (1924) (holding the Kansas Industrial Relations Act unconstitutional as applied to the mining industry).

30. *Wolff Packing Co.*, 262 U.S. at 544.

31. *Wolff Packing v. Kansas Court of Industrial Relations*, 267 U.S. 552, 560 (1925).

32. Id. at 555.

33. Id. at 557, citing *Holden v. Hardy* and *Bunting v. Oregon*.

34. That order provided:

A basic working day of eight hours shall be observed in this industry; but a nine hour day may be observed not to exceed two days in any one week without penalty: *Provided, however,* That if the working hours of the week shall exceed forty-eight in number, all over forty-eight shall be paid for at the rate of time and one-half: furthermore, in case a day in excess of the eight hour day shall be observed more than two days in any one week, all over eight hours, except for said two days in said week, shall be paid for at the rate of time and one-half, even though the working hours of the week may be forty-eight hours or fewer. (*Wolff Packing*, 267 U.S. at 560).

35. Id. at 555. "[T]he validity of the order in question concerning hours does not depend in any respect on the public interest in the meat packing industry. This was important on the question of wages, but not as to hours of labor." In neither *Holden* nor *Bunting* "was the nature of the business considered except in its effect on the health of the worker, and practically all the industries affected thereby were impressed with no public interest whatever. . . ." Id. at 557.

36. Id. at 558.

37. Id. at 564–65, 569. This interpretation was confirmed by Justice Sutherland in his opinion for the majority in *Tyson & Brother v. Banton*, 273 U.S. 418, 431 (1927):

In the *Wolff* case, this court held invalid the wage fixing provision of the compulsory arbitration statute of Kansas as applied to a meat packing establishment. The power of a legislature, under any circumstances, to fix prices or wages in the business of preparing and selling food was seriously doubted, but the court concluded that, even if the legislature could do so in a public emergency, no such emergency appeared, and, in any event, the power would not extend to giving compulsory continuity to the business by compulsory arbitration.

See also Edward Corwin, *The Constitution of the United States of America: Analysis and Interpretation* (Washington, D.C., 1964), 1102–3, n. 60.

38. Brandeis wrote on Taft's draft of *Wolff Packing I*: "Yes. This will clarify thought and bury the ashes of a sometime presidential boom. In Wilson v. New there was 'clear and present danger' and the 'curse was in the bigness.'" Papers of William Howard Taft, Library of Congress Manuscript Division, Reel 639.

39. Brandeis also authored the Court's unanimous opinion in *Dorchy v. Kansas*, 264 U.S. 286 (1924), applying the holding of *Wolff Packing I* to the mining industry.

40. See *Morehead v. Tipaldo*, 298 U.S. 587, 631–36 (1936) (Stone, Brandeis, and Cardozo, JJ., dissenting); *West Coast Hotel v. Parrish*, 300 U.S. 379 (1937). Indeed, if Stone believed when ascending the bench that minimum wage regulation was constitutional, there were by 1925 five members of the Court holding that view. See D. O. McGovney, "Reorganization of the Supreme Court," *Cal. L. Rev.* 25 (1937): 389, 396.

41. In *Tyson & Brother v. Banton*, 273 U.S. 418 (1927), a bare majority of the Court struck down a New York statute limiting resale prices of theater tickets on the ground that the business in question was not affected with a public interest. Although the brief for the appellant argued that the regulation effectively fixed both prices for tickets and fees for brokerage services, Brief for the Appellant at 17, 19, 22–23, the opinion treated the statute as a price regulation rather than a wage regulation.

42. *Ribnik v. McBride*, 277 U.S. 350, 357 (1928). The vote was this time 6 to 3. The four justices joining Sutherland's majority opinion in *Tyson* again joined him in *Ribnik*. Justice Sanford, who had dissented in *Tyson*, concurred specially on the ground that *Tyson* was controlling authority. Id. at 359. Stone, joined by Holmes and Brandeis, dissented.

43. *Tagg Bros. & Moorhead v. United States*, 280 U.S. 420 (1930).

44. Id. at 433.

45. *Stafford v. Wallace*, 258 U.S. 495, 516 (1922).

46. Separate Brief for the Appellants on the Question of the Constitutionality of the Rate Making Provisions of the Packers and Stockyards Act of 1921, insofar as they apply (as

claimed by Appellees) to the Commissions of the Commission Men (hereinafter "Separate Brief") at 5. Appellants contended that the regulation violated the principle of neutrality. It was "a redistribution of wealth, . . . a *taking* . . . from A and handing it over to B." Separate Brief at 4. "To prescribe a common maximum of earning power is to penalize the skillful for the benefit of the unskillful." Separate Brief at 3.

47. "The question is similar to that presented to the Court in [*Adkins, Wolff Packing I, Tyson, Ribnik,* and *Murphy v. Sardell,* 269 U.S. 530 (1925), a per curiam application of *Adkins*]. We submit that these decisions are conclusive. . . ." Separate Brief at 1–2.

48. *Tagg Bros. & Moorhead,* 280 U.S. at 423.

49. Id. at 423; Separate Brief at 2. "His only implements of trade are a horse on which to ride and a desk to keep his accounts." Separate Brief at 2.

50. *Tagg Bros. & Moorhead,* 280 U.S. at 424; Separate Brief at 3–4.

51. *Tagg Bros. & Moorhead,* 280 U.S. at 425–27; Separate Brief at 10–12, 21. The "simple rule is that the legislative rate-making power extends to the use of property under certain circumstances and conditions—devotion to public use, just compensation, etc.; it does *not* extend to personal services at all (excluding, of course, fees for securing bounty from the government, work for the government itself, and stipulations as to fees and wages in government contracts)." Id. at 21.

52. Separate brief at 24.

53. "The commission business of appellants is affected with a public interest because of its vital importance to interstate commerce and its monopolistic character." *Tagg Bros. & Moorhead,* 280 U.S. at 430; Brief for Appellees at 22–28.

54. *Tagg Bros. & Moorhead,* 280 U.S. at 438–39.

55. Id. at 439.

56. *Adkins,* 261 U.S. at 554.

57. *O'Gorman & Young v. Hartford Fire Ins. Co.,* 282 U.S. 251 (1931). The statute provided in pertinent part: "In order that rates of insurance against the hazards of fire shall be reasonable it shall be unlawful for any such insurer licensed in this State to . . . allow . . . any commission . . . in excess of a reasonable amount, to any person acting as its agent in respect to any class of such insurance, nor . . . to allow . . . any commission . . . to any person for acting as its local agent in respect to any class of such insurance, in excess of that . . . allowed to any one of its local agents on such risks in this State." New Jersey Laws 1928, c. 128, p. 258.

58. *German Alliance Ins. Co. v. Lewis,* 233 U.S. 389 (1914); Brief for Appellees.

59. Brief for Appellant at 9, 12, 25, 32.

60. Brief for Appellant at 12–18, 21–23, 32.

61. 280 U.S. iii; 281 U.S. iii; *O'Gorman & Young,* 282 U.S. 251.

62. Id. at 257.

63. Indeed, much of Van Devanter's dissenting opinion constituted a paraphrase of the *Wilson*-inspired "internal vs. external contracts" argument that had been made by the appellant. *German Alliance,* Van Devanter acknowledged, had established that the business of fire insurance was sufficiently affected with a public interest to permit rate regulation. However, "[n]othing there determined would permit regulation of all the undertakings of an insurance company. . . . certainly it does not follow that because the state has power to regulate the rate for insurance she may control every agreement having any possible relation thereto." Id. at 266–67. "Certainly we cannot say that exercise by the companies of the ordinary right freely to contract touching compensation for services will tend materially to interfere with reasonable rates for insurance. Rates constitute the matter of public concern, not the compensation of employees or representatives, which is, after all, only an item of expense." Id. at 270. The statute therefore restricted "the right of both company and agent to make reasonable private agreements in respect of compensation for ordinary services; and the restrictions have no

immediate or necessary relation to the maintenance of insurance rates fair to the public." Id. at 268–69. Indeed, Van Devanter offered his own parade of horribles sure to ensue if the statute in question was upheld: "The public has no direct, immediate interest in the agency contract here set up. Its concern is with rates. Like any other expense item, brokers' commissions may ultimately affect the rate charged for policies; but this is true of the wages of office boys, printers, bookkeepers, actuaries, officers; the price paid for pens, ink, or other supplies—indeed whatever expense may be incurred." Id. at 267.

64. Id. at 268–69, citing *Wilson v. New*.

65. Id. at 257–58.

66. Comment, *Harv. L. Rev.* 49 (1931): 643, 644.

67. Norman J. Macbeth Jr., "Present Status of the Adkins Case," *Ky. L. J.* 24 (1935): 59, 64–65.

68. *Nebbia*, 291 U.S. 502, 506–10, 531.

69. Id. at 505–6.

70. Id. at 511–14.

71. Id. at 525.

72. Id. at 531–32. "Contract is not specially mentioned in the text that we have to construe," Holmes had written. "It is merely an example of doing what you want to do, embodied in the word liberty. But pretty much all law consists in forbidding men to do some things that they want to do, and contract is no more exempt from law than other acts." *Adkins*, 261 U.S. at 568.

73. *Nebbia*, 291 U.S. at 533.

74. Id. at 532–37.

75. Id. 536–37, 539, 552–54. The question this narrative raises and leaves unanswered is why the Court decided to abandon the public/private distinction in *Nebbia*. As the argument for the State of New York demonstrates, there were far more conventional means by which the Court might have sustained the challenged regulation. Scholars familiar with the period could no doubt offer plausible hypotheses, but such speculations simply cannot be confirmed. Justice Roberts, author of the landmark opinion, left no papers. Nor do the surviving papers of his colleagues on the Court shed any light on how Roberts came to write the sweeping majority opinion that he ultimately produced. The origins of *Nebbia* must regrettably remain forever shrouded in mystery. This book, however, is not about the sources of *Nebbia*. It is instead about *Nebbia*'s consequences. Those consequences, I contend, were far more dramatic, epochal, revolutionary, and far-reaching than we have heretofore recognized.

76. *Nebbia*, 291 U.S. at 537. Professor Gillman downplays the significance of *Nebbia*, observing that Hughes and Roberts remained "committed to the public-purpose limit" in assessing the validity of police power legislation. Gillman, *The Constitution Besieged* 180–81. As I shall argue, however, this was also true of Hughes and Roberts in *West Coast Hotel*. The significance of *Nebbia* lies not in a rejection of the notion of public purpose, but in its expansive construction of that notion, and in its deferential posture toward legislative determinations in that regard, all of which was replicated in *West Coast Hotel*.

Gillman's modest reading of *Nebbia* appears to have been inspired by the positions that Hughes and Roberts took in two other cases. In *New State Ice v. Liebmann*, 285 U.S. 262 (1932), both Hughes and Roberts joined Sutherland's opinion striking down an Oklahoma statute prohibiting the manufacture, distribution, or sale of ice without a license, and conditioning grants of licenses on the applicant's successful showing that existing licensed facilities in the community in question were inadequate to meet the public's needs. The opinion held that the ice business, being private in nature, did not admit of such regulation. Two things should be noted with respect to the *Liebmann* decision.

First, as Professor Richard Friedman has observed, the statute there involved not the regulation of the price at which ice was sold, but instead the far more dramatic exclusion of certain persons from the pursuit of one of the ordinary callings. Friedman, "Switching Time," 1909–12. Despite his general aversion to substantive due process, Hughes had long before expressed his opposition to such legislation. "It requires no argument," he had written in *Truax v. Raich*, 239 U.S. 33, 41 (1915), "to show that the right to work for a living in the common occupations of the community is of the very essence of the personal freedom and opportunity that it was the purpose of the [Fourteenth] Amendment to secure." In *Nebbia*, New York was not preventing anyone from engaging in the ordinary calling of producing or selling milk—in fact, the price supports were probably keeping in business dairy farmers who would have been squeezed out by competition in a glutted market. This is perhaps why Hughes did not regard *Nebbia* as a sharp break with *Liebmann*. Pusey, *Charles Evans Hughes*, 700. Professor William Nelson reports that the New York courts, which had sustained below the regulation eventually upheld by the Supreme Court in *Nebbia*, see *People v. Nebbia*, 262 N.Y. 259 (1933), contemporaneously invalidated regulations that, as in *Liebmann*, established barriers to market entry. See, e.g., *Picone v. Commissioner of Licenses of New York City*, 241 N.Y. 157 (1925) (Commissioner could not deny a license to operate a junk boat simply because he thought it desirable to limit the number of junk dealers in the city); *People v. Kozanowski*, 239 N.Y.S. 706 (City Ct. Buffalo, 1930) (Buffalo Commissioner of Licenses could not deny a license to operate a theater simply because the owner had failed to serve a six-month apprenticeship under a union operator); *Sausser v. Department of Health of City of New York*, 242 N.Y. 66 (1926) (overturning the department's refusal to issue to a chiropractor a permit to operate an X-ray laboratory). See William E. Nelson, "Government Power as a Tool for Redistributing Wealth in Twentieth Century New York" (unpublished manuscript, 1995), 71–84.

Second, *Liebmann* was decided two years *before Nebbia*. Even assuming that Hughes and Roberts would in 1932 have struck down a statute regulating the price of ice, perhaps they had changed their views in the meantime. Hughes later expressed to his biographer the view that the *Liebmann* case "was near the border line." Pusey, *Charles Evans Hughes*, 698. If Roberts had wished in *Nebbia* to write an opinion that concluded merely that "this law promoted the health of the community as a whole," Gillman, *The Constitution Besieged*, 181, he certainly could have done so. He did not.

The second case inspiring Gillman's limited reading of *Nebbia* is *Morehead v. New York ex rel. Tipaldo*, 298 U.S. 587 (1936), in which Roberts joined the majority opinion striking down New York's minimum wage statute. As I will argue, there is good reason to believe that Roberts' vote in that case was not on the merits, and did not actually reflect his views of the constitutionality of such legislation.

Professor Michael Ariens' reasons for doubting *Nebbia's* significance are more difficult to understand. In addition to *Liebmann* he cites as support for the proposition that "Nebbia did not indicate a change in philosophical position by Roberts" the cases of *Ashton v. Cameron County Water Improvement Dist.*, 298 U.S. 513 (1936) and *Mayflower Farms, Inc. v. Ten Eyck*, 297 U.S. 251 (1936). Ariens, "A Thrice-Told Tale," 643–45. In *Ashton* the Court struck down the Municipal Bankruptcy Act on Tenth Amendment grounds; *Ten Eyck* struck down a provision of the New York Milk Control Act on equal protection grounds. Yet Ariens believes that these non-substantive due process decisions are more indicative of Roberts' views with respect to minimum wage regulation than Roberts' pronouncements in the substantive due process, price regulation case of *Nebbia v. New York*.

Ariens apparently cleaves to this view because he sees *Nebbia* as having retained the requirement that "socioeconomic legislation" not be unreasonable, arbitrary, or capricious—a requirement that he misleadingly suggests was abandoned by the Court in *Parrish*. Ariens,

"A Thrice-Told Tale," 642–45. See infra. For a critique of Ariens' reading of *Nebbia*, see Friedman, "Switching Time," 1891, 1920–22.

77. Id. at 537–39 (emphasis mine).

78. *Adkins*, 261 U.S. at 558–59.

79. *Nebbia*, 291 U.S. at 555, 557–58 (emphasis mine).

80. Willis, *Constitutional Law of the United States*, 736; Note, "Nebbia v. People: A Milestone," *U. Pa. L. Rev.* 82 (1934): 619, 622; Note, *Notre Dame Lawyer* 13 (1934): 468, 470; Thomas Raeburn White, "Constitutional Protection of Liberty of Contract: Does It Still Exist?" *U. Pa. L. Rev.* 83 (1935): 425, 438, 440.

81. Robert L. Hale, "Minimum Wages and the Constitution," *Colum. L. Rev.* 36 (1936): 629, 633. For a similar view, see Note, *Iowa L. Rev.* 22 (1937): 565, 570–71.

82. Note, *U. Pa. L. Rev.* 85 (1936): 117, 118.

83. Morris Duane, "Government Regulation of Prices in Competitive Business," *Temp. L. Rev.* 10 (1936): 262, 264, citing, inter alia, *Adkins*, *Wolff Packing I*, *Lochner*, *Ribnik*, and *Tyson*. See also Note, *Ill. B. J.* 23 (1934): 89, 91.

84. John E. Hannigan, "Minimum Wage Legislation and Litigation," *B. U. L. Rev.* 16 (1936): 845, 865; Alpheus Thomas Mason, "Labor, the Courts, and Section 7(a)," *Am. Pol. Sci. Rev.* 28 (1934): 999, 1007–8.

85. Macbeth, "Present Status of the Adkins Case," 59, 66.

5. *The Minimum Wage Cases Revisited*

1. *West Coast Hotel v. Parrish*, 300 U.S. 379, 386–88 (1937).

2. *Parrish v. West Coast Hotel*, 55 P.2d 1083, 1088–89 (Wash. 1936).

3. Id. at 1084, quoting *Larsen v. Rice*, 100 Wash. 642, 171 P. 1037, 1039. See also *Parrish*, 55 P.2d at 1090.

4. If the state Legislature and the state Supreme Court find that the statute is of a public interest, the Supreme Court of the United States will accept such judgment in the absence of facts to support the contrary conclusion. Unless the Supreme Court of the United States can find beyond question that [the minimum wage statute] is a plain, palpable invasion of rights secured by the fundamental law and has no real or substantial relation to public morals or public welfare, then the law must be sustained. (Id.)

5. Id. at 1084, 1089–90.

6. See Appellant's Brief on the Law, pp. 2–4, and Brief of Amici Curiae at 26, emphasizing the presumption of constitutionality and the requirement only that the legislation be reasonably adapted to addressing an existing evil.

7. Brief of Amici Curiae at 12–13; *Parrish*, 300 U.S. at 386.

8. Id. at 391. Compare Roberts' observation in *Nebbia*: "The due process clause makes no mention of sales or of prices any more than it speaks of business or *contracts* or buildings or other incidents of property. The thought seems nevertheless to have persisted that there is something peculiarly sacrosanct about the price one may charge for what he makes or sells. . . ." *Nebbia*, 291 U.S. at 532 (emphasis mine).

9. *Parrish*, 300 U.S. at 391. This was of course merely a paraphrase of what Roberts had written in *Nebbia*: "The Fifth Amendment in the field of federal activity, and the Fourteenth, as respects state action, do not prohibit governmental regulation for the public welfare. They merely condition the exertion of the admitted power, by securing that the end shall be accomplished by methods consistent with due process. And the guaranty of due process, as has often been held, demands only that the law shall not be unreasonable, arbitrary or capricious, and that the means selected shall have a real and substantial relation to

the object sought to be attained." *Nebbia*, 291 U.S. at 525. Indeed, Hughes himself had made this point twenty-six years earlier as an associate justice: "Liberty implies the absence of arbitrary restraint, not immunity from reasonable regulations and prohibitions imposed in the interests of the community," that is, in the public interest. *Chicago, B. & Q. R. Co. v. McGuire*, 219 U.S. 549, 567 (1911), quoted in *Parrish*, 300 U.S. at 392.

10. *Parrish*, 300 U.S. at 392.

11. For a discussion of Hughes' application of these skills in the commerce clause context, see ch. 10, infra.

12. *Parrish*, 300 U.S. 391–93.

13. Id. at 394–95.

14. Id. at 397–98.

15. Id. at 398–99.

16. Id. at 399–400.

17. Sunstein, "Lochner's Legacy," 873, 876–83, 917; *Adkins*, 261 U.S. at 558. Sunstein mischaracterizes the extent to which the Court constitutionalized common law/market allocations of wealth and power in the early twentieth century: "In the *Lochner* era itself, of course, the police power could not be used to help those unable to protect themselves in the marketplace." Sunstein, "Lochner's Legacy," 880. Sunstein confesses that "This oversimplifies a complicated framework," ibid., 880, n. 40; in my view, Sunstein just plain gets it wrong. It is difficult to reconcile such a characterization with, for example, cases upholding price regulation and time and manner regulations concerning payment of wages. Such misleading generalizations about early-twentieth-century jurisprudence have led many to misunderstand decisions like *West Coast Hotel* as "revolutionary."

18. Compare Gillman's view that Hughes was "jettisoning a constitutional tradition that was a century and a half old." Gillman, *The Constitution Beseiged*, 191.

19. Moreover, Sunstein mischaracterizes the nature of the baseline change. In *West Coast Hotel*, he says, "The Court's claim is that the failure to impose a minimum wage is not nonintervention at all but simply another form of action—a decision to rely on traditional market mechanisms, within the common law framework, as the basis for regulation." Sunstein, "Lochner's Legacy," 880–81. "When the *Lochner* framework was abandoned in *West Coast Hotel*, the common law system itself appeared to be a subsidy to employers. The *West Coast Hotel* Court thus adopted an alternative baseline and rejected *Lochner* era understandings of neutrality and action." Ibid., 917. This is not at all what Hughes' opinion accomplished. Hughes did not opine that the common law was unnatural or non-neutral, nor did he suggest that the common law and market forces alone afforded the employer a subsidy. Had this been his position, he would have characterized the common law as extracting a subsidy from the employee rather than from the public. Moreover, the suggestion that the common law itself redistributed property would have rendered a large body of established judge-made law constitutionally suspect. Hughes was instead more modestly suggesting that the common law and market distributions of power and property, in concert with state-supported poor relief, afforded the employer a subsidy. This was admittedly an important change in perspective, but it was not nearly so revolutionary as Sunstein makes it out to be.

20. Sunstein notes that the Court had construed the police power (not to mention the closely associated concepts of public purpose and public interest) "very broadly" in the contracts clause context in *Home Building & Loan Assn. v. Blaisdell*, 290 U.S. 398 (1934) (note, however, that Hughes even there defended the Minnesota Mortgage Moratorium statute against charges that it violated the principle of neutrality, remarking that it was "not for the mere advantage of particular individuals but for the protection of a basic interest of society," id. at 445; indeed, Hughes opined that the considerations sustaining the statute against the contracts clause challenge also disposed of the contention that the statute violated the due

process clause, 290 U.S. at 448). Yet Sunstein does not recognize that *Nebbia*, decided during the same term of Court, accomplished precisely the same result in the due process context. Moreover, Sunstein's analysis of the relationship between *Blaisdell* and *West Coast Hotel* is strikingly anachronistic. In *Blaisdell*, he writes, "the Court read the police power very broadly—thus replicating the outcome in *West Coast Hotel* and rendering the contracts clause functionally identical to the due process clause." Sunstein, "Lochner's Legacy," 891. If we are to indulge the typical historical assumption that time is linear, it would be more appropriate to say that *West Coast Hotel* replicated the outcomes in *Blaisdell* and *Nebbia*, the latter of which had rendered the due process clause functionally identical to the contracts clause. Of course, Roberts and Hughes were part of the majority, and the Four Horsemen dissented, in all three of these cases.

21. *Nebbia*, 291 U.S. at 538. "[G]overnment," he remarked, "cannot exist if the citizen may at will use his property to the detriment of his fellows, or exercise his freedom of contract to work them harm." Id. at 523. See also Hughes' opinion in *Blaisdell*, which Roberts joined:

> It is manifest . . . that there has been a growing appreciation of public needs and of the necessity of finding ground for a rational compromise between individual rights and public welfare. The settlement and consequent contraction of the public domain, the pressure of a constantly increasing density of population, the interrelation of the activities of our people and the complexity of our economic interests, have inevitably led to an increased use of the organization of society in order to protect the very bases of individual opportunity. Where, in earlier days, it was thought that only the concerns of individuals or of classes were involved, and that those of the State itself were touched only remotely, it has later been found that the fundamental interests of the State are directly affected; and the question is no longer merely that of one party to a contract as against another, but of the use of reasonable means to safeguard the economic structure upon which the good of all depends. (*Blaisdell*, 290 U.S. at 442.)

The justices were not abandoning the notion that the state could interfere with individual contractual liberty only for a valid public purpose; they were instead noting that the concept of what constituted a valid public purpose had expanded as economic interdependence had increased.

22. Gillman, *The Constitution Besieged*, 200.

23. Ibid., 123, 125, 138–39.

24. *Adkins*, 261 U.S. at 547.

25. Gillman, *The Constitution Beseiged*, 173. These criticisms should not be taken as a general disparagement of Gillman's fine book.

26. *Wolff Packing*, 262 U.S. at 535, 538.

27. See Siegel, "Understanding the *Lochner* Era," 201–7.

28. *Brass v. Stoeser*, 153 U.S. 391 (1894); *German Alliance Ins. Co. v. Lewis*, 233 U.S. 389 (1914); *Levy Leasing Co. v. Siegel*, 258 U.S. 242 (1922); *Marcus Brown Holding Co. v. Feldman*, 256 U.S. 170 (1921), and *Block v. Hirsh*, 256 U.S. 135 (1921).

29. McCurdy, "The Roots of 'Liberty of Contract' Reconsidered," 20. See also Forbath, "The Ambiguities of Free Labor," 767, 772–800; Nelson, "The Impact of the Antislavery Movement," 513.

30. See ch. 6, infra, and sources cited therein; Herbert Hovenkamp, "Labor Conspiracies in American Law, 1880–1930," *Tex. L. Rev.* 66 (1988): 919, 930–31.

31. *Adkins*, 261 U.S. at 560.

32. See Stuart Bruchey, *The Wealth of the Nation: An Economic History of the United States* (New York, 1988), 157–58; Stanley Lebergott, *Manpower in Economic Growth: The American Record Since 1800* (New York, 1964), 189.

33. *Parrish*, 300 U.S. at 390.

34. Id. at 400, 402–3 (Sutherland, J., dissenting).

35. *Williams v. Standard Oil Co.*, 278 U.S. 235 (1929); *Ribnik v. McBride*, 277 U.S. 350 (1928); *Tyson & Bros. v. Banton*, 273 U.S. 418 (1927); *Wolff Packing Co. v. Kansas Court of Industrial Relations*, 267 U.S. 552 (1925); *Dorchy v. Kansas*, 264 U.S. 286 (1924); *Wolff Packing Co. v. Kansas Court of Industrial Relations*, 262 U.S. 522 (1923).

36. *Nebbia*, 291 U.S. at 502, 530.

37. Friedman, "Switching Time," 1976.

38. Thomas C. Chapin, "Stare Decisis and Minimum Wages," *Rocky Mt. L. Rev.* 9 (1937): 297, 306–7, 309, and n. 81. For a similar view, see Comment, *Ill. B. J.* 25 (1937): 284, 285–86.

39. *Morehead v. New York ex rel. Tipaldo*, 298 U.S. 587 (1936).

40. *A.L.A. Schechter Poultry Corp. v. United States*, 295 U.S. 495, 529–51 (1935); Act of June 16, 1933, ch. 90, 48 Stat. 195 (1933).

41. Pusey, *Charles Evans Hughes*, 701; see *Donham v. West-Nelson Mfg. Co.*, 273 U.S. 657 (1927) (Brandeis, J., dissenting); *Murphy v. Sardell*, 269 U.S. 530 (1925) (Brandeis, J., dissenting).

42. *Carter v. Carter Coal Co.*, 298 U.S. 238, 304, 310–19 (1936).

43. See *Schechter*, 295 U.S. at 502, 551; *Carter*, 298 U.S. at 275, 286.

44. *Murphy v. Sardell*, 269 U.S. 530 (1925).

45. See *Tipaldo*, 298 U.S. at 618.

46. *Murphy*, 269 U.S. 530.

47. *Donham v. West-Nelson Mfg. Co.*, 273 U.S. 657 (1927).

48. See *Tipaldo*, 298 U.S. at 618.

49. *Donham*, 273 U.S. at 657.

50. Curtis, *Lions Under the Throne*, 163–64.

51. Mason, *Harlan Fiske Stone*, 482–83, quoting Harlan Fiske Stone to Felix Frankfurter, April 13, 1939; *Brush v. Commissioner*, 300 U.S. 352, 356–59, 374 (1937). Stone had similarly followed an opinion with which he disagreed in *Miles v. Graham*, 268 U.S. 501 (1925), which held that income taxation of a federal judicial salary was an unconstitutional diminution of compensation. He wrote to his sons in 1939 after *Graham* had been overruled:

> The Graham case was argued shortly after I came on the Court, and you will be interested to know that I joined Holmes and Brandeis in voting against the immunity of the judge's salary from income tax. The same principle as in the Graham case had been laid down in *Evans v. Gore*, 253 U.S. 245 (1920), decided a year or two before I came on the Court. Holmes had written a dissent but he thought the Graham case indistinguishable in principle from the Gore case and therefore he and I concluded that we would not record a dissent. I have since regretted my action because it puts me apparently on record as supporting the majority decision which I thought then and still think wrong. (Mason, *Harlan Fiske Stone*, 790 n.)

Mason noted, "Such things happened under Hughes as well," a remark with which Roberts most certainly would have concurred. Ibid.

Stone's own personal history in these matters of stare decisis apparently inclined him to sympathize with Roberts' explanation for his behavior. Stone was the only member of the *Tipaldo/Parrish* Court still on the bench when Roberts retired in 1945 and, as chief justice, he was responsible for the drafting of the ill-fated farewell letter to Justice Roberts. That letter contained the encomium, "You have made fidelity to principle your guide to decision." Justice Black objected to that sentence, and no letter was ever sent. Richard Friedman, "A Reaffirmation," 1985, 1989–90. In response to Black's objection, Frankfurter assured his colleagues that Justice Brandeis, another *Tipaldo* dissenter, would have approved of the language in question. See FF to HFS, August 20, 1945, Frankfurter MSS, LC, Reel 64; FF to "Dear Brethren," August 30, 1945, Frankfurter MSS, LC, Reel 64.

52. The memorandum is reproduced in Frankfurter, "Mr. Justice Roberts," 311, 314–15.

53. Ibid., 314.

54. See Chambers, "The Big Switch," 52.

55. Frankfurter, "Mr. Justice Roberts," 315.

56. Ibid. As Michael Ariens has pointed out, this recollection cannot be accurate. As of October 10, when Roberts voted to note probable jurisdiction in *Parrish*, the Court had before it only the jurisdictional statement submitted by the hotel company, which of course did not challenge the authority of *Adkins*. Ariens, "A Thrice-Told Tale," 639–40 n. 108, 641. Yet because the Washington statute was indistinguishable from the statute *Adkins* had held unconstitutional, see supra, because the Washington Supreme Court opinion upholding the statute had suggested that *Adkins* was no longer binding authority, see supra, and because the *Tipaldo* opinion signaled the litigants that a minimum wage statute could be sustained only if *Adkins* were abandoned, see infra, Roberts must have anticipated that the appellee would request that the Court overrule *Adkins*.

57. Actually, Roberts was confronted with a petition for rehearing in the *Tipaldo* case when he returned to the Court in October of 1936. New York sought a rehearing on the ground that it had indeed requested that the *Adkins* case be overruled. Roberts did not vote to rehear the *Tipaldo* case, but he did vote that same week to note probable jurisdiction in *Parrish*. Chambers, "The Big Switch," 56. As Professor Friedman has pointed out, voting to rehear *Tipaldo* would have been both unusual and awkward, while *Parrish*, which differed from *Tipaldo* in that the statute there involved was indistinguishable from the District of Columbia statute, offered a more attractive vehicle for overruling *Adkins*. Friedman, "Switching Time," 1947.

58. Professor Bobbitt has noted that such a technical explanation is generally consistent with Roberts' commitment to "doctrinal argument." Philip Bobbitt, *Constitutional Fate* (New York, 1982), 39–42; and Professor Freund agreed that the explanation was "entirely in keeping with Roberts' character, which led him to react violently against what he thought was intellectual slipperiness. . . ." Freund, "Charles Evans Hughes as Chief Justice," 30. See also Pusey, "Justice Roberts' 1937 Turnaround," 106.

Professor Friedman has argued that the memorandum's explanation is also consistent with Roberts' preference to avoid reaching great questions of constitutional law where possible. Friedman, "Switching Time," at 1945 (noting Roberts' reluctance to reach the merits in *Helvering v. Davis*, 301 U.S. 619, 639–40 (1937)) and *Ashwander v. TVA*, 297 U.S. 288 (1936). Friedman sees this characteristic as one among several manifestations of Roberts' "judicial timidity," and suggests that this timidity accounts for Roberts' behavior in *Tipaldo*. (". . . one would not expect [such technical] scruples . . . to cause a Justice to vote against the statute unless doing so satisfied some other interest or need. I believe the key to finding that interest or need may lie in what might be called Roberts' own judicial timidity.") Friedman, "Switching Time," 1943–44.

One would be more inclined to accept Friedman's broader "timidity" hypothesis had Roberts' behavior in this regard been more idiosyncratic. As Friedman acknowledges, Brandeis, Stone, and Cardozo shared Roberts' views in *Ashwander* and *Davis*. It may be, as Friedman suggests, this was because "in their eyes, an activist Court was far more likely to do harm than good," ibid., 1945, though Alexander Bickel suggested that Brandeis' jurisdictional scruples were grounded more in his commitments to democratic processes than in programmatic concerns. See Alexander Bickel, *The Unpublished Opinions of Mr. Justice Brandeis* (Cambridge, Mass., 1957), 1–20. In both *Ashwander* and *Davis*, the three "liberals" (with Roberts) chastised their brethren not for rendering a conservative decision, but for reaching the merits of a case in which the majority dispensed a liberal one. Had the "liberals" had their way in *Ashwander* and *Davis*, the Court would have refrained from establishing precedents approving expansive exercises of federal power. (Because Brandeis did have his way when the Child Labor Tax first came before the Court in 1919, the Court did so refrain. See Bickel, *The Unpublished Opinions of Mr. Justice Brandeis*, 1–20. When a Court with new personnel finally did reach the merits in 1922, it declared the statute unconstitutional. *Bailey v. Drexel Furniture Co.*, 259 U.S. 20 (1922)). Moreover, each of the three restrained "liberals" cast his share of votes to strike down New Deal initiatives. See, for example, *Louisville Joint Stock Land Bank v. Radford*, 295 U.S. 555 (1935); *A.L.A. Schechter Poultry Corp. v. United States*, 295 U.S. 495 (1935); *Panama Refining Co. v. Ryan*, 293 U.S. 388 (1935). There was more to the "passive virtues," even in the hands of the "liberals," than the advancement of a liberal social agenda. Seen in this light, Roberts' embrace of the passive virtues does not appear so anomalous.

Indeed, such embraces of the "passive virtues" were hardly confined to the "liberal" and the "timid." See, for example, *Massachusetts v. Mellon* and *Frothingham v. Mellon*, 262 U.S. 447 (1923), in which Justice Sutherland wrote for a unanimous Court including Van Devanter, McReynolds, Butler, and Taft an opinion rejecting challenges to the Sheppard-Towner Maternity Act on the grounds that the petitioners lacked standing. See also *Abrams v. Van Schaick*, 293 U.S. 188 (1934); *St. Louis Malleable Casting Co. v. Prendergast Construction Co.*, 260 U.S. 469 (1923); *Fairchild v. Hughes*, 258 U.S. 126 (1922). Moreover, such justices as Holmes, Taft, Stone, and Cardozo, who certainly did not do their "best not to stick out," Friedman, "Switching Time," 1944, often voted not to overrule decisions with which they disagreed when the precedent had not been attacked or where they did not consider the case before them distinguishable from the governing precedent. The "need" that Roberts was satisfying in *Tipaldo* may well have been that satisfied by these bold jurists: the need not to defend or acquiesce in distinctions they did not see.

Finally, it should be noted that Roberts did not shrink from joining controversial decisions striking down legislation, often on more than the single ground necessary to invalidate. See, for example, *Carter v. Carter Coal Co.*, 298 U.S. 238 (1936); *Colgate v. Harvey*, 296 U.S. 404 (1936); *Louisville Joint Stock Land Bank v. Radford*, 295 U.S. 555 (1935); *A.L.A. Schechter Poultry Corp. v. United States*, 295 U.S. 495 (1935); *Panama Refining Co. v. Ryan*, 293 U.S. 388 (1935); in fact, he wrote the controversial opinion striking down the Agricultural Adjustment Act of 1933 in *United States v. Butler*, 297 U.S. 1 (1936). The less obtrusive, politically expedient course might well have been to defer to the legislature. On the other hand, Roberts did not recoil from providing the crucial fifth vote in bold, pathbreaking decisions upholding legislative initiatives. See, for example, *Gold Clause Cases*, 297 U.S. 240, 317, 330 (1935); *Home Bldg. & Loan Assn. v. Blaisdell*, 290 U.S. 398 (1934); *O'Gorman & Young v. Hartford Fire Ins. Co.*, 282 U.S. 251 (1931). The less adventuresome course might well have been to cleave more closely to precedent. Here the ambiguity of the concept of "judicial timidity" suggests the limits of its analytical utility. Neither is it entirely accurate to ascribe to Roberts a "desire not to stick out his neck—or the Court's—further than necessary for deciding the case." Friedman, "Switching Time," 1945. Roberts' majority opinion in *Retirement Board v. Alton R.R. Co.*, 295 U.S. 330 (1935), in which he bludgeoned the Railroad Retirement Act to death, was hardly a model for the judicially demure; and his remarkably bold opinion in *Nebbia* went much further than was necessary to dispose of the instant controversy. See supra. When the Court delivered its "thunderbolts," Friedman, "Switching Time," 1914, Roberts was not cowering beneath ermine covers.

59. *Tipaldo*, 298 U.S. at 604–5, 605–9. The New York Court of Appeals had held that there was no material difference between the New York statute and the District of Columbia statute struck down in *Adkins*, and Butler's opinion held that the construction placed upon the statute by New York's highest court was binding on the Supreme Court. This reasoning, roundly criticized by Chief Justice Hughes in his dissent, was not presented by Roberts in

the memorandum he prepared for Frankfurter. In the memorandum, Roberts stated that he himself believed that there was no constitutionally material distinction between the two statutes.

60. See *Parrish*, 300 U.S. at 400–414 (Sutherland, Van Devanter, McReynolds, and Butler, J.J., dissenting); *Tipaldo*, 298 U.S. at 610–18.

61. See Friedman, "Switching Time," 1941.

62. *Parrish*, 300 U.S. at 389.

63. *Prudence Co. v. Fidelity & Deposit Co. of Maryland*, 297 U.S. 198, 208 (1936); *Clark v. Willard*, 294 U.S. 211, 216 (1935); *Helvering v. Taylor*, 293 U.S. 507, 511 (1935); *Zellerbach Paper Co. v. Helvering*, 293 U.S. 172, 182 (1934); *Olson v. United States*, 292 U.S. 246, 262 (1934); *Johnson v. Manhattan Ry. Co.*, 289 U.S. 479, 494 (1933); *Gunning v. Cooley*, 281 U.S. 90, 98 (1930); *Charles Warner Co. v. Independent Pier Co.*, 278 U.S. 85, 91 (1928); *Steele v. Drummond*, 275 U.S. 199, 203 (1927); *Federal Trade Comm'n v. Pacific Paper Assn.*, 273 U.S. 52, 66 (1927); *Webster Co. v. Splitdorf Co.*, 264 U.S. 463, 464 (1924); *Alice State Bank v. Houston Pasture Co.*, 247 U.S. 240, 242 (1918). See Reynolds Robertson and Francis Kirkham, *Jurisdiction of the Supreme Court of the United States* (St. Paul, Minn., 1936), 781.

64. Petition for Writ of Certiorari and Motion to Advance at 4–5, 8–9, 12–14.

65. This appears to have been the way that Chief Justice Hughes construed this language in the petition. In his dissent, in which he contended that *Tipaldo* was not controlled by *Adkins* due to material differences in the two statutes involved and the social conditions to which each was addressed, he wrote that the close divisions of the Court in *Stettler* and *Adkins* "point to the desirability of fresh consideration when there are material differences in the cases presented." *Tipaldo*, 298 U.S. at 624. Though he purported to undertake such "fresh consideration," nowhere in his opinion did he consider whether *Adkins* ought to be overruled.

66. Appellant's Brief on the Law at 16–49; Brief on Behalf of States of Connecticut, Illinois, Massachusetts, New Hampshire, New Jersey and Rhode Island, as Amici Curiae, at 15; Motion for Leave to File Brief as Amicus Curiae and Brief in Support Thereof, filed by John W. Bricker, Attorney General of Ohio, at 39.

67. Laws of Washington, Chapter 174, p. 602 (1913). The District of Columbia minimum wage act had empowered the board to prescribe wages adequate to supply the necessary cost of living to women workers to maintain them in good health and morals. In his opinion declaring the statute unconstitutional, Justice Sutherland had mused that a statute requiring an employer "to pay the value of the services rendered, even to pay with fair relation to the extent of the benefit obtained from the service, would be understandable." *Adkins*, 261 U.S. at 559. The New York statute, drafted with this dictum in mind, proscribed employment at a wage that was "*both* less than the fair and reasonable value of services rendered *and* less than sufficient to meet the minimum cost of living necessary for health." *Tipaldo*, 298 U.S. at 605 (emphasis mine). Counsel for the state sought to distinguish the two statutes based upon this difference. Id. at 592–94.

68. *Parrish*, 300 U.S. at 389–90; Appellant's Answer to Brief of Amicus Curiae, at 18.

69. *Swift v. Tyson*, 304 U.S. 64 (1938); Chambers, "The Big Switch," 66–67; Hendel, *Charles Evans Hughes and the Supreme Court*, 130; Parrish, "The Hughes Court, the Great Depression," 296; Edward Purcell, "Rethinking Constitutional Change," *Va. L. Rev.* 80 (1994): 277, 289–90. Moreover, in *Erie*, unlike in *Tipaldo*, see infra, Chief Justice Hughes suggested that the governing precedent be overruled. "'If we wish to overrule *Swift v. Tyson*,' Chief Justice Hughes announced as he laid the case before the conference, 'here is our opportunity.'" Mason, *Harlan Fiske Stone*, 478. Perhaps in part as a result of Hughes' leadership, a majority to overrule *Swift* was assembled. Hughes was not prepared in 1936 to overrule *Adkins*, and as a consequence no majority to do so could be formed. See infra.

70. Friedman, "Switching Time," 1952; Pusey, *The Supreme Court Crisis*, 51; Pusey, "Justice Roberts' 1937 Turnaround," 102, 106.

71. *Tipaldo*, 298 U.S. at 609.

72. Merlo Pusey reports that the "reactionary tone" of Butler's opinion "was very distasteful to Roberts, but he held to the position he had taken." Pusey, *Charles Evans Hughes*, 701. Indeed, Roberts wrote in his memorandum that after Butler had expanded the opinion into a full dress defense of *Adkins*, his proper course would have been to concur specially. Frankfurter, "Mr. Justice Roberts," 314–15. Felix Frankfurter, writing in the margin of Pusey's discussion of *Tipaldo* in his biography of Hughes, wrote of Roberts, "He shouldn't have suppressed his own views by silence." Pusey, *Charles Evans Hughes*, 701 (Frankfurter's personal copy), *microformed on* Harvard Frankfurter Papers, at Part III, Reel 39. Yet such suppression was by no means unusual. Consider a note that Justice Brandeis wrote to Chief Justice Taft, informing him that he would join Taft's majority opinion in *Chicago Board of Trade v. Olsen*, 262 U.S. 1 (1923). "You will recall," he wrote Taft, "that I voted the other way and the opinion has not removed my difficulties . . . [b]ut I have differed from the Court recently on three expressed dissents and concluded that in this case, I had better 'shut up.'" Alpheus Thomas Mason, *William Howard Taft: Chief Justice* (New York, 1965), 201 (quoting letter from Justice Louis D. Brandeis to Chief Justice William H. Taft (December 23, 1922). See also Bickel, *The Unpublished Opinions of Mr. Justice Brandeis*, at 21–33. Richard Friedman notes significantly that Roberts *never* filed a concurring opinion during the entire decade of the 1930s. Friedman, "Switching Time," at 1944.

73. *Tipaldo*, 298 U.S. at 611.

74. Virginia Wood, *Due Process of Law, 1932–1949* (Baton Rouge, La., 1951), 149.

75. *Tipaldo*, 298 U.S. at 631–35 (Stone, J., dissenting).

76. *Munn v. Illinois*, 94 U.S. 113 (1877); *Brass v. Stoeser*, 153 U.S. 391 (1894); *German Alliance Ins. Co.*, 233 U.S. at 409; *Terminal Taxicab Co. v. District of Columbia*, 241 U.S. 252 (1916); *Levy Leasing Co. v. Siegel*, 258 U.S. 242 (1922); *Marcus Brown Holding Co. v. Feldman*, 256 U.S. 170 (1921); *Block v. Hirsh*, 256 U.S. 135 (1921); *McLean v. Arkansas*, 211 U.S. 539 (1909); *Knoxville Iron Co. v. Harbison*, 183 U.S. 13 (1901). *Nebbia*, 291 U.S. 502; *Tipaldo*, 298 U.S. at 632–33.

77. Id. at 633–34.

78. Id. at 634, citing *Borden's Farm Products Co. v. Ten Eyck*, 297 U.S. 251 (1936), and *Hegeman Farms Corp. v. Baldwin*, 293 U.S. 163 (1934).

79. So far as the requirement of due process is concerned, and in the absence of other constitutional restriction, a state is free to adopt whatever economic policy may reasonably be deemed to promote the public welfare, and to enforce that policy by legislation adapted to its purpose. The courts are without authority either to declare such policy, or, when it is declared by the legislature, to override it. If the laws passed are seen to have a reasonable relation to a proper legislative purpose, and are neither arbitrary nor discriminatory, the requirements of due process are satisfied, and judicial determination to that effect renders a court *functus officio*. (*Tipaldo*, 298 U.S. at 634–35.)

80. Id. at 635–36. See Mason, *Harlan Fiske Stone*, 423–24.

81. See, for example, Comment, *Ill. B. J.* 25 (1936): 75, 76.

82. Louis H. Rubinstein, "The Minimum Wage Law," *St. John's L. Rev.* 11 (1936): 78, 82–83; Comment, 34 *Mich. L. Rev.* (1936): 1180, 1187; Kurt Stern, "Recent Interpretation by the Supreme Court of Liberty of Contract in Employment Cases," *U. Cinn. L. Rev.* 11 (1937): 82, 89; P. Y. Davis, "The Washington Minimum Wage Decision," *Ind. L. J.* 12 (1937): 415, 417; Chapin, "Stare Decisis and Minimum Wages," 306; Comment, *Ill. B. J.* 25 (1937): 284, 286.

83. *Tipaldo,* 298 U.S. at 618–19.

84. See Macbeth, "The Present Status of the Adkins Case," supra.

85. Frankfurter, "Mr. Justice Roberts," 314.

86. If this in fact was Roberts' position in *Tipaldo,* then his actions in *Tipaldo* and *Erie* were not inconsistent.

87. Frankfurter, "Mr. Justice Roberts," 314. In the same breath, however, the memorandum pointed to the explanation explored previously. In the ellipsis in the quoted language Roberts had written, "and [I] stated further that I was for taking the State of New York at its word."

88. On May 26, Stone wrote to Hughes in response to the latter's circulated dissenting opinion. In that same letter Stone informed Hughes that he was writing a separate dissent. Harlan Fiske Stone to Charles Evans Hughes, May 26, 1936, Stone MSS, Box 62, LC.

89. It is possible that Roberts took this view because the Four Horsemen, all of whom had been in the *Adkins* majority, did not think that the distinctions between the two statutes were constitutionally significant. As Butler's majority opinion put it, "the dominant issue in the *Adkins* case was whether Congress had power to establish minimum wages for adult workers in the District of Columbia. The opinion directly answers in the negative. The ruling that defects in the prescribed standard stamped that Act as arbitrary and invalid was an additional ground of subordinate consequence." *Tipaldo,* 298 U.S. at 614. Brandeis had not participated in the decision, and Hughes, Stone and Cardozo had not even been on the Court when the case was decided. Sutherland had written the passages of *Adkins* that the state was claiming supported the constitutionality of the New York statute. Surely, Roberts might have reasoned, Sutherland and company were in a better position to explain the meaning of *Adkins* than were the *Tipaldo* dissenters.

Even Stone, who joined Hughes' dissent, thought it "'a sad business to stand only on differences of the two statutes, especially after all the Court has decided and said on this subject in the past three years.' He could not understand why 'the Chief Justice felt it necessary to so limit his opinion.'" Mason, *Harlan Fiske Stone,* 423, quoting Harlan Fiske Stone to Felix Frankfurter, June 3, 1936.

90. Frankfurter, "Mr. Justice Roberts," 314 (emphasis mine). Paul Freund apparently concurred in this interpretation. See Freund, "Charles Evans Hughes as Chief Justice," 29–20.

91. See *Tipaldo,* 298 U.S. 587.

92. See id. at 631–36 (Stone, Brandeis, and Cardozo, J.J., dissenting).

93. See id. at 618–31 (Hughes, C.J., dissenting).

94. Freund, "Charles Evans Hughes as Chief Justice," 35 (remarking on Hughes' "talent for making nice distinctions in the interest of creative continuity. He thoroughly disliked the overruling of precedent, but his gift for differentiation fostered the controlled evolution of doctrine;" characterizing a distinction drawn by Hughes as one that "could be remembered just long enough to be stated once."); Hendel, *Charles Evans Hughes and the Supreme Court,* 279 ("He sought, virtually above all else, to maintain the dignity and prestige of the Court and this he thought in no small measure depended upon the stability of its decisions. This attitude was reflected . . . in the great lengths to which he sometimes went . . . in attempting to find distinctions to avoid overruling precedent. . . . [he] sedulously sought to protect the precedents of the Court, sometimes at the risk of offending logic. . . ."); Mason, *Harlan Fiske Stone,* 796 and n. (remarking on Hughes' capacity "to invent meaningless distinctions"); F. D. G. Ribble, "The Constitutional Doctrines of Chief Justice Hughes," *Colum. L. Rev.* 41 (1941): 1190, 1210 (Hughes possessed "a consummate skill in distinguishing adverse or apparently adverse cases"). Justice Roberts himself later noted this quality. See Owen J. Roberts, *The Court and the Constitution* (Cambridge, Mass., 1951), 18 (one of Hughes' opinions "labored valiantly, and as I think, unsuccessfully, to distinguish the earlier cases").

95. See Chambers, "The Big Switch," 53, 70; Friedman "Switching Time," 1951, n. 300; Hendel, *Charles Evans Hughes and the Supreme Court*, 130; Ribble, "The Constitutional Doctrines of Chief Justice Hughes," 1206.

96. Mason, *Harlan Fiske Stone*, 789.

97. Mason, *Harlan Fiske Stone*, 790, citing John Bassett Moore to Harlan Fiske Stone, May 16, 1932; Harlan Fiske Stone to John Bassett Moore, May 17, 1932.

98. Freund, "Charles Evans Hughes as Chief Justice," 40. Brandeis may here have been referring only to conferences at which petitions for review were considered.

99. Philip E. Urofsky, ed., "The Court Diary of Justice William O. Douglas," *J. Sup. Ct. Hist.* 1995 (1995): 77, 94.

100. *United States v. Butler*, 297 U.S. 1 (1936); Act of May 12, 1933, 48 Stat. 31 (1933); Memorandum Re: No. 401, *United States v. William M. Butler, et al., Receivers of Hoosac Mills Corporation*, Stone MSS, Box 62, LC.

101. Frankfurter, "Mr. Justice Roberts," 314.

102. Pusey, *Charles Evans Hughes*, 676.

103. Leonard, *A Search for a Judicial Philosophy*, p. 21, quoting Justice Roberts' memorial address before the New York Bar, December 12, 1948.

104. Pusey, *Charles Evans Hughes*, 676.

105. During this period many of the justices continued to work in their home libraries, coming to the Court building only for oral argument and conference. Hughes himself "continued to write his opinions at home and used his new office only for appointments and administrative work." Ibid., 689–90. This practice naturally resulted in fewer personal interactions among the justices than have occurred on more recent Courts, and accordingly produced an environment less conducive to the sort of conversation that might have enabled Hughes and Roberts to reach a better understanding.

106. Ibid., 757 (Frankfurter's personal copy), *microformed on* Harvard Frankfurter Papers, at Part III, Reel 39.

107. Felix Frankfurter to Paul Freund, *microformed on* Harvard Frankfurter Papers, at Part III, Reel 15, quoted in Ariens, "A Thrice-Told Tale," 633 n. 78.

108. *Tipaldo*, 298 U.S. at 587.

109. Harlan Fiske Stone to Charles Evans Hughes, May 26, 1936, Stone MSS, Box 62, LC.

110. On May 29, Stone circulated a memorandum alerting his colleagues to a modification in his already circulated dissenting opinion. "Memorandum in re No. 838, *Morehead v. Tipaldo*," May 29, 1936, Van Devanter MSS, Box 38, LC.

111. *Tipaldo*, 298 U.S. at 587.

112. See Mason, *Harlan Fiske Stone*, 425–26.

113. Pusey, *Charles Evans Hughes*, 757.

114. Frankfurter, "Mr. Justice Roberts," 314.

115. See, for example, Jackson, *The Struggle for Judicial Supremacy*, 208; Parrish, "The Hughes Court, the Great Depression," 297.

116. In the summer of 1945 Roberts wrote to Hughes, "To work under you was the greatest experience and the greatest satisfaction of my life. When you left the Court, the whole picture changed. For me it could never be the same." Roberts to Charles Evans Hughes, July 16, 1945, quoted in Pusey, *Charles Evans Hughes*, 802.

117. Frankfurter, "Mr. Justice Roberts," 314.

118. See Alsop and Catledge, *The 168 Days*, 142; Hendel, *Charles Evans Hughes and the Supreme Court*, 132; Jackson, *The Struggle for Judicial Supremacy*, 208.

119. *Bunting v. Oregon*, supra; *Texas & New Orleans R.R. Co. v. Brotherhood of Railway and Steamship Clerks*, 281 U.S. 548 (1930); *Adair v. United States*, 208 U.S. 161 (1908). See chs. 7 and 8, infra.

Part III. The Trail of the Yellow Dog

1. *Adair v. United States*, 208 U.S. 161 (1908).

2. *Coppage v. Kansas*, 236 U.S. 1 (1915). A "yellow-dog" contract was a contract of employment in which the employee agreed, as a condition of his employment, not to join a labor union.

3. *Washington, Virginia & Maryland Coach Co. v. NLRB*, 301 U.S. 142 (1937); *Associated Press Co. v. NLRB*, 301 U.S. 103 (1937); *NLRB v. Friedman-Harry Marks Clothing Co.*, 301 U.S. 58 (1937); *NLRB v. Fruehauf Trailer Co.*, 301 U.S. 49 (1937); *NLRB v. Jones & Laughlin Steel Corp.*, 301 U.S. 1 (1937).

4. See, for example, Irons, *The New Deal Lawyers*, 287–88; Kelly and Harbison, *The American Constitution*, 766–77; Mason and Beaney, *The Supreme Court in a Free Society*, 182–84; McCloskey, *The American Supreme Court*, 176; Paul Murphy, *The Constitution in Crisis Times*, 157–58; Rodell, *Nine Men*, 249–250; Schwartz, *The Supreme Court*, 21–22, 34–36; Swindler, *Court and Constitution*, II: 99–100; Wright, *The Growth of American Constitutional Law*, 204–5.

5. See, for example, Corwin, *Court Over Constitution*, 127; McCloskey, *The American Supreme Court*, 224; Paul Murphy, *The Constitution in Crisis Times*, 115; Walter Murphy, *Congress and the Court*, 65; Swindler, *Court and Constitution*, II: 81; Wright, *The Growth of American Constitutional Law*, 205, 222.

6. See Eric Foner, *Free Soil, Free Labor, Free Men: The Ideology of the Republican Party Before the Civil War* (New York, 1970); Forbath, "The Ambiguities of Free Labor," 767, 772–800; McCurdy, "The Roots of 'Liberty of Contract' Reconsidered," 20; Nelson, "The Impact of the Antislavery Movement," 513.

7. See John E. Nowak, Ronald D. Rotunda, and J. Nelson Young, *Constitutional Law*, §XII, 2d ed. (St. Paul, Minn., 1983), 958–59.

8. See Robert Gross, *The Minutemen and Their World* (New York, 1976), 173–75; Mary Ryan, *Cradle of the Middle Class*, ch. 3 (London, 1981); Ronald Walters, *American Reformers, 1815–1860* (New York, 1978), 29–35.

9. See Alexis de Tocqueville, *Democracy in America* (New York, 1972), II: 128–33, 138–44.

6. The Liberal Dilemma

1. *Allgeyer v. Louisiana*, 165 U.S. 578 (1897); *Godcharles v. Wigeman*, 133 Pa. 431 (1886); Foner, *Free Soil, Free Labor, Free Men*; Forbath, "The Ambiguities of Free Labor," 767; McCurdy, "The Roots of 'Liberty of Contract' Reconsidered," 20; Nelson, "The Impact of the Antislavery Movement," 513.

2. See legislative histories of H.R. 4372, S. 3653, and S. 3662, 31 Cong. Rec. 74–5566 (55–2); S. Rept. 591 (55–2); H.R. Rept. 454 (55–2). For background on the enactment of the Erdman Act, see Gerald Eggert, *Railroad Labor Disputes* (Ann Arbor, Mich., 1967).

3. 30 Stat. 424, 428, ch. 370 (55–2).

4. See Donald G. Morgan, *Congress and the Constitution: A Study of Responsibility*, ch. 7 (Cambridge, Mass., 1966).

5. *United States v. Adair*, 152 F. 737 (E.D. Ky. 1907).

6. Id. at 752, 754–56, 759.

7. *Adair v. United States*, 208 U.S. 161, 174 (1908).

8. *Holden v. Hardy*, 169 U.S. 366 (1898).

9. *Lochner v. New York*, 198 U.S. 45 (1905).

10. Id. at 53.

11. See, for example, *Swift & Co. v. United States*, 196 U.S. 375 (1905).

12. *Adair*, 208 U.S. 161, 178–79 (emphasis in original).

13. Id. at 187–89.

14. Id. at 190.

15. Justice Holmes wrote a separate dissent, in which he argued, typically, that it was not unreasonable for Congress to assume that the provisions of section 10 would advance the policy of preventing strikes tending to interrupt interstate commerce. *Adair*, 208 U.S. 190–92.

16. *Coppage v. Kansas*, 236 U.S. 1 (1915).

17. 31 Cong. Rec. 5053 (55–2).

18. *Coppage*, 236 U.S. at 13.

19. Id. at 16, 18.

20. Holmes again dissented separately, arguing that *Adair* and *Lochner* ought to be overruled. Id. at 26–27.

21. Id. at 37, 39–40.

22. *Commonwealth v. Hunt*, 4 Met. 111, 129–31, 134 (1842). See Leon Fink, "Labor, Liberty and the Law: Trade Unionism and the Problem of the American Constitutional Order," *J. Am. Hist.* 74 (1987): 904, 910; Alfred Konefsky, "'As Best to Subserve Their Own Interests': Lemuel Shaw, Labor Conspiracy, and Fellow Servants," *Law & Hist. Rev.* 7 (1989): 219; Leonard Levy, *The Law of the Commonwealth and Chief Justice Shaw* (Cambridge, Mass., 1957), 203; Christopher Tomlins, *The State and the Unions: Labor Relations, Law, and the Organized Labor Movement, 1880–1960* (Cambridge, Mass., 1985), 42–44; Anthony Woodiwiss, *Rights v. Conspiracy: A Sociological Essay on the History of Labour Law in the United States* (New York, 1990), 58–61.

23. *Hunt*, 4 Met. at 129.

24. Indeed, some courts occasionally expressed the view that the formation of such associations was not only not criminal, but positively laudable. See, for example, *Coeur D'Alene Consolidated & Mining Co. v. Miners' Union*, 51 F. 260, 263 (C.C.D. Idaho 1892); *State v. Stewart*, 9 A. 559, 566 (Vt. 1887).

25. Arnold Paul, *Conservative Crisis and the Rule of Law* (Gloucester, Mass., 1976), 106; Hovenkamp, *Enterprise and American Law, 1836–1937*, 216, 226.

26. Ibid., 233; Paul, *Conservative Crisis and the Rule of Law*, 106. See, for example, *Wyeman v. Deady*, 79 Conn. 414, 65 A. 129 (1906); *O'Brien v. People*, 216 Ill. 354, 75 N.E. 108 (1905); *Gevas v. Greek Restaurant Workers' Club*, 99 N.J. Eq. 770, 134 A. 309 (1926); *Baldwin Lumber Co. v. Local 560*, 91 N.J. Eq. 240, 109 A. 147 (1920); *Booth v. Burgess*, 72 N.J. Eq. 181, 65 A. 226 (1906); *Auburn Draying Co. v. Wardell*, 227 N.Y. 1, 124 N.E. 97 (1919); *Curran v. Galen*, 152 N.Y. 33, 46 N.E. 297 (1897); *Purvis v. Carpenters*, 214 Pa. 348, 63 A. 585 (1906); Barry Cushman, "Doctrinal Synergies and Liberal Dilemmas: The Case of the Yellow Dog Contract," *Supreme Court Review* 1992 (1992): 235, 246, n. 54, and cases there cited; John R. Commons and John B. Andrews, *Principles of Labor Legislation* (New York, 1927), 112–15, and cases there cited. See also *Connors v. Connelly*, 86 Conn. 641, 86 A. 600 (1913); *White Mt. Freezer Co. v. Murphy*, 78 N.H. 398, 101 A. 357 (1917); *Huskie v. Griffin*, 75 N.H. 345, 74 A. 595; *Brennan v. United Hatters*, 73 N.J.L. 729, 65 A. 165 (1906); *Barnes v. Berry*, 156 F. 72 (S.D. Ohio 1907).

27. *Plant v. Woods*, 176 Mass. 492, 502 (1900).

28. *Erdman v. Mitchell*, 207 Pa. 79, 89 (1903). To the same effect is *Ruddy v. Plumbers*, 79 N.J.L. 467, 75 A. 742 (1910).

29. *Casey v. Cincinnati Typographical Union*, 45 F. 135, 143 (S.D. Ohio 1891).

30. *Old Dominion Steamship Co. v. McKenna*, 30 F. 48, 50 (S.D.N.Y. 1887).

31. *Coppage*, 236 U.S. at 1, 40.

32. Id. at 8–9, 14–16, 20–21, 32, 35, 38–42.

33. *Hitchman Coal & Coke Co. v. Mitchell*, 245 U.S. 229 (1917).

34. Id. at 248, 250–51, 253, 255, 258–59, 261.

35. Id. at 271 (emphasis in original). Justice Brandeis actually concluded that neither the strike to obtain a closed shop nor a yellow-dog contract implied "coercion in a legal sense." Ibid.

36. For a discussion of the near-unanimity of state court decisions holding anti-yellow-dog contract statutes unconstitutional, see *Coppage*, 236 U.S. at 21–26. It should be noted that not all states condemned strikes to obtain a closed shop. In those states, of course, the asymmetry criticized by Brandeis was not present. See Francis B. Sayre, "Criminal Conspiracy," *Harv. L. Rev.* 35 (1922): 393, 407–8, n. 49.

37. See Paul, *Conservative Crisis and the Rule of Law*. The stronger claim that the Court was anti-worker would be harder to sustain. For example, in 1917, the year *Hitchman* was decided, the Court upheld an Oregon law limiting the working day for men to ten hours. *Bunting v. Oregon*, 243 U.S. 426 (1917).

38. Hovenkamp, "Labor Conspiracies in American Law," 919, 930.

39. Ibid., 930–31. Hovenkamp offers this observation as a means of explaining why early twentieth-century courts and political economists were inclined to treat labor combinations as analogous to, rather than different from, business combinations.

40. *Western & Atlantic R.R. Co. v. Bishop*, 50 Ga. 465 (1874).

41. *Railroad Co. v. Lockwood*, 17 Wall. 375 (1873).

42. *Bishop*, 50 Ga. at 472.

43. Ellis Hawley, *The Great War and the Search for a Modern Order* (New York, 1979), 11–12.

44. Bruchey, *The Wealth of the Nation*, 138.

45. Ibid., 137.

46. Between 1901 and 1913 the nationwide unemployment rate in the manufacturing and transportation sectors rose above 7 percent only twice, in the recession years of 1904 and 1908. In all other years, the rate was below 6 percent; in seven of those thirteen years, the rate was 4 percent or lower. John R. Commons et al., *History of Labor in the United States* (New York, 1935), III:128. The nationwide unemployment rate for the entire civilian workforce during those years rose above 6 percent only twice, in 1908 and 1911. In all other years, the rate was below 6 percent; in five of those thirteen years, the rate was 4 percent or lower. Lebergott, *Manpower in Economic Growth*, 43–47, 512. The average national unemployment rate for all civilian workers in the decade 1900–1909 was 4 percent; for the decade 1910–19, the figure was 5 percent. Ibid., 189.

47. Melvyn Dubofsky, *Industrialism and the American Worker, 1865–1920* (Arlington Heights, Ill., 1985), 119.

48. Commons et al., *History of Labor in the United States*, III:115; John Garraty, *Unemployment in History* (New York, 1979), 113–18; Lebergott, *Manpower in Economic Growth*, 166; Roy Lubove, *The Struggle for Social Security* (Cambridge, Mass., 1968), 147; Alexander Keyssar, *Out of Work: The First Century of Unemployment in Massachusetts* (Cambridge, Mass., 1986), 251–52.

49. Lebergott, *Manpower in Economic Growth*, 512.

50. Ibid. The rate for the manufacturing and transportation sectors in each of those years was 3.5 percent. Commons et al., *History of Labor in the United States*, III:128. Moreover, at least some of this unemployment was probably attributable to factors having little to do with the size of the labor supply: inability to work during certain months of the year due to weather conditions, which particularly afflicted the nation's large population of agricultural workers; a lack of paid vacations to absorb seasonal declines in demand; and perhaps in some regions a higher incidence of worker illness than we experience today. Lebergott, *Manpower in Economic Growth*, 65–71.

51. *Hitchman Coal & Coke Co.*, 245 U.S. at 229, 258. See, however, Keyssar, *Out of Work*, 301–4 (contending that in the first two decades of the twentieth century, West Virginia coal miners "suffered from chronic levels of involuntary idleness").

52. *Adkins v. Children's Hospital,* 261 U.S. 525, 560 (1923).

53. Hovenkamp, "Labor Conspiracies in American Law," 931. See also Keyssar, *Out of Work,* 257–61.

54. *Coppage,* 236 U.S. at 1, 17.

55. Hovenkamp, "Labor Conspiracies in American Law," 931; Keyssar, *Out of Work,* 123–30.

56. See generally ibid.

57. Robert D. Parmet, *Labor and Immigration in Industrial America* (Boston, 1981), 169–90.

58. Commons et al., *History of Labor in the United States,* III:128. The nationwide civilian unemployment rate of 11.7 percent was the highest since 1898. Lebergott, *Manpower in Economic Growth,* 43, 512. See also Keyssar, *Out of Work,* 278.

59. Lubove, *The Struggle for Social Security,* ch. 7.

60. Parmet, *Labor and Immigration,* 169–90.

61. In 1932, more than 13 million adult men were unemployed. Leuchtenburg, *Franklin D. Roosevelt and the New Deal,* 1. In 1933, fully 25 percent of the labor force was unemployed. Bruchey, *The Wealth of the Nation,* 157–58. In the decade of 1930–1939, the average national unemployment rate was 18 percent. Lebergott, *Manpower in Economic Growth,* 189. "Despite two substantial recoveries from the depths of the depression, unemployment during the decade never fell below 14 per cent of the civilian labor force or 21 per cent of the nonagricultural work force." Dubofsky, "Not So 'Turbulent Years'," 5, 7.

62. For an early analysis of the concept of coercion in the employment relationship and other contexts, see Robert Hale, "Coercion and Distribution in a Supposedly Non-Coercive State," *Pol. Sci. Q.* 38 (1923): 470.

63. Tomlins, *The State and the Unions,* 33.

7. Associationalism Ascendant

1. Joel Seidman, *The Yellow Dog Contract* (Baltimore, Md., 1932), 25.

2. Ibid.; Valerie Jean Conner, *The National War Labor Board* (Chapel Hill, N.C., 1983), ch. 2; Henry F. Pringle, *The Life and Times of William Howard Taft: A Biography* (New York, 1939), 915; Foster Rhea Dulles, *Labor in America* (New York, 1949), 226–27.

3. Conner, *The National War Labor Board;* Pringle, *The Life and Times of William Howard Taft,* 916, 918.

4. U.S. Bureau of Labor Statistics, "National War Labor Board," Bulletin No. 287, 30–34 (1922), quoted in Philip Taft, "Collective Bargaining Before the New Deal," in Harry A. Millis, ed., *How Collective Bargaining Works* (New York, 1942), 901–2; presidential proclamation, April 8, 1918, cited in Pringle, *The Life and Times of William Howard Taft,* 917–18.

5. Conner, *The National War Labor Board;* Taft, "Collective Bargaining Before the New Deal," 902.

6. Conner, *The National War Labor Board,* ch. 7; Daniel Ernst, "The Yellow Dog Contract and Liberal Reform, 1917–1932," *Labor History* 30 (1989): 251, 254; Edwin Witte, *The Government in Labor Disputes* (New York, 1932), 222.

7. See *Block v. Hirsh,* 256 U.S. 135, 155 (1921).

8. See David Brody, "The American Worker in the Progressive Age: A Comprehensive Analysis," in Brody, *Workers in Industrial America* (New York, 1980), 42; Brody, "The Emergence of Mass Production Unionism," in John Braeman, et al., eds., *Change and Continuity in Twentieth Century America* (Columbus, Ohio, 1964), 243.

9. Tomlins, *The State and the Unions,* 54–59, 74.

10. Ibid., quoting Robert F. Hoxie in *Trade Unionism in the United States* (New York, 1923), 274–75; Forbath, "The Ambiguities of Free Labor," 800–817; Dulles, *Labor in America,* 208–20.

11. Tomlins, *The State and the Unions*, 74–75, 77; see David Brody, "The Expansion of the American Labor Movement: Institutional Sources of Stimulus and Restraint," in Brody, ed., *The American Labor Movement* (New York, 1971), 121; Samuel Gompers, *Labor and the Employer* (New York, 1920), 286.

12. Tomlins, *The State and the Unions*, 77.

13. William Forbath, *Law and the Shaping of the American Labor Movement* (Cambridge, Mass., 1991), 147. See also Ronald Radosh, "The Corporate Ideology of American Labor Leaders from Gompers to Hillman," in James Weinstein and David W. Eakins, eds., *For a New America* (New York, 1970), 125–52.

14. Woodiwiss, *Rights v. Conspiracy*, 139; see Eugene T. Sweeney, "The A.F.L.'s Good Citizen, 1920–1940," *Labor History* 13 (1972): 200. The effects of this transformation began to be felt as early as the first decade of the twentieth century, by the end of which several business leaders had come around to the view that labor unions were either unobjectionable or desirable, insofar as they provided the only viable alternative to state socialism. James Weinstein, "Gompers and the New Liberalism, 1900–1909," in Weinstein and Eakins, eds., *For a New America*, 106, 109.

15. Joseph Rayback, *A History of American Labor* (New York, 1968), 282, 289–90; see Joseph R. Conlin, *Bread and Roses Too: Studies of the Wobblies* (Westport, Conn., 1969); Melvyn Dubofsky, *We Shall Be All: A History of the Industrial Workers of the World* (Chicago, 1969).

16. Hawley, *The Great War*, 130–31.

17. Tomlins, *The State and the Unions*, 91; see Forbath, *Law and the Shaping of the American Labor Movement*, 128–35.

18. Ernst, "The Yellow Dog Contract and Liberal Reform," 263; Felix Frankfurter and Nathan Greene, "Congressional Power over the Labor Injunction," *Col. L. Rev.* 31 (1931): 385, 396; Edwin Witte, "'Yellow Dog' Contracts," *Wis. L. Rev.* 6 (1930): 21, 31; Cornelius Cochrane, "Why Organized Labor is Fighting 'Yellow Dog' Contracts," *Am. Lab. Legis. Rev.* 15 (1925): 227, 232; Cochrane, "'Yellow Dog' Abolished in Wisconsin," *Am. Lab. Legis. Rev.* 19 (1929): 315, 316; Donald Richberg, "Constitutional Aspects of the New Deal," *The Annals of the American Academy of Political and Social Science* 178 (1935): 25, 30; Seidman, *The Yellow Dog Contract*, 31–32.

19. See *Interborough Rapid Transit Co. v. Lavin*, 247 N.Y. 65, 159 N.E. 863 (1928); *Exchange Bakery and Restaurant, Inc. v. Rifkin*, 245 N.Y. 260, 157 N.E. 130 (1927); *Interborough Rapid Transit Co. v. Green*, 131 Misc. 682, 227 N.Y.S. 258 (1928); Homer F. Carey and Herman Oliphant, "The Present Status of the Hitchman Case," *Colum. L. Rev.* 29 (1929): 441; Cochrane, "Branding 'Yellow Dog' Contracts," *Am. Lab. Legis. Rev.* 18 (1928): 115; Witte, "'Yellow Dog' Contracts."

20. Irving Bernstein, *The Lean Years: A History of the American Worker, 1920–1933* (Boston, 1960), 394, 411. The proliferation of state anti-yellow-dog statutes continued throughout the 1930s. See Osmond K. Fraenkel, "Recent Statutes Affecting Labor Injunctions and Yellow Dog Contracts," *Ill. L. Rev.* 30 (1936): 854, 858–59; Commons and Andrews, *Principles of Labor Legislation*, 407–8, 415; Mason, "Labor, the Courts, and Section 7(a)," 999, 1008. Many of these statutes sought to preserve associational liberty by prohibiting not only yellow-dog contracts, but agreements requiring the employee to *join* a union as well. Fraenkel, "Recent Statutes Affecting Labor Injunctions," 859, n. 29.

21. *United Mine Workers v. Red Jacket Consolidated Coal & Coke Co.*, 18 F. 2d 839 (C.C.A. 4th, 1927), cert. denied, 275 U.S. 536 (1927); Bernstein, *The Lean Years*, 406–9; Cochrane, "Public Opinion Flays Judicial Approval of 'Yellow Dog' Contracts," *Am. Lab. Legis. Rev.* 20 (1930): 181.

22. Bernstein, *The Lean Years*, 407.

23. Ernst, "The Yellow Dog Contract and Liberal Reform," 255; Seidman, *The Yellow Dog Contract*, 36; see Peter Graham Fish, "Red Jacket Revisited: The Case That Unraveled John J. Parker's Supreme Court Appointment," *Law and Hist. Rev.* 5 (1987): 51.

24. *Texas & New Orleans Railroad Co. v. Brotherhood of Railway and Steamship Clerks*, 281 U.S. 548 (1930); 44 Stat. 577, ch. 347; *Texas & New Orleans Railroad Co.*, 281 U.S. at 555, 557. The text of the temporary injunction is reproduced at 281 U.S. 555–56, n. 1.

25. *Texas & N.O.R. Co. et al. v. Brotherhood of Railway and Steamship Clerks et al.*, 25 F.2d 873, 876 (S.D. Texas, 1928), aff'd, 33 F.2d 13 (5th Cir. 1929), cert. granted, 280 U.S. 550 (1929).

26. 67 Cong. Rec. 4507, 4519, 4648, 4669, 8815, 9048; S. Rept. 606 (69–1) at 2–3; H. Rept. 328 (69–1) at 6.

27. 67 Cong. Rec. 8817, 8893.

28. Brief for the Petitioner at 86, *Texas & N.O.R. Co.*, 280 U.S. 550 (emphasis in original).

29. Id. at 93–94.

30. Ernst, "The Yellow Dog Contract and Liberal Reform," 267, 271–73; Irons, *The New Deal Lawyers*, 29.

31. See Thomas E. Vadney, *The Wayward Liberal: A Political Biography of Donald Richberg* (Lexington, Ky., 1970).

32. *Wilson v. New*, 243 U.S. 332 (1917).

33. Brief for the Respondent at 93–94, *Texas & N.O.R. Co.*, 280 U.S. 550.

34. Brief for the Respondent at 86–87, *Texas & N.O.R. Co.*, 280 U.S. 550. On the politics and legislative history of the Transportation Act of 1920, see K. Austin Kerr, *American Railroad Politics, 1914–1920* (Pittsburgh, Pa., 1968).

35. Brief for the Respondent at 92–93, *Texas & N.O.R. Co.*, 280 U.S. 550.

36. Id. at 89–90.

37. Id. at 93, 101–2 (emphasis in original).

38. The unanimity of the Court was apparently readily obtained. Justice Van Devanter, who had voted with the majority in *Coppage*, wrote Chief Justice Hughes that he considered the opinion "as near perfect as is humanly possible." Pusey, *Charles Evans Hughes*, 713.

39. *Texas & N.O.R. Co. et al.*, 281 U.S. at 548, 570.

40. Id. at 560, 568.

41. Id.

42. Id. at 571.

43. Freund, "Charles Evans Hughes as Chief Justice," 4, 35.

44. Seidman, *The Yellow Dog Contract*, 35, n. 109; Edward Berman, "The Supreme Court Interprets the Railway Labor Act," *Am. Econ. Rev.* 20 (1930): 619; Richard Cortner, *The Jones & Laughlin Case*, 22; B. C. Gavit, *The Commerce Clause of the United States Constitution* (Bloomington, Ind., 1932), 231–33; Thomas R. Fisher, *Industrial Disputes and Federal Legislation* (New York, 1940), 170, n. 21; Comment, *W. Va. L. Q.* 37 (1930): 101; Comment, *Yale L. J.* 4 (1930): 92; Comment, *Ill. L. Rev.* 25 (1930): 307; Hendel, *Charles Evans Hughes and the Supreme Court*, 228, 260; see Fraenkel, "Recent Statutes Affecting Labor Injunctions," 854, 862, n. 46. One commentator opined that the *Texas & New Orleans* decision "would seem to bring [the Court] still closer to complete realization that 'liberty to contract' may mean a liberty to join voluntary associations of workmen unhindered by the 'yellow dog' contract." Comment, *U. Pa. L. Rev.* 81 (1932): 68, 73. For a perceptive contemporary understanding of the limited implications of the *Texas & New Orleans* decision, see Richard B. Johns, "The Validity of Federal Labor Legislation with Special Emphasis upon the National Labor Relations Act," *Marq. L. Rev.* 20 (1936): 57, 70–71.

45. See Comment, *Ill. L. Rev.* 30 (1936): 884, 904 (*Texas & New Orleans* decision "recognize[d] the power of Congress to preserve the right of freedom of association of employees").

46. 47 Stat. 70, ch. 90 (72-1).

47. 75 Cong. Rec. 4503, 4504, 4626–28, 4677, 4762, 4917, 5463, 5469; S. Rept. 163 (72-1) at 11–14; H. Rept. 669 (72-1) at 7. See Witte, "The Federal Anti-Injunction Act," *Minn. L. Rev.* 16 (1932): 638, 655.

48. 75 Cong. Rec. 4628 (72-1).

49. 75 Cong. Rec. 5469 (72-1).

50. H. Rept. 821 (72-1) at 6.

51. 75 Cong. Rec. 5551, 5720.

52. 47 Stat. 70, ch. 90 (72-1).

53. Comment, "An Advance in Labor Legislation—The Anti-Injunction Act," *Geo. L. J.* 21 (1933): 344, 345.

54. 47 Stat. 1467 (72-2), ch. 204.

55. 76 Cong. Rec. 5118–5122 (72-2). The House agreed to the amendment at 76 Cong. Rec. 5360 (72-2).

56. 47 Stat. 1467, 1481 (72-2).

57. 76 Cong. Rec. 5119 (72-2).

58. Irving Bernstein, *The New Deal Collective Bargaining Policy* (Berkeley, Calif., 1950), 44.

59. 48 Stat. 211, 214 (73-1), ch. 91. See Bernstein, *The New Deal Collective Bargaining Policy,* 44–46. Norris and his colleagues contemporaneously sought to protect workers' freedom of association through section 7(a) of the National Industrial Recovery Act (NIRA), the precursor of the Wagner Act. Donald Richberg was again the principal author. R. W. Fleming, "The Significance of the Wagner Act," in Derber and Young, eds., *Labor and the New Deal,* 126. Section 7(a) required that every code of fair competition propounded pursuant to the NIRA provide: (1) that employees be free to organize to bargain collectively free from employer interference or coercion; and (2) "that no employee and no one seeking employment shall be required as a condition of employment to join any company union or to refrain from joining, organizing, or assisting a labor organization of his own choosing." 48 Stat. 195, 198–99, ch. 90 (73-1). The Act's aberrationally permissive posture regarding the closed shop was in large measure the quid pro quo for the AFL's acceptance of the trade association provisions sponsored by the Chamber of Commerce. Irving Bernstein, *The Turbulent Years: A History of the American Worker, 1933–1941* (New York, 1969), 32. With both business and organized labor happy to have more room to maneuver than conventional antitrust law might have permitted, the freedom of non-union workers not to associate with a labor organization got lost in the shuffle.

60. H. Rept. 1994 (73-2) at 1–2, 5, 6; 78 Cong. Rec. 11717, 11720, 12553–55.

61. 78 Cong. Rec. 12550, 12553–55.

62. Bernstein, *The Turbulent Years,* 212.

63. *Virginia Railway Co. v. System Federation, No. 40,* 300 U.S. 515, 538–41, 543–44 (1937).

64. *Arguments in Cases Arising Under Labor Acts Before the Supreme Court,* Sen. Doc. 52 (75-1), at 13–14 (hereinafter cited as *Arguments*); Brief for the Petitioner at 38–47.

65. Brief for the Respondent at 48–49; Brief for the United States at 82, 84 (emphasis in original).

66. Id. at 89; Brief for the Respondent at 55–56; see also id. at 57, 63.

67. Brief for the United States at 7; Brief for the Respondent at 52.

68. *Arguments,* at 13, 39–40.

69. *Virginian Railway Co.,* 300 U.S. at 552.

70. Id. at 548–49, 557, 559.

71. Id. at 553–57.

8. Doctrinal Synergies

1. 49 Stat. 449, 452 (74-1), ch. 372.

2. Ibid. See Fisher, *Industrial Disputes and Federal Legislation*, 273.

3. See, for example, remarks of Senator Hastings, *Legislative History of the National Labor Relations Act* (Washington, Government Printing Office, 1949), II:2403–11 (hereinafter cited as *NLRB, Legislative History*); Statement of James A. Emery, Hearings before the Senate Committee on Education and Labor on S. 1958 (74-1) at 854, reprinted in *NLRB, Legislative History*, 2240.

4. Statement of Senator Wagner, Hearings before the Senate Committee on Education and Labor on S. 1958 (74-1) at 52–53, reprinted in *NLRB, Legislative History*, 1428–29. See also S. Rept. 573 (74-1) at 17, reprinted in *NLRB, Legislative History*, 2317; remarks of Senator Wagner, *NLRB, Legislative History*, 2338; Statement of Professor Milton Handler, Hearing of the Senate Committee on Education and Labor on S. 1958 (74-1) at 233, reprinted in *NLRB, Legislative History*, 1613.

5. 49 Stat. 449, 450 (74-1), ch. 372. See Comment, *Ill. L. Rev.* 30 (1936): 884, 906 ("the protection of employees in their right of freedom of association is reasonably calculated to promote the amicable settlement of disputes").

6. See Bernstein, *The Turbulent Years*, 332–33.

7. *NLRB, Legislative History*, 2357 (emphasis in original). This had been the position taken by the administration in settling the Automobile Strike of 1934. That strike's "Principles of Settlement" had provided, "The government makes it clear that it favors no particular union or particular form of employee organization or representation. The government's only duty is to secure absolute and uninfluenced freedom of choice without coercion, restraint, or intimidation from any source." Administrative Order No. X-11, March 26, 1934, quoted in Mason, "Labor, the Courts, and Section 7(a)," 999, 1009.

8. See remarks of Senators Tydings, Couzens, Hastings, Norris, Wagner, Barkley, and Walsh, *NLRB, Legislative History*, 2357–96.

9. *NLRB, Legislative History*, 2399–2400. Tydings' amendment was rejected in the House without debate, ibid., 3216, and was later rejected by the conference committee despite the importunings of the secretary of commerce. Bernstein, *The New Deal Collective Bargaining Policy*, 127; Cortner, *The Wagner Act Cases*, 84.

10. 49 Stat. 449, 453. For Senator Hastings' unsuccessful associational objections to this provision, see *NLRB, Legislative History*, 2361, 2389–93. See also Samuel Blumberg, "The National Labor Relations Act: A Presentation of Some Constitutional and Economic Objections," *Com. L. J.* 41 (1936): 136, 138; Henry P. Chandler, "The National Labor Relations Act," *A.B.A. J.* 22 (1936): 245, 250, 281–82; Comment, *Ill. L. Rev.* 30 (1936): 884, 919.

11. Bernstein, *The Turbulent Years*, 184–85; Perkins, *The New Age of Franklin Roosevelt*, 218–19.

12. 49 Stat. 449, 452; *NLRB, Legislative History*, 2394–95. Several members of the Senate also had misgivings toward the Act's imposition of the duty to bargain. In 1934, the Senate Committee on Education and Labor had shelved Wagner's bill, S. 2926, and had instead reported favorably a substitute bill introduced by Senator David I. Walsh, Democrat of Massachusetts. "Walsh believed that the government should only protect the civil right of association in a voluntary organization and that Wagner had gone too far in urging affirmative encouragement of collective bargaining." Bernstein, *The Turbulent Years*, 195.

13. Gross, *The Makings of the National Labor Relation Board*, 187. Alpheus Thomas Mason identified the problem in 1936. In *Hitchman*, Justice Pitney had written for the majority, "Whatever may be the advantages of 'collective bargaining,' it is not bargaining at all, in any just sense, unless it is voluntary on both sides. The same liberty that enables men to form unions, and through the unions to enter into agreements with employers willing to agree,

entitles other men to remain independent of the union. . . ." 245 U.S. 229, 250–51. Mason believed that the banning of yellow-dog contracts by the Norris-LaGuardia and Wagner Acts was "constitutional if it be regarded (as obviously it should be) as part and parcel of the more general provisions guaranteeing the workers, in the exercise of their lawful rights of self-organization, freedom from interference, restraint, and coercion by employers." However, Mason continued, if "collective bargaining is not bargaining at all unless it is voluntary, those who remain nonunion are deprived of freedom of contract under any statute which forces them to accept conditions of work as established by representatives of the majority." Mason, "Labor and Judicial Interpretation," *The Annals of the American Academy of Political and Social Science* 184 (1936): 112, 120. See also Mason, "Labor, the Courts, and Section 7(a)," 999, 1012–13.

14. Gross, *The Making of the National Labor Relations Board*, 187. Charles Wyzanski, who successfully defended the Act before the Supreme Court, had objected to the majority rule, exclusive representation, and closed-shop provisions at the drafting stage. See Kenneth Casebeer, "Drafting Wagner's Act: Leon Keyserling and the Precommittee Drafts of the Labor Disputes Act and the National Labor Relations Act," *Ind. Rel. L. J.* 11 (1989): 73, 93.

15. See *Stafford v. Wallace*, 258 U.S. 495 (1922); *Swift & Co. v. United States*, 196 U.S. 375 (1905). For a detailed discussion of the origins and development of the current of commerce doctrine, see Part IV, infra. For a detailed discussion of the case selection, briefing, arguing, and resolution of the commerce clause issues in the Wagner Act cases, see ch. 10, infra; Irons, *The New Deal Lawyers*, chs. 11–13.

16. *Washington, Virginia & Maryland Coach Co. v. NLRB*, 301 U.S. 142 (1937); *Associated Press Co. v. NLRB*, 301 U.S. 103 (1937); *NLRB v. Friedman-Harry Marks Clothing Co.*, 301 U.S. 58 (1937); *NLRB v. Fruehauf Trailer Co.*, 301 U.S. 49 (1937); *NLRB v. Jones & Laughlin Steel Corp.*, 301 U.S. 1 (1937).

17. Brief for the Petitioner, at 10, 23–24, 41, *Washington, Virginia & Maryland Coach Co.*, 301 U.S. 142.

18. Brief for the Respondent at 33, 112, 116–17, *Jones & Laughlin Steel Corp.*, 301 U.S. 1.

19. Brief for Respondent at 68–69, *Friedman-Harry Marks Clothing Co.*, 301 U.S. 58 (emphasis in original).

20. Brief for the Petitioner at 68, 70, *Associated Press Co.*, 301 U.S. 103; *Arguments*, at 67.

21. *Nebbia*, 291 U.S. at 536–39; Brief for the Respondent at 89, *Associated Press Co.*, 301 U.S. 103; Brief of the American Federation of Labor, Amicus Curiae, at 15–16, *Washington, Virginia & Maryland Coach Co.*, 301 U.S. 142; *Arguments*, at 129–31.

22. Brief for Respondent at 96, *Associated Press Co.*, 301 U.S. 103; see also id. at 93, 99–100; *Arguments*, at 86, 89.

23. Brief of the American Newspaper Guild, Amicus Curiae, at 22, *Associated Press Co.*, 301 U.S. 103.

24. The majority opinions in the *Fruehauf* and *Friedman-Harry Marks* cases simply recited the facts and summarily sustained the application of the Act on the authority of the *Jones & Laughlin* decision. 301 U.S. 49 (1937); 301 U.S. 58 (1937). The Four Horsemen offered a single consolidated dissent from the three manufacturing cases. 301 U.S. at 76. Justice Roberts wrote the majority opinion in the *Associated Press* case, in which he summarily rebuffed due process objections, citing *Jones & Laughlin* and the *Texas & New Orleans* case. 301 U.S. 103, 133 (1937). The Four Horsemen, having offered their liberty of contract objections to the Act in their consolidated dissent from the manufacturing cases, confined themselves to dissenting from Roberts' opinion on the ground that the application of the Act to the Associated Press violated the First Amendment. 301 U.S. at 133. For a thorough discussion of the opinions' treatment of the commercial police power issue, see ch. 10, infra.

25. *Jones & Laughlin*, 301 U.S. at 33, 44.

26. Id. at 44–45.

27. See Corwin, *Court Over Constitution*, 124–25; Corwin, *Constitutional Revolution, Ltd.*, 66–67, 79; Hendel, *Charles Evans Hughes and the Supreme Court*, 260; Wood, *Due Process of Law, 1932–1949*, 160–61.

28. *Washington, Virginia & Maryland Coach Co. v. NLRB*, 301 U.S. 142 (1937); *Virginian Railway Co. v. System Federation, No. 40*, 300 U.S. 515 (1937); *Texas & New Orleans Railroad Co. v. Brotherhood of Railway and Steamship Clerks*, 281 U.S. 548 (1930).

29. *Friedman-Harry Marks Clothing Co.*, 301 U.S. at 97–99, 101, 103. See ch. 10, *infra*.

30. *Friedman-Harry Marks Clothing Co.*, 301 U.S. at 103.

31. See *supra*, ch. 1.

32. See Karl Klare, "Judicial Deradicalization of the Wagner Act and the Origins of Modern Legal Consciousness, 1937–1941," *Minn. L. Rev.* 62 (1978): 265, 318–25; Nowak, Rotunda, and Young, *Constitutional Law*, 967–69.

33. Klare, "Judicial Deradicalization of the Wagner Act," 293–310.

34. For a discussion of historians' assessment of the Hughes Court, see Parrish, "The Hughes Court, the Great Depression," 286.

Part IV. The Levee Breaks

1. *Washington, Virginia & Maryland Coach Co. v. NLRB*, 301 U.S. 142 (1937); *Associated Press Co. v. NLRB*, 301 U.S. 103 (1937); *NLRB v. Friedman-Harry Marks Clothing Co.*, 301 U.S. 58 (1937); *NLRB v. Fruehauf Trailer Co.*, 301 U.S. 49 (1937); *NLRB v. Jones and Laughlin Steel Corp.*, 301 U.S. 1 (1937).

2. See, for example, Corwin, *Court Over Constitution*, 156 and n. 60; Corwin, *Constitutional Revolution, Ltd.*, 53, 72; Cortner, *The Wagner Act Cases*, vi, 176–77; Schwartz, *The Supreme Court*, 16, 35; Jackson, The Struggle for Judicial Supremacy, 191–92, 218, 235; Swindler, *Court and Constitution*, II: 99–100, 137; Mason, *Harlan Fiske Stone*, 455, 458; McCloskey, *The American Supreme Court*, 176–77; Leuchtenburg, "Franklin D. Roosevelt's Supreme Court 'Packing' Plan," 94; Rodell, *Nine Men*, 249–50; Alsop and Catledge, *The 168 Days*, 143, 146; Wright, *The Growth of American Constitutional Law*, 179; Paul Murphy, *The Constitution in Crisis Times*, 153–54.

3. Wright, *The Growth of American Constitutional Law*, 222; Walter Murphy, *Congress and the Court*, 65; McCloskey, *The American Supreme Court*, 224; Cortner, *The Wagner Act Cases*, 188.

4. McCurdy, "The Roots of 'Liberty of Contract' Reconsidered," 20; Benedict, "Laissez-Faire and Liberty," 293; Forbath, "The Ambiguities of Free Labor," 672.

5. Harry N. Scheiber, "American Federalism and the Diffusion of Power: Historical and Contemporary Perspectives," *U. Toledo L. Rev.* 9 (1978): 619, 635, 676; Bernard Bailyn, *The Ideological Origins of the American Revolution* (Cambridge, Mass., 1967); Gordon Wood, *The Creation of the American Republic, 1776–1787* (New York, 1969).

6. Charles McCurdy, "Melville W. Fuller," in Leonard W. Levy, Kenneth L. Karst, and Dennis J. Mahoney, eds., 2 *Encyclopedia of the American Constitution* (New York, 1986), 812, quoting Fuller, Melville, *Address in Commemoration of the Inauguration of George Washinton as First President of the United States, Delivered Before the Two Houses of Congress, December 11, 1889* (New York, 1890).

9. A Stream of Legal Consciousness

1. *Texas v. White*, 74 U.S. 700, 725 (1869).

2. Charles McCurdy, "Federalism and the Judicial Mind in a Conservative Age: Stephen Field," in Harry Scheiber and Malcolm Feeley, eds., *Power Divided: Essays on the Theory and Practice of Federalism* (Berkeley, Calif., 1989), 33.

3. Edward Corwin, *The Commerce Power versus States Rights*, (Princeton, N.J., 1936), esp. ch. 5; Corwin, *Twilight of the Supreme Court*, 11–12; Corwin, *Court Over Constitution*, 131; McCurdy, "Federalism and the Judicial Mind," 32–35.

4. *United States v. E. C. Knight Co.*, 156 U.S. 1, 12–13, 16–17 (1895); *Kidd v. Pearson*, 128 U.S. 1 (1888).

5. *Hopkins v. United States*, 171 U.S. 578, 588 (1898).

6. *Munn v. Illinois*, 94 U.S. 113, 132 (1877).

7. See cases discussed, infra. Waite's opinion was modeled on a memorandum written by fellow Justice Joseph Bradley, in which Bradley had defended the Illinois regulations on the basis of the common law notion of a business affected with a public interest innovated by Lord Matthew Hale in his works *De Jure Maris* and *De Portibus Maris*. See Hargrave, *A Collection of Tracts*. Hale had in those writings supported public regulation of ferries, wharves, wharf cranes, and port warehouses on the ground that they were so peculiarly situated in the commercial market that they might exact "arbitrary and excessive duties." Hale, *De Portibus Maris*, part II, ch. 6, in Hargrave, *A Collection of Tracts*, 77; Hale, *De Jure Maris*, part I, ch. 2, in Hargrave, *A Collection of Tracts*, 6. The use of each of these instrumentalities was a necessary incident of the movement of people or goods in the furtherance of commercial intercourse, and each of them was situated at a choke point in that movement. The exaction of such "arbitrary and excessive duties" might therefore impede the ordinary course of commercial traffic. As Charles Fairman noted, these were for Hale "situations where the private interest of the owner is subordinated to *the general interest in the flow of commerce*" (emphasis mine). Fairman, "The So-Called Granger Cases," 587, 655–56, 670–71. The gateway notion in which due process and commerce clause doctrine were to converge was thus present in the thought of the innovator of the public interest doctrine. Though the doctrine was imported into our constitutional law through the due process clause, it was clearly designed in part to remove impediments to the flow of commercial traffic. It is therefore not surprising that later justices would welcome the concept into their commerce clause jurisprudence. See cases discussed, infra. In fact, Waite conceded that the grain elevators *might* have been so closely connected to interstate commerce as to be subject to congressional regulation. In the absence of such congressional action, however, he and his brethren were not prepared to deny to the state the power to regulate what was quite naturally at the time considered a "domestic concern." *Munn*, 94 U.S. at 135. See Fairman, "The So-Called Granger Cases," 647.

8. *Munn*, 94 U.S. at 146–47, 152.

9. *Wolff Packing Co. v. Industrial Court*, 262 U.S. 522, 535 (1923) (citations omitted).

10. Id. at 535–36.

11. Id. at 537–38 (emphasis mine). Taft's reference to "exorbitant charges and arbitrary control" echoed Hale's advertence to the exaction of "arbitrary and excessive duties."

12. *Swift & Co. v. United States*, 196 U.S. 375, 394 (1905).

13. Id. at 398–99.

14. *United States v. Hopkins*, 82 F. 529 (C.C.D. Kansas, 1897); *Hopkins v. United States*, 171 U.S. 578 (1898), Brief for Appellee, at 132. See David Gordon, "*Swift & Co. v. United States*: The Beef Trust and the Stream of Commerce Doctrine," *Am. J. Leg. Hist.* 28 (1984): 244.

15. *Swift*, 196 U.S. at 397 (emphasis mine).

16. *Stafford v. Wallace*, 258 U.S. 495, 524–25 (1922).

17. See *Cotting v. Kansas City Stock Yards Co.*, 183 U.S. 79, 85 (1901).

18. For the contrary, conventional view that *Swift* overruled *Knight*, see, for example, Corwin, *Twilight of the Supreme Court*, 40; Edward Corwin, "The Schechter Case—Landmark or What?" *N.Y.U. L. Q. Rev.* 13 (1936): 151; Corwin, *Court Over Constitution*, 120;

Wright, *The Growth of American Constitutional Law*, 118; Powell, *Vagaries and Varieties in Constitutional Interpretation*, 59.

19. *Stafford v. Wallace*, 258 U.S. 495 (1922); 45 Stat. 159, ch. 64.

20. 42 Stat. at 160; H. Rep. 77 (67–1) 7920, pp. 13–14.

21. See 61 Cong. Rec., pp. 1804, 1813, 1868–73, 1886–87, 1928–30, 2670.

22. *Stafford*, 258 U.S. at 521.

23. Mason and Beaney, *The Supreme Court in a Free Society*, 162. Indeed, intracurial correspondence reveals that Taft, Clarke, and Taft's fellow "conservative" Van Devanter formed the core around which the *Stafford* supermajority was constructed. Taft sent Van Devanter a draft of the *Stafford* opinion with a note saying, "I am sending this to you and Judge Clarke, because we three are very clear in our judgment, and I would like the benefit of your criticism before I send it on to other members of the Court who are more doubtful." Taft to Van Devanter, April 20, 1922, Van Devanter MSS, Box 32, LC.

24. The object to be secured by the Act is the free and unburdened flow of live stock from the ranges and farms of the West and the Southwest through the great stockyards and slaughtering centers on the borders of that region, and thence in the form of meat products to the consuming cities of the country in the Middle West and East, or still as live stock, to the feeding places and fattening farms in the Middle West or East for further preparation for the market. . . . [An] evil which [Congress] sought to provide against by the act, was exorbitant charges. . . . Expenses incurred in the passage through the stockyards necessarily reduce the price received by the shipper, and increase the price to be paid by the consumer. If they be exorbitant or unreasonable, they are an undue burden on the commerce which the stockyards are intended to facilitate. Any unjust or deceptive practice or combination that unduly and directly enhances them is an unjust obstruction to that commerce. (*Stafford*, 258 U.S. at 514–15.)

25. Id. at 515–16 (emphasis mine).

26. Id. at 516–17 (emphasis mine).

27. Id. at 518–19.

28. 42 Stat. 187, ch. 86; *Hill v. Wallace*, 259 U.S. 44 (1922).

29. There is not a word in the act from which it can be gathered that it is confined in its operation to interstate commerce. The words "interstate commerce" are not to be found in any part of the act from the title to the closing section. . . . [Congress] did not have the exercise of its power under the commerce clause in mind and so did not introduce into the act limitations which certainly would accompany and mark an exercise of the power under the latter clause. . . . It follows that sales for future delivery on the Board of Trade are not in and of themselves interstate commerce. They can not come within the regulatory power of Congress as such, unless they are regarded by Congress, from the evidence before it, as directly interfering with interstate commerce so as to be an obstruction or burden thereon [citation omitted]. It was upon this principle that in *Stafford v. Wallace*, 258 U.S. 495, we held it to be within the power of Congress to regulate business in the stockyards of the country, and include therein the regulation of commission men and of traders there, although they had to do only with sales completed and ended within the yards, because Congress had concluded that through exorbitant charges, dishonest practices and collusion they were likely, unless regulated, to impose a direct burden on the interstate commerce passing through. (*Hill*, 259 U.S. at 68–69.)

30. 42 Stat. 998, ch. 369.

31. Section 2(b) provided in part: "a transaction in respect to any article shall be considered to be in interstate commerce if such article is part of that current of commerce usual in

the grain trade whereby grain and grain products and by-products thereof are sent from one state with the expectation that they will end their transit, after purchase, in another. . . ." 42 Stat. at 999.

32. Transactions in grain involving the sale thereof for future delivery as commonly conducted on boards of trade and known as "futures" are affected with a national public interest. . . . the transactions and prices of grain on such boards of trade are susceptible to speculation, manipulation, and control, and sudden or unreasonable fluctuations in the prices thereof frequently occur as a result of such speculation, manipulation or control, which are detrimental to the producer or the consumer and the persons handling grain and products and by-products thereof in interstate commerce, and that such fluctuations in prices are an obstruction to and a burden upon interstate commerce in grain and the products and by-products thereof and render regulation imperative for the protection of such commerce and the national public interest therein. (Id.)

33. *New York and Chicago Grain & Stock Exchange v. Chicago Board of Trade*, 127 Ill. 153 (1889); S. Rep. 871 (67–2), 4–7; see 61 Cong. Rec. 9404–7, 9411, 9423, 9430, 9440–41, 9447, 12720–25.

34. *Chicago Board of Trade v. Olsen*, 262 U.S. 1 (1923). The "liberal" Brandeis, who joined Taft's opinion, was actually inclined to dissent. "You will recall," he wrote Taft, "that I voted the other way and the opinion has not removed my difficulties. . . . But I have differed from the Court recently on three expressed dissents and concluded that in this case, I had better 'shut up.'" LDB to WHT, December 23, 1922, quoted in Mason, *William Howard Taft*, 201.

35. The railroads of the country accommodate themselves to the interstate function of the Chicago market by giving shippers bills of lading through Chicago to points in eastern States with the right to remove the grain at Chicago for temporary purposes of storing, weighing, grading or mixing, and changing the ownership, consignee or destination and then to continue the shipment under the same contract and at a through rate. Such a contract does not take [the grain] out of interstate commerce in such a way as to deprive Congress of the power to regulate it, as is . . . expressly recognized in *Stafford v. Wallace* . . . [citations omitted]. (*Olsen*, 262 U.S. at 33.)

36. "The sales on the Chicago Board of Trade are just as indispensable to the continuity of the flow of wheat from the West to the mills and distributing points of the East and Europe, as are the Chicago sales of cattle to the flow of stock toward the feeding places and slaughter and packing houses of the East." Id. at 36.

37. Id.

38. Id. at 37–41.

39. *Tagg. Bros & Moorhead v. United States*, 280 U.S. 420, 433, 437–38 (1930).

40. Id. at 438–39 (emphasis mine).

41. The only case in which the current of commerce theory would have appeared to be applicable but was nevertheless rejected by the Court was *Hopkins*. The Kansas City Livestock Exchange was as clearly located in a current of interstate commerce as were the Chicago stockyards in *Swift* and *Stafford*, the Chicago Board of Trade in *Olsen*, and the Omaha Livestock Exchange in *Tagg Bros*. However, as Holmes pointed out in *Swift*, and as Taft reiterated in *Stafford*, the government in *Hopkins* had not shown that the Kansas City commission merchants were capable of exacting exorbitant charges. The effect of the merchants' activities on interstate commerce was therefore indirect.

42. Corwin, "The Schechter Case," 151, 159–60.

43. *United Mine Workers v. Coronado Coal Co.*, 259 U.S. 344 (1922); *United Leather Workers v. Herkert & Meisel Trunk Co.*, 265 U.S. 457 (1924). See also *Champlin Refining Co.*

v. Corporation Commission of Oklahoma, 286 U.S. 210 (1932); *Utah Power & Light Co. v. Pfost*, 286 U.S. 165 (1932); *Hope Gas Co. v. Hall*, 274 U.S. 284 (1927); *Oliver Mining Co. v. Lord*, 262 U.S. 172 (1923); *Heisler v. Thomas Colliery Co.*, 260 U.S. 245 (1922).

44. *Sonneborn Bros. v. Cureton*, 262 U.S. 506 (1923); *Hygrade Provision Co. v. Sherman*, 266 U.S. 497, 503 (1925). See also *Levering & Garrigues Co. v. Morrin*, 289 U.S. 98 (1933); *Industrial Assn. v. United States*, 268 U.S. 64 (1925).

45. Edward Corwin, "Congress' Power to Prohibit Commerce," *Cornell L. Q.* 18 (1934): 477, 495 (emphasis in original).

46. F. D. G. Ribble, "The 'Current of Commerce': A Note on the Commerce Clause and the National Industrial Recovery Act," *Minn. L. Rev.* 18 (1934): 296, 312.

47. Corwin, "The Schechter Case," 166 (emphasis in original). To similar effect, see Robert Stern, "That Commerce Which Concerns More States Than One," *Harv. L. Rev.* 47 (1934): 1335, 1336, 1347–48, 1360–61, noting in defense of the NIRA at 1363 that "although the Court has generally talked of interstate commerce as if it meant interstate movement, there has heretofore been no need for a broader definition."

48. Ribble, "The 'Current of Commerce,'" 314.

49. Ibid., 301–02, 316–17.

50. Stern, "That Commerce Which Concerns More States Than One," 1361. See also Jane Alvies, "The Commerce Power — From Gibbons v. Ogden to the Wagner Act Cases," *Ohio State L. J.* 3 (1937): 307, 313, 326.

51. Paschal, *Mr. Justice Sutherland*, 193–94; Mason and Beaney, *The Supreme Court in a Free Society*, 160.

52. See, for example, Ribble, "The 'Current of Commerce,'" 315.

53. Edward Corwin, "Social Planning Under the Constitution," *Am. Pol. Sci. Rev.* 26 (1932): 1; Corwin, *Twilight of the Supreme Court*, 43; Robert K. Carr, *Democracy and the Supreme Court* (Norman, Okla., 1936), 30.

54. Herbert Goodrich and Paul Wolkin, *The Story of the American Law Institute, 1923–1961* (St. Paul, Minn., 1961), 5. See also William Lewis, "History of the American Law Institute and the First Restatement of the Law: 'How We Did It'" in *Restatement in the Courts* (St. Paul, Minn., 1945), 1–4; Herbert Goodrich, "The Story of the American Law Institute," *Wash. U. L. Q.* 1951 (1951): 283; Arthur Corbin, "The Restatement of the Common Law by the American Law Institute," *Iowa L. Rev.* 15 (1929): 19; Herbert Wechsler, "The Course of the Restatements," *A.B.A. J.* 55 (1969): 147; Norris Darrell and Paul Wolkin, "The American Law Institute," *N.Y.S.B.J.* 52 (1980): 99; William P. LaPiana, "'A Task of No Common Magnitude': The Founding of the American Law Institute," *Nova L. Rev.* 11 (1987): 1085; N. E. H. Hull, "Restatement and Reform: A New Perspective on the Origins of the American Law Institute," *Law & Hist. Rev.* 8 (1990): 55; G. Edward White, "The American Law Institute and the Triumph of Modernist Jurisprudence," *Law & Hist. Rev.* 15 (1997): 1; Lawrence Friedman, *A History of American Law*, 2d ed. (New York, 1985), 676; Edward Purcell, *The Crisis of Democratic Theory: Scientific Naturalism and the Problem of Value* (Lexington, Ky. 1973), 79–80.

55. Wechsler, "The Course of the Restatements," 147; Goodrich and Wolkin, *The Story of the American Law Institute*, 5–6.

56. Ibid., 5–11; Purcell, *The Crisis of Democratic Theory*, 79–80. In May of 1922, Elihu Root gathered members of the Association of American Law Schools (AALS) and a group of distinguished practitioners together to form the Committee on the Establishment of a Permanent Organization for the Improvement of the Law. The committee later issued a report bemoaning the uncertainty and complexity of American law, its consequent lack of orderly development, and the disrespect for law that such defects engendered. The report took the view that the legal profession had a duty "to the American people to promote the certainty

and simplicity of the law, and its adaptation to the needs of life." The committee's objective was reminiscent of the goal of the dormant American Academy of Jurisprudence, which had formed in 1914 in order to inquire "into all important principles of law which at the present time are in a confused, conflicting, and uncertain stage by reason of conflicting judicial decisions, to the end that the sound principles of right and justice may be discovered and such logical reasons therefore given as will preclude as far as possible future uncertainty and discussion and in this manner unify and clarify the law." William P. LaPiana, *Logic and Experience: The Origin of Modern American Legal Education* (New York, 1994), 159–62.

57. Purcell, *The Crisis of Democratic Theory*, 79; see LaPiana, *Logic and Experience*, 103–5.

58. Goodrich and Wolkin, *The Story of the American Law Institute*, 15.

59. Ibid., 8.

60. Goodrich, "The Story of the American Law Institute," 283, 285–86.

61. Friedman, *A History of American Law*, 676. For the definitive treatment of Langdell's thought and his influence on legal education, see LaPiana, *Logic and Experience*.

62. Both G. Edward White and N. E. H. Hull have persuasively argued (from different perspectives and to differing degrees) that many of the restaters, including Cardozo, were not full-fledged Langdellians, but rather transitional figures positioned between classical "formalism" and "realism." White, "The American Law Institute and the Triumph of Modernist Jurisprudence," 21–26; Hull, "Restatement and Reform," 83–85. As White puts it,

> the Restatement project might first appear to be a reincarnation of Langdell's methodology. One could hardly state principles as integral generalizations unless one read inconsistent cases out of the system, treating them as "wrong." But the founders of the Institute did not anticipate that the Reporters would be engaging in Langdellian radical simplification. Instead they expected the Reporters to employ a methodology . . . that rested on a precise and comprehensive formulation of "core" principles that permitted ingenious application of those principles to cases as they appeared over time.

And while perceptively noting that Cardozo "retained a methodological allegiance to the tradition of Langdellian conceptualism," see ch. 10, infra, White acknowledges that "Cardozo endorsed a vision of law as responding creatively to changing social conditions."

The same might be said, with some qualification, of Hughes, Stone, Brandeis, and perhaps Roberts. All trained in Langdell's heyday, their jurisprudence retained some of the qualities associated with "formalism." Yet they were by no means entirely wedded to the categories, the deductivism, or the essentialism associated with formalism. See, for example, *Nebbia v. New York*, discussed infra. Indeed, as I contend next, they were able to embrace strikingly noncategorical modes of constitutional analysis at the same time that they were engaged in the quintessentially Langdellian enterprise of synthesizing the disparate doctrinal formulations of existing cases into lean rules of general application.

63. Friedman, *A History of American Law*, 676; Purcell, *The Crisis of Democratic Theory*, 80; Grant Gilmore, *The Ages of American Law* (New Haven, Conn., 1977), 70–74; Laura Kalman, *Legal Realism at Yale, 1927–1960* (Chapel Hill, N.C., 1986), 14; LaPiana, *Logic and Experience*, 160; Thomas C. Grey, "Langdell's Orthodoxy," *U. Pitt. L. Rev.* 45 (1983): 1, 43.

64. White, "The American Law Institute and the Triumph of Modernist Jurisprudence," 9.

65. *Restatement of the Law of Contracts* (St. Paul, Minn., 1932); *Restatement of the Law of Agency* (St. Paul, Minn., 1933); *Restatement of the Law of Torts* (St. Paul, Minn., 1934); *Restatement of the Law of Conflict of Laws* (St. Paul, Minn., 1934); *Restatement of the Law of Trusts* (St. Paul, Minn., 1935); Wechsler, "The Course of the Restatements," 147.

66. *Restatement of the Law of Business Associations: tentative draft* (Philadelphia, Pa., 1928); *Restatement of the Law of Property: tentative draft* (Philadelphia, Pa., 1929); *Restatement of the Law of Sales of Land: tentative draft* (Philadelphia, Pa., 1935).

67. For Hughes' continuing enthusiasm for the Restatement enterprise, see "Address of Chief Justice Hughes," *A.B.A. J.* 19 (1933): 325, 326.

68. *Nebbia v. New York*, 291 U.S. 502 (1934).

69. Justice Roberts, who wrote the majority opinion, "paced the floor of his Washington home till the early hours of the morning before he finally decided how he should vote." Corwin, *Constitutional Revolution, Ltd.*, 75–76.

70. *Nebbia*, 291 U.S. at 521–30.

71. Id. at 531–36.

72. *Peik v. C. & N.W. Ry. Co.*, 94 U.S. 164 (1876); *Chicago, Burlington & Quincy R. Co. v. Iowa*, 94 U.S. 155 (1876).

73. *Munn*, 94 U.S. at 113; *Brass v. North Dakota*, 153 U.S. 391 (1894).

74. *German Alliance Insurance Co. v. Lewis*, 233 U.S. 389 (1914).

75. *Griffith v. Connecticut*, 218 U.S. 563 (1910).

76. *O'Gorman & Young v. Hartford Fire Ins. Co.*, 282 U.S. 251 (1931).

77. *Margolin v. United States*, 269 U.S. 93 (1925); *Yeiser v. Dysart*, 267 U.S. 540 (1925); *Newman v. Moyers*, 253 U.S. 182 (1920); *Calhoun v. Massie*, 253 U.S. 170 (1920); *Capital Trust Co. v. Calhoun*, 250 U.S. 208 (1919); *Frisbie v. United States*, 157 U.S. 160 (1895).

78. *Cotting v. Kansas City Stockyards Co.*, 183 U.S. 79 (1901).

79. *Stephenson v. Binford*, 287 U.S. 251 (1932).

80. *Nebbia*, 291 U.S. at 536.

10. *Catching the Current*

1. *Schechter Corp. v. United States*, 295 U.S. 495 (1935). The full title of the code was the "Code of Fair Competition for the Live Poultry Industry of the Metropolitan Area in and about the City of New York." Id. at 519.

2. Act of June 16, 1933, ch. 90, 48 Stat. 195.

3. *Appeal dismissed, United States v. Belcher*, 294 U.S. 736 (1935).

4. Irons, *The New Deal Lawyers*, 75–82; Emerson, *Young Lawyer for the New Deal*, 24.

5. Irons, *The New Deal Lawyers*, 85; see also Emerson, *Young Lawyer for the New Deal*, 24.

6. *New York Times*, April 2, 1935, p. 20; Irons, *The New Deal Lawyers*, 82.

7. *United States v. A.L.A. Schechter Poultry Corp. et al.*, 76 F. 2d 617 (2nd Cir. 1935).

8. Freund, "Charles Evans Hughes as Chief Justice," 4, 32; "Memorandum to the Solicitor General, Re: *United States v. Schechter et al.*," from Harold M. Stephens, assistant attorney general, by Carl McFarland, special assistant to the attorney general, April 3, 1935, Stanley Reed MSS, Box 7, University of Kentucky; Interview with Paul Freund, October 18, 1982, Stanley Reed Oral History Project, University of Kentucky, 25–26.

9. Freund, "Charles Evans Hughes as Chief Justice," 32; "Radiogram to the President," from Donald R. Richberg, April 3, 1935, Stanley Reed MSS, Box 7, University of Kentucky.

10. Freund, "Charles Evans Hughes as Chief Justice," 32; Irons, *The New Deal Lawyers*, 83–85; Telegram, Tommy Corcoran to FDR, April 4, 1935, in Freedman, ed., *Roosevelt and Frankfurter*, 259–60; Joseph Lash, *Dealers and Dreamers*, 250–52.

11. Irons, *The New Deal Lawyers*, 91.

12. "Memorandum to the Attorney General, Re: U.S. v. Schechter," from Blackwell Smith, April 9, 1935, Stanley Reed MSS, Box 7, University of Kentucky.

13. "Memorandum, *United States v. Schechter, et al., Re: Nature of acts affecting interstate commerce* (unsigned), April 13, 1935, Stanley Reed MSS, Box 7, University of Kentucky.

Curiously, Smith continued to press this argument two weeks after the date of the memorandum. See "Memorandum, Re: Schechter Case, to Mr. Richberg, Mr. Stanley Reed and Mr. Stanleigh Arnold," from Blackwell Smith, April 27, 1935, Stanley Reed MSS, Box 7, University of Kentucky.

14. "Memorandum, *United States v. Schechter, Relationship between the Labor Provisions of the Poultry Code and Interstate Commerce,*" from Robert Stern, April 6, 1935, Stanley Reed MSS, Box 7, University of Kentucky.

15. Robert Stern, "The Solicitor General," in Louchheim, ed., *The Making of the New Deal*, 81.

16. Reed to FDR, April 11, 1935, Stanley Reed MSS, Box 7, University of Kentucky.

17. Irons, *The New Deal Lawyers*, 85; Emerson, *Young Lawyer for the New Deal*, 25.

18. *Schechter*, 295 U.S. at 543 (emphasis in original).

19. Id. at 548–49.

20. "If the federal government may determine the wages and hours of employees in the internal commerce of a State, because of their relation to cost and prices and their indirect effect on interstate commerce, it would seem that a similar control might be exerted over other elements of cost, also affecting prices, such as the number of employees, rents, advertising, methods of doing business, etc. All the processes of production and distribution that enter into cost could likewise be controlled." Id. at 549.

21. Id. at 554.

22. Corwin, "The Schechter Case," 151, 170. For an indictment of both Cardozo and Brandeis as spouters of "transcendental nonsense" in the "classical" style of the Langdellians, see Felix Cohen, "Transcendental Nonsense and the Functional Approach," *Colum. L. Rev.* 35 (1935): 809, 811–12.

23. *The New Republic*, June 12, 1935, quoted in Schlesinger, *The Politics of Upheaval*, 284.

24. Cardozo had observed in his opinion, "[a] society such as ours 'is an elastic medium which transmits all tremors throughout its territory; the only question is of their size.' . . . The law is not indifferent to considerations of degree." *Schechter*, 295 U.S. at 554. He nevertheless betrayed his embrace of traditional categories by remarking, "[t]o find *immediacy or directness* here is to find it almost everywhere" (emphasis mine). Id.

25. See, for example, *Wickard v. Filburn*, 317 U.S. 111 (1942).

26. Owen N. Nee, Comment, *Wisc. L. Rev.* 11 (1935): 88, 99.

27. 49 Stat. 991, ch. 824.

28. See discussion of the Wagner Act, infra.

29. Ralph Baker, *The National Bituminous Coal Commission* (Baltimore, Md., 1941), 49–50.

30. Irons, *The New Deal Lawyers*, 248.

31. *New York Times*, July 6, 1935, p. 2, cited in Baker, *The National Bituminous Coal Commission*, 50.

32. Ibid.

33. FDR to Samuel B. Hill, July 5, 1935, reprinted at 79 Cong. Rec. 13449 (74-1).

34. Baker, *The National Bituminous Coal Commission*, 51; remarks of Rep. Allen Treadway of North Carolina, 79 Cong. Rec. 13437 (74-1).

35. Baker, *The National Bituminous Coal Commission*, 51; remarks of Rep. Allen Treadway of North Carolina, 79 Cong. Rec. 13437 (74-1).

36. H. Rept. 1800, p. 57 (74-1).

37. Ibid.

38. 79 Cong. Rec. 13435–37, 13481–85 (Rep. Treadway); 13438 (Rep. Cox); 13446–48 (Rep. Knutson); 13457–60 (Rep. Fuller); 13460–65 (Rep. Cooper); 13465 (Rep. McCormack);

13466–69 (Rep. Church); 13568 (Rep. Hobbs); 13771–73 (Sen. Tydings); 14066 (Sen. Connally); 14073 (Sen. King); 14083 (Sen. Walsh).

39. 79 Cong. Rec. 13482 (74-1).

40. 79 Cong. Rec. 13482–83.

41. Leuchtenburg, *Franklin D. Roosevelt and the New Deal*, 116.

42. 79 Cong. Rec. 13666–67 (74-1). Ninety-three Democrats joined seventy-three Republicans and two Progressives in voting against the bill. See Thomas C. Longin, "Coal, Congress and the Courts: The Bituminous Coal Industry and the New Deal," *West Virginia History* 35 (1974): 101, 110.

43. Leuchtenburg, *Franklin D. Roosevelt and the New Deal*, 116.

44. 79 Cong. Rec. 14084 (74-1). Here, twenty-four Democrats joined twelve Republicans and one Farm-Laborite in opposition. See Longin, "Coal, Congress and the Courts," 111.

45. Baker, *The National Bituminous Coal Commission*, 51–52. On the legislative history of the Act generally, see also James P. Johnson, *The Politics of Soft Coal* (Urbana, Ill., 1979), 220–24.

46. Quoted in Johnson, *The Politics of Soft Coal*, 224.

47. James Patterson reports that "on the seven key bills of the 1935 session . . . the average anti-New Deal bloc [in the Senate] had been composed of twelve Republicans and but fourteen Democrats." Patterson, *Congressional Conservatism and the New Deal*, 160. The votes against the Wagner Act numbered twelve, fourteen fewer than this average; the votes against the Guffey Coal Act numbered thirty-seven, eleven more than the average. Irving Bernstein has contended that "many senators, convinced that the bill [the Wagner Act] was unconstitutional, wished to shift the onus of its defeat to the Supreme Court. They would gain labor's political support while certain that the measure would not take effect because employers would fail to comply until the court declared it void." Bernstein, *The Turbulent Years*, 341. This may have been true of some senators, though Bernstein did not identify those to whom he was referring. But it does not explain the discrepancy between the vote on the Wagner Act and the vote on the Guffey Coal Act taken later that same summer. Both acts were supported by organized labor, yet the Guffey Coal Act garnered twenty-five more negative votes than did the Wagner Act. It seems unlikely that more than a quarter of the Senate took such a curious approach to courting the labor vote. Nor does it seem likely that so large a bloc of senators would have refused to pass the buck to the Court regarding the Guffey Act's constitutionality when asked to by President Roosevelt, yet willingly done so with respect to the Wagner Act when the President made no such request.

48. Quoted in Johnson, *The Politics of Soft Coal*, 224.

49. *Carter v. Carter Coal*, 298 U.S. 238, 305 (1936).

50. Id. at 306.

51. The *Carter* majority had taken a comparable approach to a severability clause in *Railroad Retirement Board v. Alton*, 295 U.S. 330, 361–62 (1935).

52. Id. at 319.

53. Id. at 327–28.

54. Irons, *The New Deal Lawyers*, 227.

55. S. 1958 (74-1), printed in *Legislative History of the National Labor Relations Act* (Washington, D.C., 1949), I:1295–97 (hereinafter cited as, NLRB, *Legislative History*).

56. "Comparison of S. 2926 (73d Congress) and S. 1958 (74th Congress) Senate Committee Print," printed in NLRB, *Legislative History*, 1319, 1338.

57. NLRB, *Legislative History*, 1339–42, 1347–48, 1358.

58. S. 1958 (74-1), printed in NLRB, *Legislative History*, 1295. Identical language may be found in competing versions of the bill. See H.R. 6187 (74-1), printed in NLRB, *Legislative History*, 2445; H.R. 6288 (74-1), printed in NLRB, *Legislative History*, 2459.

59. The Committee's reformulation of the purchasing power theory stated:

The inequality of bargaining power between employer and individual employees which arises out of the organization of employers in corporate forms of ownership and out of numerous other modern industrial conditions, impairs and affects commerce by creating variations and instability in wage rates and working conditions within and between industries and by depressing the purchasing power of wage earners in industry, thus increasing the disparity between production and consumption, reducing the amount of commerce, and tending to produce and aggravate recurrent business depressions. The protection of the right of employees to organize and bargain collectively tends to restore equality of bargaining power and thereby fosters, protects, and promotes commerce among the several States. (S. Rept. 573 (74-1), printed in NLRB, *Legislative History*, 2285–86.)

Identical language may be found in competing versions of the bill. See H.R. 7937 (74-1), printed in NLRB, *Legislative History*, 2845; H.R. 7978 (74-1), printed in NLRB, *Legislative History*, 2857.

60. 79 Cong. Rec. 7681 (74-1).

61. Cortner, *The Wagner Act Cases*, 82; Gross, *The Making of the National Labor Relations Board*, 144.

62. Ibid., 144, quoting from the author's oral history interview with Philip Levy. Charles Wyzanski, who successfully defended the Wagner Act before the Court, had urged such a course from the outset. See Kenneth Casebeer, "Drafting Wagner's Act," 73, 93–95.

63. H. Rept. 1147 (74-1), printed in NLRB, *Legislative History*, 3032–33.

64. Ibid., 3034.

65. Ibid., 3035.

66. NLRB, *Legislative History*, 3187.

67. 79 Cong. Rec. 9731 (74-1).

68. H. Rept. 1371 (74-1).

69. NLRB, *Legislative History*, 3260, 3269.

70. Cortner, *The Wagner Act Cases*, 85.

71. Irons, *The New Deal Lawyers*, 240–41. See also Emerson, "The National Labor Relations Board," in Louchheim, ed., *The Making of the New Deal*, 210; Fuchs and Freedman, "The Wagner Act Decisions," 510, 512–13.

72. Irons, *The New Deal Lawyers*, 241–42.

73. Ibid., 243.

74. Leonard, *A Search for a Judicial Philosophy*, 110.

75. Irons, *The New Deal Lawyers*, 252–53, 268.

76. *United States Law Week* 3 (1936): 1041.

77. Ibid., 1041–42.

78. Ibid. "'Since a strike of the packing house employees would stop the flow of animals into and of products out of the packing plant,' the Chairman of the Labor Relations Board continued, 'it would stop a stream of interstate commerce. The Federal Government, which has the power to protect such commerce, would seem clearly to have the power to apply remedial measures, such as the Wagner Act, to prevent such a strike.'" Ibid.

79. Ibid.

80. Emerson, *Young Lawyer for the New Deal*, ch. 4.

81. *NLRB v. Jones & Laughlin Steel Corp.*, 301 U.S. 1 (1937), Brief for the Appellant at 77.

82. Id. at 66.

83. Id. at 67–69.

84. Id. at 78, 90–91.

85. *Arguments in Cases Arising Under Labor Acts Before the Supreme Court*, Sen. Doc. 52 (75-1) (hereinafter *Arguments*), 116.

86. Ibid., 116–17.

87. Cortner, *The Jones & Laughlin Case*, 148–49.

88. *Arguments*, 173–74.

89. See cases discussed, infra.

90. *NLRB v. Jones & Laughlin Steel Corp.*, 301 U.S. 1, 37–38 (1937), citing *Florida v. United States*, 282 U.S. 194 (1931); *Wisconsin Railroad Commission v. Chicago, B. & Q. R. Co.*, 257 U.S. 563 (1922); *Shreveport Case*, 234 U.S. 342 (1914).

91. *Jones & Laughlin Steel Corp.*, 301 U.S. at 38, citing *Baltimore & Ohio R. Co. v. ICC*, 221 U.S. 612 (1911); *Southern Railway v. United States*, 222 U.S. 20 (1911).

92. *United States v. American Tobacco Co.*, 221 U.S. 106 (1911); *Standard Oil v. United States*, 221 U.S. 1 (1911).

93. *Jones & Laughlin Steel Corp.*, 301 U.S. at 39–40, citing *Local 167 v. United States*, 291 U.S. 293 (1934); *Bedford Cut Stone v. Stone Cutters' Assn.*, 274 U.S. 37 (1927); *Coronado Coal v. United Mine Workers*, 268 U.S. 295 (1925); *Loewe v. Lawlor*, 208 U.S. 274 (1908).

94. *Jones & Laughlin Steel Corp.*, 301 U.S. at 37.

95. Id. Hughes noted that if, as Jones & Laughlin contended, the Act were an attempt to regulate *all* industry, "the Act would necessarily fall by reason of the limitation upon the federal power which inheres in the constitutional grant, as well as because of the explicit reservation of the Tenth Amendment." Id. at 29. As authority for this proposition Hughes cited *Schechter*. Continuing, he wrote,

> The authority of the federal government may not be pushed to such an extreme as to destroy the distinction, which the commerce clause itself establishes, between commerce "among the several states" and the internal concerns of a State. That distinction between what is national and what is local in the activities of commerce is vital to the maintenance of our federal system. (Id. at 29–30.)

Here Hughes made it clear that the local/national distinction remained a vital component of commerce clause jurisprudence. It was only because of the facts of this particular case that the Act could be applied without violating the Constitution. In other words, the NLRB lawyers had properly understood the importance of carefully selecting cases with which to test the Act's constitutionality.

In a similar vein, Hughes offered a nod of appreciation to those who had drafted the Act's provisions. Again responding to the contention that the Act regulated all industry, Hughes wrote:

> The grant of authority to the Board does not purport to extend to the relationship between all industrial employees and employers. Its terms do not impose collective bargaining upon all industry regardless of effects upon interstate or foreign commerce. It purports to reach only what may be deemed to burden or obstruct that commerce and, thus qualified, it must be construed as contemplating the exercise of control within constitutional bounds. . . . Whether or not particular action does affect commerce in so close and intimate a fashion as to be subject to federal control, and hence to lie within the authority conferred upon the Board, is left by the statute to be determined as individual cases arise. (Id. at 31–32.)

96. Indeed, one finds Justice Roberts employing the notion of direct and indirect burdens on commerce in a majority opinion as late as 1939. See *Milk Control Board v. Eisenberg Farm Products*, 306 U.S. 346 (1939).

97. *Jones & Laughlin Steel Corp.*, 301 U.S. at 41–42.

98. *Schechter*, 295 U.S. at 554.

99. Grant Gilmore, *The Death of Contract* (Columbus, Ohio, 1974), ch. 3.

100. The corporation, Hughes wrote, was

> the fourth largest producer of steel in the United States. With its subsidiaries—
> nineteen in number—it is a completely integrated enterprise, owning and operat-
> ing ore, coal and limestone properties, lake and river transportation facilities and
> terminal railroads located at its manufacturing plants. It owns or controls mines in
> Michigan and Minnesota. It operates four ore steamships on the Great Lakes,
> used in the transportation of ore to its facilities. . . . It owns limestone properties in
> various places in Pennsylvania and West Virginia. . . . Much of its product is
> shipped to its warehouses in Chicago, Detroit, Cincinnati and Memphis. . . . In
> Long Island City, New York, and in New Orleans it operates structural steel fabri-
> cating shops in connection with the warehousing of semi-finished materials sent
> from its works. . . . It has sales offices in twenty cities in the United States and a
> wholly-owned subsidiary which is devoted exclusively to distributing its product in
> Canada. Approximately 75 per cent of its product is shipped out of Pennsylvania.
> (*Jones & Laughlin Steel Corp.*, 301 U.S. at 26–27.)

101. "To carry on the activities of the entire steel industry, 33,000 men mine ore, 44,000 men mine coal, 4,000 men quarry limestone, 16,000 men manufacture coke, 343,000 men manufacture steel, and 83,000 men transport its product. Respondent has about 10,000 employees in its Aliquippa plant, which is located in a community of about 30,000 persons." Id. at 27. In a decade of chronic unemployment, there could be little doubt that the steel industry was affected with a national public interest.

102. Id.

103. *NLRB v. Fruehauf Trailer Co.*, 301 U.S. 49 (1937); *NLRB v. Friedman-Harry Marks Clothing Co.*, 301 U.S. 58 (1937).

104. *Fruehauf Trailer Co.*, 301 U.S. at 53.

105. Id. at 53–54.

106. *Friedman-Harry Marks Clothing Co.*, 301 U.S. at 72–73.

107. Id. at 72–74.

108. Id. at 75; see also *Fruehauf Trailer Co.*, 301 U.S. at 57.

109. In determining that the labor relations of the various manufacturing enterprises were sufficiently related to the free flow of commerce to warrant federal regulation under the commerce power, Hughes outlined the commercial police power rationale justifying the statute's intrusion upon the employer's common law prerogatives. The stoppage of Jones & Laughlin's manufacturing operations "by industrial strife," wrote Hughes,

> would have a most serious effect on interstate commerce. In view of respondent's
> far-flung activities, it is idle to say that the effect would be indirect or remote. It is
> obvious that it would be immediate and might be catastrophic. . . . When indus-
> tries organize themselves on a national scale, making their relation to interstate
> commerce the dominant factor in their activities, how can it be maintained that
> their industrial labor relations constitute a forbidden field into which Congress
> may not enter when it is necessary to protect interstate commerce from the para-
> lyzing consequences of industrial war? (*Jones & Laughlin Steel Co.*, 301 U.S. at 41.)

Revealing the extent to which the wartime experience had exposed the *Adair* Court's naivete, Hughes concluded:

> Experience has abundantly demonstrated that the recognition of the right of
> employees to self-organization and to have representatives of their own choosing
> for the purpose of collective bargaining is often an essential condition of industrial
> peace. Refusal to confer and negotiate has been one of the most prolific causes of
> strife. This is such an outstanding fact in the history of labor disturbances that it is
> a proper subject of judicial notice and requires no citation of instances. (Id. at 42.)

110. Had the Court intended to overrule *Carter Coal*, the fact that each enterprise relied extensively on the importation from other states of raw or semi-finished materials would have been irrelevant—the fact that they exported the vast bulk of their goods to other states would have been sufficient warrant for federal regulation.

111. Owen J. Roberts, "American Constitutional Government: The Blueprint and Structure," *B. U. L. Rev.* 29 (1949): 1, 25.

112. See *Santa Cruz Fruit Packing Co. v. NLRB*, 303 U.S. 453, 466 (1938), wherein Hughes quotes a passage from Cardozo's *Schechter* concurrence as if it were from his own majority opinion. See n. 58, ch. 11, infra.

113. See Danelski and Tulchin, eds., *The Autobiographical Notes of Charles Evans Hughes*, 312–13, where Hughes maintained that his opinions for the majority upholding the Wagner Act "were in no sense a departure from the views I had long held and expressed." Hughes asserted that he had stated "with clarity and precision" the principles upon which he had later sustained the Wagner Act in the *Minnesota Rate Cases*, 230 U.S. 352 (1913), where Hughes had remarked that the federal government had power to regulate intrastate commerce where such regulation was necessary to protect interstate commerce. Hughes did not explain how these principles dictated the conclusion he had reached in *Carter Coal*, which neither Cardozo nor Stone thought Hughes had given a decent "burial" in *Jones & Laughlin*. See Joseph L. Rauh Jr., "An Unabashed Liberal Looks at a Half-Century of the Supreme Court," *N.C. L. Rev.* 69 (1990): 213, 217; Mason, *Harlan Fiske Stone*, 459. If Hughes thought that the difference between *Carter Coal* and *Jones & Laughlin* was adequately captured by the abstract principle articulated in the *Minnesota Rate Cases*, while Roberts, as his subsequent remarks may suggest, thought the difference lay in the applicability of the current of commerce doctrine, it would appear that Hughes had more explaining to do than Roberts.

114. See ch. 11, infra.

115. *Friedman-Harry Marks Clothing Co.*, 301 U.S. at 97–99, 103. See infra.

116. *Washington, Virginia & Maryland Coach Co. v. NLRB*, 301 U.S. 142 (1937); *Virginian Railway Co. v. System Federation No. 40*, 300 U.S. 515 (1937). Lest it be thought that these votes were sacrifices made to appease backers of the Court-packing plan, it should be remembered that the Horsemen also voted unanimously to uphold the collective bargaining provisions of the original Railway Labor Act in 1930. *Texas & N.O.R. Co. v. Railway Clerks*, 281 U.S. 548 (1930).

117. *Friedman-Harry Marks Clothing Co.*, 301 U.S. at 100.

118. Id. at 97–98. McReynolds, who had dissented in both *Stafford* and *Olsen*, continued:

> [I]f this theory of a continuous "stream of commerce" as now defined is correct, will it become the duty of the Federal Government hereafter to suppress every strike which by possibility may cause a blockade in that stream? . . . There is no ground on which reasonably to hold that refusal by a manufacturer, whose raw materials come from states other than that of his factory and whose products are regularly carried to other states, to bargain collectively with employees in his manufacturing plant, directly affects interstate commerce. In such business, there is not one but two distinct movements or streams in interstate transportation. The first brings in raw materials and there ends. Then follows manufacture, a separate and local activity. Upon completion of this, and not before, the second distinct movement or stream in interstate commerce begins and the products go to other states. (Id. at 98.)

The custom in dissenting opinions is not to refute every argument advanced by the prevailing party, but rather to critique only those arguments accepted by the majority. It would have been highly irregular for the Four Horsemen to have devoted so much effort to refuting the current of commerce argument had they not understood the Court's opinion to embrace it.

119. See Thomas Kuhn, *The Structure of Scientific Revolutions* (Chicago, 1970).

11. *The Persistence of Memory*

1. Stanley Reed, Memorandum for the Attorney General, April 22, 1937, National Archives, Washington, D.C., Dept. of Justice 114-115-2, quoted in Leuchtenburg, *The Supreme Court Reborn*, 318–19; Charles Fahy, "Notes on Developments in Constitutional Law, 1936–1949," *Geo. L. J.* 38 (1949): 1, 11; Robert E. Cushman, "Constitutional Law in 1936–37," *Am. Pol. Sci. Rev.* 32 (1938): 278, 283–84. For another analysis noting the importance of the facts of the particular cases, though prepared to generalize beyond them, see Henry Rottschaefer, *Handbook of American Constitutional Law* (St. Paul, Minn., 1939), 267–68.

2. Alvies, "The Commerce Power," 307, 307–08.

3. Note, "Interstate Commerce: Jurisdiction of the National Labor Relations Board," *Cal. L. Rev.* 26 (1938): 273, 274; Paul H. Douglas and Joseph Hackman, "The Fair Labor Standards Act of 1938 I," *Pol. Sci. Q.* 53 (1938): 491, 493; John J. Trenam, Note, "Commerce Power Since the Schechter Case," *Geo. L. J.* 31 (1943): 201, 205; D. J. Farage, "That Which 'Directly' Affects Interstate Commerce," *Dick. L. Rev.* 42 (1937): 1, 8–9; Burton A. Finberg, Note, *B.U. L. Rev.* 17 (1937): 710, 721; Donald R. Harter, Note, "Constitutional Law: A Survey of Recent Decisions on the Commerce Clause," *Corn. L. Q.* 26 (1941): 464, 466–67. See also P. N. Cooper, Comment, "Constitutional Law—Interstate Commerce—National Labor Relations (Wagner) Act," *So. Cal. L. Rev.* 11 (1938): 240, 250–52.

4. See Justice McReynolds' dissent, which focused on the operations of the Friedman-Harry Marks company: "The business of the Company is so small that to close its factory would have no direct or material effect upon the volume of interstate commerce in clothing." *Friedman-Harry Marks Clothing Co.*, 301 U.S. at 94. "If closed today, the ultimate effect on commerce in clothing obviously would be negligible." Id. at 87.

5. Warren Woods and Altha Connor Wheatley, "The Wagner Act Decisions—A Charter of Liberty for Labor?" *G.W. L. Rev.* 5 (1937): 846, 853–54.

6. Walter L. Daykin, "Interstate Commerce as Defined in the National Labor Relations Act," *B. U. L. Rev.* 19 (1939): 586, 598; Ribble, "The Constitutional Doctrines of Chief Justice Hughes," 1207. See also Alvies, "The Commerce Power," 326.

7. Note, "Constitutional Law—Interstate Commerce—Constitutionality of National Labor Relations Act as Applied to Manufacturing," *Brooklyn L. Rev.* 6 (1937): 467, 469.

8. Joseph H. Mueller, "Businesses Subject to the National Labor Relations Act," *Mich. L. Rev.* 35 (1937): 1286, 1297–98.

9. Alvies, "The Commerce Power," 319–20.

10. Ibid., 309.

11. Lloyd Garrison, "Government and Labor: The Latest Phase," *Colum. L. Rev.* 37 (1937): 897, 898–99.

12. Mason, *Harlan Fiske Stone*, 553.

13. See *Humble Oil & Refining Co. v. NLRB*, 113 F. 2d 85 (5th Cir., 1940); *NLRB v. Crowe Coal Co.*, 104 F. 2d 633 (8th Cir., 1939); *NLRB v. Kentucky Fire Brick Co.*, 99 F. 2d 89 (6th Cir., 1938); *NLRB v. Carlisle Lumber Co.*, 94 F. 2d 138 (9th Cir., 1937); *NLRB v. Santa Cruz Fruit Packing Co.*, 91 F. 2d 790 (9th Cir., 1937); *Edwards v. United States*, 91 F. 2d 767 (9th Cir., 1937); *Divine v. Levy*, 39 F. Supp. 44 (W.D. La., 1941).

14. See *United States v. Adler's Creamery, Inc.*, 107 F. 2d 987 (2d Cir., 1939); *Moore v. Chicago Mercantile Exchange*, 90 F. 2d 735 (7th Cir., 1937); *United States v. Barr & Bloomfield Shoe Mfg. Co.*, 35 F. Supp. 75 (Dist. N.H., 1940); *United States v. F. W. Darby Lumber Co.*, 32 F. Supp. 47 (S.D. Ga., 1940); *Bagby v. Cleveland Wrecking Co.*, 28 F. Supp. 271 (W.D. Ky., 1939); *City of Atlanta v. National Bituminous Coal Commission*, 26 F. Supp. 606 (Dist. D.C., 1939); *Currin v. Wallace*, 19 F. Supp. 211 (E.D. N.C., 1937).

15. Shackleford Miller Jr. See Harold Chase, et al., *Biographical Dictionary of the Federal Judiciary* (Detroit, Mich., 1976), 195.

16. *Bagby v. Cleveland Wrecking Co.*, 28 F. Supp. 271, 272 (W.D. Ky., 1939). See also *Foote Bros. Gear & Machine Corp. v. NLRB*, 114 F. 2d 611, 614 (7th Cir., 1940) (upholding the jurisdiction of the board, emphasizing the corporation's acquisition of most of its raw materials from states other than Illinois and its sale of most of its finished products to purchasers outside the state).

17. 82 Cong. Rec. 1006–7 (1937).

18. *Santa Cruz Fruit Packing Co. v. NLRB*, 303 U.S. 453, 460–61, 463–64 (1938).

19. Cardozo and Reed did not participate; Butler and McReynolds dissented. Id. at 469.

20. Id. at 464.

21. Stern, "The Commerce Clause and the National Economy," 645, 683.

22. *Santa Cruz Fruit Packing Co.*, 303 U.S. at 462, 468; see also Brief for the NLRB at 7–8, 17.

23. *Santa Cruz Fruit Packing Co.*, 303 U.S. at 462.

24. Brief for the NLRB in Opposition to Petition for Writ of Certiorari at 6.

25. *Santa Cruz Fruit Packing Co.*, 303 U.S. at 461; see also Brief for the NLRB at 6–7.

26. *Santa Cruz Fruit Packing Co.*, 303 U.S. at 469.

27. John J. Trenam, Note, "Commerce Power Since the Schechter Case," 201, 207, n. 40; Ward P. Allen, Comment, "Labor Law—Extent of Jurisdiction of the National Labor Relations Board," *Mich. L. Rev.* 37 (1939): 934, 936.

28. *Consolidated Edison Co. v. NLRB*, 305 U.S. 188 (1938).

29. Brief of the NLRB in Opposition to Petition for Certiorari at 18–19, 21; Brief for the NLRB at 14, 24, 28, 30–31.

30. Id. at 22; see also Brief for the NLRB in Opposition to Petition for Certiorari at 20.

31. *Consolidated Edison Co.*, 305 U.S. at 220.

32. See Brief for the NLRB in Opposition to Petition for Certiorari at 19–20; Brief for the NLRB at 13, 20–24. See also Brief for United Electrical and Radio Workers of America, Intervenor-Respondent at 22, 56–63.

33. *Consolidated Edison Co.*, 305 U.S. at 220–21.

34. "Constitutional Law—Interstate Commerce—Jurisdiction of the NLRB over Intrastate Power Company," *U. Pa. L. Rev.* 87 (1939): 480, 482, n. 21.

35. *Virginian Railway v. System Federation No. 40*, 300 U.S. 515 (1937). See ch. 7, supra.

36. "Interstate Commerce and the NLRB," *Harv. L. Rev.* 52 (1939): 491, 495.

37. Mueller, "Businesses Subject to the National Labor Relations Act," 1286, 1291 (citations omitted).

38. See Brief of the NLRB in Opposition to Petition for Writ of Certiorari at 23, n. 8 and *passim*; Brief for the NLRB at 29, n. 16 and *passim*.

39. Brief for United Electrical and Radio Workers of America, Intervenor-Respondent at 62–63 (emphasis in original).

40. *Consolidated Edison Co.*, 305 U.S. at 221. For commentary noting the finding that the effects of a labor dispute at Consolidated Edison would produce direct rather than indirect effects on interstate commerce, see "Constitutional Law—Effect of N.L.R.A. on Commerce Clause," *N.Y.U. L. Q.* 16 (1939): 298; "Labor Law—NLRB—Jurisdiction—Power to Issue Affirmative Orders," *St. John's L. Rev.* 13 (1939): 387, 389; "Federal Regulation of Local Transactions Affecting Interstate Commerce: Consolidated Edison Company of New York v. National Labor Relations Board," *Md. L. Rev.* 3 (1939): 194, 197.

41. *NLRB v. Fainblatt*, 306 U.S. 601 (1939).

42. See Chase, et al., *Biographical Dictionary of the Federal Judiciary*, 21.

43. *NLRB v. Fainblatt*, 98 F. 2d 615, 619 (3d Cir., 1938).

44. Petition for Writ of Certiorari at 2–3; Brief for Petitioner at 2.

45. Id. at 17.

46. Id. at 6. See also Petition for Certiorari at 5–6: "Throughout the year there is a constant flow of raw material from points outside the State of New Jersey to respondents' plant, and of finished goods from the plant to New York City and other points outside New Jersey"; id. at 9: "a constant flow of goods moves in interstate commerce to respondents' plant in New Jersey, and that after prompt manufacture into finished products the goods pass again through the channels of interstate commerce to all parts of the United States."

47. Brief for Petitioner at 18; Petition for Certiorari at 11.

48. Brief for Petitioner at 13–14.

49. Brief on Behalf of the International Ladies Garment Workers' Union, as Amicus Curiae at 5–6.

50. Id. at 8 (emphasis in original).

51. Id. at 7 (citing language from *Schechter* distinguishing the facts in that case from those present in the current of commerce cases).

52. *Fainblatt*, 306 U.S. at 602.

53. Id. at 603, 605–6.

54. *Gibbons v. Ogden*, 9 Wheat. 1 (1824); *Champion v. Ames*, 188 U.S. 321 (1903).

55. Opinion draft, *NLRB v. Fainblatt*, No. 514, March 27, 1939, Hugo Black MSS, Box 255, LC, p. 4.

56. *Fainblatt*, 306 U.S. at 608.

57. Opinion draft, *NLRB v. Fainblatt*, No. 514, March 27, 1939, Black MSS, Box 255, LC, 5–6.

58. "[W]here federal control is sought to be exercised over activities which separately considered are intrastate, it must appear that there is a close and substantial relation to interstate commerce in order to justify the federal intervention for its protection. However difficult in its application, this principle is essential to our constitutional system. The subject of federal power is still 'commerce,' and not all commerce but commerce with foreign nations and among the several States. The expansion of enterprise has vastly increased the interests of interstate commerce but the constitutional differentiation still obtains. *Schechter Corporation v. United States*, 295 U.S. 495, 546. 'Activities local in their immediacy do not become interstate and national because of distant repercussions.' Id. at 554." Note that Hughes here is quoting from and citing to the pages of Cardozo's concurring opinion without indicating as much in his citation, thereby appropriating the views expressed in Cardozo's *Schechter* concurrence as his own by assimilating the Cardozo opinion to his own (uncited) majority opinion.

59. HLB to HFS, March 16, 1939, Stone MSS, Box 64, LC, 1; HLB to FF (undated), Black MSS, Box 255, LC.

60. HLB to HFS, March 16, 1939, Stone MSS, Box 64, LC, 2; HLB to FF (undated), Black MSS, Box 255, LC.

61. FF to HFS, March 15, 1939, Stone MSS, Box 64, LC, 2.

62. HFS to FF, March 15, 1939, Stone MSS, Box 64, LC. Note that Stone here refers to strikes that prevent shipment of goods in interstate commerce, not to strikes that prevent the manufacture of goods to be shipped in interstate commerce. See discussion of *Santa Cruz Fruit*, supra.

63. See ch. 12, infra.

64. HLB to HFS, March 16, 1939, Stone MSS, Box 64, LC, 2.

65. See *Fainblatt*, 306 U.S. at 609–14 (McReynolds, J., dissenting).

66. HLB to HFS, March 17, 1939, Stone MSS, Box 64, LC.

67. Compare *Fainblatt*, 306 U.S. at 605 and n. 1 with Draft Opinion, *NLRB v. Fainblatt*, No. 514, March 27, 1939, Stone MSS, Box 64, LC, and *idem.*, Black MSS, Box 255, LC.

68. Robert E. Cushman, "Constitutional Law in 1938–39," *Am. Pol. Sci. Rev.* 34 (1940): 249, 257; John G. Somers, "The Commerce Clause of the Constitution Since the Schechter Case, or From Chickens to Children," *J.B.A. Kansas* 8 (1940): 311, 331; John C. Griffin, "Labor Law—National Labor Relations Act—Jurisdiction of the National Labor Relations Board," *Mich. L. Rev.* 37 (1939): 1328, 1330; Philip Treibitch, "The Supreme Court of the United States: Validity of the Agricultural Adjustment Act of 1938," *Geo. L. J.* 27 (1939): 1082, 1090. See also "National Labor Relations Act—Interstate Commerce—Application to Contract Manufacture," *G. W. L. Rev.* 7 (1939): 1028, 1029; "Interstate Commerce—Jurisdiction of N.L.R.B. Over Employer Processing Materials for Extrastate Owner," *Va. L. Rev.* 25 (1939): 856, 857.

69. *Currin v. Wallace*, 306 U.S. 1 (1939); 49 Stat. 731. Section 1(i) of the Act invoked the current of commerce metaphor, providing that "a transaction in tobacco shall be considered to be in commerce if such tobacco is part of that current of commerce usual in the tobacco industry whereby tobacco or products manufactured therefrom are sent from one State with the expectation that they will end their transit, after purchase, in another. . . ."

70. "Diseased livestock [citing Act of May 29, 1884, c. 60, 23 Stat. 31] and diseased plants [citing Act of March 4, 1917, c. 179, 39 Stat. 1165] have been excluded from interstate commerce. Likewise grain, [citing Act of August 11, 1916, c. 313, 39 Stat. 482] and rosin and spirits of turpentine [citing Act of March 3, 1923, c. 217, 42 Stat. 1435] are required to be inspected and graded, or referred to according to prescribed standards, as a condition to their entering interstate commerce. Apples and pears may not be received for foreign shipment unless they are certified as conforming with prescribed standards of quality. [citing Act of June 10, 1933, c. 59, 48 Stat. 123]." Brief for the United States at 26–27.

71. Id. at 27, citing *Pittsburgh Melting Co. v. Totten*, 248 U.S. 1 (1918).

72. Brief for the United States at 27. For the cases "tacitly approving" federal grain standards legislation, see infra.

73. *Currin*, 306 U.S. at 9.

74. See remarks of Rep. Carpenter, 79 Cong. Rec. 11807 (1935); remarks of Rep. Chapman, 79 Cong. Rec. 11875, 11879 (1935).

75. 79 Cong. Rec. 11807, 11876 (1935).

76. Ibid., 11879.

77. The panel consisted of Elliott Northcott and John J. Parker, appointed by President Coolidge, and Morris Soper, a Hoover appointment. Chase, et al., *Biographical Dictionary of the Federal Judiciary*, 209, 214, 258–59.

78. *Wallace v. Currin*, 95 F. 2d 856 (4th Cir., 1938).

79. Brief for the United States at 17, n. 5.

80. *Shafer v. Farmer's Grain Co.*, 268 U.S. 189, 198 (1925).

81. *Currin*, 306 U.S. at 11, quoting 268 U.S. at 198–99. See also *Flanagan v. Federal Coal Co.*, 267 U.S. 222 (1924).

82. *Lemke v. Farmer's Grain Co.*, 258 U.S. 50, 60–61 (1922).

83. *Dahnke-Walker Co. v. Bondurant*, 257 U.S. 282 (1921).

84. See Willis, *Constitutional Law of the United States*, 290.

85. *Swift*, 196 U.S. at 398–99; *Stafford*, 258 U.S. at 519. The Court's opinion takes up these authorities at *Currin*, 306 U.S. at 10–11; the Fourth Circuit's opinion considers them at *Currin*, 95 F. 2d at 862–63; the Government pursues these lines of argument and authority throughout its brief, especially at 18–21.

86. *Currin*, 306 U.S. at 9–11. "Congress has long exercised this authority in enacting laws for inspection and the establishment of standards in relation to various commodities involved in transactions in interstate or foreign commerce." Id. at 12, citing the United States Cotton Standards Act, the Pure Food and Drugs Act, the United States Warehouse

Act, the Farm Products Inspection Act, and the Perishable Agricultural Commodities Act.

87. Somers, "The Commerce Clause of the Constitution," 330; Jackson, *The Struggle for Judicial Supremacy*, 237; *United States v. Rock-Royal Co-operative, Inc.*, 307 U.S. 533, 568–69 (1939); Stern, "The Commerce Clause and the National Economy," 688. By the time the milk cases reached the Supreme Court, Stern reported, the contention that the regulations "did not come within the Commerce Clause had been abandoned by most of the parties, and the Court dealt with the point summarily." Ibid.

88. Brief for the United States at 30.

89. *Currin*, 306 U.S. at 11.

90. *Shreveport Case*, 234 U.S. 342 (1914). Also cited for this proposition were *Wisconsin Railroad Commission v. Chicago, B. & Q. R. Co.*, 257 U.S. 563 (1922), and the *Minnesota Rate Cases*, 230 U.S. 352 (1913). The lower court had reached the same conclusion invoking the same line of authority. See *Wallace v. Currin*, 95 F. 2d 856, 860–62 (4th Cir., 1938).

91. *Railroad Commission of Wisconsin v. Chicago, B. & Q. R. Co.*, 257 U.S. 563, 588 (1922).

92. See, for example, *Ohio v. United States*, 292 U.S. 498 (1934); *Florida v. United States*, 292 U.S. 1 (1934); *United States v. Louisiana*, 290 U.S. 70 (1933); *Alabama v. United States*, 279 U.S. 229 (1928); *Colorado v. United States*, 271 U.S. 153 (1926) ; *United States v. Village of Hubbard*, 266 U.S. 474 (1925); *Dayton-Goose Creek Ry. Co. v. United States*, 263 U.S. 456 (1924); *Illinois Central R.R. Co. v. Public Utilities Commission of Illinois*, 245 U.S. 493 (1918); *American Express Co. v. Caldwell*, 244 U.S. 617 (1917).

93. See *Heiner v. Donnan*, 285 U.S. 312, 316 (1932) (holding that the requirements of due process under the Fifth and Fourteenth Amendments are identical).

94. Baker, *The National Bituminous Coal Commission*, 63–64; Longin, "Coal, Congress and the Courts,"101, 123–24.

95. Baker, *The National Bituminous Coal Commission*, 66.

96. 81 Cong. Rec. 2032 (1937).

97. 81 Cong. Rec. 3010 (1937); see also remarks of Sen. Barkley, 81 Cong. Rec. 2959 (1937).

98. 81 Cong. Rec. 2033 (1937).

99. See remarks of Rep. Vinson, 81 Cong. Rec. 2034, 2038–39 (1937); remarks of Rep. Jenkins, 81 Cong. Rec. 2042 (1937); remarks of Sen. Guffey, 81 Cong. Rec. 2953 (1937).

100. 81 Cong. Rec. 2039 (1937).

101. 81 Cong. Rec. 2030 (1937).

102. 81 Cong. Rec. 2959 (1937).

103. 81 Cong. Rec. 2034 (1937). See also remarks of Sen. Barkley, 81 Cong. Rec. 2959, 3010 (1937).

104. H. Rept. 294 (75–1), 14. Sponsors of the 1935 Guffey Coal Act had relied upon these same lines of authority as support for the Act's provisions authorizing price regulation. See H. Rept. 1800 (74–1), 9–10.

105. 81 Cong. Rec. 2048 (1937).

106. 81 Cong. Rec. 3014 (1937).

107. 79 Cong. Rec. 13666–67 (1935).

108. 81 Cong. Rec. 2128 (1937).

109. 79 Cong. Rec. 14084 (1935).

110. 81 Cong. Rec. 3145 (1937).

111. The Senate agreed to the conference report without a record vote on April 9, 81 Cong. Rec. 3315 (1937); the House similarly accepted the report without a record vote on April 12, 81 Cong. Rec. 3390 (1937).

112. S. Rept. 252 (75–1), 5.

113. Note, "Agricultural Adjustment and Marketing Control," *Yale L. J.* 46 (1936): 130, 138–39. See also H. Rept. 468 (75–1), 1; S. Rept. 565 (75–1), 2.

114. See remarks of Sen. Pope, 82 Cong. Rec. 343, 345 (1938).

115. H. Rept. 1645 (75–2), 1, 5, 17. See also remarks of Rep. Cooley, 82 Cong. Rec. 661–62 (1938); Brief for the United States at 36, *Mulford v. Smith*.

116. H. Rept. 1645 (75–2), 4–5.

117. 82 Cong. Rec. 345 (1938).

118. 82 Cong. Rec. 1062 (1938).

119. 82 Cong. Rec. 343 (1938).

120. See remarks of Senator Austin, 82 Cong. Rec. 831–32 (1938). Austin had expressed similar views with respect to the regulation of intrastate sales of coal in the debates over the Bituminous Coal Conservation Act of 1937. See 81 Cong. Rec. 3008 (1937).

121. See remarks of Rep. Mapes, 82 Cong. Rec. 479 (1938); remarks of Rep. Mott, 82 Cong. Rec. 702 (1938); remarks of Rep. Short, 82 Cong. Rec. 766 (1938); remarks of Sen. Walsh, 82 Cong. Rec. 1075 (1938); remarks of Sen. King, 82 Cong. Rec. 881, 883 (1938). Some of these remarks are ambiguous, and may have been directed only at the provisions of the bill establishing acreage allotments for wheat, cotton, corn and rice (there was no acreage allotment provision for tobacco). See, for example, remarks of Rep. Tarver, 82 Cong. Rec. 649 (1938); remarks of Sen. Borah, 82 Cong. Rec. 1006 (1938).

122. *Mulford v. Smith*, 307 U.S. 38 (1939).

123. Brief of Appellants at 12–19.

124. Brief for the United States at 45–49 (emphasis in original).

125. Id. at 41–42, 109–111.

126. Id. at 37–38, 50–51, 54 (emphasis in original).

127. Id. at 60.

128. Id. at 68; see also id. at 60. Even assuming that marketing quotas influenced production, tobacco presented a special case. Tobacco could be "stored for a long period of time. Indeed practically all tobacco is stored for a period of one to five years before it is used. If an amount in excess of marketing quotas is grown, that excess can be stored for sale in years when marketing quotas are not in effect, or when a grower produces less than his quota." Id. at 64.

129. Id. at 68–69 (citations omitted).

130. Id. at 69–70.

131. 28 Stat. 963 (1895); *Champion v. Ames*, 188 U.S. 321 (1903); 34 Stat. 768 (1906); *Hipolite Egg Co. v. United States*, 220 U.S. 45 (1911); 36 Stat. 825 (1910); *Hoke v. United States*, 227 U.S. 308 (1913); 41 Stat. 324 (1919); *Brooks v. United States*, 267 U.S. 432 (1925); 47 Stat. 326 (1932), as amended by 48 Stat. 781 (1934); *Gooch v. United States*, 287 U.S. 124 (1936).

132. Brief for the United States at 83–84.

133. Id. at 40, 88–89 (citations omitted).

134. "That a regulation of the quantity of interstate commerce is a regulation of such commerce would seem to be plain upon its face." Id. at 51.

135. Id. at 112–13. The United States also argued that *Hammer* had been wrongly decided and had been effectively overruled *sub silentio* by such subsequent cases as *Kentucky Whip & Collar Co. v. I.C.R. Co.*, 299 U.S. 334 (1937) and *Brooks v. United States*, 267 U.S. 432 (1925). Id. at 113–19.

136. Note, "Agricultural Adjustment and Marketing Control," 140.

137. Brief for the United States at 88. "A statute which is designed to aid and protect an interstate industry, including producers who sell in interstate commerce, is designed to benefit commerce. . . . Commerce is benefitted when an over-supply which unduly depresses

prices is kept off the market, as well as when an obstruction to trade is removed." Id. at 94–95.

138. Id. at 53, 94.

139. Id. at 40–41, 91–94. "The Act is designed to raise or stabilize prices. It achieves that result by controlling the amount marketed rather than the amount grown. . . . The purpose of stabilizing commerce through providing an orderly, adequate and balanced flow of commodities in lean years as well as in good is likewise accomplished by controlling marketing rather than production. . . . An even flow of commerce at reasonable prices can be achieved without regulating production by keeping surpluses in fat years from being marketed until years of shortage. This is what the Act contemplates, not limitation of production." The House Agriculture Committee report stated "that legislation to meet the farm problem" should "encourage the abundant production of agricultural commodities, and provide for the storage or warehousing of the production above current needs in order to have such commodities available at reasonable prices in years of drought or other adverse conditions. . . . The emphasis throughout is on keeping excessive supplies *off the market,* not on prohibiting their production." Id. at 62–64 (emphasis in original).

140. Id. at 94. The 1936 note in the *Yale Law Journal,* discussed supra, had foreseen these arguments in 1936. See Note, "Agricultural Adjustment and Marketing Control," 139–40.

141. Brief for the United States at 52–53, citing *Wallace v. Hudson-Duncan & Co.,* 98 F. 2d 985 (9th Cir., 1938); *Edwards v. United States,* 91 F. 2d 767 (9th Cir., 1937); *United States v. David Buttrick Co.,* 91 F. 2d. 66 (1st Cir., 1937), cert. den. 302 U.S. 737; *United States v. Whiting Milk Co.,* 21 F. Supp. 321 (Dist. Mass., 1937); *United States v. Goldsmith Fruit Co.,* 19 F. Supp. 147 (S.D. Fla., 1937). The brief also noted several unreported cases in which district courts had granted temporary restraining orders or preliminary injunctions enforcing orders of the secretary of agriculture issued under the earlier marketing provisions. Brief for the United States at 53, n. 41, citing *United States v. Babcock Dairy Co.* (N.D. Ohio); *United States v. Herman M. Sheffield* (S.D. Texas); *United States v. Melvin Child Andrews* (D. Mass.); *United States v. Corinth Creamery, Inc.,* 21 F. Supp. 265 (D. Vt., 1937). The only unreversed district court case holding such orders invalid, the brief reported, was *Chester C. Fosgate Co. v. Kirkland,* 19 F. Supp. 152 (S.D. Fla., 1937), "which in effect has been overruled by the decision of the Circuit Court of Appeals for the Fifth Circuit in *Whittenburg v. United States,* 100 F. (2d) 520." Brief for the United States at 52, n. 40. This argument was again rehearsed and expanded when the provisions of the Act regulating milk sales were attacked in *United States v. Rock Royal Co-operative,* 307 U.S. 533 (1939), discussed infra. See Brief for the United States, *Rock Royal,* 150–54. See also Stern, "The Commerce Clause and the National Economy," 687–88.

142. Bascom Deaver, appointed by Coolidge, and Charles Kennamer and Samuel Sibley, appointed by Hoover. See Chase, et al., *Biographical Dictionary of the Federal Judiciary,* 69, 149, 252.

143. Comment, "Constitutional Law—Agriculture as Interstate Commerce," *Ind. L. J.* 18 (1943): 242, 245.

144. *Mulford v. Smith,* 24 F. Supp. 919, 922 (M.D. Ga., 1938).

145. Edward H. Adzigan, "Constitutional Law—Agricultural Adjustment Act of 1938," *Geo. L. J.* 27 (1938): 89, 90–91.

146. *Mulford,* 307 U.S. at 47, 51.

147. Brief for the United States at 40, 60–61.

148. *Mulford,* 307 U.S. at 49–50. See also Brief for Appellants at 5–8.

149. Brief for the United States at 61–62.

150. *Mulford,* 307 U.S. at 51.

151. Id. at 47.

152. 82 Cong. Rec. 344.

153. Brief for the United States at 45.

154. *Mulford*, 307 U.S. at 47–48. Having implied that the intent of the statute was an important consideration, Roberts went on apparently to contradict himself a mere two sentences later: "The motive of Congress in exerting the power is irrelevant to the validity of the legislation." Id.

155. Id.

156. Id. at 47. The district court had reached the same conclusion invoking the same line of reasoning. See *Mulford v. Smith*, 24 F. Supp. 919, 922–23. Both the district court and Supreme Court opinions followed the line of argument set out in the Brief for the United States at 28–29, 38, 45–46. This argument, too, had been foreseen in 1936. See Note, "Agricultural Adjustment and Marketing Control," 140.

157. *Mulford*, 307 U.S. at 51–57.

158. For some examples of the literature to which Jackson was referring, see Comment, *G.W. L. Rev.* 8 (1939): 228, 229, 230; Comment, *U. Pa. L. Rev.* 87 (1939): 1005, 1006; Stern, "The Commerce Clause and the National Economy," 692.

159. Jackson, *The Struggle for Judicial Supremacy*, 238. For commentary consonant with Jackson's view, see Comment, "Constitutional Law—Commerce Clause—Agricultural Adjustment Act of 1938," *U. Cinn. L. Rev.* 14 (1940): 192, 193; Comment, "Constitutional Law—Agriculture as Interstate Commerce," *Ind. L. J.* 18 (1943): 242, 245; Comment, "Interstate Commerce—Federal Regulation of Tobacco Marketing Held Constitutional," *Harv. L. Rev.* 52 (1939): 1364. Jackson went on to say, however, that he "would agree, however, that the latter opinion indicates a broader and more tolerant approach to the constitutional problem than did his first opinion." Jackson, *The Struggle for Judicial Supremacy*, 238.

Carl Swisher took a similar view. "The Mulford decision did not overrule its predecessor [*Butler*]," he wrote.

> The Court as constituted in 1939 might still have held direct federal control of agricultural production to be unconstitutional. But here the control of production was only indirect. It was an incidental effect of the power of Congress to regulate interstate and foreign commerce. The decision undoubtedly reflected a trend in judicial attitude toward the exercise of federal regulatory power, but not too much stress should be laid on this point. On numerous occasions the Court has shown a preference for regulations based on the commerce power, which is specifically a regulatory power, rather than on the taxing power where the primary constitutional purpose is to raise revenue rather than to regulate. (Swisher, *American Constitutional Development*, 2d ed., 957.)

160. 82 Cong. Rec. 341 (1938) (remarks of Sen. Pope), quoting *United States v. Butler*, 297 U.S. 1, 63–64 (1936).

161. 82 Cong. Rec. 341 (1938).

162. Brief for the United States at 110 (citations omitted). See ch. 9, supra.

163. See Lincoln Caplan, *The Tenth Justice: The Solicitor General and the Rule of Law* (New York, 1987).

164. See Stern, "The Commerce Clause and the National Economy," 687; remarks of Rep. Hope, 79 Cong. Rec. 9559 (1935).

165. 49 Stat. 750.

166. See remarks of Rep. Jones, 79 Cong. Rec. 9462, 9464 (1935); remarks of Rep. Cooley, 79 Cong. Rec. 9484 (1935); H. Rept. 1241 (74-1), 10. Senators Bankhead and Black also gamely defended the statute on the authority of *Champion v. Ames* and *Hoke v. United States*, see 79 Cong. Rec. 11154–55, 11157–59 (1935), and other supporters distinguished *Hammer v. Dagenhart* by employing lines of argument appropriated by the Government in *Mul-*

ford v. Smith. See remarks of Rep. Jones, 79 Cong. Rec. 9462 (1935); remarks of Rep. Cooley, 79 Cong. Rec. 9485 (1935).

167. See remarks of Rep. Jones, 79 Cong. Rec. 9461–62 (1935); remarks of Rep. Cooley, 79 Cong. Rec. 9485 (1935); remarks of Sen. Bankhead, 79 Cong. Rec. 11150–54, 11158, 11219 (1935); H. Rept. 1241 (74–1), 10.

168. 79 Cong. Rec. 9485 (1935).

169. See remarks of Rep. Cooley, 79 Cong. Rec. 9485 (1935); remarks of Sen. Borah, 79 Cong. Rec. 11138 (1935); remarks of Sen. Murphy, 79 Cong. Rec. 11139 (1935). See also Note, "Agricultural Adjustment and Marketing Control," *Yale L. J.* 46 (1936): 130, 140.

170. 79 Cong. Rec. 9595 (1935).

171. 79 Cong. Rec. 11658 (1935). The vote on accepting the conference committee report was 174 to 40 in the House, 79 Cong. Rec. 13026 (1935), with the Senate acquiescing by a voice vote. 79 Cong. Rec. 13231 (1935).

172. 50 Stat. 246. The bill passed both houses without a record vote. 81 Cong. Rec. 3594 (1937) (House), 79 Cong. Rec. 4969 (1937) (Senate).

173. *United States v. Rock Royal Co-operative,* 307 U.S. 533 (1939); *H. P. Hood & Sons v. United States,* 307 U.S. 588 (1939).

174. Brief for the United States at 84–86, 96–105, 119–24. In *Hood* the petitioners raised an exceedingly brief commerce clause objection to the Act in their petition for certiorari, which they dropped entirely in their brief. Petition for a Writ of Certiorari at 7. The United States accordingly responded summarily in its brief. "Petitioner's argument does not differ substantially from the views urged upon this Court by the appellants" in *Currin* and *Mulford.* "The decisions of this Court in rejecting those views are a complete answer to petitioner's argument." Brief for the Respondent at 48. See Stern, "The Commerce Clause and the National Economy," 688.

175. Brief for the Appellee, Central New York Co-operative Assn., Inc. at 27.

176. *Rock Royal Co-operative,* 307 U.S. at 568.

177. Id. at 568–71.

178. Id. at 569–70. See Stern, "The Commerce Clause and the National Economy," 688.

179. *Jones & Laughlin, Fruehauf, Friedman-Harry Marks, Consolidated Edison,* and *Fainblatt* all made cameo appearances in footnotes to Reed's opinion, alongside *Stafford, Olsen, Shreveport, Currin,* and *Mulford.* See *Rock Royal Co-operative,* 307 U.S. at 568–69.

180. *Hood,* 307 U.S. at 603–8.

181. *Rock Royal Co-operative,* 307 U.S. at 583–87.

182. Id. at 582–83. As he had in his dissent in the Wagner Act cases, McReynolds conflated Tenth and Fifth Amendment cavils, asserting "the absence of Congressional authority to manage *private* business affairs under the transparent guise of regulating interstate commerce. True, production and distribution of milk are most important enterprises, not easy of wise execution; but so is breeding the cows, authors of the commodity; also, sowing and reaping the fodder which inspires them" (emphasis added).

183. Memorandum, No. 804 (undated), *Sunshine Anthracite Coal v. Adkins,* Douglas MSS, Box 49, LC.

184. Brief for the Appellee at 19–22.

185. *Sunshine Anthracite Coal Co. v. Adkins,* 310 U.S. 381, 393–94 (1940).

186. Id. at 394.

187. Id. at 396–97. Compare Johnson, *The Politics of Soft Coal,* 232–33 ("The Supreme Court reversed itself dramatically on its interpretation of the commerce power and specifically upheld the law in the *Sunshine Anthracite* case.")

188. Douglas' conference notes reveal that Hughes had no reservations about upholding the Act. Douglas records Hughes' remarks as follows: "Constitutionality—Carter case

maj. of ct. declined to pass on price fixing features of old Act—Act remodelled [illegible] definitely applies to interstate commerce. C.J. sees no reason for holding it invalid." Conference Notes, No. 804, *Sunshine Anthracite Coal v. Adkins*, May 4, 1940, Douglas MSS, Box 49, LC. The notes go on to record that "McR thinks Act is bad," and leave off there. Douglas made no record of Roberts' remarks, which presumably echoed those of Hughes.

189. In *Sunshine*, practically the entire output of the company was sold to purchasers outside the state in which it was mined. *Sunshine Anthracite Coal Co.*, 310 U.S. at 392. Accordingly, no question of the constitutionality of regulating intrastate sales of coal was raised in the case.

190. *Rock Royal Co-operative*, 307 U.S. at 568. Here Reed cited not only *Shreveport, Currin, Mulford,* and the *Minnesota Rate Cases* but also *Stafford, Olsen,* the *Labor Board Cases,* and *Fainblatt.*

191. *Rock Royal Co-operative*, 307 U.S. at 569. See Stern, "The Commerce Clause and the National Economy," 688–89.

192. Sherman Minton and Otto Kerner. See Chase, et al., *Biographical Dictionary of the Federal Judiciary,* 150, 196.

193. *United States v. Wrightwood Dairy Co.*, 123 F. 2d 100 (7th Cir. 1941). Robert Stern characterized the decision as "inexplicable." Stern, "The Commerce Clause and the National Economy," 689.

194. *Wrightwood Dairy Co.*, 123 F. 2d at 101–2.

195. Id. at 103.

196. Id.

197. Petitioner's Brief at 17–18, citing *United States v. Krechting*, 26 F. Supp. 266 (S.D. Ohio); *United States v. Andrews*, 26 F. Supp. 123 (D. Mass., Judge Brewster); *United States v. H. P. Hood & Sons*, 26 F. Supp. 672 (D. Mass., Judge Sweeney); *United States v. Schwarz et al.*, Civil Action No. 1480 (N.D. Ill.), decided January 30, 1941 (Judge Barnes). See also Petition for Writ of Certiorari at 6; Stern, "The Commerce Clause and the National Economy," 688.

198. Petition for a Writ of Certiorari at 6–7. The petition also cited *Olsen* and *Jones & Laughlin,* among other cases.

199. Petitioner's Brief at 24.

200. Petition for a Writ of Certiorari at 7. See also Petitioner's Brief at 23–24.

201. Respondent's Brief at 22–23 (emphasis in original).

202. Respondent's Brief at 39.

203. For commentary noting that the holding in *Wrightwood* was the logical outcome of combining *Rock Royal* with the *Shreveport* line of cases, see J. N. E. Jr., "Constitutional Law—Intrastate Competition as Burden on Interstate Commerce," *Tul. L. Rev.* 16 (1942): 619; "Constitutional Law—Commerce Clause—Power to Regulate Intrastate Transactions—Milk Prices," *Mich. L. Rev.* 40 (1942): 1097, 1097–98; "Commerce—Regulation by Congress—Power to Regulate Intrastate Commerce," *Minn. L. Rev.* 26 (1942): 746, 747; "Constitutional Law—Effect of Competition of Intrastate Commerce on Interstate Commerce as Justifying Regulation of Former," *Colum. L. Rev.* 42 (1942): 694, 695; Harold Hoffman, "Constitutional Law—Commerce Clause—Competition with Interstate Commerce," *Tex. L. Rev.* 20 (1942): 612, 613–14; "Constitutional Law—Interstate Commerce Clause—Agricultural Marketing Agreement Act of 1937," *U. Pitt. L. Rev.* 8 (1942): 139, 140.

204. *United States v. Wrightwood Dairy Co.*, 315 U.S. 110, 118–19 (1942).

205. Id. at 120. Here Stone also cited *Jones & Laughlin* and *United States v. Darby*, 312 U.S. 100 (1941).

206. *Wrightwood Dairy Co.*, 315 U.S. at 120–21. Justice Roberts did not participate. *Jones & Laughlin* and *Consolidated Edison* again made only brief appearances in string citations. See id. at 119–20.

207. "Constitutional Law—Interstate Commerce Clause—Agricultural Marketing Agreement Act of 1937," *U. Pitt. L. Rev.* 8 (1942): 139, 140 (emphasis in original).

208. "Constitutional Law—Effect of Competition of Intrastate Commerce on Interstate Commerce as Justifying Regulation of the Former," *Colum. L. Rev.* 42 (1942): 694, 696.

209. "Commerce—Regulation by Congress—Power to Regulate Intrastate Commerce," *Minn. L. Rev.* 26 (1942): 746, 748.

210. "Constitutional Law—Effect of Competition of Intrastate Commerce on Interstate Commerce as Justifying Regulation of Former," *Colum. L. Rev.* 42 (1942): 694, 699.

12. *The Struggle with Judicial Supremacy*

1. *United States v. Darby*, 312 U.S. 100 (1941).

2. *Hammer v. Dagenhart*, 247 U.S. 251 (1918).

3. Act of September 1, 1916, c. 432, 39 Stat. 675.

4. *Bailey v. Drexel Furniture Co.*, 259 U.S. 20 (1922), which struck down the Child Labor Tax, Act of February 24, 1919, Title XII, c. 18, 40 Stat. 1057, 1138.

5. Swisher, *American Constitutional Development*, 729–32; Richard B. Bernstein, *Amending America: If We Love the Constitution So Much, Why Do We Keep Trying to Change It?* (New York, 1993), 179–81.

6. Mason, *Harlan Fiske Stone*, 551; Pusey, *Charles Evans Hughes*, 678.

7. Conference Notes, No. 82, *United States v. F. W. Darby Lumber Co.*, December 21, 1940, W.O. Douglas MSS, Box 51, LC; Conference Notes, No. 82, *United States v. F. W. Darby Lumber Co.*, Frank Murphy MSS, Reel 123, University of Michigan.

8. Id. McReynolds also passed at the conference vote, and he retired before the opinion was handed down.

9. Hughes to Stone, January 27, 1941, Stone MSS, Box 66, LC.

10. Opinion draft dated February 3, 1941, Stone MSS, Box 66, LC.

11. Conference Notes, No. 82, *United States v. F.W. Darby Lumber Co.*, Reel 123, Frank Murphy MSS, University of Michigan (emphasis mine).

12. *A. B. Kirschbaum v. Walling*, 316 U.S. 517 (1942).

13. Id. at 518–19.

14. Id. at 520–22.

15. Id. at 522–24.

16. Id. at 524–25 (emphasis mine).

17. Id. at 526.

18. Roberts differed with the majority over this question's resolution, however. "I am convinced," he wrote, "that Congress never intended by the statute to reach the employees of the petitioners. Neither the words of the Act, nor its legislative history, nor the purpose to be served, requires the application of the statute in these cases." Id. at 527.

19. Id. at 527.

20. *Wickard v. Filburn*, 317 U.S. 111 (1942).

21. Conference Notes, No. 1080, *Wickard v. Filburn*, Frank Murphy MSS, Reel 125, University of Michigan. Justice Reed took no part in the decision.

22. Opinion draft, *Wickard v. Filburn* (undated); Opinion draft, *Wickard v. Filburn* (May 22, 1942), Jackson MSS, Box 125, LC.

23. Opinion draft, *Wickard v. Filburn*, at 3 (undated); Box 125, Jackson MSS, LC.

24. *Jones & Laughlin Steel Co.*, 301 U.S. at 37; Opinion draft, *Wickard v. Filburn*, at 10 (May 22, 1942), Jackson MSS, Box 125, LC.

25. Id. at 11.

26. RHJ to HFS, May 25, 1942, Jackson MSS, Box 125, LC.

27. Opinion draft, *Wickard v. Filburn*, at 10–12 (May 22, 1942), Jackson MSS, Box 125, LC.

28. Id. at 12.

29. Id. at 13.

30. Justice Reed asked to be disqualified. Returns of opinion drafts, *Wickard v. Filburn* (May 22, 1942), Jackson MSS, Box 125, LC.

31. See HFS, "Memorandum in Re: No. 1080—Wickard v. Filburn" (May 22, 1942), Jackson MSS, Box 125, LC.

32. Id.; WOD, "Memorandum to Justice Jackson, Re: No. 1080, *Wickard v. Filburn*" (May 25, 1942), Jackson MSS, Box 125, LC; HFS, "Memorandum Re: No. 1080—Wickard v. Filburn" (May 27, 1942), Jackson MSS, Box 125, LC.

33. FF to HFS, May 26, 1942, Stone MSS, Box 74, LC.

34. HFS, "Memorandum Re: No. 1080—Wickard v. Filburn" (May 27, 1942), Jackson MSS, Box 125, LC.

35. RHJ, "Memorandum for the Members of the Court, Re: No. 1080—*Wickard v. Filburn*" (undated), Jackson MSS, Box 125, LC.

36. RHJ to HFS, May 25, 1942, Jackson MSS, Box 125, LC (emphasis in original). Alpheus Thomas Mason characterized this letter as Jackson "pour[ing] out his doubts" in "language reminiscent of the Old Guard." Mason, *Harlan Fiske Stone*, 594.

37. RHJ to HFS at 2, May 25, 1942, Jackson MSS, Box 125, LC.

38. Id. at 1–2.

39. See Jackson, *The Struggle for Judicial Supremacy*, 69–70 ("the Court had held that the power to regulate interstate commerce may not be exercised where in the opinion of the Court its effect or purpose is to regulate a subject exclusively within state control, even though nothing in the Constitution indicates that any particular subject is within the exclusive control of the states"); ibid., 114 (criticizing the *Schechter* decision).

40. Ibid., 125–39, 153–65, 162.

41. Ibid., vii.

42. Ibid., 313–14.

43. "Memorandum for Mr. Costelloe, Re: *Wickard* Case," 1 (June 19, 1942), Jackson MSS, Box 125, LC.

44. "Memorandum for Mr. Costelloe, Re: *Wickard* Case," 1 (July 10, 1942), Jackson MSS, Box 125, LC.

45. "Memorandum for Mr. Costelloe, Re: *Wickard* Case," 1 (June 19, 1942), Jackson MSS, Box 125, LC.

46. Id.

47. *Wickard v. Filburn*, Memorandum by Mr. Justice Jackson at 10 (undated), Jackson MSS, Box 125, LC.

48. Id.

> [T]hroughout this era the prevailing tests of federal jurisdiction under the interstate commerce clause were legalistic and not economic. It was marked by a belief that our self-defined legal system should be impressed on our economic life, rather than that the unity and interdependence of our economic system should be reflected in the interpretation of our legal institutions. It was thought neither futile nor harmful to attempt to impose the political pattern with its many state lines upon all the activities of life, and cases under the commerce clause were exhaustively argued without presenting economic facts and were decided in the same

way. It was thought that the partitioning of power between federal and state governments could be applied without difficulty to economic life by simply knowing the precepts of the Constitution, precedents and decisions of the courts, and the maxims of the law. ("Memorandum for Mr. Costelloe, Re: *Wickard* Case," at 9–10 (July 10, 1942), Jackson MSS, Box 125, LC.)

49. Id.

50. "Memorandum for Mr. Costelloe, Re: *Wickard* Case," 2 (June 19, 1942), Jackson MSS, Box 125, LC.

Gradually working its way through the constitutional habits of thought and eventually predominating in constitutional interpretation was the idea that political patterns could no longer disregard economic patterns in the interpretation of the commerce clause. . . . there was a rising appreciation that a national system of railroads, efficient and indiscriminating, was of more importance than theories of national power. Economic thinking was entering into the law. . . . The argument of cases came to include the presentation of economic backgrounds and identification of economic evils, at which legislation was aimed. . . . ("Memorandum for Mr. Costelloe, Re: *Wickard* Case," at 10–11 (July 10, 1942), Jackson MSS, Box 125, LC.)

51. "Memorandum for Mr. Costelloe, Re: *Wickard* Case," 2 (June 19, 1942), Jackson MSS, Box 125, LC. "A difficulty which may not have been foreseen in adopting economic, in addition to legal, standards for the measurement of the commerce power grows out of the indefiniteness of economic lines. The political lines are definitely drawn but economic lines are not." "Memorandum for Mr. Costelloe, Re: *Wickard* Case," at 12 (July 10, 1942), Jackson MSS, Box 125, LC.

52. Id. at 13.

The comparatively simple, and perhaps oversimplified, concepts of the law lose their validity when applied to economic data. It has been an easy thing to say that the power to regulate commerce included the power to protect that commerce against competition, for the legal concept of competition was a fairly definite and simple one. But what is competition in an economic sense? While competition in a legal sense would arise only between men dealing in the same kind of goods and hence attempting to fulfill the same customer desires, the economic concept of competition might be very much broader and more difficult of ascertainment. In the economic sense, fuel oil competes with coal. Both are rivals of electricity, and all three of them are competitors with every other commodity in the market for the consumer's dollar. (Id. at 12–13.)

53. Id. at 13. "[T]he truth is that we have not yet evolved any set judicial standard by which to determine what effects upon interstate commerce are adequate to confer jurisdiction on the federal government and what are not." Id. at 14.

54. Id. at 14–18.

55. "Memorandum for Mr. Costelloe, Re: *Wickard* Case," at 3 (June 19, 1942), Jackson MSS, Box 125, LC; *see also* "Memorandum for Mr. Costelloe, Re: *Wickard* Case," at 13–18 (July 10, 1942), Jackson MSS, Box 125, LC.

56. Jackson's intellectual debt to Cardozo's *Schechter* concurrence is apparent in the metaphors deployed in the following passage: "Economic effects seem almost as persistent as physical force which, it is said, once exerted is never lost. An economic impulse continues indefinitely and may be overcome or its identity lost but it is too illusive and subtle for tracing out in legal proceedings. First impacts shade off in force as they expand, like the concentric rings caused by throwing a stone in the water." Id. at 15.

57. "At what point these effects have enough vitality to confer federal jurisdiction and at what point they have passed outside it, we have no standards to determine, and I am not at

all sure of our capacity to invent a standard that would have any validity upon the immediate case to which it is applied." Id. at 15.

58. Id. at 15. "[S]ince the economic test is to be applied, the extent of the commerce power is no longer a legal question but an economic, and hence policy, one." "Memorandum for Mr. Costelloe, Re: *Wickard* Case," at 4 (June 19, 1942), Jackson MSS, Box 125, LC.

59. "All of this raises seriously the question whether the extent of power under the commerce clause is appropriate for judicial decision and brings us to the question of whether Congress by determining what is 'appropriate' to its own regulatory schemes may in effect define the extent of its own power under the commerce clause." Id. at 3.

60. "Memorandum for Mr. Costelloe, Re: *Wickard* Case," at 15 (July 10, 1942) Jackson MSS, Box 125, LC.

61. "While we have not yet expressly recognized it, it seems clear to result from our decisions that that which Congress finds appropriate to regulate as a matter of policy we find it appropriate to regulate as a matter of law." Id. at 16. "For some time this Court has, in effect, exerted no restraint upon the exercise of the commerce power in practice. It cannot do so under the existing standards. Once breaking away from a legalistic interpretation of the Constitution and adopting an economic basis, it becomes impossible for this Court to maintain a position that a subject which Congress and the President regard as appropriate for regulation is not in fact appropriate, or that one where Congress and a President perceive a relationship and an effect is in fact nonexistent." Id. at 16–17.

62. "Memorandum for Mr. Costelloe, Re: *Wickard* Case," at 4 (June 19, 1942), Jackson MSS, Box 125, LC.

63. "Memorandum for Mr. Costelloe, Re: *Wickard* Case," at 16–17 (July 10, 1942), Jackson MSS, Box 125, LC.

64. "Memorandum for Mr. Costelloe, Re: *Wickard* Case," at 5 (June 19, 1942), Jackson MSS, Box 125, LC.

65. "Memorandum for Mr. Costelloe, Re: *Wickard* Case," at 16 (July 10, 1942), Jackson MSS, Box 125, LC.

66. "Memorandum for Mr. Costelloe, Re: *Wickard* Case," at 6 (June 19, 1942), Jackson MSS, Box 125, LC.

67. Id. at 5.

68. "[T]he necessity of waiting for a quibbling judicial review leads to the framing of legislation in a disrespectably indirect and inefficient manner." Ibid. "Much of the fantastic complexity and indirectness of federal regulatory statutes has been directed toward meeting some judicial objections to the direct and forthright exercise of the commerce power." "Memorandum for Mr. Costelloe, Re: *Wickard* Case," at 18–19 (July 10, 1942), Jackson MSS, Box 125, LC.

69. "Memorandum for Mr. Costelloe, Re: *Wickard* Case," at 6 (June 19, 1942), Jackson MSS, Box 125, LC.

70. "[I]f we have really reached the point where we are dealing only with the shadow of judicial review, I think we should not allow ourselves to stand as a symbol of protection to states' rights which have vanished." Id. at 5.

71. Id. at 4.

72. "Memorandum for Mr. Costelloe, Re: *Wickard* Case," at 20 (July 10, 1942), Jackson MSS, Box 125, LC. "Congress has said that [growth of wheat for home consumption] . . . is . . . appropriate to regulation, and the Court is without power to gainsay this Congressional determination." Id. at 22.

73. Id.

74. Id.

75. Jackson's law clerk was apparently somewhat taken aback by the forcefulness of the memoranda. "Are *all* the old formulae and tests junked?" he asked with seeming incredulity.

"Is the Court never to seek to preserve our 'dual system of government' by denying that the Commerce Power can reach to 'effects upon interstate commerce so indirect and remote that to embrace them, in view of our complex society, would effectually obliterate the distinction between what is national and what is local and create a completely centralized government'?" Memorandum, "AAA," at 1, Jackson MSS, Box 125, LC.

76. *Wickard*, 317 U.S. at 125–27.

77. Brief of Appellant at 44.

78. Opinion draft, *Wickard v. Filburn*, at 12 (May 22, 1942), Jackson MSS, Box 125, LC. There Jackson had written:

> Perhaps we could assume in the present case without proof that if a farmer is not permitted to feed his own wheat to his livestock he will be forced into the market as a feed buyer and thereby help swell the volume and sustain prices of the interstate market, or perhaps we should as reasonably assume that he will be forced into the market as a livestock seller. So, also, might we assume that if he and his family are forbidden to eat his home-grown wheat, he might be forced into the market as a buyer of wheat products or perhaps we should as reasonably expect him to turn for sustenance to other products. Whether the production of wheat for consumption on the farm does have a substantial effect upon interstate commerce by taking such a producer out of the consumer market or by the possibility that the wheat so produced may actually be put upon the market directly or by the sale of stock to which it is fed, are far from clear on the record and the legislative history presented.

79. "Memorandum for Mr. Costelloe, Re: *Wickard* Case," at 4–8 (July 10, 1942), Jackson MSS, Box 125, LC. "[W]e are furnished an extensive agreement as to the economics of the wheat industry," the memorandum stated. "From it we may determine roughly the relationship between wheat that is produced for commerce and that produced for home use. . . ." Id. at 4–5. Following a lengthy discussion of wheat economics, Jackson concluded that "There is no doubt of the interest of wheat produced for commerce to regulate and to restrain wheat grown for home use. It is obvious that if the self-supplier can be forced into the market to become a purchaser instead of becoming a self-supplier . . . the market demand will be broadened and the price easier to sustain." Id. at 7. What had in May been a mere speculative hypothesis requiring empirical support was by mid-July "obvious." Jackson's reconceptualization of the judicial role in commerce clause cases apparently facilitated his achievement of epistemological certitude. It was much easier to assent to the Government's claim when it was no longer his duty to determine whether it was true.

80. *Wickard*, 317 U.S. at 127–28.

81. Id. at 124.

82. Jackson MSS, Box 125, LC.

83. *Wickard*, 317 U.S. at 124–25.

84. Id. at 128–29.

85. Compare Stone's draft in *Fainblatt*, in which he described circumstances under which the Court might invalidate a statute enacted under the commerce power. See ch. 11, supra.

86. *Wickard v. Filburn*, Memorandum by Mr. Justice Jackson at 10–12 (undated), Jackson MSS, Box 125, LC.

87. Jackson to Sherman Minton, December 21, 1942, Jackson MSS, Box 125, LC.

88. *United States v. Carolene Products Co.*, 304 U.S. 144 (1938).

89. *Helvering v. Gerhardt*, 304 U.S. 405, 416 (1938):

> [T]he people of all the states have created the national government and are represented in Congress. Through that representation they exercise the national taxing power. The very fact that when they are exercising it they are taxing themselves,

serves to guard against its abuse through the possibility of resort to the usual processes of political action which provides a readier and more adaptable means than any other which courts can afford, for securing accommodation of the competing demands for national revenue, on the one hand, and for reasonable scope for the independence of state action, on the other.

90. *South Carolina Highway Dept. v. Barnwell Bros.*, 303 U.S. 177 (1938).

State regulations affecting interstate commerce, whose purpose or effect is to gain for those within the state an advantage at the expense of those without, or to burden those out of the state without any corresponding advantage to those within, have been thought to impinge upon the constitutional prohibition even though the Congress has not acted. . . . Underlying the stated rule has been the thought, often expressed in judicial opinion, that when the regulation is of such a character that its burden falls principally upon those without the state, legislative action is not likely to be subjected to those political constraints which are normally exerted on legislation where it affects adversely some interests within the state. (Id. at 184–85, n. 2.)

On the other hand, Stone noted, the need for a judicial remedy in such cases was diminished by virtue of the fact that "Congress, in the exercise of its plenary power to regulate interstate commerce, may determine whether the burdens imposed on it by state regulation . . . are too great, and may, by legislation designed to secure uniformity or in other respects to protect the national interest in commerce, curtail to some extent the state's regulatory power." But in the absence of such congressional legislation, the sole judicial inquiry was whether the end was permissible and the means rationally related to the end. The judgment of the state legislature concerning the means to be employed was "presumed to be supported by facts known to the legislature unless facts judicially known or proved preclude that possibility. Hence . . . we examine the record, not to see whether the findings of the court below are supported by evidence, but to ascertain upon the whole record whether it is possible to say that the legislative choice is without rational basis." Id. at 190–92.

Of course, in the spring of 1942, Jackson had thought that the judgment of Congress that growth of wheat for home consumption affected interstate commerce *did* have to be supported by evidence in the record. By the autumn, however, he was prepared to employ the same standard of review (if not an even more lenient one) for exercises of the commerce power that Stone had prescribed for the dormant commerce clause context.

91. RHJ to HFS, May 25, 1942, "Re: 1080—*Wickard v. Filburn*," Jackson MSS, Box 125, LC.

92. "Memorandum for Mr. Costelloe, Re: *Wickard* Case," at 6–7 (June 19, 1942), Jackson MSS, Box 125. LC. This last sentence, interestingly enough, was obviously a quotation from another, much older due process case. In *Munn v. Illinois*, Chief Justice Waite had remarked, "For protection against abuse by legislatures the people must resort to the polls, not the courts." *Munn*, 94 U.S. at 134 (1877).

One detects here the germ of Herbert Wechsler's famous article, "The Political Safeguards of Federalism: The Role of the States in the Composition and Selection of the National Government," *Colum. L. Rev.* 54 (1954): 543, which played such a prominent role in Justice Brennan's dissenting opinion in *National League of Cities v. Usery*, 426 U.S. 833, 856, 877 (1976), and in Justice Blackmun's opinion for the majority in *Garcia v. San Antonio Metropolitan Transit Authority*, 469 U.S. 528, 551 (1985).

93. *Wickard*, 317 U.S. at 120.

94. See chs. 6 and 9, supra.

95. See chs. 8 and 10, supra.

96. See *Carolene Products*, supra.

97. See, for example, *NLRB v. Fainblatt*, 306 U.S. 601 (1939); *Consolidated Edison Co. v. NLRB*, 305 U.S. 197 (1938); *Santa Cruz Fruit Packing Co. v. NLRB*, 303 U.S. 453 (1938).

98. It is clear that Jackson had brought the political process rationale, though perhaps in understated fashion, into the domain of commerce clause jurisprudence; it is not similarly clear that he had transplanted the rationality standard of review. As I have shown, Jackson's opinion failed to clarify the standard to be applied in commerce clause cases, if indeed there was to be any judicially enforced standard at all. This obscurity in Jackson's opinion may have been designed to mediate a dispute between Stone and Black. Stone's *Carolene Products* opinion had explicitly claimed judicial power to invalidate legislation under the due process clause where the rationality test was not met. 304 U.S. at 152–54. Black denied that any such judicial power existed, see Louis Lusky, "Footnote Redux: A *Carolene Products* Remembrance," *Colum. L. Rev.* 82 (1982): 1093, 1097, and refused to join that portion of Stone's opinion. See *Carolene Products Co.*, 304 U.S. at 155; HLB to HFS, April 21, 1938, reprinted in Lusky, "Footnote Redux," 1109. In his letter to Stone rejecting Stone's due process analogy in *Wickard*, Jackson had suggested that they "avoid the row with Black (I notice he dissented for that part of your *Carolene Products* opinion) on the method and with such meagre help as we will get from reargument settle down in the fall to deciding the merits." RHJ to HFS, May 25, 1942, "Re: 1080—*Wickard v. Filburn*," Jackson MSS, Box 125, LC. Studied ambiguity may have been Jackson's method for avoiding such a row. By splitting the difference—giving Stone the political process rationale while sparing Black the rationality test—he was able to secure a single, unanimous opinion of the Court.

The brevity of Jackson's allusion to the political process rationale may have been an attempt to assuage not only Black, but also Frankfurter and Douglas. For it is clear that neither of them was fully prepared to abandon all federalism restraints on national regulatory power. See *United States v. Kahriger*, 345 U.S. 22, 37–40 (1953) (Frankfurter and Douglas, JJ., dissenting).

99. *Warren-Bradshaw Drilling Co. v. Hall*, 317 U.S. 88, 89–91 (1942).

100. Id. at 93–95 (Roberts, J., dissenting).

101. *Walton v. Southern Packaging Corp.*, 320 U.S. 540, 543 (1944) (Roberts, J., concurring). See also *Armour & Co. v. Wantock*, 323 U.S. 126 (1944), where Roberts joined a unanimous opinion upholding application of the Act to auxiliary firefighters employed at the plant of a soap manufacturer producing goods for interstate commerce, on the authority of *Kirschbaum* and *Walton*.

102. See *Overnight Motor Transportation Co., Inc. v. Missel*, 316 U.S. 572 (1942), in which Justice Roberts dissented without opinion from a decision holding the Act applicable to an employee of an interstate motor transportation company, who acted as a rate clerk and performed other incidental duties.

103. See *Borden Co. v. Borella*, 325 U.S. 679 (1945), in which the Court held that where a large manufacturing concern maintained its central executive and administrative offices in an office building that it owned and in which it occupied 58 percent of the rented space, the maintenance employees of the building were engaged in an "occupation necessary to the production" of goods for interstate commerce and therefore subject to the Act. Justice Stone, joined by Justice Roberts, filed a dissenting opinion reminiscent of Roberts' dissent in *Hall*:

> No doubt there are philosophers who would argue, what is implicit in the decision now rendered, that in a complex modern society there is such interdependence of its members that the activities of most of them are necessary to the activities of most others. But I think that Congress did not make that philosophy the basis of the coverage of the Fair Labor Standards Act. It did not, by a "house-that-Jack-built" chain of causation, bring within the sweep of the statute the ultimate *causa causarum* which result in the production of goods for commerce. . . . The services rendered in this case would seem to be no more related, and no more necessary to the processes of production than the services of the cook who prepares the meals of the

president of the company or the chauffeur who drives him to his office. . . . All are too remote from the physical process of production to be said to be, in any practical sense, a part of or necessary to it. (Id. at 685–86.)

See also *Overstreet v. North Shore Corp.*, 318 U.S. 120 (1943), in which Justices Roberts and Jackson dissented without opinion from a decision holding the Act applicable to employees of a private corporation who were engaged in the operation and maintenance of a drawbridge that was part of a toll road used extensively by persons and vehicles traveling in interstate commerce, and that spanned an intercoastal waterway used in interstate commerce.

104. See, for example, *McLeod v. Threlkeld*, 319 U.S. 491 (1943), where Justice Reed, in an opinion joined by Stone, Roberts, Frankfurter, and Jackson, construed the statute not to apply to a cook who prepared and served meals to maintenance-of-way employees of an interstate railroad pursuant to a contract between his employer and the railroad company. "In the Fair Labor Standards Act," wrote Reed, "Congress did not intend that the regulation of hours and wages should extend to the furthest reaches of federal authority." Id. at 493.

See also *Western Union Telegraph Co. v. Lenroot*, 323 U.S. 490 (1945), where Justice Jackson, in an opinion joined by Stone, Roberts, Reed, and Frankfurter, construed the statute not to apply to local Western Union messengers; and *10 East 40th Street Building, Inc. v. Callus*, 325 U.S. 578 (1945), where Justice Frankfurter, in an opinion joined by Stone, Roberts, Douglas, and Jackson, held that maintenance employees of a metropolitan office building, operated as an independent enterprise, which was used and to be used for offices by a wide variety of tenants, including some producers of goods for commerce, were not covered by the Act. "In enacting this statute," wrote Frankfurter in an opinion echoing Roberts' dissent in *Hall*, "Congress did not see fit . . . to exhaust its constitutional power over commerce." Id. at 579.

> We must be alert . . . not to absorb by adjudication activities that Congress did not see fit to take over by legislation. Renting office space in a building exclusively set aside for an unrestricted variety of office work spontaneously satisfies the common understanding of what is local business and makes the employees of such a building engaged in local business. Mere separation of an occupation from the physical process of production does not preclude application of the Fair Labor Standards Act. But remoteness of a particular occupation from the physical process is a relevant factor in drawing the line. Running an office building as an entirely independent enterprise is too many steps removed from the physical process of the production of goods. Such remoteness is insulated from the Fair Labor Standards Act by those considerations pertinent to the federal system which led Congress not to sweep predominantly local situations within the confines of the Act. To assign the maintenance men of such an office building to the productive process because some proportion of the offices in the building may, for the time being, be offices of manufacturing enterprises is to indulge in an analysis too attenuated for appropriate regard to the regulatory power of the States which Congress saw fit to reserve to them. Dialectic inconsistencies do not weaken the validity of practical adjustments, as between the State and federal authority, when Congress has cast the duty of making them upon the courts. Our problem is not an exercise in scholastic logic. (Id. at 582–83.)

105. *Darby*, 312 U.S. at 119.

106. Indeed, there is reason to doubt that Stone and Jackson believed that *Jones & Laughlin* had overruled *Carter Coal*. In *Darby*, Stone stated that *Carter* had been "limited in principle" rather than overruled by the Wagner Act cases. Id. at 123. And in a draft of the *Wickard* opinion, Jackson cited *Darby*, rather than *Jones & Laughlin*, as the case having overruled *Carter Coal*. *Wickard v. Filburn*, Memorandum by Mr. Justice Jackson, at 7 (undated), Jackson MSS, Box 125, LC.

107. The transformations in commerce clause jurisprudence wrought by *Darby* and *Wickard*, which rendered the federal commerce power virtually plenary, were similarly felt in the arena of collective bargaining. Taken in conjunction with the Court's decision in *Nebbia*, these expansions of the commercial police power made it clear that *Adair's* analytical model had dissolved. In 1941, Hughes' final year on the Court, Justice Frankfurter stated what must have been obvious to all. "The course of decisions in this Court since *Adair v. United States* and *Coppage v. Kansas*," he wrote, "have completely sapped those cases of their authority." *Phelps-Dodge Corp. v. NLRB*, 313 U.S. 177, 187 (1941) (citations omitted).

108. In particular one might wonder whether Roberts would have voted the same way in *Wickard* had his colleagues been those with whom he decided *Schechter*.

109. Max Planck, *Scientific Autobiography and Other Papers*, trans. F. Gaynor (New York, 1949), 33–34.

110. See *Williams v. Standard Oil Co.*, 278 U.S. 235 (1929); *Ribnik v. McBride*, 277 U.S. 350 (1928); *Tyson & Bros. v. Banton*, 273 U.S. 418 (1927).

111. WHT to Horace Taft, Nov. 14, 1929, quoted in Pringle, *The Life and Times of William Howard Taft*, 967.

112. WHT to Horace Taft, December 1, 1929, quoted in Pringle, *The Life and Times of William Howard Taft*, 967.

113. WHT to Pierce Butler, September 14, 1929, quoted in Mason, *William Howard Taft: Chief Justice*, 296–97.

114. In the contracts clause area, the three Hoover appointees also provided the margin of victory in *Blaisdell* and the *Gold Clause Cases*. See ch. 2, supra.

115. Among the works repudiating the notion that Hoover was a conservative, laissez-faire ideologue are Murray N. Rothbard, "The Hoover Myth," in Weinstein and Eakins, eds., *For a New America*, 162–79.

Index